Comparative urban land use planning

Best practice

Leslie A. Stein

SYDNEY UNIVERSITY PRESS

First published by Sydney University Press
© Leslie A. Stein 2017
© Sydney University Press 2017

Reproduction and communication for other purposes
Except as permitted under the Act, no part of this edition may be reproduced, stored in a retrieval system, or communicated in any form or by any means without prior written permission. All requests for reproduction or communication should be made to Sydney University Press at the address below:

Sydney University Press
Fisher Library F03
The University of Sydney NSW 2006
AUSTRALIA
Email: sup.info@sydney.edu.au
sydney.edu.au/sup

National Library of Australia Cataloguing-in-Publication Data

Creator:	Stein, Leslie A., author
Title:	Comparative urban land use planning : best practice / Leslie A. Stein.
ISBN:	9781743324677 (paperback)
	9781743324684 (ebook: epub)
	9781743324691 (ebook: kindle)
	9781743325582 (ebook: PDF)
Notes:	Includes bibliographical references and index.
Subjects:	Sociology, Urban.
	Urbanization--Social aspects.
	Land use--Planning--Social aspects
	City planning--Social aspects.

Cover image: *HOME*, ink pen and marker on sketch paper, Celeste Stein (2016).
Cover design by Miguel Yamin

Contents

List of figures   v

Preface   ix

Introduction   xi

1 **The planning process**   1
    1   Strategic planning   3
    2   Planning scale   49
    3   Community participation   91

2 **Implementing the plan**   121
    4   The bases of regulatory controls   123
    5   Zoning   137
    6   Development control   163

3 **Planning and climate change**   203
    7   Planning and greenhouse gas mitigation   205
    8   Adaptation for climate change   227

Conclusion   245

Appendix 1   253

Appendix 2   257

Works cited   270

Index   295

List of figures

Figure 1-1 Archimedean point of reference? A city is more than a set of buildings, roads, and open spaces. — 4

Figure 1-2 An example of a rational comprehensive planning process, adapted from Malaysia's Federal Department of Town and Country Planning. — 8

Figure 1-3 46th Street and 8th Avenue, Manhattan. — 12

Figure 1-4 Dong Koi Street in Ho Chi Minh City, Vietnam. — 14

Figure 1-5 Traditional neighbourhood elements in Letchworth Garden City, Hertfordshire. — 15

Figure 1-6 Material flows between the national and rest of world (ROW) economies and the environment. — 18

Figure 1-7 Tverskaya Street, Moscow. — 41

Figure 2-1 Kuala Lumpur Sentral, Malaysia. — 56

Figure 2-2 Sprawl in Lisbon, Portugal. — 72

Figure 2-3 Ribbon development in Flanders, Belgium. — 76

Figure 2-4 New Urbanist development in Seaside, Florida. — 77

Figure 2-5 Urban growth boundary in Helvitia, Oregon. — 81

Figure 2-6 Integrated transport in Charlotte, North Carolina. — 84

Figure 4-1 Telegraph Avenue in Berkeley, California. — 131

Figure 5-1 Industrial zones separated from residential areas. — 138

Figure 5-2 The Meadowhall Regional Shopping Centre in Sheffield. — 143

Figure 5-3 The Shinjuku renaissance district, Tokyo. — 148

Figure 6-1 Affordable housing in Edinburgh. — 193

Figure 6-2 Diagram adapted from the Smart Code of Lauderhill, Florida. — 196

Figure 7-1 Toyoma prefecture compact city, Japan. — 214

Figure 7-2 Transport-oriented design (TOD) in Emerson Park East, St Louis, Illinois. — 218

To the memory of Professor Patrick McAuslan

Preface

This work began in 2012 as a series of reports I prepared on international best practice in planning law for the Department of Planning in New South Wales, Australia. At that time, I had direct knowledge of the planning regimes of Argentina, Australia, Austria, Bangladesh, Belgium, Brazil, Canada, Croatia, France, Germany, Hong Kong, India, Ireland, Israel, Italy, the Netherlands, New Zealand, Pakistan, Russia, Singapore, Sri Lanka, Thailand, Ukraine, the United Arab Emirates, the United Kingdom, and the United States of America. The knowledge was gained over decades from on-the-ground experience of these systems through research for the United Nations, as a practising lawyer offering advice on these systems, and as an academic studying their operation. The New South Wales reports were my first attempt to compare the systems I already understood to explore their similarities and differences. Thereafter, in preparation for this work, I expanded the comparisons by visits, discussions with officials, and studying city plans and policies in relation to Denmark, Finland, Indonesia, Japan, Kenya, Malaysia, the Marshall Islands, Mexico, Nigeria, Norway, the Philippines, Poland, South Africa, South Korea, Spain, Sweden, Switzerland, Turkey, and Vietnam. That accounts for only 45 countries out of a possible 193. To understand the systems of more countries, in particular China and Cuba, I turned to the library of Columbia University, where I was a visiting scholar at the Sabin Center for Climate Change Law, to undertake research into the planning regimes to the extent that they were explained in contemporary studies and papers.

The task was time consuming but not overwhelming because the systems have common characteristics. To 'plan' is to attempt to improve the urban environment and there are only so many methods that can be used. As an analogy, if one looks ahead in a personal plan, there is an assessment of resources, goals, and some method to implement that vision. That sequence applies equally to planning in all its forms.

What has most surprised me in preparing this work is how most plans begin full of hope and promise for a brighter future but then have little to do with the urban ills that face communities. In many instances, I studied a planning system in detail before travelling to a country, but when I arrived I searched in vain for how the plan had any impact on the problems faced by a city. This was especially the case in developing countries where the neoliberal, economic imperative to create wealth contrasted sharply with insecure land tenure, urban chaos, and environmental degradation. In countries with massive populations and poor infrastructure, the problems of traffic, crowding, depersonalisation, slums, pollution, crime, and unemployment seem beyond the capacity of any plan.

In most developed countries as well, there appears to be little connection between planning as seen in laws and maps and what is revealed on the ground. Studying the *Istanbul transportation master plan*, one would think that traffic was under control, but a short ride in a taxi demonstrates immediately why Istanbul has the worst traffic conditions in the world. The disconnect between the lofty goals of a plan and the human condition is striking. South Korea has an exemplary national planning system with carefully revealed five-year plans for a 'happy' city, yet has the highest suicide rate in the world.

Occasionally in the literature, planning gives up and questions its own usefulness and legitimacy in the face of insoluble problems. Yet all countries continue to plan. The theme of this book is that best practices exist to assist planning to at least deliver a sense of community satisfaction with the process as well as increasing its efficacy.

I would first like to thank Evan Jones, one of Australia's leading planners, for his help in formulating the first chapter on strategic planning. The work of Professor Bart van Klink at Vrije Universiteit Amsterdam and our discussions on symbolic legislation provided a crucial framework to organise disparate material.

Sam Haddad, then director of the New South Wales Department of Planning, kindly granted me permission to use any and all of the consulting reports I prepared for the department in this work. Copyright to the last chapter, which represents a revised version of work I completed for a book of essays on *Land solutions to climate displacement,* was reserved.

This book is dedicated to the memory of Professor Patrick McAuslan, who was the first to explain planning and planning laws as a clash of ideologies, thus freeing others to open their minds to the dynamics of cities. He was a friend and mentor and his brilliance, humour, and humility made land use planning come alive for me and countless colleagues.

Leslie A. Stein
Pushkar, India
1 February 2017

Introduction

The purpose of this book is twofold. The first is to explore common themes and issues that arise in planning regimes all over the world. The second is to offer examples of the best practice that has emerged for these themes and issues.

Urban land use planning is a universal phenomenon and exists in one form or another in every country; no exceptions can be found. Even in countries such as Malawi in southeast Africa, where property rights arise within a customary system of land tenure related to tribe and clan, there is the *Town and Country Planning Act 1988* to provide a framework for the planning of urban centres. In some places a land use planning framework exists but is not implemented; the Marshall Islands *Planning and Zoning Act 1987*, for example, is not in use because of a lack of interest by local government. Nevertheless, every government, irrespective of politics, crises, orientation, and religion, has believed that some form of land use planning is of such importance that it should be the subject of laws and processes. This applies to democratic and autocratic systems equally: in 2002, for instance, the fifth session of the 10th Supreme People's Assembly of the Democratic People's Republic of Korea (DPRK, North Korea) adopted a land use planning law.

City problems are no longer solved by the skills of a good planner and a set of maps. When Patrick Geddes went to British Dhaka in 1917 for only a week and then divided the city into zones and suggested development around Ramna Park, it was how planning was done. Now, with racial tensions, overwhelming displacement of entire populations, income inequality, poverty, global warming, and alcohol and drug dependencies, a few markings on a map are no longer going to be effective.

Urban problems beset all cities in the 193 countries of the world and they all struggle to find solutions, at least in part, through urban planning. The faith that planning will provide solutions is derived from the harmony and order that flows from design. Le Corbusier's plan for Buenos Aires in the 1930s contains the seeds of that vision by offering an unbridled, simple design that opened up streets to light and air and pointedly shortened the distance between residences and the business centre, the latter then becoming the mainstay of his plan for Moscow. His sensitive ideas in his 1930 book of lectures *Precision*[1] offered a pure aesthetic of city design as the utopian paradigm of urban life. This idea, that

---

1 Le Corbusier 1991.

design could improve the urban setting and that harmony and order may be achieved, has never faded.

A planner views the city as a set of objects – buildings, roads, open spaces – that are already in place and need to accord with a design, rather than a system under constant change that can never be ordered. As a consequence, planners work to manipulate the urban objects rather than just allowing an organic change over time and thereby attempt to impose 'a futile certainty on a contingent, uncertain world'.[2] Thus, harmony and order, as the underpinnings of certainty, are the natural goals of urban design. In fact, harmony and order are indeed necessary in an uncertain world because, without a sense of predictability, all appears lost. George Kelly, the psychologist, speaks of individuals construing their experiences in a manner necessary to make the world predictable, then constantly readjusting for unexpected events to maintain that basic need.[3] As a result, to a greater or lesser degree, every city falls under the influence of planning as a means to achieve predictability.

Planning is concerned with more than just harmony and order. It postulates an imagined future that will also result in a better way of life. As it is not possible to explain what form that better way of life may take in 20 or more years, what is primarily being expressed is removal of some existing problem, rather than how the city might ultimately look or function. Planners then are urban doctors healing a problem of decay or dysfunction. Nothing utopian is needed to fix urban ills, yet projecting forward an ideal, imagined future is inevitable. Idealisation is a legitimate, creative capacity that is not diminished by an argument that no one knows how the urban fabric will evolve. Planning systems therefore provide a means to maintain the hope of delivering the ideals of harmony, order, and a better future, no matter how defined.

It is a recurring theme in this work that harmony, order, and a better life cannot be vouchsafed by a planning system. Some aspects of planning, such as the placement of a park near an inner-city neighbourhood, may contribute to a greater sense of wellbeing. However, deeper issues such as depression, anxiety, and substance dependency are not relieved by the locational placement of buildings, roads and open space. A city really suffers from social problems more than from planning problems.

The *Fiji Town Planning Act 1978* is as good a place as any to describe the end product of planning:

> A scheme may be made, in accordance with the provisions of this Act, with respect to any land with the general object of controlling the development of the land to which such scheme applies, and of securing suitable provision for traffic, transportation, disposition of commercial, residential, and industrial areas, proper sanitary conditions, amenities and conveniences, parks, gardens and reserves, and of making suitable provision for the use of land for building or other purposes . . .
> (Cap. 129, s.16(1)).

Controlling the development of land, as the Act proposes, is the tool that is used to achieve harmony and order. 'Development' is always widely defined to encompass the carrying out of any building on land, or any use of land, so planning provides for control of the physical environment as it may affect the community: how land is used and how buildings appear.

---

2   Hillier 2007, 15.
3   Kelly 1963.

Introduction

Papua New Guinea is perhaps unique in realistically naming its planning framework the *Physical Planning Act 1989*, in recognition that the process is really about the physical manipulation of objects on land – roads, buildings, open space – and is not a social welfare tool for a better life or for fighting the myriad ills that face urban centres.

I.1 Planning culture

The factors that constitute a better life vary across different cultures. In one culture, such as the Netherlands, historic liberalism, a sense of pride, and tolerance for diversity may underpin the aspirations of urban life, while in another, such as the United Arab Emirates, traditional conservatism, exclusiveness, and display of wealth may be more important. As a result, the approach of this book is not to unravel the complex cultural, and political subtleties behind each system's orientation. Rather it attempts to describe the common processes of urban planning and to determine any best practices that can be found or extrapolated. The details of the systems of various countries are therefore used, where appropriate, as illustrations that highlight good planning practice. There is no attempt made to drill down to the individual cultural or political complexities of each regime or to canvass all regimes on a particular process unless there is something on offer in terms of best practice.

Ignoring cultural nuances is necessary because they extend to so many layers of urban existence that their influence ceases to be explicable. The culture of a country, its values, its history, its predicates, are ultimately more important than the forms of planning controls in determining planning outcomes. The attitude of the citizenry to imposed government control, the degree to which rights are important, the expectations of wealth distribution, and the current economic situation are examples of factors that will manifest in the devices used to carry out planning and the manner in which the city functions. For instance, planning may be perceived as the critical engine of economic growth, forcing a change in use to bring land on stream to provide employment or increase government revenue, in spite of the consequences. The rush to exploit the lucrative global demand for palm oil led Indonesia to alter the land use of forested conservation areas to allow intense exploitation to the detriment of local inhabitants.[4] Such underlying cultural factors are constantly in flux, although rarely articulated in government reports or planning literature.[5]

In addition to the culture of a nation, local culture and values influence the operation of planning systems. For example, cumulative problems with a potential high-rise development may motivate activism by residents and make them more aware of their right to object. This in turn may lead to the amendment of local laws to exclude high-density developments. More subtly, the details and operation of a planning regime must be understood, not only in the context of the culture of the country or local area, but in the specific *planning culture* of the area. This phrase can be used to describe the shared understanding of how the system operates, where the source of power and decision making lies, what the interests of residents are meant to be, and the arc of previous projects over time. A planning culture is created in the practical day-to-day operation of planning controls: the legal or

---

4 Resosudarmo et al. 2012, chapter 3.
5 Friedmann 2005.

understood interpretations of written rules, the nuances of unwritten conventions, and the ways to accomplish outcomes through the system.

To shift a planning regime from one form to another, say, from an emphasis on case-by-case determination of projects to a greater reliance on an overall strategic plan for the future, creates tensions in the established planning culture no matter how poorly the existing regime is operating. Often, the largest obstacle to change from inefficient aspects of a planning system to more efficient functioning or international best practice is that the stakeholders in the system are accustomed to the regime and are comfortable with navigating its intricacies. Power has also been distributed in subtle ways by the existing system to developers, politicians, planners, consultants, and lawyers, so a change represents an alteration of entrenched interests.

When the property market is rising, it is possible that deficiencies in the planning system will not be recognised. Even if the procedures for obtaining approval to develop are cumbersome, obstructionist, or inefficient, the community will be tolerant because the market value of land increases. A developer who has to wait years for approval can make up costs by the rise in the price of what is sold. As with a well, when it goes dry and property prices fall, the muck at the bottom becomes evident and an inadequate planning system will then be scrutinised and called into question. It is at that time that grafting on a new procedure or fixing issues at the fringe are no longer enough and greater change or new practices are required.

If there is a desire or push to change a system, the drafter of the new framework looks through the lens of the planning culture they know and tries to fit the changes into what is understood. This is a highly technical exercise because the planning culture and the rules of the planning regime are so complex that they are only understood by experts. As a consequence, change, even arising from consistent failures, is most often incremental and exceedingly slow to yield new devices to accomplish the same goal or even to add or subtract relatively small instances of change. Each step requires consultation, expert opinion and political debate, and will inevitably receive criticism by some sector of the community. Changes are measured in years and not months.

A clear example of the difficulty of changing the form of a planning regime can be found in New South Wales, Australia. This is an interesting case to start with as it gives a flavour of the significant influence of the planning culture. The planning legislation, the *Environmental Planning and Assessment Act 1979*, was heralded at its inception as innovative because it integrated environmental assessment with planning issues when there was an application to develop land. Due to the manner in which the act was drafted, local authorities were given the power to decide applications for development: a full system of what is called 'development control'. The act also allowed the state to create state environmental planning policies to direct and override the decisions of local authorities. Looked at from a distance as forms of law and policy, the system suggested an efficient, although costly, regime of development control. However, the state policies were used frequently to set standards for particular developments and became another, complex layer for consideration by the local authority in deciding applications. Some of the 40 or so policies as of 2015 regulate specific sites, but most impose a level of control on a local authority's consideration of applications for many issues.

As Sydney is a large region, the state mandated a Sydney Metropolitan Strategy, a strategic plan that indicated how the area should grow, what greenfield areas should be released for new housing, and what policies should be applied to increase density and activity in specific areas. When this was completed in 2005, there was a view held by the minister of planning that the existing controls in the act could implement that strategy or that perhaps another policy could be made. This occurred because of the familiarity of the stakeholders with the operation of the current controls and a reluctance to give even more power to state government. The power therefore remained in the hands of local councils, who were often reluctant to implement the metropolitan strategy when it conflicted with local desires. As there was no effective mechanism put in place to override local councils, the goals of the strategy were not carried out. This resulted in the state minister for planning creating a new regime where larger applications could be sent to him so he had the capacity to override local objections. This was, of course, anathema to the democratic functioning of the state, and the opposing political party won an election partly on a platform of abolishing that regime.

Once that regime was abolished, the new minister for planning proceeded with the goal of correcting the system by abolishing ad hoc ministerial decisions. He then extended his goals to a complete overhaul of the many levels of decisions that were bogged down in delay. The proposed new system suggested a radical shift away from development control so that most uses would be permitted as of right on the basis of an agreed strategic plan. The proposal incorporated an exemplary, wide, and efficient system for obtaining the views of residents in the formation of the strategic plan, thereby reducing the battles that inevitably took place between neighbours when a new development was proposed under the system of development control.

As the old system had become so unwieldy and combative, local residents considered the ability to protest and fight it out as a right that should not be lost. Community action groups had been formed and were well equipped to do battle. As a result, even though the system proposed would have offered much greater community participation for residents in the creation of a strategic plan, the fact that it would also allow more development without permission stirred community protest. The rival political party saw a way to align with the residents and was able to defeat the proposed changes in parliament.

The lesson from the New South Wales experience is that a complete change in a planning system is extremely difficult no matter how well thought out. What was proposed in the new legislation was clearly a great improvement on the complicated system that had developed over time. However, the negativity that had surfaced in response to the previous minister's ad hoc control of development following the failure to implement the metropolitan strategy led to the creation and entrenchment of well-organised community interest groups. The new proposed regime, which would have benefited the community and was itself the subject of full consultation, was examined in terms of the reduction in the right to protest and the possible loss of resident influence. This meant that the *planning culture* overrode sound planning, throwing the state into a whole range of ad hoc fixes, including a new Greater Sydney Commission, in an attempt to prop up an unwieldy system.

Another example of an unsuccessful attempt to change a planning regime is found in the Netherlands. In Europe, the system of development control – a case-by-case determination of an application – is common. Contrary to that trend, the *Dutch Spatial Planning Act 2008* provided that there should be greater reliance on a strategic land use plan and less on development control. The 2008 act had one exemption: a 'project decision' that allowed a separate decision to be made outside the strategic plan on a particular development proposal. It provided that the exception was only effective if the local authority amended the strategic plan within a year to include that decision. If it failed to do so, it could not charge any fees for the application (this was considered to be a major discouragement). A detailed study[6] raised the question of whether the previous Dutch system that was relied on by developers and the public (the 'planning culture') would in fact undergo significant change following the amendments to the 2008 act. It concluded that the change from flexibility to more rigid reliance on a strategic plan would ultimately be ineffectual because of the planning culture in the Netherlands.

In practice, the system remained one of development control and, after the global financial crisis, a further amendment was made to the act so that the plan had to be amended within ten years and not one, resulting in approval of more project decisions. The study stated, in explaining what was occurring: 'Planning law is not only institutionalised in local practices: local practices are also formalised and institutionalised into planning law.'

Some authors have suggested that due to variations between planning cultures, there are no universal laws or ideal forms for a planning system and each can be understood 'only in the context of distinct political and legal regimes'.[7] This includes not only the current planning culture, but the unarticulated ways that it has evolved into a particular form, making the underlying goals of the system and the changes that have occurred over time often unknowable or obtuse. As a prime example, a push for neoliberalism is behind the United Kingdom's *Localism Act 2012*, but that sentiment is not apparent on the face of the act. It is only evident in speeches surrounding its enactment and in the more general emphasis of government policy.

I.2 Best practice methodology

There have been few attempts to derive best practice from a comparative view of land use planning. In the work *Comparative planning cultures*,[8] various authors explore many factors that account for differences in planning cultures in the countries examined. These factors include differences in legal systems, a centralised state as opposed to a decentralised devolution of power, the willingness of individuals to sacrifice their interests for a higher public cause, and also religious traditions. With this wide and complex matrix of background issues, comparative research has its detractors, as it is not possible to take into account all the contexts in which a planning system and controls have developed.[9] It has been observed that:

> these planning cultures seem to have evolved with social, political, and economic influences, both internal and external, creating hybrid cultures whose complexity can only be understood through deep historical analysis.[10]

In the comprehensive work *Spatial planning systems and practices in Europe: a comparative perspective on continuity and changes*,[11] the editors gathered explanations from local schol-

---

6   Buitelaar et al. 2011.
7   White 1999.
8   Sanyal 2005.
9   Kantor and Savich 2005.
10 Sanyal 2005, 15.

Introduction

ars of the scope and objects of spatial planning in each place: the tools used, the networks formed, the planning culture and bureaucratic styles. However, no conclusions are attempted, no comparisons made, nor does a summary of best practices emerge from the analysis. This is because each system developed by a series of complex changes and emerges from the historical narrative rather than from a clear analysis of best practice.

The editors instead suggest that the only form of comparative research that is appropriate, and the first task to undertake, is an examination of common categories, concepts, or variables that can be understood as applicable to all systems.[12] Although each planning control arises in the context of a particular political and legal regime, as well as a specific planning culture, the existence of common categories makes possible the second task: deducing the best practices for each. This is a cogent analysis, as the forms of planning controls are fundamentally the same in every place and, even more importantly, the issues facing land use planning are largely common among jurisdictions.

There is a natural hesitation to take one best practice out of a planning culture and suggest that it might work in another. However, as one commentator on comparative planning law expressed, there is still a need to seek out best practices in spite of cultural differences:

> But since there is frequently a quest for better, more just, or more operational planning laws, and since the variety of alternatives is usually not intuitively apparent, the capacity to learn systematically from other countries' laws and their implementation is a valuable policy resource.[13]

The approach I take in this book is not an inquiry into the historical bases of the planning culture of a particular country or an attempt to explain a planning system by a resort to the national or local culture. Rather, it is that there indeed are practices and ideas that have a universal appeal because of their cogency. This is therefore an examination of planning systems and an exploration of the best practice that can be found for all common planning forms. It looks at the end products of planning – how practices work and what has fallen out of the planning culture. As one study defined it:

> Planning culture might be understood as the way in which a society possesses institutionalised or shared planning practices. It refers to the interpretation of planning tasks, the way of recognising and addressing problems, the handling and use of certain rules, procedures and instruments, or ways and methods of public participation.[14]

An example of a commonality underlying all systems, which makes a search for best practice appropriate, is that the need for planning arises from population increases: it is necessary to find areas for new housing and employment and to provide appropriate services. New housing is created by changing the land use classification of farmland or moribund industrial land on the urban fringe and by increasing the density of housing in existing areas. These are the only methods possible to accommodate increased population, short of restricting the free movement and relocation of individuals. As new areas require

---

11   Reimer, Gitimis and Blotevogel 2014.
12   Kantor and Savich 2005, 136.
13   Alterman 2011.
14   Knieling and Othengrafen 2009, 43.

transportation infrastructure and services, there is a common set of land use problems that arise in choosing areas for increased density and then timing the growth. As signalling a new area is ripe for growth will lead to developer expectations of an increase in land value, some means is also necessary to control rampant speculation, which can drive up house prices. In existing areas, increased density raises the concern that it may destroy the expectations of residents who have come to enjoy a certain level of amenity. The exact mix of population growth, housing policy, economic development, and environmental considerations in growth areas is complex and variable, but the planning issues are the same.

The search for international best practice in planning perhaps had its origins in the UN Habitat Conference in Dubai in 1995 where a prize was established for new, successful techniques to improve the environment. It was a recognition that there are common issues in all planning systems that foster a need to innovate by best practice. There are no exceptions to this need as all systems create anxiety requiring change as their capacities are tested daily.

This anxiety arises when a new developments in existing areas spark fears that the character of the locality will be destroyed and residents therefore distrust developers. This creates polarisation, which then highlights shortcomings in community participation or the weakness of the controls. In the case of new areas, similar anxiety can arise because of suspicion as to why certain greenfield sites are permitted to change to allow residential development instead of others, giving some landowners a large windfall.

The anxiety and resultant tensions mean that the planning system is never static, never just right. The idea of planning as a form of collective bargaining, first suggested by Charles Lindblom,[15] and of planning as a clash of ideologies, as analysed by the late Patrick McAuslan,[16] indicate that planning is dynamic, controversial, chaotic, and always under attack. It has been said that all planning issues are defined by:

> a geographic scope, a substantive issue, and a population of hundreds of active stakeholders from all levels of government, multiple interest groups, the media and research institutions [that] . . . compete over whose policy objectives are translated into government policy.[17]

Planning systems respond to conflict by modifying the planning regime to address the tensions and therefore are always in motion. Governments constantly struggle to develop new methods, which are implemented by laws or policy. A good example is the gradual introduction in the United States of more development control, which now is common practice in the strategic planning systems of all states. The requirement that an applicant obtain a 'special permit', overriding an as-of-right authorisation for a development, was historically seen as a process alien to American planning.[18] Now that it has been accepted as a useful method, new devices need to be developed to prevent the arbitrary application of the discretion to issue or refuse a permit. Accordingly, there is a move to modify the planning regime further: a 'model statute' has been developed by the American Bar Association.

---

15 Lindblom 1959.
16 McAuslan 1980.
17 Weible and Sabatier 2005, 181.
18 Mandelker 1963, note 87.

Introduction

In all countries, there are similar issues that can be analysed for best practice. When a best practice has been developed from the tensions in a particular system, there is a universal imperative that these best practices be shared. The United Nations' *International guidelines on urban and territorial planning*, released in 2015, enunciates the critical importance of developing new tools for planning and of transferring this knowledge across borders.[19]

To be a 'best practice' for each issue or a 'good practice', the planning solution must be one that offers some form of improvement, such as greater efficiency, or reduced conflict between governance levels and between government and its inhabitants. It must have a measure of fairness and, when analysed, be valued by its users. A report for the United Nations Educational, Scientific and Cultural Organization (UNESCO) offered the overarching test that a best practice is one which is innovative in providing solutions to local problems, has effects that are sustainable rather than faddish, and is replicable.[20]

The idea of 'efficiency' in terms of a best practice in planning goes further than good procedural operation and requires 'bounded efficiency', a concept that measures effectiveness in achieving a pre-existing goal.[21] Best practice in this purview embraces procedural and substantive change directed at the fundamental goal of reducing conflicts in planning and also offering openness and fairness in the administration of the regime:

> At the core of this process is a democratic struggle for inclusiveness in democratic procedures, for transparency in government transactions, for accountability of the state and planners to the citizens they work for, for the right of citizens to be heard and to have a creative input in matters affecting their interests and concerns at different scale levels, and for reducing or eliminating unequal power structures between social groups and classes . . .[22]

These goals – reducing conflict, transparency, and the right to be heard – are what are to be analysed and discovered as best practice as they create a shared respect for the system by all stakeholders and are therefore sustainable. It is not enough if the practice speeds up a process and causes more conflict by, say, excluding the right to be heard. To be a best practice, it must reflect the higher order goals to improve the regime and the conflicts it generates. This approach to best practice requires that a practice carry with it a heightened degree of interaction between the planning authority and the community. This is not just an altruistic ideal, but is based on the idea that the most efficiently functioning planning system is one based on consensus that reduces conflict between stakeholders, creating a sense of empowerment and improving the relationship between citizens and government. Viewed through this lens, autocratically forcing a development on a local community is not as effective as arriving at acceptance by way of consensus, once residents are satisfied that the proposal is consistent with the fabric of their existing environment.

Making *consensus* a primary evaluative criterion is appropriate given that the the ethical tests of a functioning governance system are not historically part of the planning process. Ethical considerations such as distributive justice, social equity, and the fair dis-

---

19   United Nations 2015.
20   Bendixsen and Guchteneire 2003.
21   Keogh and D'Arcy 1999.
22   Albrechts 2004, 750.

tribution of opportunities are rarely apparent in land use planning, which, by its nature, discriminates between uses and so advantages some while disadvantaging others. For example, public policy dictates that the supply of urban public goods such as services and open space should be distributed equitably among stakeholders, but this has never been a recognised aspect of the planning process. A classic paper on planning explains that this is because no planning system has ever adequately delivered the wide scope of public policy, as the obligations to which planning must respond are not understood and there is confusion as to whether it can be a social welfare instrument.[23] The planning system, accordingly, does not measure its own ability to offer equitable solutions. Instead, it relies on the cold efficiency of its controls, and judges its success according to whether the right procedures have been carried out.

The key to best practice employed in this work is that it makes a difference to the relationship between a community and government in terms of consensus: it should improve participatory democracy, transparency, and other values by relieving the tensions in the system. The core issues covered in this book cause anxiety to arise, which in turn causes destructive planning battles, ideological struggles, and poor outcomes. A best practice solution is one that takes into account multiple and conflicting interests, offers a safety valve for community tension, addresses the main pressure points, and is mindful of the history of past failures. It therefore has some chance of success.

Any analysis of best practice, as I am undertaking here, inevitably results in a charge that the author's choices are derived from a deeply held opinion on what is right and what is wrong, based on subjective ethical standards. This occurs inevitably because any practice that appears efficient, fairer, more transparent, or conducive to better outcomes necessarily puts other practices in the spotlight as deficient and, by excluding them, implies that they are examples of poor practice. This is a natural consequence of looking for *better* practices in any system. I accept that in making such evaluations, I may in fact be incorrect. Furthermore, practices that appear noteworthy may be fraught with complications arising from multifaceted cultural phenomena that are not apparent when a practice is isolated for observation. There may also be practical problems in its use that are not reported. Therefore, when gathering resource material in English or in translation, I have attempted to approach each best practice through as many objective sources as possible, as well as subjective opinions. For many of the practices examined it was necessary to go back and forth between subjective views and objective operation, calling on personal experience to assess the bias or interpret the experience of practitioners, and unravelling the evaluations in the literature. If this needs justification as a research method it arises from 'triangulation', the post-positivist concept that qualitative and quantitative data can be mixed to try to understand the subject matter. This *ex culpa* is necessary for any analysis of best practice and should be considered a prelude to every section of this book.

I.3 Developing countries

The urban issues in developing countries are different from those of many developed countries. Rapid urbanisation in developing countries is often characterised by a rise in gated, protected communities, as well as the proliferation of randomly constructed slums. The

---

23 Rittel and Webber 1973.

effects of globalisation have advantaged only some of the population, leaving a wide economic gap between rich and poor. The gated communities and the slums are not part of the planned urban fabric but are enclaves with their backs to the other inhabitants, making comprehensive urban land use planning difficult. This splitting away from the urban core by the wealthy has come about for many reasons, including fear of kidnapping and other crimes in cities such as Bogota, Managua, and Rio de Janeiro.

The rate of economic growth in developing countries has been inconsistent and has given rise to a need for increased housing because of the so-called south-to-south migration in Latin America, where there is emigration to countries with greater opportunity at a pace that defies careful, considered planning. As well, environmental degradation, resource exploitation, and the growth of tourism to the detriment of inhabitants, as has happened for example in Jamaica, make many planning issues, such as sustainability or strategic environmental assessment of plans, seem irrelevant.

There is a long documented history of failed planning in developing countries. One distinct reason is that in an attempt to join the global flow of capital, a concentration on local, community development gave way to market-led imperatives, such as in Costa Rica, with its planning system focused on the exigencies of commercial success. In Latin America, some recognition of the need to plan more effectively in the midst of an onslaught of economic growth has occurred, using the so-called Barcelona Model arising from Barcelona's systematic planning for the 1992 Olympics. This model dictates that there should be concentration on individual projects rather than a plan for the entirety of the city, with public space serving to link different areas, and a governance model that embraces public as well as private interests.

The planning process in developing countries is both formal, via various planning models, and informal, through squatter settlements and local self-help. Self-help often adds to the integrity of neighbourhoods, as occurred in the squatter settlements of Lima or the barrios of Caracas, where it is palpable that residents have created social capital and a sense of community. These informal arrangements often improve on the formal structures, such as occurred in the highly planned Ciudad Guayana in Venezuela.

In many cases, traditional forms of planning in developing countries have not been adapted to current urban problems and conditions. There is therefore a large gap between the rational planning process embraced by developed countries and that undertaken in developing countries. A 2013 report by the Joint Center of Housing Studies of Harvard University, *Advancing inclusive sustainable development: correcting planning failures and connecting community capital*,[24] analysed urban planning in developing countries. The report reveals the complex interactions of the planning systems, and emphasises that it is has become crucial to identify and invest in best practices. Within this mix of formal and informal planning methods, best practices offer governments a greater capacity to plan, to link private investment to public needs by providing a higher level of certainty, and to create respect for the rights of residents. As well, given the pressing issues in developing countries of poor infrastructure and disenfranchisement, the best practices must also facilitate infrastructure development and participatory planning.

The best practice examples that emerge in this work are oriented to embrace the imbalance caused by economic inequality, to enhance the social capital that is developed by community involvement, and to increase the capacity to provide infrastructure. Best

---

24 Belsky et al. 2013.

practices are not chosen simply for those reasons but, where they serve these goals, they enhance the arguments for their inclusion. Given the integrity of these goals, where possible, the best practices address the issues of the developing world as much as those of the developed world.

I.4 Laws and policies

The laws and policies that govern the planning process are based on a structural matrix that varies greatly. That matrix in turn reflects the degree to which individual property rights are considered a fundamental right, which determines when and how intervention for the public good is allowed. For instance, the primary position in the United States is that private property is sacrosanct under the Constitution and, if planning goes too far and amounts to a taking of those rights, compensation should be paid. In Italy, property rights are not recognised in the Constitution as a fundamental right and greater intrusion through planning is considered acceptable for the public good.[25]

The subject matter of planning laws is therefore concerned with striking the cultural balance between private rights and public interests, and, as a matter of form, is clustered around the legal concern about the exercise of discretion: distribution of decision-making powers and the need for judicial or administrative review of those decisions. The laws then vary in myriad ways, influenced by the local legal tradition, the politics of the day, different modes of drafting, and the constant, complicating appearance of new ideas. It is therefore impossible to create a universally ideal set of laws as the underlying foundation is subtle and not transferable between countries. It is no wonder that the editor of a book comparing the approach of different countries as to when a planning law amounts to a taking of property rights leading to compensation expressed this sentiment:

> Time and again I have witnessed how misleading are my own and others' tendencies to extrapolate from our own country's laws and practices or to assume that we can deduce about a specific legal arrangement based on our knowledge about some foreign country.[26]

I have therefore not attempted in this book to draft a set of laws that represent best practice. A best practice of creating, say, a sustainability charter, may face difficulties in implementation in one country if there is no enabling legal mechanism, or a lengthy pattern for passing new legislation, but be easily implemented in another because ad hoc policies that carry legislative force can be made rapidly. However, some attempt at drafting a code for community participation has been undertaken, to illustrate what full participation can look like should it fit within a planning culture.

Lawyers tend to seek a legal peg on which to hang any change in planning practice. As a result, practices that may be more efficient are not adopted because of lacunae in legislation. For example, an idea for a charter of rights for individuals faced with a new land use plan may be a worthwhile concept but may fade away if it cannot be supported by the existing local framework of laws. Nevertheless, experience tells us that a good idea will

---

25 Calavita 1984.
26 Alterman 2010, xix.

linger in the background and eventually may find its way through as legislation changes, or through some other mechanism that allows its implementation. The absence of legal capacity is therefore no barrier to the efficacy of a best practice.

It should also be added that the implementation of best practice is not guaranteed even if there is a legal mechanism to bring it to fruition and it is compatible with the planning culture. Governments are engaged in carrying forward a panoply of their own ideas, and introducing a best practice may be inconsistent with the existing agenda, unfilled promises, the interests of stakeholders, the distribution of powers in a bureaucracy, the influence of lobby groups, or the personal power of the minister or head of department. For a best practice to have traction as a legal device, it must be incontrovertible, easily implemented, and seen to offer political gain.

The structure of the book reflects the fundamental issues that underpin the planning regimes of all countries. Planning regimes are predicated on employing a strategic planning process, making a choice of geographical scale for carrying out the process, attending to governance issues, allowing community participation in the process, and relying on the two predominant forms of planning control: zoning and development control. These are the essential chapters of the work. As well, particular attention is paid to the role of planning in the mitigation of greenhouse gases and adaptation to climate change. These topics are emerging as critical issues for planning control; they cannot be denied a significant place in any discussion of land use planning.

Except in the case of studies of a particular place, references have been chosen selectively as offering directions for further study and elaboration rather than as justification for principles and ideas. The currency of planning literature is not important as the same conundrums have been occupying the minds of planners for the last 60 years. Planning is a never-ending series of experiments, begun with enthusiasm, full of false promises and starts, and leading to yet further experiments in search of an elusive solution to the complexities of urban life. Between the time of writing this and when it is read, there will be new experiments, adding to or consolidating existing ideas. That is a reflection of how planning works: it can never be satisfied and it is always responding to tensions in the community.

I have quoted extensively from laws, documents, and reports that reflect the principles of good practice and less from other works. The wording and the means of expression in laws, planning schemes and policy may be helpful in understanding how best practice may be implemented. In some cases, two or three quotations on the same issue are used to indicate how an emphasis may be developed by subtle alterations in language.

At the end of each chapter is an analysis of best practice as it falls out of the discussion of the topic. The reasoning in the text is consistently oriented towards discovering what makes sense and can be useful and applicable in any regime. What is a best practice may not be enforced. It may be sidelined by stakeholders, or be contrary to the planning culture. Its relationship to the existing built environment may also not be clear. The most that a writer on comparative planning can do is to stand on a street, whether in Dubrovnik, Buenos Aires, Utrecht or Moscow, and ask what is it that works here? Why am I having this pleasant experience and what is it in the planning system, as opposed to the culture, that might have made this work? The conclusion then must be drawn that there is something in the system that is worth finding and isolating. That something is what I address in this work.

1
The planning process

1
Strategic planning

'Planning' is essentially whatever planners do rather than a specific process arising from coherent professional practice or the application of a particular theory. In fact, it has been asserted that there is no close relationship between planning theory and the manner in which decisions about the future of cities are actually made.[1]

All planning, by definition, is about wrestling with the question of how to get from here to there: how to make the urban environment better while accommodating an increasing population. The scope of land use planning is contained entirely in the two meanings of the word 'plan': to create some direction for the future, and to indicate concretely what is necessary to accomplish that vision. The traditional view of planning is that it involves implementing a vision of the future by allocating land to various uses. These uses are then arrayed on a map, which becomes the concrete representation of the vision.

It bears pointing out from the start that a city cannot be so easily viewed from an Archimedean point of reference as just a set of buildings, roads, and open spaces subject to spatial placement. The French poet Georges Perec perhaps explains it best when he says that a city is a subtle, almost indefinable, interaction of people and spaces, and that one must therefore 'stop thinking in ready-made terms, forget what the town planners and sociologists have said.'[2] Walking up Marylebone High Street in London offers a different sense of order and values then wandering down Sukhumvit Road in Bangkok. Both are the subject of land use plans, both involve a mix of uses along a linear road, but the two streets do not, to say the least, offer similar experiences. Each road reflects something deeper: a collective mind or psyche that manifests in how the city unfolds. That psyche contains an amalgam of forces, such as intergenerational aspirations, symbols, and organising principles that are largely outside conscious awareness. The fabric of a city reveals a pattern, the nature of which cannot always be articulated in a plan.

Formally, the planning process involves the description of a problem, predictions of what is necessary to correct it, and a projection of a solution into the future. The solution always carries a hope or promise of some superior state and a belief that, with time, the problem will be fixed and all will be well. All plans are therefore imbued with hope, and in most cases they point towards a grand vision or some utopian end point. Any process

---

1 Flyvbjerg 2001, 292.
2 Perec 1997, 62.

Figure 1-1 Archimedean point of reference? A city is more than a set of buildings, roads, and open spaces. Source: Google Earth.

that envisages what might be better naturally suggests end goals. It is therefore less likely to simply say that some urban ill can be improved only slightly when the possibility of a complete solution can be envisaged.

Planners want to solve urban problems; that is their imperative and *leitmotiv*. These urban problems are human problems, so issues of urban alienation, depression, loneliness, health, poverty, crime, to name but a few, should be as much a part of a plan as any other aspect, such as increasing housing density for a growing population or allocating land for development on the urban fringe. Real, difficult urban, human problems are, however, mostly excluded from the planning process. To take but one startling example, Pueblo, Colorado, is unique in having generations of crippling gang activity leading to the most murders and the highest crime rate in that state. The *Pueblo comprehensive plan*, the guiding land use plan for the area, does not even mention crime, even though crime unfortunately defines the nature of the place.

The reason that the vision does not extend to such human problems is that the subjective life of an individual is not directly assumed to be part of the planning process. There is no concern expressed when coming up with a strategy for urban expansion that the inhabitants might feel isolated or depressed at the urban fringe or become more prone to abuse alcohol or prescription drugs. Land use planning cannot turn away from the human problems of poverty, illness and the like, but makes the bet – the only bet it has the capacity to make – that, by controlling the use to which land can be put, the quality of life will be improved. Improved how, or why, or to what extent, is never expressed, as that would raise questions that are impossible to answer.

The orientation of planning is towards the resultant effects of how land can be used: housing, public open spaces, public transport, building heights, streetscapes, bike lanes, parking spaces, community facilities and tourism uses. Planners, it is said, 'use places and things to give a sense of reality to their reflections on practice and to connect to the world they find unjust and intolerable.'[3] The social goals of planning, to the extent that there is an attempt to include them, can only be marginally addressed through a narrative of what the manipulation of the physical environment may produce.

Even if planning is unable to address the many urban problems, there is a germ of an idea present in all planning regimes that urban ills of all types and the subjective feelings of the inhabitants will benefit from this manipulation of land use. Sometimes the idea is addressed directly, such as relieving the effects of economic hardship by requiring the development of affordable housing or maintaining a sense of community continuity by historic preservation. Most often the idea is indirect, found, for instance, in a requirement for development near transportation hubs to make it more convenient for the inhabitants and to prevent the alienation caused by urban sprawl.

The importance for planning of subjective feelings (discontent, alienation, loneliness, fear, depression, anger) and the consequent problems such as increased medication or substance abuse, is therefore confused, not articulated, and certainly never precise. As a consequence, there is always a disconnect between a city as lived and the city as planned. Planners can only think about uses of land; when they crossover into the themes of the collective psyche of the inhabitants, the chasm widens. A good example, found everywhere, is an idealised plan for a suburb, close to shopping facilities, jobs and schools, embodied in a city plan with lofty goals of improving the health and welfare of its inhabitants. The plan has no means to reduce depression or prevent the possible sources of family dysfunction, such as parents coming home late from the commute to work. This is because planners, at best, can only generalise about how people think and feel from their life experience and their own idealised views as to how life should be lived, and try to breathe this into the plan. Yet, with this glaring lacuna – the inability of planning to address the real urban problems – planning continues because not to plan seems anathema, leading to chaos, unpredictability and far greater urban decay. It is then accepted that, at least from a government point of view, the best that is possible can be derived by careful strategising and visioning as there is no alternative.

Perhaps the fault lies in visions being too grand and planners allowing themselves to hope that they can affect outcomes in terms of wellbeing. Much of the blame must be on the cult-like acceptance of the ideas of Jane Jacobs in *Death and life of great American cities*[4] that a person's subjective relationship with a city can be improved by greater interactions with other residents and a diversity of uses. This continues to be wholeheartedly embraced as a link between the urban environment and mental processes and is used by planners to justify introducing areas of mixed commercial and residential uses to encourage 'diversity,' employing the catchphrase of 'vital neighbourhoods'. Her ideas have powerful acceptance because the concepts appeal to planners as a chance to take their profession to a higher level by emulating what appears to be successful practices in Europe and in Greenwich Vil-

---

3 Beauregard 2012, 183.
4 Jacobs 1961.

lage. There is no doubt that an interesting mix of uses makes an area more stimulating, but how that counteracts isolation, loneliness, depression and the like is far from clear. Most importantly, it is used because it justifies the planning process as it offers a 'better' vision; it puts a mundane plan on the footing of a loftier ideal. The negative effect, apparent in almost all strategic plans, is to give a licence to planners to think too large, to speak in idealised tones and to make planning work too hard for unreachable goals.

There are so many examples of lofty goals that are so unrealistic that the plan can never be realised. In the case of Kathmandu, Nepal, one of the poorest of developing countries, the 1969 UN-financed land-use plan, *The physical development plan for Kathmandu Valley*, recommended the development of a sophisticated urban complex as a model city. The drawings suggested a utopian vision of perfect interaction of residents. None of the goals have been achieved, even before the devastating earthquake of 2016, and the plan is dutifully updated every five years to reflect the unplanned, intense real-estate boom and new developments that have taken place in the interim. Planning in Kathmandu, in spite of the goals, has abandoned the development plan and has instead taken the form of what has been called 'insurgency planning', where citizens employ informal methods to accomplish planning goals, such as forming social movements or using non-governmental organisations (NGOs) as mediators. The main problem, not addressed in the utopian plan, was that squatters were being evicted to make way for government projects on the basis that they held no proprietary interests. An NGO worked with the squatters, who formed themselves into an organisation, started protests and filed court proceedings to secure an agreement that 'genuine squatters' had recognisable rights and were entitled to compensation.[5]

In spite of the disservice done by unrealistic goals, they can never be curtailed as the utopian vision is a natural, human expression of a paradisiacal state. In October 2016, participants from 170 countries attended the UN Habitat conference in Ecuador and produced a *New urban agenda*. One of the items in the draft agenda indicates how it is impossible not to think of higher goals:

> We share a vision of cities for all, referring to the equal use and enjoyment of cities and human settlements, seeking to promote inclusivity and ensure that all inhabitants, of present and future generations, without discrimination of any kind, are able to inhabit and produce just, safe, healthy, accessible, affordable, resilient and sustainable cities and human settlements to foster prosperity and quality of life for all. We note the efforts of some national and local governments to enshrine this vision, referred to as 'right to the city', in their legislation, political declarations and charters.[6]

1.1 The logic of strategic planning

Planners work with the limited tools they have: extrapolating, forecasting, predicting. No matter how varied it may be in practice, the logical means of planning can be described as fundamentally a mix of 'strategic planning', directed towards the development of a strategy to correct problems and reach a goal, and 'spatial planning', where the results of the strategy produce a spatial allocation of uses and future development patterns. These two

---

5   Shrestha and Aranya 2015.
6   United Nations 2016, para. 11.

phases are not concerned with producing legal instruments for restricting land use, but rather occur prior to such legislative controls. The initial planning phases are concentrated on developing a positive and rational expression of a vision for a community and the direction for the realisation of that vision; it is 'planning intended for development and action, beyond the idea of planning as control.'[7]

'Spatial planning' is the inevitable result of the 'strategic planning' process: it is showing what should happen in an area displayed on a map. Together, they form an overarching process often referred to as 'strategic spatial planning'. This planning process appears to be the dominant modern form, although in practice it varies in different local contexts. The order in which its components are employed also varies:[8] the land use map or spatial plan may come first, followed by a strategic plan to define priorities for action. The spatial plan and strategic plan sometimes occur at the same time, or a strategic plan may be used to transition from one spatial plan to another.

A review of the planning systems of various countries highlights an interesting possibility that an insistence on strategic planning is embedded in subtle cultural nuances. In those countries where there is a Western influence, the notion of a strategic spatial planning process is most evident. In Singapore, India and Malaysia, highly structured, strategic planning processes reflect a strong British hierarchical arrangement. For example, in Malaysia, British laws, including planning law, were incorporated before its independence in 1957. Malaysia has a classic strategic planning process with a *National physical plan* that creates a spatial framework based on comprehensive strategic planning, which then filters down to state structure plans, local plans, and special area plans. Although there are some difficulties in local government comprehension and enforcement of these plans, there is a consensus that the Malaysian planning process has led to a 'well-structured hierarchy of development plans.'[9]

There are various theories that can be offered as to why Western countries and those with a Western institutional history have all developed, with local variations, a strategic planning system based on a similar logical, structured hierarchy.[10] One idea is that the Western concern for private property rights and the common law of nuisance dictate that incompatible uses must separate from each other, a concept at the heart of strategic spatial planning. Yet prior to that utilitarian idea of private property and nuisance is the supposition that logic and thought are the means to overcome what are essentially social and psychological issues. The basis of planning in the West is that the interiority of thought can somehow manage the external elements of life that have yet to take place.

This Western approach contrasts with that of countries where there is no history of structured, strategic planning and, in fact, no emphasis on the power of logic to overcome potential future social issues. In Bangkok, the *Bangkok comprehensive plan of 1999* is a series of spatial plans derived with the help of Western consultants. It consists of a strategic land use plan, a transportation system plan, and an open space plan. There was an earlier, traditional strategic plan completed in 1960 with the ambitious title *Greater Bangkok master plan 2033* carried out by the architectural firm Litchfield, Whiting, Bowne & Associates. One might speculate that it was perhaps so foreign to the culture that it took 32

---

7   Balducci 2011, 534.
8   Salet and Faludi 2000.
9   Ahmed et al. 2013, 16.
10 Reimer, Getimis and Blotevogel 2014.

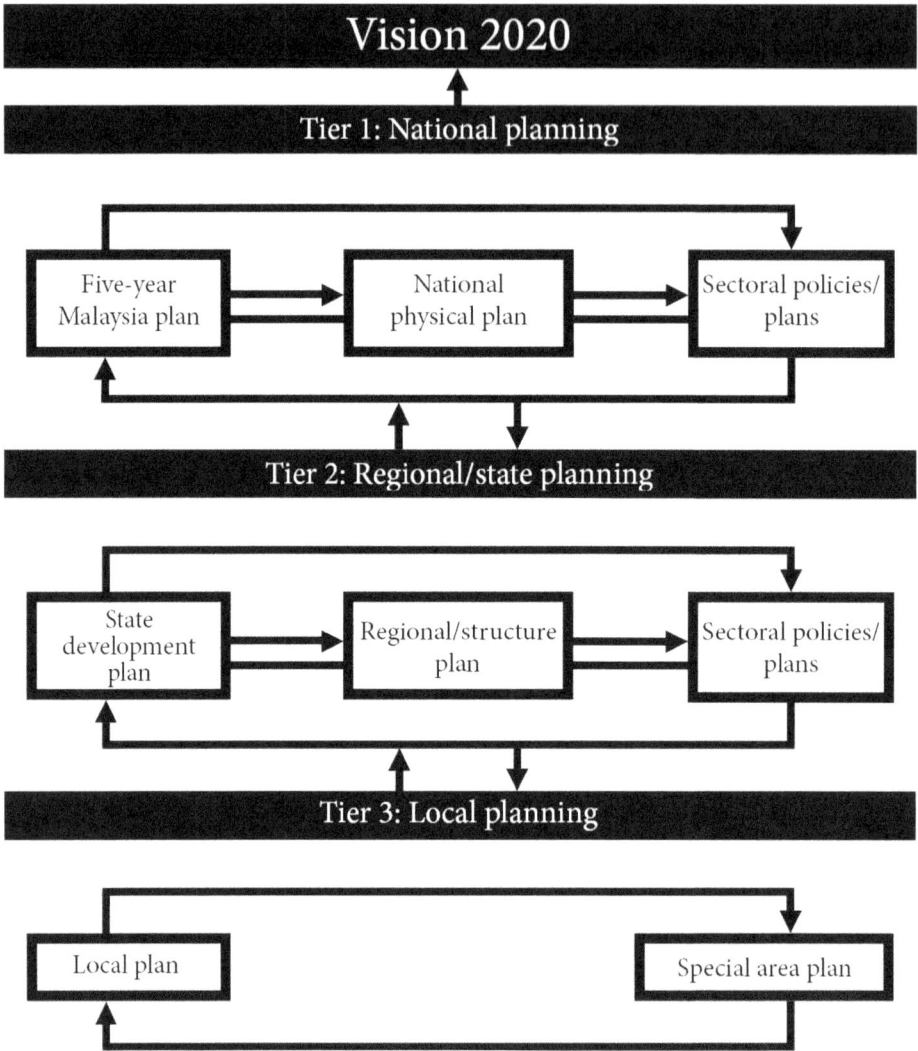

Figure 1-2 An example of a rational comprehensive planning process. Adapted from Malaysia's Federal Department of Town and Country Planning (2010), 1.1.

years for a new strategic exercise to begin. By that time, the city had grown to a population of over eight million, and it was easier to resort to a spatial plan with Western help. Sri Lanka is another case in point where, until recently, there was only ad hoc decision making and no strategic planning. In 1970, a Land Use Policy Planning Division was established in the Ministry of Lands but no strategic planning was carried out. In the case of Myanmar, the very first attempts to create a land use policy with Western aid began in 2013.

There appears, in the case of Thailand, Sri Lanka, and Myanmar, some difficulty with the idea that a sequence of steps can be taken to create an imagined future; it is as if there is a different view of time and of the capacity of planning to influence external events. This is a speculative assertion, but these countries embrace Theravada Buddhism, in which the future is considered 'as yet undetermined'.[11] It has been said that in Theravada Buddhism there is a 'thin' description of time that does not necessarily yield an appropriate course of future action, rather than a 'thick' concept as arises in the West.[12]

In any event, whatever its cultural and religious underpinnings, strategic land use planning encompasses any attempt to establish a vision for the future of an area and to seek its realisation by controlling how land is used. Strategic planning has existed for centuries, and, it is noted, 'the many types of strategic planning actually applied involve, in different ways and with different focuses, various aspects of practice absorbed at different times in planning history.'[13]

1.2 The popularity of strategic planning

A strategic planning process is the paramount means of controlling land use in most countries. Even though it has had limited success in resolving many real urban problems, it has now been adopted almost universally because it has a logical sequence, it offers the opportunity for consensus, and it is wide in scope. As such, it is widely perceived as the basis for harmony, order, and a better way of life.

A 'vision' of the future is the fulcrum of strategic planning as it is the means by which the aspirations of a community are implied and expressed. It does not matter if the vision could be different, more refined or expanded; the fact that it is enunciated is sufficient to give it all the gravitas it needs. It will then be imposed by a planning authority convinced it has the perfect set of goals.

Where community participation is allowed and the aspirations are agreed upon by consensus, belief in the vision and its importance is even stronger. In Latin America, for example, the 'vision' stage is particularly important because it is the product of a forum for participatory democracy, something lacking in many other governmental matters in the region,[14] and community participation thereby provides the imprimatur for the imposition of strategic planning. There is nothing more powerful for governments than consensus, and strategic planning therefore serves a higher goal when a vision has arisen from common understandings, agreement as to the alternatives, and a shared belief that the implementation of that vision is incontrovertibly the best thing for an area.

Logic would suggest that a consensual vision should not be random, concerned with stopping development or progress, but based on what has been called 'value rationality': values agreed upon by a community based on evidence, testing, visioning, and dialogue: '[t]he introduction of value rationality is thus a clear reaction against a future that extrapolates the past and maintains the status quo.'[15] The emphasis on evidence may conflict with a vision arising from consensus. For instance, economic analysis may suggest that a shopping area is moribund, when in fact the residents enjoy their close relationship with the

---

11   Kalupahana 1974, 183.
12   Hallisey 2013, 95.
13   Sartorio 2005, 28.
14   Steinberg 2005.
15   Albrechts 2004, 750.

vendors and would rather leave it as it is. This apparent split between evidence and consensus comes about because of limited dialogue and discussion during the participation process, whereby residents react rather than consider.

Consensus that has considered the evidence is a more complete form of community consultation than evidence alone. When strategic planning relies upon full community participation, the resultant plan is a consensual document incorporating an amalgam of the views of the planning authority, owners, residents, other stakeholders, and community advisory groups. It stands then as the highest form of strategic planning. When there is agreement about what is going to happen in the future and in what sequence, which areas are to be maintained as they are, which are going to change, and how that change is going to unfold, consultation about issues regarding individual development proposals is not as essential. An emphasis on consensual strategic planning prompts a shift away from ad hoc decision making to one of congruence with a shared vision. If a proposal does need assessment, there is at least a vision to weigh it against and a means to assess its relationship to the agreed common values. In that sense, the consensual strategic plan is the most logical form of planning, as decisions about the future of an area do not merely arise as a consequence of a dispute over particular proposals or from political debates about planning options.[16]

Strategic planning, as the logical form of making decisions and the basis of a consensual future, has become increasingly important because of the need for 'sustainable development', which requires careful analysis of all of the social and environmental aspects of development. This topic deserves, and will receive, further analysis, but by way of introduction it can be said that there is a clear link between strategic planning and sustainability. This link was declared an essential element of the strategic planning process in the European Union's *Leipzig charter on sustainable cities* in 2007:

> We recommend that European cities consider drawing up integrated urban development programmes for the city as a whole. These implementation-oriented planning tools should
>
> - describe the strengths and the weaknesses of cities and neighbourhoods based upon an analysis of the current situation,
> - define consistent development objectives for the urban area and develop a vision for the city,
> - co-ordinate the different neighbourhood, sectoral and technical plans and policies, and ensure that the planned investments will help to promote a well-balanced development of the urban area,
> - co-ordinate and spatially focus the use of funds by public and private sector players and
> - be co-ordinated at local and city-regional level and involve citizens and other partners who can contribute substantially to shaping the future economic, social, cultural and environmental quality of each area.[17]

---

16   Nadin 2000.
17   European Union 2007, 2–3.

The concept of an integrated sustainability program that describes, defines and co-ordinates invites consideration of how the the city as a whole can be advantaged. It views, as it says, the urban area in its entirety rather than concentrating on separate areas.[18] Of course, taking a whole-of-city approach to each of these tasks is formidable; how do you examine the cultural and environmental quality of an entire city? Yet, this is indisputably a rational process, with an added awareness of social and economic values that suggests it should result in a higher-order outcome. This expanded concept of strategic planning derived from the goal of sustainability does not dictate a rigid set of requirements but encourages a particular emphasis on how potential development is considered within the strategic plan. It has been said that it involves 'encouraging the emergence of particular development trajectories, thus providing orientation for local and regional actors as well as other agencies that supply infrastructure.'[19]

The strategic plan, which is the result of the strategic planning process with goals based on consensus and social and environmental values, is not to be confused with the legal, regulatory plan that imposes controls over land use in order to implement the vision. The strategic plan, in most cases, comes before the spatial plan and before any regulatory instrument used to implement it. The *San Diego regional comprehensive plan* (RCP), a strategic plan, is clear about that distinction:[20]

> [T]he RCP is not based upon a 'top down' approach of consistency and conformity, and does not include mandates regarding local staffing positions or committees. Instead, it is a collaborative planning approach that builds up from the local level into a regional framework to establish stronger connections between transportation and land use, connect local and regional plans, and foster co-operative approaches to implementing the actions identified in the plan.

1.3 Unsaid goals

On 46th Street and 8th Avenue in Manhattan there is a 43-storey residential building with floor-to-ceiling windows in the living and dining rooms, designed to be without blinds or drapes, giving the residents views to the Hudson River. Directly across 8th Avenue is the Riu Hotel, built in 2016, with 29 storeys and 640 hotel rooms, 150 of them facing the residents of the apartment building opposite. That means that at any one time perhaps 300 people can gaze into an apartment's living and dining rooms. The zoning resolution for the Special Clinton District, where the hotel is situated, sets out explicit goals to strengthen the residential character of the area and to move to lower-scale residential development from the existing mixed uses. This is just one example where it appears that a decision was made to allow a development that makes little sense.

What could be the thinking of planners? What line of reasoning prompts planners or elected officials to allow an outcome that will be deleterious to many existing residents? The only explanation is that it reflects a view that the interests of developers should be given priority, or that the city should promote a particular image. Wanting a city to be

---

18   Friedmann et al. 2004.
19   Healey 2008, 8.
20   San Diego Association of Governments 2004, 396.

Figure 1-3 46th Street and 8th Avenue, Manhattan. The Riu Hotel is on the left. Source: Google Street View.

grand, full of significant buildings, presenting a proud image, is a statement of economic power. Dubai immediately comes to mind. Its skyline announces that it is a city to be respected because of its attractiveness to investors local and foreign. Developers are allowed to make large profits from land development and are encouraged to add to the statement of the city's power. These are not the explicit goals of planning, either in theory or in practice, yet they constitute a profound and important backdrop to modern city planning.

Unsaid goals often lack rational examination of what is being provided to the developer. The development of a building such as a hotel relies upon public expenditure for infrastructure, so the government is contributing to the profit. The Riu Plaza Hotel on 46th Street is supported by transportation, electricity, sewerage, and roads, and takes advantage of other decisions and investments, such as its proximity to the revitalised Times Square. The profit of the developer is not recognised as an express consideration in planning but has, more recently, been revisited in the form of a levy on developers, an example of what is sometimes called ' value capture'. The UK *Town and Country Planning Act 1947* introduced a betterment levy to capture some of the increase in land value contributed by the public purse, an idea that failed because of its complexity rather than its theory; the 2004 UK Barker Review of Land Use Planning recommended a 'planning-gain' supplement to be paid by the developer. In many countries, levies are imposed on developers to fund the infrastructure necessary for their developments to take place. This takes many forms, such as direct contributions to pay for affordable housing, a requirement that land be handed over for public infrastructure or that developers make mandatory contributions to public infrastructure, or elaborate value-capture levy schemes to pay for transportation links, such as that being used in China's Pearl River Delta.[21]

However, even with such policies, promoting the skyscraper as an indicia of success or progress is one of the most powerful yet least articulated influences on planning. The sentiment has an effect on all public officials and planners even though it is never expressed. A good example, bordering on the ridiculous, is the City of South Perth in Western Australia, which was prepared to allow a completely incongruent 29-storey building in a low-rise neighbourhood against the wishes of the residents, who successfully took proceedings in a desperate attempt to stop the planners' inflated aspirations for their sleepy town.[22] The city attempted to amend the planning scheme to fix the problem, but in the meantime the developer applied again, in a cynical exercise, this time for a 44-storey monstrosity. The state government then altered the amendment to allow the new building and others, opening up the floodgates for South Perth to become a shining, high-rise metropolis even though it lacked sufficient services and infrastructure.

The will to power, to borrow a phrase from Nietzsche, is a driving force for developers, officials and planners. It is seldom overt, because factors such as pride, competitiveness, and the desire for large profits and power are not associated with orderly and proper planning; they have pejorative connotations. The power/profit motive is theoretically ameliorated in some cases by the concept of environmental sustainability but, as sustainability is achieved incrementally, other motives often do not meet resistance until after there already is a critical mass of development. In downtown Ho Chi Minh City in Vietnam, the Art Deco character is being lost to modern development incrementally, with hundreds of colonial-era buildings having being destroyed over a ten-year period. This has so changed the character of the major thoroughfares, such as Dong Koi Street, that the area is now more a modern, commercial centre rather than a charming, evocative colonial street.

It is developers who take the initiative to build what city planners contemplate and it is understood that they must be rewarded by profit. The need for a sufficient rate of return to justify the risk means that the developer will want to maximise the yield of the project. If land costs are high, an increase in height is required: the higher apartments sell for more because of their views. The appearance of several high-rise buildings in a previously mid- or low-rise area may trigger an impression that the area can perhaps absorb more high rise, which may lead to a new vision for the area, such as occurred in Surfers Paradise in Queensland, which now houses New York-style apartments of over 70 floors.

Underlying many unsaid goals of planning, even in the case of high-rise buildings, is the aim of constructing a pleasing experience for inhabitants and visitors. It may be couched it terms of 'maintaining the character' of existing areas or 'creating vitality' for new areas or similar vague phrases. A 'pleasing experience' does not easily permit of a clear means of expression. A person's experience of an area is created by the juxtaposition of various design aspects, the relationship of buildings to surrounding structures and to the environment, and their relative scales. Scale determines an individual's experience of their relationship with the built form. The best example of deliberately using scale to create an aesthetic experience is probably Rossi Street in St Petersburg, where the buildings are 22 metres in height, the street is 22 metres wide, and the street's length is ten times its width:

---

21 Li, Yang and Lin 2013.
22 *Nairn v. Metro-Central Joint Development Assessment Panel* [2016] WASC 56.

Figure 1-4 Dong Koi Street in Ho Chi Minh City, Vietnam.

220 metres. This is the 'golden ratio', a rectangle with a set ratio of length to width, adopted by many, including Le Corbusier, to produce a form that is aesthetically pleasing.

Aesthetics is often substituted for the vaguer formulation of a 'pleasing experience', and can be articulated as an aspect of land use planning for various reasons. The first is the integral, historic ties of planners with architects as designers and city builders. When aesthetics is a relevant consideration in planning decisions, it is to the architects that governments turn. The second is that it would be anathema for planning to say that it does not care how an area looks. Thus, restrictions on billboards for aesthetic reasons have always made sense, as has the restriction of modernist buildings in historical residential areas. It has been suggested that aesthetics in this sense is part of the shared community values that are the essence of a planning vision.[23] The unarticulated basis of aesthetics is that planning should create something pleasing and, where possible, offer an experience that is not alienating or that creates an unwelcome feeling of being trapped by the built environment.

The garden city movement in the United Kingdom in the late 19th century was a clear, articulated attempt to inform a subjective experience of pleasantness. The intention was to surround communities with green spaces and, with the city beautiful movement of the same period in North America, the results of which can be seen in Washington, D.C., suggested that beautification should be the primary goal. This aesthetic emphasis arose historically as a reaction to the squalor of overcrowding. Letchworth in the United Kingdom is an example of a town built on these principles and it has a particular quaint aesthetic that is undeniable.

The difficulty with making aesthetics the 'basis' for planning, rather than just another goal, is that it relies upon a romantic notion that an aesthetically pleasing city will forever

---

23 Costonis 1982.

1 Strategic planning

Figure 1-5 Traditional neighbourhood elements in Letchworth Garden City, Hertfordshire. Source: Google Street View.

stay that way.[24] In the Westelijke Tuinsteden district of Amsterdam, part of the *Great expansion plan* of 1934, a longstanding desire for renewal and beautification of the area led to reliance on the garden city movement. The government mandated massive areas of open space and greenery but there was little direction as to how the space was to be used and how it was to blend with the modernist architecture that became the norm in Western Europe at that time. The area has now become a focus of migration and lacks real social cohesion, far from the grand vision of the garden city movement.

Aesthetics is often used to justify planning choices as it is an accepted goal that has historical precedent. It is not often used as a main or primary goal but finds its way into various planning ideas, such as gentrification. The sequence of gentrification is that an area, previously in decay, will become a hub initially for artists and then gather momentum in attracting new shops and uses. This is consistent with the idea that planners want to make things better: get rid of the decay and revitalise an area. The negative consequences are obvious: old inhabitants are forced out and the character of the area in its decay and diversity is lost. The demand for economic progress ripples through all cities and the issues of displacement and economic inequality are never discussed as part of the planning process, in which the primacy of the new, aesthetic experience has pride of place.

An interesting case of the effects of gentrification, based on economic prosperity and justified by aesthetics, is the Little India section of Singapore. The area contains old, crumbling buildings, street food stalls and markets that create an intense, visceral experience in contrast to much of that highly planned city. The driver for gentrification has not been

---

24 Scott 1998.

artists seeking out the area, but rather the government mandating artistic uses in order to create a successful commercial area.[25] This was accomplished by offering subsidised rent for arts groups and by running a lottery for space. The consequence is that the urban fabric has been altered to make the area fit for tourism. The district now has its own commercial aesthetic, but the history and character of the place have been lost in the push to improve economic productivity.

These unarticulated goals of power, greed, and pleasantness remain mostly unsaid because they cannot be translated into adequate words. A vision statement in a strategic plan will use terms to describe a future state where things are generally better but without saying *how* they will be better for residents. For instance, in Burlington, Vermont, the 2014 *Municipal development plan* refers to the need to 'conserve and strengthen residential neighborhoods' and 'Strengthen the City Center District . . . while ensuring it meets the needs of city residents, particularly those in adjacent neighborhoods.'[26] This high level of abstraction is inevitable, as the subjective experience of a strong residential neighbourhood cannot be expressed.

The inevitable conclusion is that the goals of land use planning cannnot be directly linked to subjective experience and must instead exist at the level of abstraction. Planning hides many of the drivers of land use decisions because they appear to be impossible to articulate. The *Development strategy for the City of Warsaw until 2020* approaches this difficulty by offering a narrative that captures the general aspirations behind the plan:

> The status of capital city results in Warsaw being the most dynamically growing Polish metropolis, offering the greatest access to good jobs, good salaries and prospects of overall development and thereby attracting new inhabitants from all regions of Poland. Newer inhabitants of Warsaw are largely young and well-educated. They are motivated to succeed and gain high material rewards. They offer Warsaw the opportunity to grow, therefore we will strive to make them think of the capital as a place to live, work and relax.[27]

1.4 Neoliberalism and planning

From the 1960s, industrial cities faced unemployment and urban decay due to the closing down of industry. A master plan made little sense in the face of these economic problems. In the 1980s, the relationship of cities to the global economy became a major consideration in planning forums, although little direction emerged initially as to how planning could be useful. By the 1990s, an awareness developed that the movement of manufacturing to Asia and Latin America, and of populations from rural to urban centres, were threatening the economy of cities. In 1991, the World Bank and the United Nations Development Programme (UNDP) focused on this issue in the World Bank's *Urban policy and economic development* report and the UNDP's *Cities, people and poverty*. As one commentator explains:

---

25 Chang 2016.
26 See http://bit.ly/2gdzLbj.
27 Korcelli-Olejniczak et al. 2005, 35.

Urban policy needed therefore to go beyond issues of housing and residential infrastructure to address directly the question of urban productivity and the removal of the constraints on growth.

The World Bank introduced the idea of 'city development strategies' that went beyond manipulation of the urban environment for the purposes of harmony and order and linked planning to financial programs for urban economic development. The result, undertaken intensely in Asia with World Bank support, was the linking of strategic plans to economic plans. This link took different forms: the economic and strategic plans might be integrated, or might remain separate but take each other into account. A good example is South Korea. The pattern of five-year economic plans began in the 1960s. In 2004, the *Special Act for Balanced National Development* created a new five-year plan that sought to improve national living standards and was a prelude to the involvement of planning. In 2009, three zones were established for a five-year plan for regional development: a 'basic living zone', a 'wide-area economic zone', and a 'super-wide living zone'. In these zones, improvement of living standards as well as creation of employment are emphasised. Fifty-six areas were designated 'living areas of happiness', to be developed by increased infrastructure and planning.

The emphasis on economic development in strategic planning may be a necessity in developing countries. In Bangladesh, *Vision 2021* is a policy document that directs that the country should aim to increase its population of middle income earners. The *Sixth five-year plan*, as of 2016, therefore includes every possibility for accelerating growth and reducing poverty, including strengthening the role of local government and providing for the introduction of a more elaborate urban planning system. Although current strategic plans for Dhaka and the *pourashavas* (the cities) do not link directly to the five-year pan, the plans required for the *upazilas* (districts) suggest the possibility of a greater linking to economic goals.

Economic development or neoliberalism are the underlying goals of nearly all current strategic plans. It is hard to resist in all its aspects and has even been extrapolated to the sensitive environment as it is a worldwide phenomenon, although opposition is often expressed:

> It is important to note that even state functionaries can resist the wholesale implementation of neoliberal development paths (especially the veneer of liberal democratic politics), such as those who insist on 'Asian-style democracy' in the midst of establishing open markets and free trade.[28]

Consequently, neoliberal economic development in all its forms, with its stress on competition, free markets, the reduction of individual liberty and limited government, is a primary goal of strategic planning in all societies. Margaret Thatcher's statement that 'there is no alternative' to neoliberalism and the idea that it is the best way to build wealth and improve societies predominates as the backdrop to all planning structures, controls, and plans.

The idea of economic growth as the true measure of public and individual welfare is essential to a government's self-image. All countries have strategic plans based on wealth

---

28   Mittelman 2000, 177.

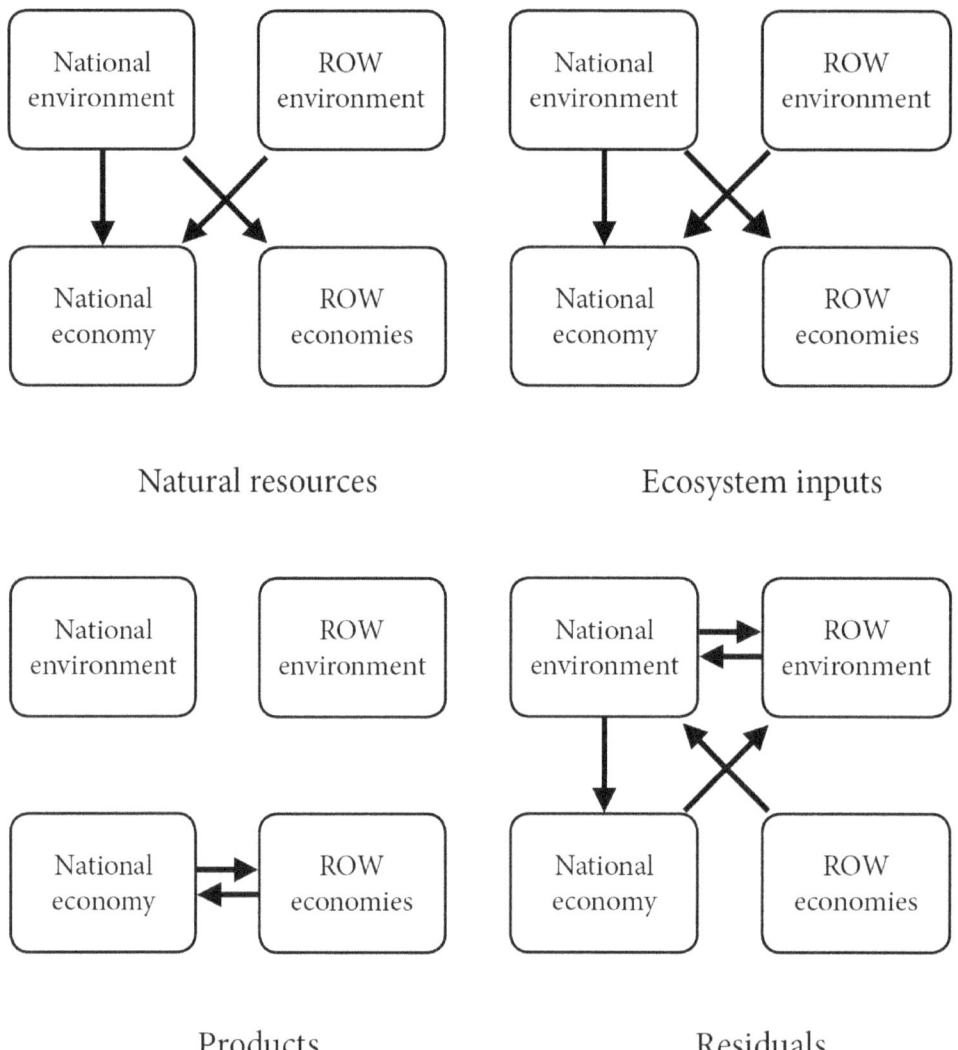

Figure 1-6 Material flows between the national and rest of world (ROW) economies and the environment. Adapted from United Nations et al. 2003, 31.

creation; they are a direct result of World Bank and International Monetary Fund requirements for developing countries. It has been observed that in India, 'neoliberal growth produces glittering cities, with ostentatious new tall buildings, streets with cars, and well-dressed young people who are incessantly on the cell phone, all of which makes it look like "everyone is doing well".[29]

---

[29] Peet 2011, 17–18.

The continuous push for economic growth and the neoliberal agenda affects cities in several ways. Primarily, they become competitive with each other for private investment, they tend to monetise public land by making protected land available for development, and they enter into public–private funding arrangements or create value-capture schemes to accelerate infrastructure development. The basis of this competitive movement is always the belief that an increase in wealth provides the highest form of benefit for the citizenry. In planning terms, this is manifested by the desire of the state to push for growth, fast track applications, allow the market to dictate the form of development, and demonstrate urban power through powerful statements such as sports stadiums and other iconic projects. A government is both captured by the need for economic growth and frightened of its effect. The fear comes from the formation of elite power structures, abuse of official power for monetary gain, and the grumbling of inhabitants who must do battle to maintain a semblance of the status quo.

A study of Brussels, caught up in the EU's push to foster urban competitiveness and decentralisation, analysed the *Brussels international development plan,* which aimed to attract foreign investors by establishing large infrastructure projects and opening up previously reserved and protected land for development.[30] The plan was given such priority that it existed outside the regional planning process and had the effect of fragmenting planning policy and bypassing planning controls. It did not consider sustainability or participatory planning. The plan is representative of other initiatives with the same goals, such as a metropolitan commission imposing projects on local governments or the use of separate development corporations to implement large projects. However manifested, the desire for economic growth easily provides the means to override the fundamental format of structure planning.

An alternative to the onslaught of neoliberalism is to enhance public participation, place greater reliance on the emergent vision, and approve development according to that vision. This process is, however, fragile in the wake of an economic growth agenda because the public's view is seen as weaker than that of the experts, and because visions are subjective and promote local or individual interests that may be perceived as parochial. This has led to reactionary attempts to focus on residents' political and planning rights. The 2001 Brazil *City statute* provides that all branches of government must recognise the 'social function' of the city by prioritising the collective interest over private ownership and the efficient use of land over increasing land value. This echoes the philosopher Henri Lefebvre's concept that the social function of property should have priority over individual rights of exploitation; what he called the 'right to the city'. For many years, this led to a call for a world charter for the right to the city, in recognition perhaps that cities are a source of imposed neoliberalism and inequity, and that they lack participatory democracy and ignore sustainable development.

The UN's *New urban agenda* of 2016 is that world charter, adopted by 170 countries recognising the 'right to the city'. It sets out major goals for the future of urban areas with three underlying principles: to end oppression in the form of poverty and discrimination; to ensure sustainable urban economies; and to guarantee environmental sustainability. The specific goal related to urban planning is:

---

30   Vermuelen 2008.

We commit ourselves to promoting the development of urban spatial frameworks, including urban planning and design instruments that support sustainable management and use of natural resources and land, appropriate compactness and density, polycentrism and mixed uses, through infill or planned urban extension strategies as applicable, to trigger economies of scale and agglomeration, strengthen food system planning, and enhance resource efficiency, urban resilience and environmental sustainability.[31]

The *New urban agenda* offers, in its words, a 'paradigm shift', which is obviously a reaction to the inequalities caused by neoliberalism and the weakening of participation in the face of progress. The agenda suggests that the consequences of the rush to progress in urban areas are patent and that a counterforce is necessary. What that urban spatial framework might look like is not easy to imagine because development is how a city grows and developers will always desire profit to offset their risk. Their expectations of future profit and growth are not readily curtailed and the idea of 'appropriate compactness and density' is confusing but seems to suggest containing urban sprawl and encouraging increased density near transport hubs. Although it is vague and aspirational, the importance of the *New urban agenda* should not be underestimated as it is perhaps the first coherent cry to redress the hidden neoliberal drivers of the planning process. In a planning culture based on neoliberalism, the planning process is often perceived as a stumbling block to growth, forcing amendments, exceptions, legal challenges and political interference. Seeking to move projects along, governments limit community involvement to token participation, pay lip service to the vision, or espouse grand ecological plans in order to legitimise a bias in favour of development. This issue can only be solved by a paradigm shift and the *New urban agenda* may be that harbinger of change.

1.5 Sustainability and 'smart cities'

Sustainability is the name given to the goal of protecting the environment while maintaining economic growth. It deserves special attention as it is an underlying theme of planning theory and practice in all countries. As one example, the *STEP 2025: Urban development plan for Vienna* pointedly explains that sustainability is the driver of investment and innovation in the plan.[32]

Many historical eventsour and ideas converged to elevate sustainability to the peak criterion in strategic planning. If any one source can be highlighted as most important, it is perhaps the obvious failure of strategic planning to address urban ills, which fostered a desperate need for hope of an alternative. As an example, Lord Rogers' report, published in the United Kingdom in 2000, *Our towns and cities – the future – the urban white paper* emphasised that compact cities with social and environmental sustainability were the only means to redeem urban failures. Planners and governments needed a rallying cry to justify strategic planning as offering a better quality of life.[33]

There is much in the word itself that offers hope as it implies creating an urban future that can continue indefinitely because the right choices are made. It is general enough to

---

31 United Nations 2016, para. 51.
32 Municipal Department, Urban Development and Planning 2014.
33 Department for Communities and Local Government 2000.

support any number of other planning goals, such as quality of life, good social relations, health, or prosperity. It contains a powerful symbolism, promising a world where growth and the environment are balanced so that massive increases in population and the endless need for more housing and infrastructure will not be destructive. It is far more powerful than pleasantness, aesthetics, or diversity and has therefore become the catchword for all plans, policies, and strategies.

The dual aspects of sustainability – economic growth and protection of the environment – are expressed as one positive concept: the environment must be protected for future generations, and economic prosperity, achieved by increased production of goods and services, is necessary for all. The two goals are independently incontrovertible and within the notion of 'sustainability' are in theory balanced. Sustainable economic growth is sometimes characterised as 'green growth' or, more commonly, 'sustainable development'. Cities that adopt these goals have been labelled 'smart cities'.

This concept of smart cities carrying out the sustainability agenda appears straightforward and useful, but being labelled a smart city has become a means of attracting government funding to stimulate economic growth. Thus a commitment to sustainability is often co-opted for solely economic ends. The Smart Cities Mission, an initiative of the Central Indian government, allocated billions of rupees to 20 cities to redevelop derelict areas. The project aimed to make a statement that the growth of the urban population to almost 400 million people could be managed sustainably by economic means, but in practice it has increased property values without concern for broader environmental issues. This is one illustration of how the concept of sustainability does not offer an inherently balanced process and is capable of being manipulated.

The definition and scope of sustainability in strategic planning has gone through several phases. Before its adoption by strategic planning, the term appeared in the 1987 report of the World Commission on Environment and Development of the United Nations, *Our common future*, also known as the Brundtland report. It defined 'sustainable development' as 'development that meets the needs of the present without compromising the ability of future generations to meet their own needs'. The report explained:

> In essence, sustainable development is a process of change in which the exploitation of resources, the direction of investments, the orientation of technological development; and institutional change are all in harmony and enhance both current and future potential to meet human needs and aspirations.[34]

The UN Conference on Environment and Development's *Rio declaration on environment and development* in 1992 refered to the Brundtland report's definition of 'sustainable development' and outlined the principles for its achievement. These principles became the starting point for making sustainability a focus of planning. The two relevant principles are:

> Principle 4: In order to achieve sustainable development, environmental protection shall constitute an integral part of the development process and cannot be considered in isolation from it . . .

---

34 United Nations 1987, chap. 2, sect. I.15.

Principle 15: In order to protect the environment, the precautionary approach shall be widely applied by States according to their capabilities. Where there are threats of serious or irreversible damage, lack of full scientific certainty shall not be used as a reason for postponing cost-effective measures to prevent environmental degradation.[35]

The Rio declaration makes environmental considerations an integral aspect of the definition of 'sustainable development' and the precautionary principle, used to protect the environment against scientific doubt, a fundamental, underlying proposition. The precautionary principle is particularly applicable to planning as it requires that land uses that *may* cause environmental harm be refused. The outcomes document from revisiting the Rio Principles at the Rio+20 conference in 2012, *The future we want*, did not change the definition or scope of sustainability but added a decisive change in emphasis:

We recognize that urgent action on unsustainable patterns of production and consumption where they occur remains fundamental in addressing environmental sustainability and promoting conservation and sustainable use of biodiversity and ecosystems, regeneration of natural resources and the promotion of sustained, inclusive and equitable global growth.[36]

The concept of taking action on 'unsustainable patterns of production and consumption', and the meaning behind this change in emphasis, was addressed in a report prepared in 2011 for the Rio Conference by the United Nations Environment Programme, *Towards a green economy: pathways to sustainable development and poverty eradication*. The report attempted to realign economic growth as *dependent* upon a 'green economy' that prioritises the environment. It suggested that economic growth should be restricted where environmental limitations required and that this should apply to every aspect of urban growth, so that all patterns of production and consumption would become sustainable by explicitly taking into account environmental values. It stated:

In a green economy, growth in income and employment should be driven by public and private investments that reduce carbon emissions and pollution, enhance energy and resource efficiency, and prevent the loss of biodiversity and ecosystem services. These investments need to be catalysed and supported by targeted public expenditure, policy reforms and regulation changes.[37]

In such an economy, economic growth would serve environmental concerns. The programs suggested in the report made land use planning the primary method for delivering a green economy, as planning offers a means of controlling production and consumption so that they fulfil environmental objectives. Even though the Rio+20 outcomes are not binding, and have received criticism for ignoring particular requirements such as biodiversity,[38] they represent a shift in the use of the concept of sustainable development in land use planning.

---

35 United Nations 1992.
36 United Nations 2012, para. 61.
37 United Nations Environment Programme 2011.
38 Carriere et al. 2012.

The definition of 'sustainable development' from the *Brundtland report* has remained the operative international definition in use in strategic planning, and has not followed the change in emphasis suggested in *Rio+20*; it does not favour either growth or environmental concerns, but provides that all decisions embrace economic development *as well as* environmental values in a manner that does not detract from the needs of future generations.

Applying this definition, the use of land for economic purposes should not be permitted unless it is at least in harmony with environmental values. This, however, is where the problems begin, as the balance between the two is confusing. The difficulty of achieving some form of harmony between the two probably fostered the branch of economics called 'ecological economics',[39] in an attempt to meld disparate sciences. Economics is concerned with continued growth, the engine of progress, and ecology is concerned with the natural environment, with no concern for economic needs. Ecological economics has been at the forefront of demanding equal importance for both and has suggested the phrase 'ecologically sustainable development' (ESD) to emphasise the ecological aspect of sustainability. 'Development', which denotes progress and economic growth, should not be given pride of place.

Two schools of thought have developed as to the balance to be struck: the first is referred to as 'weak' ESD and accepts that there are instances when natural capital (the natural world in economic terms) can, in fact, be sacrificed for economic growth. The second is 'strong' ESD, which provides that, in order to preserve the environment for the benefit of future generations (the essence of sustainability), maintaining the natural environment must be given the higher priority.

Some have argued that 'ecological sustainability', with its emphasis on environmental values, and 'sustainable development' as an economic concept should never be joined together under a single definition of 'sustainability' because doing so dilutes the importance of environmental preservation.[40] In this view, any wide definition of 'sustainability' that encompasses economic as well as environmental considerations improperly links economic, social and environmental concerns when in fact the environment requires primary consideration.[41]

'Ecologically sustainable development' has not gained favour as a general phrase in strategic planning except in Australia and in other countries where there are delicate issues of threatened ecosystems, such as coastal reserves.[42] In these countries, there may have been a change in emphasis to favour the primacy of the environment rather than attempting to strike a balance. When planning uses the term 'sustainable development' alone, the primacy of economic development is implied. In practice, however, the inclusion of 'ecologically' may not always be sufficient to change the emphasis, if that is what is desired. For example, if there is a need for new housing development for a rising population, issues of economic growth will predominate because of the policy orientation of government agencies to carry out their duties of distributing population increases.[43] In a study of sustainability in Birmingham,[44] it was concluded that, although the term 'sustainabil-

---

39   Splash 2012.
40   Langhelle 2000.
41   Hopwood, Mellor and O'Brien 2005.
42   Mavrommati and Richardson 2012.
43   Ehrenfeld 2000.

ity' in policies squarely encompassed environmental considerations, these considerations in practice were subservient to the need for housing growth and economic investment.

It is clear in this Birmingham study, and others of insotances where ESD has been expressed but ignored,[45] that the application of the principles of sustainability, however it is defined, depends on political positions rather than linguistic subtleties. An example is the strong orientation towards economic development in the UK *Localism Act 2012*, which was derived from a political agenda to aid a rapid public-sector deficit reduction plan in which economic growth was given priority.[46] No definition of sustainability, however cast, could meet that political juggernaut. This leads to the conclusion that any definition will be less important than a government's desire to implement sustainability to its greatest extent.

1.6 Approaches to sustainability

In the United Kingdom, the 1999 report *A better quality of life: a strategy for sustainable development for the UK* included a reminder that protection of the environment is a critical aspect of sustainability and suggested that planning systems should recognise this goal. This was to be accomplished through an environmental review of draft strategic plans rather than by an expanded definition of sustainability.[47] In the environmental review, factors such as ecosystems and vulnerable areas could be identified, and growth limited in response. In 1999, *Planning policy guidance 12* was published to specifically require a full environmental appraisal of draft strategic plans. In 2012, as part of the *Localism Act*, this and other policies were subsumed in the single *National planning policy framework* (NPPF). *Statement 165* of the NPPF provides:

> A sustainability appraisal which meets the requirements of the European Directive on strategic environmental assessment should be an integral part of the plan preparation process, and should consider all the likely significant effects on the environment, economic and social factors.[48]

The *European directive* outlines methods to carry out a sustainability appraisal of all plans.[49] Prior to the NPPF, there was a much stronger and wider statement in a specific planning policy (*Planning policy statement 1*) that provided:[50]

> Planning authorities should ensure that sustainable development is treated in an integrated way in their development plans. In particular, they should carefully consider the inter-relationship between social inclusion, protecting and enhancing the environment, the prudent use of natural resources and economic development.

---

44 Lombardi et al. 2011a.
45 Wieglib et al. 2012.
46 Bentley and Pugalis 2013.
47 Benson and Jordan 2004.
48 Department for Communities and Local Government 2012.
49 European SEA Directive 2001/42/EC.
50 *Planning policy statement 1 (PPS1): Delivering sustainable development*, para. 24.

It was argued in a note in *The Architects' Journal*, no doubt making patent what many were thinking, that references to 'sustainable development' and a 'sustainability appraisal' without any specific reference to the primacy of the environment meant that the NPPF was concerned with economic growth but not environmental protection.[51] The note mentions that the local government minister stated:

> Six years on, there are some respects where thinking on sustainability has progressed. For example, there is the idea that the separate pillars of the economy, the environment and the social aspects of sustainability can be traded off against the other . . . Our intention was to make sure that we are not stranded in our thinking when we might have a more progressive approach to sustainability.

Prior to the NPPF coming into effect in March 2012, the former chair of the Sustainable Development Commission stated that, because of the primary emphasis on economic growth as proclaimed by the use of the term 'sustainable development' in *Planning policy 1*, 'sustainable development as a mediating framework in planning is essentially dead'.[52] The emphasis was taken to be on economic growth, even though the policy was indeed wider.

The essence of the *Localism Act* is that individual communities will decide their own future direction. Local plans become the means for respecting environmental values and introducing ecological sustainability to strategic plans. The *City of Westminster core strategy of 2011*, after revisions in 2013, suggests that the NPPF definition of sustainability has had no limiting effect on the city and its efforts to balance 'competing requirements and demands to deliver against economic, social and environmental objectives'.[53]

Since 2005, the Greater London Authority has had a policy, *Sustainable design and construction: supplementary planning guidelines*, that provides a sustainability checklist for evaluation of development proposals.[54] This concept of a checklist has been adopted by other local authorities (e.g. Milton Keynes) and brings in all aspects of ecologically sustainable development. Rather than using sustainability to appraise draft plans, this approach considers sustainability in determining applications to develop land.

These local interpretations of how to effect a balance arise because the NPPF does not provide guidance as to what a sustainability appraisal entails and, more importantly, how to strike a balance or what really is being implied. Perhaps because of the vagueness of the NPPF, other means of environmental evaluation have developed through the Natural England program and the *Environmental Damage (Prevention and Remediation) Regulations 2009* that were introduced on 1 March 2009 to implement the provisions of the European Commission's *Environmental liability directive* for environmental offsets.

Sustainability as a means of embedding environmental considerations in strategic planning, in the absence of any guidance, takes its strength from the application of the precautionary principle at the time of considering an application for development rather than by resorting to a definition or a statement in a vision or policy. It requires that for any proposed development, environmental considerations be investigated and given priority if there will be environmental harm, even in the face of scientific doubt. The precautionary

---

51 Murray 2011.
52 Hickley 2011.
53 City of Westminster 2011.
54 Greater London Authority 2014.

principle is a matter of EU law[55] and the Health Safety Executive of the United Kingdom, at an early stage, developed policies and methods for its use and implementation.[56] As a consequence, the precautionary principle is subsumed in the general law and does not need separate expression in the NPPF. However, it appears to be most effective when the two are combined specifically so there is no doubt about the orientation.

Northern Ireland is a good example of an all-of-government approach leaving nothing to chance, using all aspects of ESD and resulting in strong ESD in decision making. The *Northern Ireland (Miscellaneous Provisions) Act 2006* (sect. 25) provides that every public authority must act in a way that it 'considers best calculated to contribute to the achievement of sustainable development' and must have regard to any strategy or guidance relating to sustainable development.

Northern Ireland's *Sustainable development strategy* of 2010 provides for the creation of a sustainability implementation plan that includes 'local government commitments' to ESD. This was followed by the *Sustainable development implementation plan* of April 2011. The strategy expresses the goals of sustainability:

> Sustainable development aims to bring viability, stability and opportunity to all of our social, economic and environmental activities and programmes. It does not aim to stop us from growing our economy. It does not seek to obstruct our attempts to improve our society and communities. It does not prevent us from using and capitalising on our natural resources. Rather its goal is to put in place economic, social and environmental measures to ensure that we can continue to do all of these things effectively in the years to come.

In addition, the Northern Ireland Planning Service, in *Planning policy statement 1 (PPS1): general principles*, emphasises both a wide definition of sustainability and the precautionary principle. This sustainability agenda is then implemented by local councils, such as in the *Belfast sustainable development action plan 2009–2011*. The critical concept that underlies the success of the Northern Ireland sustainability agenda is the continuous coordination of activities on all levels of government so as to provide a clear direction for local governments to balance the different measures.[57]

The UK sustainability agenda as set out in the NPPF, in contrast, reflects a weak ESD, depleted by a development-driven requirement for housing for a growing population. As such, the emphasis is on development and not on environmental considerations. The environmental component is devolved by the governance arrangements of the *Localism Act* to local governments, leading to some reported difficulty in matching wide, international sustainability goals to local interests.[58]

The notion of sustainability has more recently expanded beyond environmental concerns balanced with economic growth and has become all embracing. In 2015, the UN released 17 sustainable development goals and 169 targets to be met by 2030 in the document *Transforming our world: the 2030 agenda for sustainable development*.[59] These goals include ending poverty and hunger, achieving gender equality, conservation of oceans,

---

55   European Commission 2000.
56   United Kingdom Interdepartment Liaison Group on Risk Assessment 2002.
57   Wilde et al. 2006.
58   Cowell 2013.
59   United Nations 2015b.

and reducing inequality within and between countries. Although a guidance statement followed (*Mainstreaming the 2030 agenda for sustainable development*) suggesting ways to include these wider goals in state and local plans, little in the original document is directed at strategic planning or balancing economic growth with the environment.

As can be seen by the *Northern Ireland planning policy* and local initiatives, the essence of sustainability is in fact contained in local sentiments derived from country-wide commitments. Local initiatives derive their legitimacy from a wider state policy. However, even if this link is established, and even where there is an overarching state or regional policy, it is clear that local concerns define the scope of sustainability in strategic planning, as was suggested in studies in the Netherlands.[60]

Where a planning system does not place adequate importance on the environment, or where a weak ESD policy is in place, a counterbalance can be achieved by having community participation so that sustainability concerns can be expressed, and by implementing local requirements that sustainability be considered in the development process.[61] The development checklist of the Greater London Authority is one example, but there are others; the emphasis on economic sustainability is not necessarily at the cost of environmental considerations.

New Zealand was an early adopter of a sustainability agenda and has a comprehensive, co-operative scheme. The 1991 *Resource Management Act* (sect. 5.2) defines 'sustainable management' as:

> managing the use, development, and protection of natural and physical resources in a way, or at a rate, which enables people and communities to provide for their social, economic, and cultural wellbeing and for their health and safety while –
>
> a. sustaining the potential of natural and physical resources (excluding minerals) to meet the reasonably foreseeable needs of future generations; and
> b. safeguarding the life-supporting capacity of air, water, soil, and ecosystems; and
> c. avoiding, remedying, or mitigating any adverse effects of activities on the environment.

In section 7, a list of sustainability matters is presented for consideration for all decision makers under the act. This is an extensive list that includes such matters as 'intrinsic values of ecosystems' and 'maintenance and enhancement of the quality of the environment'. The Environment Court of New Zealand initially concluded that these provisions do not override other relevant consent issues for planning permission and this was affirmed by the High Court. However, the New Zealand parliament amended the act to add that decision makers must give prime consideration to the list of matters under the act.[62]

A comprehensive study of the act states that 'the guiding rationale for decision makers remains economic, despite intentions to the contrary' and that the intent of the act has not been realised.[63] The conclusion of this study was that local or community environmental

---

60 Runhaar 2009.
61 Lombardi et al. 2011b; Menchini and Rosati 2013.
62 Birdsong 2002.
63 Knight-Lenihan 2007.

initiatives are needed to enhance and orient the central government sustainability agenda, even though it is technically relevant to local decision making.

What can be understood from the New Zealand experience is that the best approach is to include in legislation the most comprehensive definition of sustainability possible that lists specific matters to be taken into account by decision makers. It is then the list of specific matters to which a decision maker must turn and not just a definition. This offers local governments an opportunity to embrace strong ESD *if* that accords with local ideas.

The deficiency appears to be that local or regional decisions are influenced by neoliberal ideas for economic growth and any checklist of consideration does not have force against this imperative. As the checklist contains all the elements of sustainability, it is possible it will draw attention to matters of environmental concern even if it ultimately defers instead to economic growth. The definition of 'sustainability' is at least more effective when it is combined with specific indicators.

Germany has an integrated system of sustainability. It carries out spatial planning in a comprehensive manner according to a constitutional framework: the national government makes policies, and the communities and regions (Gemeinden and Länder) create the formal instruments for spatial planning. Co-operation is the nature of the system. The Federal Office for Building and Regional Planning reports on the progress of spatial planning to the federal parliament, providing an examination of the success of these plans.[64] The *Federal Spatial Planning Act of 1998* introduced the notion of sustainability as:

> a sustainable spatial development which reconciles the social and economical demands of space with its ecological function, leading to a lasting, spaciously balanced order.

Elaborating on this act and the requirement to reconcile completing demands, a set of indicators was developed to assess sustainable spatial development according to 17 core tests that cover all aspects of economic competitiveness as well as ecological sustainability. This makes sustainability, according to the strategy, an 'interregional and intergenerational norm of justice'. The 2012 *Report on sustainability in Germany* expanded the core to 21 criteria, all of which are rated across the country for individual cities.[65] The essence of the German system is vertical integration of federal sustainability principles into regional strategic and spatial planning by use of benchmarks. The Länder were involved in the formulation of the federal strategy and various co-operative sustainability groups were established, including the German Council for Sustainable Development and the Parliamentarian Council for Sustainable Development, and sustainability was expressly recognised in a statement of the Association of Municipalities.

The concept of inter-government relationships and co-operation between the state and local government may be more important in carrying out sustainability goals than even indicators. In a report by the Netherlands Environmental Assessment Agency, *The energetic society: in search of a governance philosophy for a clean economy*, it was argued that 'There is no blueprint for the sustainable city. The sustainable city is rather a collective quest that begins with a willingness to address the problem.'[66] This concept of the sustainable city in the Netherlands therefore requires community participation so that sustainability con-

---

64 Manderscheid 2012.
65 Statistisches Bundesamt 2012.
66 Hajer 2011.

cerns are balanced with growth according to a local consensus. However, the report makes it clear that even with an emphasis on environmental issues, growth cannot be ignored:

> A government wants to achieve something with a regional city: it needs to be capable of generating high levels of economic dynamism, it must attract individuals and businesses, and it needs to challenge residents as well as giving them a feeling of security.[67]

Germany and the Netherlands offer two examples of how sustainability can be integrated into strategic and spatial planning at all levels. The German approach is that of converting the definition of sustainability into a set of objective or audit criteria that makes its scope beyond controversy as the criteria can include all principles of ESD. The Dutch approach is a dynamic evaluation of sustainability in a local context according to continuous dialogue and the creation of policy.[68]

What is noteworthy about Germany and the Netherlands is that the strategic planning process is, at its core, aspirational and based on a vision for a community, thus allowing sustainability to form a significant part of that vision.[69] It is in the visioning process that the scope of sustainability becomes clear. This does not conflict with the fact that the main basis for planning in Europe is a neoliberal approach that is focused on economic growth.

Where the primary priority is economic growth, a wide range of considerations under the heading of 'sustainablity' can offer a counterbalance.[70] This has both the advantage of a flexible concept and the disadvantage of encouraging unrealistic aspirations which cannot be addressed successfully through a plan. Sustainability is, therefore, becoming one of those concepts that means everything and nothing. It is best understood in the fears and concerns of local residents or as part of the political governance structure between state goals and local or regional acceptance. It does not matter whether there is a checklist or indicators or a narrow definition – it lives as a concept in the will of the people at a particular point in time.

Planning remains the focus of sustainability in making land use decisions, even when there are strategies or policies outside planning. In the USA, the comprehensive plan contains all of the goals of strategic planning in a single document. The elements of this plan can therefore include local expressions of sustainability in any aspect. For example, the *San Francisco general plan* contains approximately 90 specific statements relating to environmental issues in addition to general policies, such as the following (policy 1.4):

> In reviewing all proposed development for probable environmental impact, careful attention should be paid to upholding high environmental quality standards. Granted that growth provides new economic and social opportunities, uncontrolled growth can also seriously aggravate environmental deterioration. Development projects, therefore, should not disrupt natural or ecological balance, degrade the visual character of natural areas, or otherwise conflict with the objectives and policies of the General Plan.[71]

---

67 Hajer 2011, 38.
68 Healey 2007.
69 Aiginger and Guger 2006.
70 Keil 2009.
71 Department of City Planning 1988.

In San Francisco, a sustainable development program has been created outside the comprehensive plan and focuses on greenhouse gas emissions and sustainable infrastructure systems. This has been accomplished by the establishment of 'eco-districts' such as the central corridor transport-oriented development and the creation of other land use plans that specifically take into account environmental considerations. These are limited extensions to sustainability and the focus is still on planning. *The Sustainable Communities and Climate Change Act 2008* of California requires a metropolitan planning organisation for each region to prepare a 'sustainable communities strategy'. *Plan Bay Area* is the strategy that encompasses San Francisco and contains an environmental impact report for possible future development as well as a separate section for an 'equity analysis'. This analysis is tied into the public participation plan that takes into account the community vision.

The important characteristic of these examples is that sustainability is perceived to be at the core of planning by the planning authority and the local community, and is not something merely imposed by a definition or a checklist. A specific case in point is the City of Mountain View in California, which established a citizen group called the Environmental Sustainability Task Force, which led to a city approved *Environmental sustainability action plan*.[72] This was separate to, but fed into, the general plan process and to other activities that reflect environmental concerns.

What is apparent in a review of the sustainability plans for individual cities in the United States is that, where there is specific attention paid to the environmental consequences of development in a particular location, this will be more important than general government statements as to the scope or definition of sustainability.[73] In those places that benefit from participation in relation to sustainability, the understanding and implementation of sustainability goals go beyond mere baselines or goals or definitions and offer a consensual vision of community sustainability values.

In creating such a sustainability vision, it is most useful when an explanation of the community views of the reasons behind sustainability choices is provided. For example, the *Philadelphia Greenworks plan* consists of well-explained, general statements, as well as baselines, although it has still been criticised for a lack of specificity.[74] However, the sentiment that explains the community vision is important because general baselines are more likely to be incomplete and confusing because of the incompatible notions of economic growth and environmental restraints. To be even more complete, a detailed index or a set of measures for sustainability can be added in conjunction with the explanation of the general concepts. The combination of explanations of concepts and baselines with specific indices offers the most comprehensive understanding of what is possible as a sustainability platform within a strategic plan. In analysing the possibilities for Philadelphia, it is stated:

> Our survey and focus groups thus suggest a comprehensive model (or set of models) of sustainability in which land-use policies (e.g., open space requirements, restrictions on impervious surfaces, or zoning bonus provisions for meeting energy efficiency goals) serve as independent variables and sustainability metrics (derived from the baselines that we have begun to establish, such as those associated with a return to the prehuman hy-

---

72 Attinger 2011.
73 Guy and Marvin 2000.
74 Dilworth 2011.

drologic cycle or a reduction in nonrenewable energy consumption) serve as dependent variables.[75]

The concept of developing sustainability metrics in addition to participation relates sustainability to expressed outcomes or goals and clarifies their scope. It is not necessary to construct an index from scratch as there are many that have been created that dovetail with strategic planning. For example, the United Nations Centre for Human Settlements has developed the City Development Index, which examines all aspects of lifestyle quality and economic growth.[76] The UN Statistics Institution published *Integrated environmental and economic accounting*, which provides resources for understanding how to quantify the different aspects of sustainability.[77] The importance of these metrics is that they are more effective than general statements in legislation or in policies alone where it is not clear as to the operational conditions for environmental sustainability.[78] It has also been argued that the lack of a full enunciation of the concept of sustainability creates confusion as to why the sustainable metrics are being used, so that it is probably more effective for the two to be combined.[79]

1.7 Use of external forms for sustainability

A wider vision for sustainability beyond land use planning is made patent in Bavaria:

> Many municipalities are developing (strategic) plans or visions, which they are not obliged to do. On the one hand, this shows that spatial planning, unlike in some other European countries, is not confined to land use planning, regulating exclusively the use of a certain piece of ground. It clearly indicates that spatial planning is rather an activity that seeks to coordinate all spatially relevant interests, functions, programs, and projects.[80]

The Bavarian explanation is saying that, as a country, it has decided that sustainability should not be confined merely to land use but should include all of the wider elements now being addressed by the *New urban agenda* and the *UN agenda* for 2030.

The British Columbia *Local Government Act*,[81] which regulates planning, makes no mention of sustainability. The act only authorises the making of official community plans: a federal–state union of municipalities agreement relating to distribution of funding from a tax on petrol, tying this funding to sustainability, or 'Integrated Community Sustainability Planning' defined as:

> 'Integrated Community Sustainability Planning' means long-term planning, in consultation with community members, that provides direction for the community to realize

---

75 Greenworks, 32.
76 Bohringer and Jochem 2007; Mori and Christodoulou 2012.
77 Bartelmus 2007.
78 Bithas and Chrisofakis 2006.
79 Tanguay et al. 2010.
80 Waterhout et al. 2012, 151.
81 RSBC 1996, chap. 323, part 323.

sustainability objectives it has for the environmental, cultural, social and economic dimensions of its identity . . .

The BC intergovernmental agreement took sustainability on its own path, not dependent on planning. The city of Vancouver developed the *Greenest city 2020* plan with general targets for sustainability *external* to the strategic plan. It states that the co-operation of the regional planning agency, Metro Vancouver, is necessary, but indicates that the *Greenest* plan has the highest priority. Since 1990, the city has placed emphasis on sustainability through a Special Office of the Environment, followed in 2002 by the *City of Vancouver sustainability statement* that sets out the definitions and principles to follow. The operative definition was: 'Sustainability requires integrated decision-making that takes into account economic, ecological, and social impacts as a whole.'

The *Metro Vancouver regional growth strategy of 2010* added sustainability objectives in similarly broad terms to the regional planning policy. It is reported that various other municipalities adopted sustainability strategies but with a wide range of ideas and definitions about what constituted the relevant aspects.[82]

The conclusion that can be drawn from Vancouver and other municipalities in British Columbia is that the scope of sustainability is not fully derived by a form of planning legislation or policy, but is more successfully expanded and explained in the initiatives of local authorities expressed as an external, overarching approach. For instance, the City of Surrey in British Columbia has a *Sustainability charter* that is described as an 'overarching policy document'. It is in this document that the definition of sustainability emerges.

There is a distinct advantage in keeping the sustainability goals outside the strategic plan. Community participation in a strategic plan is complex enough because of the various land use decisions related to growth areas and infrastructure. Adding to this the broad, all-encompassing aspects of sustainability makes participation more difficult. It has been noted that community members may be overwhelmed by the complexity of choices and trade-offs as a consequence of wide community participation on the broad issues of sustainability.[83] As well, participation on a strategic plan is finite, but can become an ongoing forum for discussion if sustainability is included within its own agenda. This has cogency because it is often feared that participation will slow down the process in strategic planning. The issues of what a community believes about environmental, social and economic matters can be safely discussed under sustainability and then used as a point of reference for the strategic plan. The City of Toronto sustainability effort has been bolstered by a sustainability roundtable that meets periodically. Half of its members are representatives of relevant agencies and half are community members. This idea is consistent with the *Toronto sustainability charter*, which states: 'Sustainability acknowledges and considers the impact of our decisions and actions beyond the City of Toronto recognizing that continuous commitment is essential.'

The *Ontario Planning Act*[84] specifically emphasises economic development:

The purposes of this Act are,

---

82 Holden 2012.
83 Robinson, et al. 2011.
84 RSO 1990, chap. 13, sect. 1.1.

a. to promote sustainable economic development in a healthy natural environment within the policy and by the means provided under this Act . . .

The emphasis on economic development has had no limiting effect on Toronto's development of external sustainability strategies as the *Planning Act* does not enunciate policy but only enables local initiatives and local policy.[85] The Toronto Waterfront Revitalization Corporation, a separate development corporation, created its own definition of sustainability as a balance of the three pillars of economic development, social growth and environmental protection. It was in the action policies and plans that the definition became activated and not in the wording. In a study of this process, it was stated:

> An emphasis on implementing a broad definition of sustainability into specific and tangible implementation strategies of planning and real estate development on the waterfront has turned policy and planning attention towards how the concept of 'sustainability' will be adapted in practice.[86]

1.8 Triple bottom line

The 'triple bottom line' (TBL) of sustainability, the alternative formulation of ESD, is that attention must be given to the three variables of environmental protection, economic prosperity, and social justice. This concept has not been used extensively in strategic planning. In Metro Washington, TBL is mentioned in the *Regional plan region forward*, and is also used in several other comprehensive plans, such as the City of Ithaca and New York's comprehensive plan, which uses the USA Economic Development Administration's TBL tool.

Even in the absence of specific sustainability indices, as in New York, or of a complete exposition of the nature of sustainability, TBL is still useful as a touchstone for analyses of equity and environment protection in relation to economic growth. There is, however, no clear method to balance the three pillars and it is therefore more a statement of purpose than a guideline.[87]

As TBL is a conceptual grouping of the elements of sustainability, it is subject to revision. The 'quadruple bottom line' is an idea to add culture, spirituality, and faith, such as maintenance of an indigenous culture, and relating development to individual meaning. It is also interpreted as adding appropriate governance arrangements, such as ethical practices or cohesive policy frameworks. Yet another fourth element is progress for an expanding population.

The *New urban agenda* indicates that, although not defined specifically or in accordance with a triple or quadruple bottom line, the sustainability ideas contained in these expressions are wider. When seen as a reaction to true urban ills, such as poverty, discrimination, and inequality, the agenda is supporting not only the various aspects of the bottom line but a basic human right to live with dignity in urban areas. Equating the 'right to the city' as a fundamental right has led to many other expressions in different forms, such as

---

85 Sorenson 2011, chap. 11.
86 Bunce 2009, x.
87 Halpern 2013.

the 'ethical city', a movement to incorporate social justice, and 'thrivability', to be able to meet one's potential.

The strength of the TBL, augmented by other factors, and expressed more passionately in the *New urban agenda*, is a statement of a heartfelt longing to address urban problems that are endemic in cities. It is a non-mechanistic attempt to give life to all the feelings and emotions that have been ignored in the rapid rise of economic growth and that have been left out of planning. The weakness is that it gives planning the hope that it can be the lever to create a world in which urban ills are controlled and eliminated. In reading the *New urban agenda*, which gives voice to decades of unresolved problems, planning has only a limited purpose and the achievement of the wide, interlocking goals of urban survival is an all-of-government approach centred on social welfare at the expense of neoliberalism.

Triple bottom line reporting is still a useful adjunct to the planning system because it forces the authority to look at the consequences of its decisions. This reporting is popular, for instance, in Melbourne, Australia; the city has worked with the International Council for Local Environmental Initiatives to develop TBL indicators. The Coffs Harbour City Council in New South Wales has also used these indicators, as have the City of Albany, New York, the City of Eugene, Oregon, and Long Island; and they are the cornerstone of the land use plan for Buffalo, New York: *The Buffalo green code draft land use plan*.

In the places where TBL is used, the definition of sustainability is less relevant than the imperative to balance the elements of the TBL. It is TBL that then substitutes for a definition of sustainability when there are no specific indicators.[88] Where there are specific indicators or baselines, the concepts behind TBL are incorporated by implication in the metrics.

An effective alternative used in the United States is to divorce TBL from planning and deal with it in an overarching sustainability plan. This split can be confusing unless the relationship is made clear between the external measures and the strategic plan. As an example of that confusion, the *Sustainable Chicago 2015* plan makes sustainability plans and actions (the latter set out in a separate plan) the basis for the future of the city. However, the City of Chicago *Go to 2040* is the comprehensive strategic plan and has its own sustainability goals relating to liveability, transportation, open space and other issues that relate exclusively to land use. The comprehensive plan does not address the *Sustainable Chicago plan* nor does the latter address the former, in essence dividing the functions of sustainability.

Although the case has already been made for addressing sustainability in an external document covering a very wide range of issues rather than including these issues in the strategic plan, sustainability does have a natural place in the planning process during the creation of a vision for the future. The supposition that underpins the concept of an external document is that the community can continue to be involved in an evolving sustainability process and is not excluded from participation as it is after a strategic plan is created. The conclusions of this ongoing participation can then be integrated into the planning process.

Where there is robust participation and respect for a sustainability agenda, it may not matter where the sustainability principles are addressed. In Oregon, the *Portland plan of 2012* was the result of a visioning process during the preparation of the strategic plan called *visionPDX*. The process specifically and fully addressed the elements of TBL during

---

88   Mitra 2003.

the community participation phase of creating the strategic plan. The Portland Planning and Sustainability Commission provided recommendations to the Portland Plan Advisory Group reinforcing the relevant sustainability issues, so there was input from a specialised body as well as the local community. The single *Portland plan* combines all of the TBL aspects in a comprehensive document addressing the needs of Portland; there is no mention of competing elements of sustainability or an emphasis on economic growth over environmental protection. The plan has also incorporated sustainability indices as a crucial aspect for the general growth of the region. In adopting the plan in April 2012, the city summarised the measures as a mix of equity provisions, economic development, and environmental goals. What is unique about the *Portland plan* is that it views sustainability in all its dimensions as a normal factor in planning, as is economic growth. There was no need in this plan to give priority to any of the TBL elements or to confine them to an external document, but rather the emphasis was on integrating all matters relating to sustainability expanded and developed during the visioning process.

This pattern of separate development of sustainability goals or TBL outside of, or in addition to, planning is becoming more the rule than the exception in systems that are not as open and transparent as those in Oregon. It is a recognition that sustainability is complicated, divisive and technical. Having an external sustainability policy is more logical as it can be treated to an ongoing analysis not subject to the time constraints of preparing a strategic plan. Ideally, it may be preferable to implement the ideas of *Agenda 21* – adopted in 1992 by the UN Conference on Environment and Development as a guideline for sustainability – which suggests consideration of all aspects of the concept in *all* plans. However, as a matter of practice, although sustainability issues will arise in a visioning process that is part of strategic planning, it has the greatest effect when it is part of intergovernmental co-ordination that informs all agencies and is not confined to planning.

1.9 The appropriate place of sustainability in planning

A consideration of environmental issues does not follow naturally from a planning agenda for economic growth, such as making up a shortage of housing for an increasing population. Economic issues like these are driven entirely by the imperative of growth first and only reluctantly forced into some consideration of how to make room for the natural world.

When there is an attempt to bring environmental issues into a growth imperative, the language becomes awkward and counterintuitive. For instance, the primary indicator of economic growth is the standard of gross domestic product (GDP), which ignores the environment. The UN Department of Economic and Social Affairs therefore created the concept of 'green GDP' as one indicator to examine the negative effects of a development and the damage to the environment. In 2000, an 'ecological domestic product indicator' was developed for *Agenda 21* that included more specific measures of the consequences of economic development.

Unlike economic growth, ecological sustainability cannot be measured without considering the impact on the economy. Yet it is formulated in a manner that is not concerned with economic growth. Accordingly, the means to formulate a set of independent measures for ecological sustainable development has been unclear. The consequence has not been an accommodation of economic issues within environmental issues but rather an insistence that priority must be given to ecological concerns no matter what the growth potential. Often, the measures hone in on the specifics of the environment to emphasise their importance; for instance:

> The biological crucial level (BCL) approach suggests such maintenance of the biologically and ecologically critical levels (BCLs) of the environmental system's species and processes as ensures the biological and ecological integrity of ecosystems.[89]

The difficulty then is how to measure ESD in a strategic planning context and how to combine it with the economic imperatives for growth when the two do not share common characteristics or methods. It may not be surprising that there do not appear to be any concrete measures that allow or calculate a clear balance between the two. The question is whether this balance should even be attempted in planning systems, as the issues of relative weight are political and cultural.

In an editorial in the journal *Sustainable development*, it was argued that the concept of sustainable development – suggesting economic growth – and ecologically sustainable development – favouring the environment – are always, in reality, a matter of political positions:

> The ways in which the concept is employed reveal the ideological persuasion of both critics and supporters of sustainable development, and the paradigms resulting from these ideological struggles are social constructs that carry strongly normative associations.[90]

The international literature reflects the 'stakes in the ground' of specific groups interested in defining what the concept should mean:

> economics, ecology, environmental management, environmental philosophy, the claims and contestations of academic disciplines, views from the South (developing countries) and political and corporate positions all reveal the political, ideological, epistemological, discipline-based and philosophical approaches that compete for legitimacy.[91]

The use of the term 'sustainable development' in the original *Brundtland report* had already polarised the issue. The editorial states in this regard:

> For purists, the terms are almost diametrically opposed, sustainable development representing a threat to sustainability on account of its 'dangerous liaison' with economic growth ... particularly since the *Brundtland report*.[92]

As to the Rio+20 attempt to shift the emphasis to a green economy, the editorial states:

> While the agenda appeared to promise a different approach to economic decision-making, the fear for many was that it was little more than a maneuver to replace sustainable

---

89 Mavrommati and Bithas 2013.
90 Springett 2013, 73.
91 Springett 2013, 74.
92 Springett 2013, 75.

development with 'ecological modernization' or 'greener business as usual': many perceived 'green economy' as a pseudonym for the new OECD mantra of 'green growth' – a wolf in sheep's clothing.[93]

In the United States, there is no legislative requirement or definition for sustainability in state planning legislation, perhaps in recognition that the incompatibility would just create difficulties in planning. Planning is left to local governments, as in California, to develop community sustainability strategies according to the general requirement that planning:

> should proceed within the framework of officially approved statewide goals and policies directed to land use, population growth and distribution, development, open space, resource preservation and utilization, air and water quality, and other related physical, social and economic development factors.[94]

The state of Colorado is one example where the legislation is clear that the decisions as to sustainability are left primarily to local government. The Colorado planning enabling statute states:

> The general assembly hereby finds and declares that in order to provide for planned and orderly development within Colorado and a balancing of basic human needs of a changing population with legitimate environmental concerns, the policy of this state is to clarify and provide broad authority to local governments to plan for and regulate the use of land within their respective jurisdictions. Nothing in this article shall serve to diminish the planning functions of the state or the duties of the division of planning.[95]

Under this power, there have been significant sustainability projects in Denver.[96] The *Denver comprehensive plan 2000* specifically sets out the sustainability goals of economic development, environmental stewardship, equity, and engagement. Each is explained in detail and is woven through the strategic plan. In addition, *Blueprint Denver* is an implementation plan that divides the area into 'areas of change' and 'areas of stability'. It is then suggested that small area plans be developed with full community participation.

> Analysis of environmental sustainability should include topics such as physical setting and topography, tree canopy, street trees, flood plain, brownfields, and air and water quality. The focus and depth of the discussion will depend on the attributes of the planning area.

The concept in Denver planning is that conflicts such as growth versus environmental protection, or gentrification versus character, are best identified by the community at the time of making a local plan. It is a recognition that the scope of sustainable growth depends on the area in question and its place in the metropolitan mix of issues of transportation, community facilities, affordable housing, and other matters that define appropriate land use.

---

93 Springett 2013, 77.
94 *California Zoning and Development Laws 2011*, sect. 65030.1.
95 *Local Government Land Use Control Enabling Act*, sect. 29-20-102.
96 Godschalk 2004.

Where sustainability is found in legislation relating specifically to planning, it is usually confined to green buildings or to encouraging solar energy. For example, the Village of Albion in New York sets out that a purpose of planning is 'To provide for solar access and the implementation of solar energy systems'.[97] The planning system in these cases incorporates sustainability issues, but is not the source of its use. A 2000 study found that most comprehensive plans in the United States have little explicit support for sustainability principles even though they may draw on elements of sustainability for specific issues, such as parks or conservation areas.[98] Indirect support comes through other devices used to promote sustainability, including the development of compact cities, transit-oriented design, smart growth and New Urbanism. These latter forms concentrate on urban design to strike a balance of all aspects of sustainability, but do not contain any specific direction or statement as to its use.

This lack of specific statements about sustainability in planning legislation occurs in the United States because all of the various policy issues get resolved in the strategic planning phase and the production of the comprehensive plan. As this document is not traditionally very complex or lengthy, the difficulties engendered by sustainability goals are left to other initiatives, such as a policy document or an external sustainability policy not related to planning.

There are numerous examples of successful sustainability efforts for cities created entirely outside the planning system. An example from Madison, Wisconsin is *Building a green capital city: a blueprint for Madison's sustainable design and energy future*, which was prepared by the city council but not related to the comprehensive plan. In fact, a draft zoning code for Madison, *Updated zoning code for a more sustainable city*, is said to reflect the *Green capital city* plan, although it does not actually dictate the manner of implementation of sustainability goals. The progressive local government of Boulder, Colorado, has adopted the *Boulder County sustainable plan*, which contains strong policy statements about air quality, climate change, and 'ecological health', and which includes specific directions for the treatment of environmental issues such as forests and waterways.

There are thus several ways to balance economic growth and environmental protection in strategic planning, and these examples indicate a pattern. The first consists of a declaration of general sentiments or statements of intent as to the scope of sustainability. This is not necessarily expressed in legislation, but rather in planning policies, or other policies that are outside the formal planning regime. It is a recognition that the strategic plan should not carry the weight of balancing sustainability goals. The second consists of detailed contents in strategic plans where the balance between aspects of sustainability are developed through community consultation and applied to specific areas. This relies on the fact that these issues will necessary arise in a visioning process where they must be considered and reflected in the strategic plan. This does not exclude a separate participatory sustainability process occurring outside the planning process, perhaps lessening the need to expand the visioning process to all manner of sustainability issues. The third consists of sustainability indices that attempt to create a testing scenario for decision making in planning. However, the development of effective indices in planning schemes is a work in progress.

---

97 *New York Code*, chap. 290, art. I, sect. 290-2 2008.
98 Berke and Conroy 2000.

What is very clear is that environmental concerns arising during the strategic planning process are increasing in most places,[99] but the conflict between economic growth and environmental concerns cannot be solved merely by general statements or definitions. Instead, growing local concerns about sustainability seem best reflected in community participation and its outcomes, wherever they are expressed.

1.10 Formal contents of a strategic plan

In order to set future development trajectories, the strategic plan must initially explain the current details of the area that is being planned, the opportunities for potential development and its constraints, the shared vision for its future including environmental concerns, the priorities for the area given the range of choices, the strategies that are necessary to achieve those priorities, the policies that must be applied to clarify the actions needed, and the outcome that is expected.

The plan requires a full narrative of the area in question that confers a clear impression of its past, its current state, and its possible future. A full narrative, rather than a short summary, has the important effect of conveying the rationale for the plans for a particular area and the sentiments that underlie the ideas. The sentiments, although not precise or scientific, are necessary to evoke a sense of that place. Non-legal language, photographs where possible, and an explanation of the character, architecture and impressions of what is being described is essential. This has the advantage of setting a tone for an area so that it is possible for a reader to envision the future imagined by the planning process.

A strategic plan that serves as an example of the scope of the contents that evoke the past, current, and future states can be found in the Pottstown, Pennsylvania *Metropolitan region comprehensive plan*. The thoroughness of the topics covered assures a full explanation of the expectations and orientation of the plan. It is useful to briefly examine its ten chapters, each of which illustrates a particular topic. These chapters seek to create an evidence base of the factual elements of the area, centring on the existing state and future population increases. The plan then sets out goals and objectives relying on that evidence, describes the constraints and opportunities that will allow or deny those goals, and concludes by outlining what might need to be done to reach the level of growth required by future population increases.

The first chapter of the Pottstown plan contains a description, in narrative form, of the constituent municipalities, their history, socio-economic conditions, population forecasts, current operation of employment centres, the income of residents, their educational backgrounds, household structures, housing costs, the number of housing units in the region, and the owner versus renter balance. This is an extensive evidence base: the factual details of the region.

The presence of an evidence base has advantages and disadvantages. The principal advantage is that what follows has the legitimacy of a logical, scientific analysis based on mathematical calculations and supports any conclusions that follow. The main disadvantage is that an extensive evidence base freezes the strategic plan as an oracular document whose pronouncements are then accepted as fundamentally unchangeable. This need for evidence as opposed to impressionistic ideas of what needs to be done may stand in the

---

99 Marquart-Pyatt 2012

way of innovation. A decision, for instance, to allow mid-rise apartments in a particular area because of what the demographic numbers suggest creates a rigid vision of the area's future that is not subject to dynamic review.

Chapter 2 of the Pottstown plan explains the goals and objectives for the region in terms of general concepts (e.g. preserve open space and agriculture), but also specific needs such as housing (e.g. provide housing opportunities for a range of income levels), commercial, retail, office and light manufacturing requirements. It can be seen that as these requirements fall out of the evidence base, choices are then made that lock the areas into particular configurations. At this point, addressing social or welfare needs, such as services for the aged, takes a secondary role. This bolsters the case for planning not to cross over into social and welfare issues because the main content of a strategic plan is, in fact, the allocation of land uses arising from the evidence of the housing needs of the population.

Chapter 3 describes the constraints and opportunities for the region: geology, soils, agricultural land, water resources, wetlands, groundwater, slopes, woodlands, vegetation cover, sites of state significance, and historical districts and buildings. Chapter 4 describes the land use pattern of existing uses: residential, agricultural, open space, as well as unused land. Chapter 5 suggests future land use requirements in terms of the region's growth, identifies which growth areas are available, and then provides a future land use map to indicate the possible mix and location of these uses.

Chapter 6 is a plea for economic development, suggesting that there is a need to promote employment opportunities, enhance the tax base, and maintain commercial, office and industrial areas. Pottstown has low-income households, with 26 per cent of residents living below the poverty line, and it was affected by the financial downturn. The comprehensive plan is only one of a suite of other plans to highlight economic growth.

Chapter 7 deals with housing, examining the housing statistics and where different forms of housing can be located. Chapter 8 evaluates transportation in terms of highways, roads, and transportation corridors, indicating what changes must be made to accommodate growth areas and housing. Chapter 9 explains the open space that exists and which areas need protection, and provides an open space plan to balance resource and agricultural needs. Finally, Chapter 10 sets out community infrastructure and services that exist and are necessary for such issues as solid waste, government services, electricity and gas, emergency services, and healthcare.

This Pottstown plan *is* the strategic planning process. It relies on an evidence base, a shared vision and a direction that arises because of opportunities and constraints. It is certainly not conclusive in solving all the urban land use problems, but it is the best, it asserts, that can be done. There are variations to this range of contents in other jurisdictions, some including sustainability goals, cultural or racial diversity, mitigation of greenhouse gases, adaptation to climate change and other factors that are deemed to be important to that area. Many strategic plans include policies in relation to one or more social issues, such as for affordable housing, which flow from the analysis and offer suggestions as to how they might be implemented. However, they are all consistent with the classic strategic planning formula: an evidence base, then goal setting, acknowledgement of constraints and opportunities analysis, setting priorities, and proposing strategies for implementation.

It is for this reason that this logical process of strategic planning has also been called 'rational comprehensive planning'. It does seem rational and it is comprehensive when fully undertaken on a step-by-step basis. This process is relatively easy to carry out in a small

1 Strategic planning

Figure 1-7 Tverskaya Street, Moscow. Source: Google Street View.

town or city. No one wonders if what is proposed is a good idea and, more importantly, it is accepted as an attempt to stave off chaos and all manner of urban ills. The Pottstown plan does not mention that Pottstown has one of the highest crime rates in Pennsylvania, much greater than Chicago or New York.

A city can grow and develop without rational comprehensive planning. A good example is Moscow, where in 1935 planning was not based on a strategic plan, but rather on an enunciation of basic socialist principles underlying the city's growth. Indeed, the city grew from the influence of Stalin rather than of planners. Stalinist architecture dominates the Moscow skyline, not only in the seven major buildings called the Seven Sisters, but also in the striking avenues, such as Tverskaya Street. In more recent times, Western planners have introduced notions of comprehensive planning into Russia. It is of interest to note that the lack of strategic planning has not resulted in a planning disaster; in fact, Moscow remains one of the most vibrant cities, with a mix of uses and diversity that would make any planner happy. This is not to say that strategic comprehensive planning is not to be followed, but perhaps reinforces the notion that a city is not just a collection of buildings, open spaces and roads. Strategic planning is not the perfect solution for all urban issues and it largely derives its attractiveness from its rationality and its predicates of harmony and order.

The deficiency of a large, comprehensive plan is that it attempts to do too much. It is difficult to understand the urban vision for Pottstown because the statistics, graphs, and charts do not allow a reader to follow what is wrong and what needs adjustment. For instance, the fact that the area of East Coventry has the largest number of vacant units is taken to mean in the plan that it is a good area for growth. Driving through East Coventry reveals a mix of urban decay and empty streets. Discussions with planners and residents consist of complaints about the high cost of living and violent crime. The feel of East Coventry and its evolution, its history and the quality of life cannot be understood by such a comprehensive plan. Statements about its potential growth appear out of context and unrelated to the needs of the community. This is not the fault of the planners, but is a consequence of the strict adherence to rational comprehensive planning and the ensuing belief that it is the best that planning can accomplish.

1.11 Timeframes

The forward casting of the strategic plan is usually in the range of 15–30 years. Some examples are Delhi (16 years), Helsinki (35 years), Kuala Lumpur (20 years), London (20 years), Melbourne (35 years), and Nairobi (16 years). The ability to draw on population growth statistics that are expressed in terms of decades and the need for transportation planning far into the future are the key drivers for these timespans. In Auckland, New Zealand, the demographers' forecast that the population is to grow by a million inhabitants over 30 years made it possible to calculate that 400,000 dwellings will need to be constructed – 70 per cent in existing areas and 40 per cent outside the existing city. The timespan of the plan *Long-term strategy contributing to efficient and comprehensive growth and development of Auckland* is thus 20–30 years. In Boston, the amount of federal funding for highways is projected over 25 years so the Metropolitan Region Metropolitan Planning Organization created a plan, *Charting progress to 2040*, which is based on infrastructure and is then worked into the scenarios for the land use plan.

The actual timeframe over which a plan is to have effect is not a logically derived period and, as a result, there are constant amendments to the strategic plan. The amendments naturally arise when population forecasts and corresponding imperatives that rely on current data change over time. When a strategic plan sets out general principles not reliant entirely on such increases, it is less likely to require amendments. The *Copenhagen finger plan of 2007*, named to indicate the growth of the area along corridors with green wedges, is a strategic plan that is not often amended as it establishes only principles and urban form. It was developed in 1947 to shape the city and not to predict in detail the land use allocations, leaving that to the constituent suburbs. In contrast, the City of Ottawa has a rational comprehensive strategic plan containing the details of the population distribution plan of 30 per cent growth by 2031 and a 40 per cent growth in households and, as such, had 168 amendments from 2003 to 2016.

The methodology of population analysis is that the census data are disaggregated to understand households by type and size. Migration predictions are what remain when the current census data and recorded deaths do not account for the statistics. This is a complex science that takes these figures and manipulates them in many ways. An example of the type of calculations that are made, which shows the extent of fine detail for forecasting, can be seen in just one paragraph of the Boston Metropolitan Area Planning Council's *Methodology for land use projections in the Boston region*:

> To estimate change in households, regional headship rates (number of people who are head of households) (by household type) were applied to the population in households for 2010 and forecast years, and the difference was calculated. This change in households was added to the actual household counts by age from Census 2010 to produce future-

year household estimates by householder age. These households were then disaggregated by household type (family versus nonfamily), income (relative to the area median income defined by the US Department of Housing and Urban Development), and size, based on the distributions observed using decennial census data and ACS [American Community Survey] microdata.[100]

The more detailed the analysis, the longer will be the timeframe for the strategic plan. This is primarily because the ability to project population into the distant future opens up the imperative to calculate a myriad of possibilities, such as the housing needs for types of families, all of which must be planned for and accommodated in the long-term spatial dimension of the region.

Extending the timeframe for a strategic plan beyond a few years is the norm because, after the tedious analysis done to form the plan, there is a reluctance to go back and start again. Many local authorities were caught with grandiose plans before the global financial crisis made housing growth a fantasy. Yet no amendments to a strategic plan can be found in any country that re-invented the goals and opportunities in light of the consequential economic downturn, except to say that economic growth was needed. The strategic planning process takes many years to complete and, although a time period is set for its review in most places, the combined process of implementing the plan and reviewing may take ten years.

If plans were on a smaller time scale, they would be more concentrated and directed at specific issues or projects. This would shorten the period for their creation to possibly two years for a plan to be completed and another year or more to be implemented, assuming a co-operative milieu. This is not a prevalent form of planning because, in comparison with rational comprehensive planning, it can appear that something is missing or incomplete in a plan with such a short timeframe. However, the distinct advantage of smaller-scale plans is that they foster the one-step-at-a-time approach, which shows results and creates confidence in the process.

1.12 Best practice

The enunciation of best practices for strategic planning is guided by the ethical position of providing practical solutions to urban problems that are addressed in the plan as well as those that are formative but unarticulated, to the extent that is possible. The best practices offered are those that prevent plan failure in order to limit anxiety, to reduce the chaos of constant amendments, to reduce any loss of community faith in the strategic planning process and the effectiveness of government, and to forestall the possibility of corruption. The basis for the best practices is to keep the goals clear, choose solutions that are workable, focus only on what is achievable, and make the outcomes realistic and deliverable to all stakeholders.

---

100 Appendix E: Methodology for Land Use Projections in the Boston Region to Charting Progress to 2040.

1.12.1 Goals and visions

A basic lack of concordance between the underlying vision, the plan's goals, and success in reducing urban problems must be accepted. The tendency to express goals in utopian terms offers the hope of a high measure of success that cannot ever be achieved. It is human nature to project the best possible outcome, but it is essential to realise that doing so will result in a strategic plan that, in the end, will be deficient. The more grandiose the vision in a strategic plan, the less likely it will be realised. Failure is caused by the unattainability of the vision, or by the neglect of the vision during implementation if it is amorphous or jejune (such as a 'vibrant neighbourhood'). The discordance between the vision with what is accomplished leads to a weakening of the strategic planning process. It may also mean that the strategic plan eventually has to be forced on the community. The problem arises because land use planning is too often directed to the realisation of subjective states, such as vitality, pleasantness, excitement, or other internal or emotional reactions, but these states cannot be effectively controlled by the planning process.

Best practice is therefore to confine the operative logistics of planning to *achievable* goals and aspirations that relate to the physical environment and not subjective states. Planning should address placement of uses, protection of areas that are environmentally sensitive, density, roads, and other aspects of the area with modest goals that are a direct response to a need. *Need-based planning* can be particularly successful in the resolution of specific issues that address the mechanics of realising a particular project. As each project succeeds, the plan is strengthened. There is then less need for amendment and controversy: faith is gained in the process and the capacity to co-opt the public increases.

Utopian planning is, however, difficult to abandon. We naturally think of the ultimate solution as our creative, imaginative function is never dormant. We also observe planning successes and incorrectly believe they are not just cultural, historical, political or accidental but are the result of planning. This puts too much pressure on planners and government. Perhaps one of the most beautiful, vibrant urban places, the corner of Herengracht and Beulingstraat in Amsterdam, is a result of a random juxtaposition of forms due to the need for turning space on the canal. The success cannot be attributed to a strategic planning process with utopian goals.

Without utopian thinking or inclusion of what appear to be planning successes, the strategies and goals may appear to give way to a dry, lifeless, mechanical set of practical ends. It is indeed rare to find a plan without any aspirational objectives. An aspirational plan should then, to accord with this imperative for creative ideas, express goals, ideas, and directions as a broad, introductory vision, but should not elevate them to an operational role. A plan should attempt to relate the planning choices directly to the practical goals and workable outcomes and should therefore keep the vision very wide and non-specific and certainly not make it the indicator of success. An example might be expressing the need for vital neighbourhoods in the introduction to the planning of an area but not thereafter expanding on the relation of particular planning choices to that goal. In this manner, the aspirations are set out as a legitimate function of hope but do not become the measure of testing the efficacy of the plan. They are more like new year's resolutions rather than a road map for implementation.

It may appear cynical to state aspirational goals but then to ignore them in the same plan. The best practice is then to have a separate document that explains the aspirations as the basis for the planning process and that they have been taken into account. The plan itself need not repeat the aspirations and it can then be implied that they are behind the workings of the strategic plan. This is indeed the case in any event, whether they are expressed or unarticulated and never discussed. If the aspirations are to be expressed in the plan, it is wise to use caution in enunciating them, by acknowledging that these are indeed aspirations and hopes and that they underlie the thoughts of every member of the community.

The evidence-based, strategic planning process yields complex results that are difficult to implement entirely. Plans should rather be tightly focused: practical plans for specific projects or distinct areas without aspirational connections. The wider the scale of the planning area, the less should be the scope of those goals or visions that are related to subjective states. This best practice may seem to reduce the effectiveness of planning and to lack the potential for an urban vision. However, it is a process that is more easily implemented, free of cloudy ideas, and therefore more efficient. It does not deny the aspirational thinking of the stakeholders; it recognises the limits of planning to control subjective states.

1.12.2 Timing

Strategic plans for a period of less than ten years have greater cogency than longer plans. This is because they are not as subject to the inevitable natural changes that will occur in the urban fabric after that time. While changes to an urban area can occur slowly over a long period, they can also happen much faster, as in the case of Pottstown, which quickly accumulated vacant homes after the global financial crisis. A classic study of urban change[101] indicates that some slow changes, such as construction of transport, continue while there is also rapid change, such as an increase in traffic or a change in shopping preferences.

As strategic plans allow for reviews starting at five to six years – which can then take several years to finalise – the best timeframe is ten years. Best practice is to focus on practical issues that can be carried out *in that limited period*, further strengthening the integrity of the plan.

Detailed population forecasting, by its ability to extrapolate over time, leads in turn to longer timeframes for a strategic plan. Planning assumptions are based on this timeframe, such as an increase in retired baby boomers taking away accommodation from the urban workforce. Population forecasting and urban data are essential to the functioning of a plan, but long-range forecasting is not. It is, however, hard to move away from the longer span because long-range population forecasting is embedded as an essential tool for government and the subject of the UN Population Division that extends the outlook to 2150. Therefore, it is very difficult to wean demographers from their forecast data and to convince planners, who rely on evidence, to resist long-term thinking.

The best practice to achieve tighter accuracy is to use shorter forecasting periods, but with regular reviews and alterations. The longer-term strategic plan has the unhelpful role of enhancing aspirational goal setting because it is possible to speculate that a subjective goal may eventually be reached. As well, it adds a doubtful statement of legitimacy that the planning authority not only has the evidence, but also the skills, to deliver desired outcomes over time. Shorter plans can operate along with longer plans and carry the result that the outcomes can be directly tested and, if the plan is focused on workable solutions,

---

101   Wegener, Gnad and Vannahme 1986.

the outcomes can be realised. It should not be underestimated how the future credibility of planning, and public confidence in it, depend on the marketing of its successes.

1.12.3 Sustainability

Three observations can be made as to best practice for the incorporation of sustainability in planning legislation. First, it is better to set out a government's intention as to sustainability in narrative form in a policy document, rather than in a definition in legislation, so it can fully explain its goals and how it will apply its sustainability principles. The second is that a definition of sustainability without further explanation in policy documents leads to speculation as to its effect: does it mean strong ESD or does it allow weak ESD? The third is that, when local councils are creating plans for the full enunciation and development of all aspects of sustainability, a definition in legislation is no barrier, which makes the definition irrelevant. A legislative definition therefore has limited usefulness, except in establishing a sentiment or demonstrating the government's attention to the issues, as the efficacy of such legislation depends on its interpretation by a court or planning authority. The scope of the interpretation cannot be sufficient to guarantee the implementation of the full extent of sustainability.

The complexity of sustainability as a concept containing conflicting ideologies suggests that best practice is to remove sustainability issues and goals from a strategic plan and move them to a higher-order document such as an overarching policy. This higher-order document then has its own integrity to influence planning as well as other governmental decisions, such as environmental protection or climate change adaptation. A separate policy on sustainability can at least achieve some autonomy in the face of neoliberalism and therefore be given its due in all decisions. That policy can be the subject of ongoing community involvement and stands as a singular document that expresses views on all aspects of the sustainability spectrum.

The greatest expressions of sustainability appear to be developed not in city plans but in separate documents, such as *Sustainable Pittsburgh*, *Sustainable Seattle*, *Sustainable Cincinnati* and *Sustainable Calgary*, to name a few. These documents establish in clear language, rather than by interpretation, argument, or speculation, the scope and dimension of sustainability and how it should inform the planning process.

1.12.4 Content

Ideally, the content of a strategic plan should be limited in scope to the setting of policies and general growth directions, and to derive workable solutions for particular projects or areas.

Analysis of the strategic plans of major cities produced in the last 15 years leads to the conclusion that in attempting to justify their worth, they give the impression that the plan is the final word. In all cases, they can be seen to be generating arguments as to their correctness to justify their conclusions. Due to the sophisticated manner in which the plan is presented, the time it took to complete, and the great expertise that was needed for its completion, it becomes inflexible and assumes an oracle-like function that shapes and defines a city. Its development is so complicated that, when complete, all stakeholders quickly forget why specific outcomes were mandated or the details of the data and analyses. It appears then as a paternal document against which no argument can be made and about which, in most places, the community only gets a chance to comment after all the work has been done, by which point useful comment is impossible, given the document's complexity.

As it has a rational sequence, the strategic planning process will continue to be the main planning vehicle. It does not matter if it fails to solve urban problems or even creates more problems than solutions. Because it is both rational and comprehensive, it is a process that is hard to resist. However, there is much merit in reducing the content by creating specific plans for particular purposes and not leaving the larger plan to cover it all in detail. When the larger plan becomes more general, as with the Copenhagen finger plan, leaving the details to local government or smaller regions, the assumptions of the plan can be more easily tested and understood.

This concentration on smaller plans, with larger plans reserved for direction or goal setting, makes the plan's aspirational settings far less important than the practical completion of planning options. A case in point is Hudson Yards in New York, where all aspects of a large site were made the subject of specific analysis and a 'special district' without the immediate requirement to make it fit into the overall comprehensive planning process. This is not a new insight and harks back to the notion of creating a master plan for a specific subdivision or project. The best practice appears to be to use this methodology of smaller plans to foster planning successes that do not need to be measured by lofty goals.

The more complex the content of the strategic plan, the more difficult it is for the local community to reach consensus with its ideas and conclusions. Taking the emphasis off the strategic plan as the workhorse of planning and instead focusing on individual projects appears to satisfy the need for a plan to be responsive, flexible, understandable, and capable ofcreating measured, successful results.

2
Planning scale

The nature of strategic planning is that it has an internal, sequential logic of extrapolating a future vision based on existing facts, and then proposing a direction to achieve that vision. As the vision is not circumscribed by planning theory or practice, in all countries, it encompasses social welfare issues and economic growth as well as a myriad of aspirational ideas.[1] The logic of the process and the width of its scope to offer a utopian vision combine to make it compelling as the way to address *all* planning problems.

Strategic planning has gained popularity worldwide, not just because of its rational sequence and its capacity to extrapolate the future of towns and villages, but because of its usefulness in describing the dynamics in large cities where local boundaries do not adequately explain the economic and social relationships of constituent areas.[2] The ability to define regions and their internal interactions makes it possible to work on a larger scale than local government or county boundaries. Accordingly, strategic planning is particularly appropriate for a region or sub-region where there are recognisable interdependencies within an area.[3]

As there is always some interrelationship between local government areas, such as a common development pattern or adjoining locations along a highway, the interdependencies suggest that a process should be carried out on a scale that includes regional and sub-regional conglomerations.[4] There are also many planning issues that naturally go beyond local boundaries and suggest wider considerations, such as distribution of housing density for increasing populations among different areas, as well as the construction of regional services such as transportation, freight routes, water and electricity supply. As a consequence, examining the strategic future of areas that have a regional or sub-regional connection and co-ordinating infrastructure and services on a wider scale has become the modern, acceptable approach to land use planning.[5]

It follows, to the extent that there is a region that is defined geographically, economically or functionally, a separate strategic plan is appropriate even if there are already

---

1 Cowell and Owen 2006.
2 Smith 2012; Harrison 2012.
3 Alderson, Beckfield and Sprague-Jones 2010.
4 Healey 2006.
5 Pearce and Ayers 2006.

strategic plans for the constituent local authorities. The relationships that designate a wider area to be subject to a strategic planning exercise may be only of one kind, such as economic congruence as in Munich,[6] or transportation linkages or natural boundaries, but, if there is a reason for an area to function as a whole, it is appropriate that there be a strategic plan to reflect the interrelationships.

The choice of scale may not necessarily reflect an area bounded by functional interrelationships and may extend beyond what is apparent because of the historical development of a region. In many cases, regional divisions have already been imposed by the state, perhaps as a consequence of a power struggle between the central government and the cities. An example of this is the historic growth of territorial strategies in Thailand, which were established to exert control over the population and resources for its hundreds of principalities.[7] Another might be the forced amalgamation of municipalities, as occurred under the Thatcher administration in the United Kingdom, and in Toronto.

The choice of a wide scale is not always useful because strategising for a vast area will diminish the importance of the details emerging from problems associated with smaller areas. For instance, with cities the size of Mexico City, it is not possible to have a regional plan that can take into account all local nuances. The regional strategy may come to be at odds with what is perceived as necessary on the local level and can ignore local needs. Accordingly, the choice of the scale of the region is important and its relationship to local conditions is necessary for the proper functioning of the strategic planning process.

2.1 Plan alignment

If there is more than one level of strategic planning – a regional strategic plan, a sub-regional or district plan, as well as a local plan – it is important to allow the documents to be read together. This may appear to be self-evident but is one of the most significant problems in strategic planning. The issue arises because strategic plans are expressed as narratives concerned with a comprehensive exposition of a vision and all options. It is not a focus of the strategic planning process to make sure that the resulting vision and outcomes are divided precisely into defined sections in an exact order or explained by a certain form of description. This means that, where there are multiple levels, there may be a conflict of goals or a subtler conflict of ambitions that override local interests and sentiments. The result may cause the implementation of the regional strategy to effectively fail, be contentious, or difficult to advance.

A case of failure is the 2002 *National spatial strategy* (NSS) of Ireland. The NSS was a 20-year strategic plan for the entire country, with an emphasis on promoting further development outside Dublin. The ambitious plan designated gateway areas and specific hubs for development in order to disperse the population away from central cities. It contained goals to enhance that emphasis. This concept of re-arranging population and development as a form of urban growth is common, but it can take decades to change the priorities of developers and for the provision of the necessary infrastructure to be put in place for the new areas. The NSS created major gateways with populations of over 100,000 to develop

---

6 Lüthi, Thierstein and Goebel 2010.
7 Vandergeest and Peluso 1995.

a critical mass to spark job growth for the regions. The hubs were to have populations of 20,000–40,000 and included such towns as Kilkenny and Killarney.

The strategic plan was consistent with the 1999 European Union *European spatial development perspective 2000–2009*. This document called for:

> development of a polycentric and balanced urban system and strengthening of the partnership between urban and rural areas. This involves overcoming the outdated dualism between city and countryside.[8]

The term 'polycentric' in this context refers to the distribution of development across individual regions predicated on co-operation between different areas. It was a policy to signal a move away from the growing megacities of Europe in favour of distribution of population and development within a country and then co-operation between the new centres.

Due to the economic crises of 2008, the funding for the development of the gateways was cut. Accordingly, a national development plan that contained that funding mechanism was replaced by the *National recovery plan 2011–2014*, followed in 2014 by an act to abolish town and borough councils and merge three major city councils.

The NSS failed because there was a lack of co-ordination with small towns and proposed gateways and, most importantly, local plans conflicted in many ways. The NSS plan overreached, creating too many gateways without local co-operation, was at odds with local strategic goals, and seemed merely to be following the EU concepts of spatial distribution. Once the economic crises occurred, the weakness of the plan as a national strategy for the avowed benefit of the country became clear. As with all strategic plans that provide for population and power redistributions, it required developers to come forward as quickly as possible, which reduced reliance on a carefully thought-out local plan and encouraged opportunistic and political relationships. The replacement policy, the *National planning framework of 2015*, appears to be less ambitious and more interested in a better alignment of local and national interests.

The potential for misalignment and eventual failure also occurs when the regional or sub-regional strategic plan, accompanied by a spatial plan, is only a draft or is not implemented, yet looms over all local planning decisions for the future. This is a common phenomenon as a full strategic plan can take a decade before it is refined and complete; the Hong Kong *Territorial development strategy* was released to the public in 1998, for example, and a new revision was proposed in 2007 with a policy statement that further work needed to be done, making it as yet incomplete.

Even if the strategic plan is a work in progress, the idea that there has been solid work undertaken around the issues makes it impossible not to consider it, even if it has no official status. Various legal tests can be used, such as whether the draft is a seriously entertained proposal based on the work undertaken, the amount of community participation, and the resolution by the planning authority to accept the draft. The local authority and other stakeholders still have no clear understanding what is to be done with a draft and the planning process necessarily becomes more political. The state of Queensland, Australia, is unique in having a provision that the draft plan is binding when the minister determines that not to so declare would increase the risk of:

---

8   European Commission 1999a, 19.

a. serious harm to the environment or serious adverse cultural, economic or social conditions happening in a planning scheme area; or
b. compromising the implementation of a regional plan or proposed regional plan.[9]

As strategic plans for different scales must have consistency, it is important that the layout of the vision, goals and conclusions establish a 'line of sight' so that one element of the planning process can be examined in one document and its complementary element can be found in another. It would then be possible to understand the regional view of conservation, for example, and the local view.

There are two effective methods that can enhance line of sight. The first is to have a legislative requirement that the parts of each strategic plan have common, identifiable elements. The Wisconsin *Comprehensive Planning Law* (sect. 66.1001[2]) provides that every comprehensive plan must have nine elements: an issues element (facts on the area and a statement of overall objectives, goals, and policies); a housing element (the objectives, goals and programs for an adequate housing supply); a transportation element; a utilities and community facilities element; an agricultural, natural and cultural resources element; an economic development element; a land-use element (density and the existing and proposed future uses); and an implementation program that includes performance measures. Each element is set out in some detail in the legislation. For example, in respect of the land use element:

> Land-use element . . . The element shall analyze trends in the supply, demand and price of land, opportunities for redevelopment and existing and potential land-use conflicts. The element shall contain projections, based on the background information specified in par. (a), for 20 years, in 5-year increments, of future residential, agricultural, commercial and industrial land uses including the assumptions of net densities or other spatial assumptions upon which the projections are based. The element shall also include a series of maps that shows current land uses and future land uses that indicate productive agricultural soils, natural limitations for building site development, floodplains, wetlands and other environmentally sensitive lands, the boundaries of areas to which services of public utilities and community facilities, as those terms are used in par. (d), will be provided in the future, consistent with the timetable described in par. (d), and the general location of future land uses by net density or other classifications.

The second method for a clear line of sight between different levels of strategy is for the lower-level strategic plan to indicate how it complies, goal for goal, strategy for strategy, with the higher-level plan. As an example, in the Vancouver regional strategic plan: *Metro Vancouver 2040*, strategy 1.2.6, states that the role of a municipality in this regard is to prepare a regional context statement that:

> Include(s) policies for Urban Centres which:
> i. identify the general location, boundaries and types of Urban Centres on a map generally consistent with the guidelines set out in Table 3 (Guidelines for Urban

---

9 Queensland *Sustainable Planning Act 2009*, sect. 73.2.

Centres and Frequent Transit Development Areas) and the Regional Land Use Designations map (Map 2).

Every municipality must include in a regional context statement how that strategy is being met. In the North Vancouver district, for instance, it is stated in respect of the regional town centre:

> Lynn Valley (the District's Municipal Town Centre) is designated a Town Centre (Policy 2.1.1) Higher density residential and Commercial Residential Mixed Use land use designations are applied, including Residential Level 6 (up to 2.5 FSR), Commercial Residential Mixed Use Level 2 (up to 2.5 FSR), and Commercial Residential Mixed Use Level 3 (up to 3.5 FSR), to focus residential and commercial development.

If the strategies for each goal are not created in a line-of-sight method, the effect will be an inability to follow through a strategy from the highest level to the lowest level other than in an ad hoc manner that may cause confusion. There will also be no opportunity to evaluate the effectiveness of the higher-level goal. In practice, lack of specificity in a strategic plan and the absence of line of sight decrease the relevance of the entire process and place the emphasis on the spatial plan and the legal means of its implementation. At that point, the strategic plan becomes merely a general policy that informed the spatial plan and the goals and the vision lose clarity.

It is also important for the higher-level plan to correspond to policy documents and in-process initiatives at the lower levels. There may be existing or draft policies for resource allocation, sustainability or for infrastructure derived from local plans or other agencies. Without embracing the entirety of the policy spectrum, the higher order document will have less effect and will be confusing.

An alternative, perhaps best demonstrated in the *Paris regional plan: gcarand Paris*, launched in 2007, is for the regional plan to establish general guidelines indicating vectors of development, transport networks and major projects around those networks and not to impede local plans. The clear, underlying purpose of the plan is to rescale Paris as going beyond the municipal borders of 'petit Paris' and to include the wider region, perhaps as a response to the political unrest in the *banlieues* – the suburbs. For this purpose, networking the areas through transport is the key goal for a territorial balance and it allows the strategic plan to stay regional and to set up the progressive development of that network over time, not interfering with local plans or policies.

These methods, direct and indirect, are attempts to rationalise two different structures: planning for regions requiring local government compliance and co-operation – a 'top-down' approach; and planning primarily for local governments – a 'bottom-up' approach. Both political and planning theory suggest that ideally there be a combination of these approaches, depending on appropriate functions – regional capacity-building situated in regional institutions to carry out top-down planning, followed by bottom-up regional political mobilisation where local governments work in partnership.[10]

---

10   Amdam 2010.

2.2 Governance issues

There are common governance issues in all countries because of multi-tiered hierarchical administrative and control arrangements around planning. The governance problems emerge from two alternative, conflicting theories on planning responsibilities. The first is that the local authority, closest to residents' aspirations and problems, must have the primary responsibility to control strategic planning for the local area. The second is that the state, which establishes regional authorities, can see beyond local interests and generally should control the policy agenda for all residents.

The conflicts between city and state politics over planning are often to do with a battle for power to exert control over the social agenda. The fight, in general, turns on the cultural attitude towards 'localism', a term used to define the belief that it is local government and not the state that is morally responsible for the welfare of its inhabitants.[11] The balance struck is most related to the historical structures of government and the success of local government. In countries where there has been a vacuum in metropolitan leadership, as in Brazil, the state has traditionally taken a stronger role and there is less emphasis on localism.[12]

Localism is not just an abstract concept, but rather is justified by other aspects of the planning process. The increased use of community participation, the general push for participatory democracy, and the need for formation of social capital within a community, all point to the power of a local community to decide its own fate in terms of planning. The emphasis on localism or its opposite, centralisation, depends very much on the politics of a country and local areas, and in many countries, the degree of influence of the World Bank's policies of decentralisation. A study of the drivers of localism and the barriers it faces concluded that 'this political project will have to overcome the binary opposites such as local/global and state/civil society in order to be relevant.'[13]

The imperative used by the state to justify state intervention, and to perpetuate those binary opposites, arises primarily because of perceived distrust of the capacity and ability of local authorities to carry out their functions, even without allegations of corruption. When there is, in addition, the taint of corruption, the rationale becomes all-pervasive and remains paramount decades later, even after the corruption has long since been eradicated, continuously justifying state control. The ability of local governments to make decisions that approximate competence, fairness, lack of bias and efficiency is not a concept generally supported internationally even though there may be a high degree of trust by the local inhabitants. Perhaps this trust is because a resident has a greater voice in local government than in state government.[14]

The desire for the state directly, or through regional government, to intervene also arises because of the concern that different approaches to the same issues by local authorities might have varying outcomes. However, this basis of intervention does not follow an investigation by the state of the efficacy of local planning approaches in each case, but rather will be based on assumptions of the benefits of uniformity. Accordingly, there are often no traceable causes for increased state intervention other than a sentiment against

---

11 Geoghegan and Powell 2009.
12 Kink and Denaldi 2012.
13 Mohan and Stokke 2010, 264.
14 Fitzgerald and Wolak 2016.

localism, that the state knows better about the idealised outcomes, and that there is bound to be local corruption. These shifting views on localism perhaps explain why some states in the United States have a bottom-up approach in which the local plan has dominance and the state's guidance is informal (Washington, Maine, Wisconsin, Rhode Island, Vermont), while in others there is a top-down approach in which the state plans and policies must be adopted by the local councils (New Jersey, Oregon, Florida).

As the essence of local government is that the elected representatives have the pulse of the inhabitants, state intervention is often perceived by local government and its residents as a hostile act. The origin of this belief, traced back perhaps to Alexis de Tocqueville, the 19th-century political philosopher, is that local government is the most direct symbol of democracy.[15] The consequence is that there is always an argument that local government should be considered to have autonomy and to be protected from state interference. The Council of Europe *European charter of local self-government* (1985) provides (art. 4:3) that except to a limited extent, local governments 'may not be undermined or limited by another, central or regional, authority.' A study of the Florida system reveals that, when there is a top-down approach of state imposition of planning rules on local councils, it undermines trust in processes and has the obvious effect of polarising local councils and the state, resulting in constant litigation.[16] What can occur is that the state creates the opposites and then exploits the problems that arise as a means for increasing state power in planning.

State intervention is the international norm based on the accepted idea that the central government of a state or province should ultimately dictate the content, controls and direction of the local plan. In practice, this occurs in several ways. A state can establish a strategic plan for a region and direct, by law, that it be followed by a local authority or their local plan will become ineffective. It can indicate that certain projects or areas of state significance be taken out of the hands of the local council. It can prescribe the state-wide requirements for development or it can add planning considerations that must be taken into account by every local council.

A common form of state intervention is a mandatory policy that a local plan be guided by the philosophy of transport-oriented design: i.e., that the concentration of residential density near railway stations is the most effective way to distribute population. In Malaysia, for example, the draft *National planning and design guidelines for compact and liveable development* is a national intervention that requires transport-oriented design, which filters down to the state structure plan, and then binds the local government in the creation of its structure plan; the *Kuala Lumpur structure plan 2020* resulted in one of the largest such transport-oriented design projects, Kuala Lumpur Sentral.

This arrangement, whereby the state can impose its will, exists legally because local governments are established by state laws and therefore exist as subordinate to the state. In several countries, local governments have autonomous powers granted by the constitution, such as in the Philippines and the Panchayats of India. However, where there is legal creation of local governments by the state, it allows the state to claim its interests as superior to that of the local council. The famous quote of Justice Dillon in the United States (establishing the so-called Dillon rule) explains it conclusively:

---

15   de Tocquevile 1968.
16   Dawson 1996.

Figure 2-1 Kuala Lumpur Sentral, Malaysia. Image: Akira Mitsuda via Wikimedia Commons, CC BY 3.0.

> Municipal Corporations owe their origins to, and derive their powers and rights wholly from, the legislature ... As it creates, so it may destroy. If it can destroy, it may abridge and control ...[17]

Although there is always some state intervention because of this hierarchical arrangement, there are different degrees of intervention. It has been stated that there is a sliding scale internationally as to the degree of state intervention in local planning,[18] ranging from a mandatory imposed state planning regime completely overriding local concerns to one where there is greater local autonomy or even non-directive approaches, such as informal consultation, advice or warnings.[19]

State control of the planning system cannot be the basis for all land use decisions because the administrative work would be overwhelming. Therefore, in some countries, the intervention is confined to matters of state or regional interest, such as particular projects of state importance, large areas of open space, or an attempt at uniformity. Accordingly, no matter what the degree of state intervention, the local plan still remains critical. An interesting example of the enduring nature of a local plan is the City of Helsinki's 30-year *Strategic spatial plan: from city to city-region*, which has only one page on how it will be implemented because this depends on the co-operation of the constituent municipalities. In a similar way, regional plans are not valid in Finland where there is a local plan.[20]

---

17 *Clinton v. Cedar Rapids and M. River R. Co.*, 24 Iowa 455, 475, 1868.
18 Nelson and Duncan 1995.
19 Fleurke and Willamse 2004, 526.

In Germany,[21] there is a historical tradition of co-operation between the state and local governments that extends, because of that culture, to planning issues and creates a mixture of top-down and bottom-up approaches. The national German Federation enacts framework laws that provide guidance on spatial planning and the state and regions are required to create spatial plans to reflect that guidance. A local authority then has two plans: the *Flächennutzungsplan* (the F-plan) that is the spatial policy plan reflecting on its concordance with the guidance, and the *Bebauungsplan* (the B-plan) that is the local, binding regulatory plan. The F-plan must accord with state, regional and federal spatial plans and is binding on public authorities, who are responsible for infrastructure delivery, but not on private individuals. The B-plan affects individuals and is derived from the F-Plan.

The *Localism Act 2011* in the United Kingdom is a declared movement away from state intervention and provides for the revocation of regional strategies. It has an almost exclusive emphasis on local planning. State guidance is provided only in respect of state strategic issues. The concept of localism, reflected in the act, is an express recognition that local issues should be managed by the residents. This is an understandable perspective because it takes into account the basic fact that local decisions have the greatest impact on what is important for residents. It also implies that a sense of place is important to wellbeing and that a say in the formation of that place has high priority.

The importance of incorporating the true relationship of a resident to their local community in the concept of localism cannot be underestimated. This is an expression of the social cohesion formed within a place rather than just its physical attributes.[22] Communal bonds create predictability, a sense of purpose and a place in the social hierarchy. State intervention that alters that sense of place creates anxiety, which can be seen when a regional plan earmarks an area for a major shopping centre against the wishes of residents. Unfortunately, this type of interaction between a resident and place is amorphous and is recognised only as a minor issue compared to other agendas related to regional imperatives, such as economic growth.

Inevitably, irrespective of planning cultures, some state intervention is necessary in all planning regimes, which accounts for its ubiquity. A state can fill in deficiencies in local plans, such as requiring that there be community participation; it can direct changes to land use to protect against natural disasters or other hazards – creating a buffer zone around heavy industrial uses, for instance; or it can embed the principle of sustainability in all plans. The state, by its nature, takes a wider view and can be a source of quality assurance for a local plan. However, as there is no ideal balance between state intervention and local autonomy, the best practice must at least maintain the integrity and autonomy of residents and their sense of their own community. This self-evident argument does not mean that there should be little state intervention, but that these higher-order ideals should be specifically addressed.

One method to acknowledge local autonomy and to alleviate some of the anxiety caused by state intervention is to clearly explain the details of the governance arrangements – when the state will intervene and when the local authority has autonomy – thus creating predictability. This is to be preferred to the usual practice of discovering those arrangements by interpreting laws and trying to deduce who holds what power. As an example

---

20   Denmark Ministry of Environment 2004.
21   Akademie 2002; European Commission 1999.
22   Hidalgo and Hernandez 2001.

of that disclosure, the Oregon *Comprehensive Land Use and Planning Co-operation Act* (chapt. 197) specifically provides for the respective roles of local government and the state and also contains provisions for a problem-solving process when conflicts arise.

The scope and subject matters for which the state may intervene in the name of planning are not straightforward. The *Spatial Planning and Land Use Management Act 2013* of South Africa raises the question of whether land use planning can be used by the state to advance a general political and social agenda. The preamble to the act indicates that the past spatial planning laws promoted racial inequality and segregation. Accordingly, this new act provides that land use plans redress these past imbalances (sect. 7). Each tier of government is required to develop a spatial planning framework incorporating what is called 'spatial justice'. The use of planning to address racial injustice is novel but is authorised legally as consistent with the National Planning Commission's *National development plan 2030* and the *Restitution Act* in order to use all means to reverse the policy of dividing the country along racial lines and to undo damage caused by apartheid.[23]

The scope of state intervention in local planning on all aspects of social relevance seems potentially unlimited, as land use can be expanded to embrace every aspect of our existence. It has been pointed out that not only are there local or state issues that define the scope of planning, but there are also global issues that expand the breadth of land use, such as food production, prevention of infectious diseases, forest preservation, loss of species, fresh water and climate change.[24] It is of course possible to deal with each of these issues by separate regulation; for example, the uncontrolled deforestation in Bolivia was addressed by the 1996 *New Forestry Law* and the requirement of forest management polans, but they could also have been subsumed under planning. These global consequences can go further and encompass human rights issues as in South Africa, or address matters unrelated to the traditional sense of planning as the instrument to achieve harmony and order. Some examples of these even wider matters include the unequal distribution of land, international capital flows, fracking, power generation, use of pesticides, inflated housing markets and, in some places, land tenure issues. One current popular aspects of land use is oriented to the health issue of preventing obesity by providing for walking between local resources.

Land use and social issues always overlap. For instance, the *Mount Laurel* doctrine[25] in the United States stipulates that zoning must be used specifically to provide for a fair share of affordable housing in order to avoid exclusionary planning controls such as large-lot zoning and minimum building size, which make land and housing unaffordable for most.

Social and economic intervention in markets by the state is a necessary aspect of the political structure as the state uses land as the pivotal *prima materia* as it is tied in to indicia of wealth and the ideologies of capitalism and private interest. However, although it spans all areas of living, state intervention in planning may not be suited to the regulation of certain externalities simply from the point of view of administration. An example would be delaying a land use plan to cater for health impacts determined by a department of health.

Although it is valid for the state to include a social and economic agenda in planning, the planning system can become unwieldy if the scope is too wide, leading to anxiety and tension that require constant readjustment in the planning controls. An interesting

---

23 *Alexkor v. the Rictersveld Community* [2003] ZACC 18; 2004 (5) SA 460 (CC) 2003.
24 Foley et al. 2005.
25 *South Burlington Count NAACP v. Township of Mount Laurel*, 92 NJ 158 1983.

example of state planning controls creating complications is the use of levies to fund infrastructure by value capture, based on the historic notion of Henry George that the state owns the wealth it creates through planning. The Columbian attempt to capture the increase in value a developer obtains when farmland is rezoned or density is increased is one instance of an increasing popular economic notion. In 1997, the Congress of the Republic of Columbia enacted a requirement in the land use law that developers pay fees reflecting the increased value, which can be used by local governments for social housing.[26] This is similar to the provisions that first appeared in the *English Town and Country Planning Act 1947*. The effect has been, as it was in the English act, to induce those who have a potential profit not to sell or develop because the levy diminishes the return as well as creating a complicated administrative system of value assessment, enforcement, and distribution.[27]

The most cogent approach to striking a balance between state and local interests is to restrict state intervention in land use to those matters which are, in fact, state issues in the traditional sense: choosing land for growth, protecting the environment, providing for infrastructure, and regulating large projects. However, this is not practical because the power to use land use controls to accomplish social goals is hard to resist. Planning is an existing regime that does not require new legislative invention and is flexible enough to be turned to almost any purpose. To name a few instances, land use planning controls can be very useful to maintain social cohesion of refugees,[28] to ban or control prostitution, to condition the time of operation of existing alcohol establishments, to mitigate greenhouse gases, to adapt to climate change, or to promote even more novel ideas such as restricting fast food restaurants near schools.[29]

Accordingly, best practice does not require a limit on the use of intervention by the state to accomplish social goals. It does, however, require some means to deliberately address the autonomy and importance of local areas and residents, to provide an explanation of the exact nature of the state intervention, and to set out a defined process for full community participation in the evaluation of the intervention.

2.3 Regional forms

The clear theory behind regional government is that a central authority established by the state can better manage trans-local authority issues in a functionally defined region. In planning terms, the use of regional planning can probably be traced to the acceptance of regional government as a useful unit of government as a result of the United States census data in the 1950s that revealed that 168 metropolitan areas were administered by 16,000 local governments.[30] The earliest attempt at a metropolitan plan in North America was most likely the joinder of 13 municipalities in Metropolitan Toronto in 1953, which then produced the *Metropolitan Toronto plan*. The most recent example of regional government for a major city is probably the Greater Sydney Commission of 2015.

---

26   *Law of Land Development*, law 388.
27   Walters 2013.
28   Stein 2013.
29   Austin et al. 2005.
30   Haar 1957.

Regionalism in Western Europe arose, not from an awareness of the overwhelming number of local authorities, but from the historical development of economic co-operation after World War II, connecting countries related by geographical proximity and dependencies. Spatial planning linked to regionalism emerged early as a consequence because the concept of co-operation was already instilled. Although there are varying degrees of regional control, some aspect of regionalism in planning therefore exists in all Western European countries.[31]

The use of regions in Western Europe as planning units has led to several governance arrangements: the state provides the planning of regions as in Portugal; sets up regional authorities to work with local government as in Finland; a regional authority covers all policy issues that guide decisions of local authorities as in the Netherlands' use of provisional councils; or the regional authorities prepare reports that then guide local planning decisions as in Ireland.

Many of the governance arrangements for regional government have deep historical roots. Regional planning in Germany has multiple forms as the result of the relationship of the Länder to the federal government and the historical development of government functions on a regional scale. In one study,[32] it was found that in the Rhine-Main region there was a myriad of public and private regional associations operating at different capacities and geographic scales and embracing co-operative forms with no legislative authorisation. Berlin-Brandenburg is another example of a non-statutory regional planning association, while Stuttgart has an elected statutory authority. The observation from Germany is that having a central or regional authority does not prevent other forms of regional arrangements formed co-operatively or on an ad hoc basis, when regionalism is an historic form.

France is a good example of how the ancient settlement pattern led to the existing form of regional planning. The establishment of the provinces in feudal times resulted in disconnected areas with their own traditions and laws, later called 'departments', which were brought into a common designation as regions in 1982. The essence of this system is the historical independence of regional areas, not subject to central control. As a consequence, planning takes place primarily at the regional level. The central government creates an overarching plan of action giving its point of view for each region. The regions then create a regional spatial planning and development blueprint, which sets the guidelines for the local governments – the communes. For the large urban areas, the *Land Use Planning Act 1967* sets up Urban Planning Agencies, which function as regional bodies to provide the communes with support for local planning.

The Metro Vancouver Board developed out of a prior intergovernment arrangement of the City of Vancouver and the Districts Joint Sewerage and Drainage Board of 1914. The early collaboration led to a regional system of governance for other intermunicipal services in 1965. This is part of a system of collaboration that included other functions, such as water, after the *Greater Vancouver Water District Act of 1924*. The Metro Board is not the first such co-operative structure that existed internationally, as pointed out by the 1913 Lea report, which led to the formation of the Sewerage and Drainage Board; there was the Melbourne and Metropolitan Board of Works in 1890, the Birmingham Tame and Rea Drainage Board of 1877, and the Board of Metropolitan Sewerage Commissioners of Boston of 1889, all of which were inspirations for the Metro Board.

---

31 Larsson 2006.
32 Hoyler, Freytag and Mager 2006.

The Vancouver *Regional growth strategy* came into effect only after the local authorities agreed on its content. It is a co-operative arrangement of the Metro Vancouver Board whereby each council has one director on the board and one vote for every 20,000 residents. Thereafter, each local authority can make requests for major amendments, which require unanimous approval, or minor amendments, which require 50 per cent approval of the Metro Board and its constituent councils.

In addition to historical regionalism, there are places where co-operation rather than competition is paramount. This has led, even in the absence of formal governance arrangements, to co-operative regional associations. They are often made up of local council representatives, citizen groups and lobby interests and may have no formal status and are not necessarily recognised in the land use process. The San Diego Association of Governments (SANDAG) is an example of a collaborative, voluntary collaboration of local and county governments that began informally in the 1980s. It has since been given a legislative structure and powers as its effectiveness has been proven.[33] It now controls regional transit planning and transit capital project development and has prepared a regional plan, the *San Diego regional comprehensive plan 2004*.

In the United States, formal and informal planning structures also exist at a local level. Zoning ordinances formally create citizen advisory committees that are appointed by the mayor in order to provide advice on projects, and are given actual powers to conduct design reviews, evaluate historic preservation issues and analyse requests for rezoning.[34] In many places, interest groups have been given formal recognition in local governments and their views sought,[35] as in the City of Bend, Oregon, with its *Resolution 1: Recognition of neighborhood associations*.

Co-operation between regional and local government, no matter what the structure, is not assured. A regional authority may want land designated for a large shopping centre, while the local authority may want that land maintained in its present state because of its landscape qualities. The regional authority has the moral superiority in that it can make a claim to go beyond the local, parochial interests and act for the greater good of the entire region. When there is a failure of the local authority to co-operate, it is met swiftly by state controls, such as an automatic amendment to the local plan when it does not accord with the regional plan, or by making certain types of projects come exclusively within the jurisdiction of the regional authority.

The requirement that a local authority co-operate with regional planning is subsumed under the general constitutional and statutory powers of all planning regimes. This requirement in legislative terms is usually framed negatively, by allowing the state to enforce co-operation as a marker of the dominance of the regional authority. It is rare to see a positive duty to co-operate. Section 110 of the UK *Localism Act 2011* requires a limited duty on local authorities to co-operate, to 'engage constructively, actively and on an ongoing basis in any process by means of which activities within subsection (3) are undertaken.' The activities in subsection (3) are those that extend outside local boundaries and have an impact on sustainable development in other planning areas or on strategic infrastructure. It is also provided that the Secretary of State can offer guidance on how that co-operation is to be effected.

---

33 Hill 2006.
34 Callahan 2002.
35 White 1987, 5.

A regional authority perceived as imposing its will to the detriment of local authorities is not the case where regional control is essential for a larger agenda, such as national economic expansion. An example is the overriding Indonesian *National Development System Law 2004*, which is a blueprint for socio-economic development and thus formative for all other laws. As a result, in 2007, the *Spatial Planning Law* was amended to focus on greater economic growth and that led to the *National spatial plan of 2008*. That plan reflected the imperative and divided the areas into four groups defined by their economic purpose: national central city, inter-region central city, regional central city, and national strategic central city. A national central city is one that is an export/import centre or an international gateway. Accordingly, the creation of an authority to govern these areas, such as the Jabodetabekpunjur Development Planning Bureau in Jakarta, is not in conflict with local aspirations as it has a higher-order mission.

If there is a national imperative for economic development that is specific about its purpose rather than just complying with the neoliberal agenda for wealth creation, this will greatly decrease the relevance of local views in land use planning. This can be observed in South Korea, where there are comprehensive national territorial plans linked to the five-year plans for national development. The lesser plans, wide-area urban plans for inter-city plans, urban plans, and others, reflect this link. Where a regional authority follows these economic priorities but still allows local input and seeks the views of residents, it is usually after the plan has been drafted or where the views are trivialised and have no real influence on the regional plan. In Seoul, a city of ten million people, a group of fewer than 100 residents devised a vision called 'Happy City of Citizens with Communication and Consideration' over a two-day session as input to *The Seoul 2030 plan*.

2.4 State and regional policies

Local strategic plans may lag behind market changes or may fail as ineffective in preserving the environment. An example is the master plan for Lisbon, Portugal, which allowed a high degree of random, urban sprawl that degraded land suitable for agriculture because the plan was outdated and not enforced properly.[36] When there are such failures, the fixes that a state or regional authority needs to impart to a local authority cannot be left to the next version of the local plan, especially when there is always considerable delay in revisions. Accordingly, state or regional wishes are most often imposed by the creation of regional policies, official or unofficial, rather than regional plans, because policies can direct local authorities and are easier to create than legal instruments that require a legislature's approval. Their ease of creation means that there is no limit on the number that can be made, whether to cure a failure or for any planning matter. England at one time had 25 planning policy statements, exceeding 1300 pages in total. The *National planning policy framework* of 2012 reduced these statements to one document of 58 pages. In the foreword to the framework, the minister made these observations:

> In part, people have been put off from getting involved because planning policy itself has become so elaborate and forbidding – the preserve of specialists, rather than people in communities. This *National planning policy framework* changes that. By replacing over a

---

36 Abrantas et al. 2016.

thousand pages of national policy with around fifty, written simply and clearly, we are allowing people and communities back into planning.

The reduction in the number of policies in the framework received considerable criticism because it was argued that the detailed content of previous policies was lost in the brevity.[37] The brevity was in fact only possible because of a change in emphasis in the UK planning process that departed from the primacy of regional, spatial planning to a greater philosophical and practical reliance on local plans as well as an orientation around a presumption of sustainable development that incorporated previously disparate concepts.

Planning policy Wales does not have the same localism orientation as that of the English *National planning policy framework* but undertook a reduction down to 200 pages that has been considered a success.[38] A consolidation of planning policies is always possible theoretically, but a massive reduction such as that of the *National planning policy framework* is only feasible if there is a desire to allow greater local autonomy, as this reduces the need for regional or state control.

In Ontario, Canada, where governance is based on state or regional policies overriding local plans, there is a policy for evaluation and monitoring of these regional policies in order to justify the governance structure. The *Provincial policy statement* of 2005 sets out measures to test each policy goal in accordance with its adoption. For example, the efficacy of a policy providing that there be a range of housing types to meet population expansion is measured by the number of local plans that establish targets for the provision of multiple housing types. A review of the policy statement suggested amendments to widen the scope of policy to fulfil other goals after surveying stakeholders and local authorities as to its success.[39] The advantage of this system is that it keeps the policies under review and consequently raises awareness of their efficiency.

2.5 Metropolitan structures

Some of the examples presented in this work of regional authorities have been of *metropolitan* regions, definable as a region consisting of a discrete urban area with interrelated local governments. The advantage of a metropolitan regional authority is that is has the ability to create uniform policies and plans that transcend yet incorporate mutually shared local interests.

The actual amalgamation of constituent local governments into one metropolitan government has been said to be the most cost-effective means of regional planning, although its creation is politically fraught.[40] As an example, after dissatisfaction with the metro form, Metro Toronto was replaced in 1998 by an expanded City of Toronto through the amalgamation of seven constituent local governments into one city, combining 149 agencies, boards and commissions.

When any metropolitan commission is created, there are three basic forms for its structure. The first is that the members are appointed by the state; an example is the Min-

---

37　House of Commons 2011.
38　Kelley and Stirling 2011.
39　PEDCRC 2011.
40　Frug 2002, 1784.

neapolis–St Paul (Twin Cities) Metropolitan Councils, where members are appointed, not elected. The second is where there is an election of members to a metro commission either generally or by the residents of each constituent local government. This method appears to be more accepted because it offers citizens a greater opportunity to participate in planning decisions indirectly by voting.[41] The third method is where each constituent local government supplies a member to a metropolitan commission, appointed by a mayor. This method has its critics because such a grouping amounts to 'collections of local government officials in regional guise but ultimately accountable politically only to their local constituencies [that] cannot be expected to produce effective advocacy for state and regional interests'.[42]

An elected body of members of a metropolitan commission has been considered the best practice. It has been said:

> A representative form of government assures greater accountability to the people. Elected officials, especially those at the regional or local levels of government, can more effectively monitor smart growth implementation than unelected agency heads who often lack feedback from the citizenry or firsthand observation. Voters can remove elected officials who fail to meet their expectations, but possess very limited ability to oust appointed governmental officials.[43]

It is implicit in the arrangement that a metropolitan planning authority has a higher legislative power than constituent local authorities. The inevitable result, however, is conflict between metropolitan goals and local aspirations and it is no surprise that it usually results in state intervention to give the metropolitan authority primacy.[44] The conflicts are often, but not always, worked through behind the scenes because the metropolitan authority understands that it needs to foster relationships with local government and state agencies as much as the local government needs channels to communicate with the authority.

The co-operation of local governments with a central metropolitan authority may occur without legislative requirements. The most successful co-operative structures are the result of the historical co-ordination of local and regional interests over time and the build-up of professional and personal relationships. Vancouver Metro, as an example already presented, is a model that developed from co-operative sewerage and drainage arrangements starting in the early 20th century.[45] Vancouver Metro is a federation of 24 municipalities and other regions, including the City of Vancouver. The directors are elected (not appointed) by local government councils. Although one vote is given for every 20,000 residents of the constituent local government, there is an upper limit of five votes, so that the City of Vancouver does not control the board. The chairperson and vice-chair are not appointed by government but elected by the directors.

The core function of Metro Vancouver is to provide water and sewerage but it also has functions of regional planning, air-quality management through industrial permits, and management of regional parks. As it has the utilities and planning functions, it is well

---

41 Daniel 2001, 1956–8.
42 Saxer 1997, 680.
43 Griffith 2009, 1019.
44 Briffault 2000, 3.
45 Artibase, Cameron and Seelig 2004.

staffed, with over 1400 employees. In 2008, the *Sustainability framework* of Metro Vancouver, given the co-operative arrangement, was able to provide principles for provision of utilities integrated with the planning function. What is unique in this co-operative structure is that the board of the transportation authority (TransLink) is appointed by the Metro Vancouver Board, assuring integration of transportation with planning. TransLink is required to offer Metro Vancouver an opportunity to comment on its strategic plans and Metro Vancouver is required to obtain TransLink's acceptance of its *Regional growth strategy*.

Brazil has a well-planned collaborative system through the *Public Consortia Law 2005* (sect. 11.107) that provides for formal establishment of a legal agreement for the purpose of collaboration, consisting of state, federal, local government and agency membership with no hierarchy. This arose as part of the 1988 Constitution's recognition of inter-municipal arrangements and the need to formalise arrangements already in place. The initial purpose of the law was to create shared municipal visions. That led to a formal dialogue about regional issues, such as health care and education and, to a lesser extent, planning. Conveniently, planning ideas, such as integrating local planning with the regional vision, coincided with respect for local government autonomy, and resulted in planning consortia.[46] The *Consortia Law* indicates that, even in the absence of historic interrelationships, co-operation can best be achieved by a formal system of collaboration.

The most effective model for operation of a metropolitan commission, following the Vancouver and Brazil examples, is when there is a historic, legislative and willing collaboration between local governments and the metropolitan authority. It is clear to all planning authorities that this avoids the need for conflict between local and the wider, metropolitan interests, it reduces the need for state imposition on local governments and also limits the desire to take away local government powers. However, long-term co-operation is very difficult to achieve, as can be seen in the failure of collaboration in Toronto that eventually forced the amalgamation of all local governments into one city government.[47]

The threat that the state can intervene is eventually the main driver of co-operation. The natural belief remains, however, that only locals can understand the character of the locality and the idea of a metro commission having planning powers over local government is always viewed with suspicion. A system of collaboration is not usually embedded in the formation of a metro commission. Instead, various powers and responsibilities are assigned to the various stakeholders with different agendas that require some compromise. Without a formal collaborative system, the suspicion of imposed intervention that ignores local interests may not be alleviated by informal mechanisms as these cannot be tested or relied upon.

The theory of an 'Institutional Collective Action Framework' has been devised to evaluate the effect of governance arrangements, formal and informal. It postulates that conflicts exist on various levels but can be disaggregated and analysed. On the first level, conflicts are of the type that will arise if one of the stakeholders is either too small or too large to produce the service they propose. An example is the inability of a regional authority to manage local reserves. The second level is where a regional and a local authority pursue policy objectives which are in conflict. The third is where there is too much

---

46   Palhano et al. 2010, 307.
47   Bourdreu et al. 2007.

fragmentation of decision making, such as different authorities being responsible for transportation, environment, plannin,g and resource management.

The solutions suggested by this theoretical framework arise from recognition of the interdependencies and how actions by one government agency affect others. The framework suggests a series of appropriate mechanisms to avoid conflict for all levels, such as informal networks, interagency contracts, working groups, partnerships, networks constructed by central government, systems aimed at particular policy issues, and councils of governments that can meet regularly.[48]

Successful collaborations are rare. A review of the literature and discussions with state and local planners reveals no more than 35 instances in the last two centuries in the United States. As a consequence, no matter what attempts are made, the common forms of governance between regional strategic plans and local plans remain a mixture of state control and enforced co-operation. The methods of co-operation vary around the world between explicit regulation and self-regulation – between imposed law and co-operative structures – and it is in some balance between the two that an effective form of governance usually settles.[49] It has therefore been said that there is no one form of metropolitan governance arrangement that is to be preferred, as all forms are a complex blend of patent, formal government structures and informal governance arrangements between agencies.[50] Studies of regional governance structures reveal that the forms that are effective for strategic planning are ultimately dependent upon an area's historical development, previous legal forms, competencies, financial capabilities, economic imperatives, and a myriad of other factors such as media relationships and politics.[51]

2.6 Conflict resolution

Studies have shown that the conflict between regional or metropolitan government and local government is detrimental as it results in an uncertain planning environment because of confusion among stakeholders and planners themselves.[52] A common cause of conflict that cannot easily be overcome by co-operative arrangements is the existence of different planning styles, such as a technical or bureaucratic style in one planning authority versus a political style in another.[53] A deeply held, local parochial interest may also conflict with a sub-regional or regional imperative; there is an inevitable clash between the sustainability goal of distributive justice of land use burdens across a region and local interests.[54] The cases where this has occurred, where there is conflict and not co-operation between a local authority and a regional plan, are therefore the rule and not the exception. Co-operation issues are always at the forefront of regional planning processes in European[55] and North American cities.

---

48   Felock 2013.
49   Tolkki et al. 2011.
50   Phares 2004, 2.
51   Dieringir and Sturm 2010; Murdoch and Tewdwr-Jones 1999.
52   Domingo and Beunen 2012.
53   Innes and Gruber 2005.
54   Orenstein, Jiang and Hamburg 2011.
55   Albrechts 2006.

A continuing, conflict-ridden debate over the proper jurisdiction of regional and local authorities is a repeated theme in the history of strategic planning in all countries. For instance, in the late 1980s in England, the attempt to centrally set housing numbers for local governments failed. There were no direct mandates and there was substantial local government obstruction based on protecting existing landowners. In the late 1990s, English planning introduced the system of regional spatial strategies that removed some power for regional matters from county councils. It was specifically implemented to overcome opposition to housing allocations in the south of England.

Local governments have few tools to resist a regional imposition – delay, obfuscation, appeals to ministers, publicity and lobbying are often used if there is a view that local interests must prevail. The loss of trust in the planning process that results from this direct imposition of regional power is perhaps the single most observable reason for inaction and delay in local government planning. There are enough mechanisms in the local government's legal powers to cause the regional plans to be slow in implementation, which often leads to amendment or revision of the plans.

There are several solutions that have been attempted to resolve the inevitable conflicts between regional metropolitan planning and local planning. In the *Atlanta Region plan 2040* there is a bottom-up approach. Local comprehensive plans come first and the regional plan provides the framework to address what is covered in the local plans. Thereafter, local governments have to apply minimum standards to be consistent with regional strategies; if they fail to do so, they lose 'Qualified Local Government Status' whereby grants are allocated. This push–pull approach depends on the ultimate lever of financing, always an effective method of control. This model of the state controlling regional issues through funding also occurs in the Kainudu region of Finland.[56] A regional council is elected and controls funding for matters of regional concern, leaving the local council to carry out land use planning in other areas according to the decisions made at the regional level.

Another model is to strengthen regional authorities in certain matters to enhance the regional significance of a particular project.[57] In New Jersey, for instance, the entire range of planning options for some forms of development in an environmentally sensitive area of 3480 square kilometres was removed from the local councils and given to the Department of Environmental Protection. This, and similar models, arise because of a fear that local interests may inhibit an effective regional approach, that local governments are not interested in committing time or resources to regional co-operation, and that local interests, given a chance, may override regional interests.[58]

Reviewing the co-operative arrangements of cities around the world, Vancouver still remains the prime example of a functional, co-operative arrangement, although it has been argued that it was achieved by taking a conservative approach to avoid controversy.[59] It is also a unique case because of the historical growth of that planning authority and, for that reason, it has been suggested that it is not easily replicated.[60] In all other places, even where there are attempts at co-operative arrangements, the power of the region to override local

---

56 Finland 2004.
57 DeGrove 2005.
58 Gillette 2001.
59 Tomalty 2002.
60 Grant 2009a.

governments and to cause conflict is evident. This arises because there is always a constitutional hierarchy of power that already exists between national, state, regional and local governments – planning follows this arrangement. This can be said to be a natural order and suggests that form should follow function, allowing the planning function to be divided appropriately between the administrative layers.

It does not appear that conflict resolution is a priority when metropolitan regional authorities are established, as if the chance of co-operative structures is lost in the process or already implied because of the constitutional hierarchy. After its independence from the Soviet Union, Lithuania developed a planning law, *Law on Territorial Planning 1995*, as its first attempt to incorporate the concepts of Western planning. This law requires flow-through planning while recognising the hierarchy of national, regional, county and local plans, based on the pre-existing governmental structure. This attempt at matching the planning functions to the overriding governance arrangement is ultimately the most salient form as the means of communication and co-operation are known.

The hierarchical place of regions means that regional planning appears as the appropriate logical organisation in planning and even when it is controversial or out of favour, it will emerge again. This can be best seen in the decline of regional planning in the Thatcher years in the United Kingdom because of an anti-interventionist, neoliberal stance, leading eventually to the resurgence of loose regional groups. This was followed by the introduction of regional guidance statements in the late 1980s, making the concept of regional planning acceptable as a proper government function that respects governmental arrangements.[61] The move to localism has not prevented continuous consideration of sector or regional co-operation between local government and possible regional structures.[62]

It should be apparent that the planning culture is, in the end, the most important factor in the effectiveness of regional metropolitan government. Oregon's Metro Portland is an example of essential regional control within regional boundaries that yields proper planning and co-operation because it acts respectfully towards local interests. Attending planning meetings in Beaverton and Hillsboro led to a clear impression that there was a culture of interest in co-operating and promoting the goals of the Metro plan. It is said that this is because Metro Portland developed from a unique coalition of politicians and environmental groups.[63] As a result, it is founded on co-operation and respect for local interests as it consists of both elected and local government representatives sitting on committees that have additional power to veto Metro's actions. Local governments still carry out planning but must conform to the Metro plan, meaning that there is essential, accepted regional control over land use decisions for areas considered regional in scope. Nevertheless, the power of Metro was anathema to local constituents and there was a legal challenge to the imposition of power over local government. This challenge was dismissed on the basis that the state had created metro by statute with specific power to override local interests where necessary.[64]

The ultimate success of regional strategic planning and local government co-operation depends on these cultural and historical values. In a comparison of two regional strategic planning exercises, one that was successful and one that was not, it was stated:

---

61 Baker 1998.
62 Bafarasat 2016.
63 Abbott 1997.
64 *City of Sandy v. Metro*, 115 P.3d 960 2005.

> The outcomes ... are rooted in a complex array of factors that include differences in intergovernmental relations, the relative influence of the city on the region, history of regional planning, receptivity of suburbs to smart growth, and the mobilizing potential of issues of nature preservation versus visions of the just region in bringing together urban and suburban interests[65]

Inclusion and co-operation yield planning systems that have less delay and more successful planning outcomes, as understood by the community. The successful San Diego regional planning exercise incorporated 18 municipalities, making it less a regional imposition than a co-operative of local interests. However, there is a difficulty using this model where there are many local governments in smaller areas, such as the Boston region, which encompasses 101 cities and towns. The Boston area is divided into subregions, each of which falls under the authority of a specific subregional planning commission. These are given a specific legislative status and are easy to create. The *General Laws of Massachusetts* (sect. 3) provide:

> Any group of cities, towns, or cities and towns may, by vote of their respective city councils or town meetings, vote to become members of and thus establish a planning district, which shall constitute a public body corporate. After a planning district has been thus established, any other city or town within the district area as hereinafter defined may by vote of its city council or town meeting apply for admission. Upon the affirmative vote of two thirds of the representatives of the cities and towns comprising the district, said city or town shall become a member thereof. The area of jurisdiction of said district shall be an area defined or redefined as an effective regional planning region by the Massachusetts office of business development.

A self-generating commission is formed for each district in Boston and there is a requirement that a growth management policy be prepared and adopted. A discussion of commission amendments to a regional policy indicates that there still remains a conflict between the constituent local governments and the commission resulting in inaction for six years.[66]

Since it is not possible to design a best practice interrelationship between state, municipal and local government, it is necessary that there is a clearly understood, defined and explained rationale for the allocation of authority in the ongoing process of strategic planning. This requires a specific, stated rationale for why some matters are regional and some local. The need for a full exposition is necessary because the underlying, hidden reasons, such as personal and professional connections and the individual motives of the stakeholders, are not understood and are formed by undisclosed economic or political philosophies; it is reported, for instance, that the main reason for the development of a strong regional association in Hanover, Germany, was the desire to align interests against powerful state-government intervention.[67] It may also be that regional governance is used as a subtle way to establish and enforce power structures. For instance, an announcement of a critical housing shortage may be used to accuse local governments of delay or inaction.

---

65 Wekerle and Abbruzze 2010, 592.
66 Barnstable County Assembly of Delegates 2012.
67 Albrechts, Healey and Kunzmann 2003.

Every place has, of course, its own planning culture in which the historical relationships are responsible for the degree of co-operation. It is only when the rationale for allocation is agreed and made explicit that the relationships become apparent and conflicts can be reduced.

As a consequence, the essential question in considering the appropriate governance structure between a metropolitan region and its constituent local governments is a determination of which areas of strategic planning are best suited for collaboration and which for control. An important study analysed that the appropriate form of regional governance depends upon five functional issues: who has legislative authority to develop determinative short- and long-term priorities for the region; who has the capacity to marshal the talent and deploy expertise and staff; who has the authority to make and enforce rules and laws governing planning; who has the authority to collect revenues and allocate resources for regional planning, including the power to impose fees and otherwise raise funds; and who has the political authority to make legitimate and accountable planning decisions and to influence external and internal stakeholders.[68]

The consequence of this analysis is to divide local and metropolitan regional functions according to the capacity to plan and the power to control. It follows that there are three areas to be considered: certain matters of strategic planning that are best suited to a metropolitan regional authority; those that overlap with local governments; and those that are not suited to metropolitan plans. An examination of the background papers to the *Chicago go to 2040 regional plan*, as an example, reveals a range of matters that are best allocated to metropolitan regional strategic planning and are not matters for local government. These include the preservation of agricultural land, school siting, climate change, parks, water supply, transportation, housing needs and economic development.

One addition to having a stated rationale is to deliberately recognise informal channels, such as interagency agreements or lines of communication. In jurisdictions where there are informal planning bodies, explaining their roles and relationships is helpful. For example, the Metropolitan Area Planning Councils in the United States are given statutory form but have only an advisory role, which is important in fostering a wider view of community involvement in governance structures. There are at least 500 in the United States.[69] The Metropolitan Area Planning Council of Boston is a public agency recognised under Massachusetts law that is made up of representatives of each city and town as well as government appointees. The council is recognised in order for there to be a co-operative realisation of regional planning objectives. This is accomplished by its deep involvement in the preparation of the strategic regional plan, *MetroFuture*, advising the legislative committees on proposed planning legislation, and staffing the sub-regional Metropolitan Councils that have similar sub-regional duties. Its annual report reveals that it has worked on place-based projects, promoted forums for visioning for *MetroFuture*, carried out research on sustainable solutions, provided assistance to local planning, convened meetings for housing analysis, and generally was an active participant and often instigator in all regional issues.

---

68 Hodge and Robinson 2001, 120–32.
69 Foster 2010.

2.7 Regional growth areas

'Growth area' is a phrase used in regional plans to refer to a locality that is earmarked for increased residential density. It is either one that is a greenfield area (agricultural land on the urban fringe), a brownfield area (non-viable industrial or commercial sites that are now suitable for housing), or an infill area (an existing locality that can absorb greater density). Finding and then developing growth areas is the inevitable consequence of population increases that occur naturally, by migration, and by immigration.

The need for growth is assessed by the predicted increase in the general population of the region and the projected housing requirements for each local authority. The scale is regional because the dispersion of population into particular local areas is not certain. Accordingly, managing growth is primarily a state and regional issue, overarching local needs.

In planning terms, 'growth' is the accommodation of increased population in new housing. There are only two options: to increase housing in existing areas; or to choose new areas, greenfield or brownfield, for the development of housing. The difficulties of infill in existing areas are fundamentally land assembly, where titles have to be consolidated for sufficient space for higher density, and problems with finding developers, who may earn less profit due to the complexity of obtaining approval because of resistance from local residents to changing the nature of the neighbourhood.[70] The consequence is that there is a tendency for developers to favour growth in untouched areas to create new suburbs.

A choice of growth areas suitable for housing requires an overall, regional view in order to distribute increased density among the constituent local areas. There is an implicit assumption that the intensity of the distributed density will disadvantage the areas chosen because it will change their character. In fact, an increase in density in one suburb or area may not be deleterious. An Australian study of how areas actually become disadvantaged shows it is not by a density increase, but rather by stagnation of old, decaying housing stock, below-standard services, and other factors that lead to an exposure to violence and increased competition for limited resources.[71] As a matter of fact, the ills of increased density in the inner city are not proven. They arise most probably because of a fear of the loss of character of a neighbourhood and crowding – a concept called 'perceived density', described as a 'subjective, qualitative, and affective (emotion-laden) experience'.[72] Density is unrelated to our perception of our personal space,[73] and changes in character may result in a different area, but not necessarily one that is deleterious to the residents, as increased population creates new services, diversity, and amenities.

As a result of perceived density, there continues to be an emphasis by planning authorities on distributing the greatest opportunities for housing outside existing, already established areas. It is clear that decisions as to distribution must be made in strategic planning because, when there is no attention to the spatial opportunities for housing, significant problems arise. This certainly is what has happened in Africa; the rapid expansion of cities on the urban fringe has been unrelated to infrastructure and has occurred in haphazard patterns, destroying viable agricultural land and land which is environmentally

---

70   Farris 2001.
71   Pawson, Davison and Wiesel 2012.
72   Churchman 1999.
73   Stein 1982.

Figure 2-2 Sprawl in Lisbon, Portugal. Source: Google Earth.

precarious. This has also resulted in traffic congestion and increased car emissions.[74] The alternative of controlled development of growth areas is therefore termed 'smart growth' or 'compact cities' to distinguish it from unplanned sprawl. The content and theories of smart growth vary, but it is the usual name given to an attempt to distribute urban growth to nominated areas and to control the manner in which they develop.

Growth areas raise many common planning issues. These include the need to co-ordinate transport and energy infrastructure with growth, to expand and allocate land for community resources such as hospitals and schools, and to entice companies to relocate to provide employment opportunities for the new population. It is appropriate to assert that managing growth as a city expands by population increases is the most difficult of all planning issues. This is because it affects the market, as fortunes are made by developers assembling non-residential land and speculating that it will be zoned for housing or for infilling existing areas with new development. As a result, there is constant pressure by the development community on the state government to make zoning changes because of this rampant speculation. Each such decision that chooses one area over another will have the effect of raising house and land prices.[75] This is a universal problem because, even when there is decreasing population, as in some Eastern European countries, the demand for increased density still occurs as smaller sized households still require space and greater services.[76]

---

74 Arku 2009.
75 Buxton and Taylor 2011.

The models used for state intervention for growth areas have similar dynamics in all planning systems. The underlying theme is a requirement that the local plan must conform to the state's choice for placement of the increased population, even if the local area is unwilling to change its character by increased density. The state enforces the choice of growth areas by various means, such as requiring state approval of a local plan to make sure it accords with state growth plans – the state plan overriding a local plan where there is an inconsistency – or the state labelling growth projects as having 'state significance' to obtain complete planning control. The standard model also includes a state or metropolitan planning commission or special growth-management body being assigned responsibility to plan for and manage growth. The appointment of these bodies is a recognition that they will be able to build up a sufficient evidence base to have the ostensible power to override local concerns.

As the state has control or contributes to the construction of infrastructure – roads, electricity and water – that is the most effective lever to ensure local compliance with state growth strategies. An example is the State of Maryland funding-based system under the *Priority Funding Areas (Smart Growth) Act*. The act provides for the flow of state funds for 'growth-related projects' to existing communities and areas where growth is planned if the areas meet criteria for residential density targets and other matters relating to infrastructure. Development is not restricted outside these growth areas but state funding is not available, thus creating an incentive for localities to drive growth to state goals. It has been found that the greater the state subsidy of a project under this system, the more likely the local authority will comply with the state initiative,[77] although this is never a guarantee that the areas have been chosen wisely.[78]

One of the obvious ills of the government rezoning land for large-lot development of housing on the urban fringe is the possibility of the indiscriminate sprawl of housing, leapfrogging areas ripe for development, resulting in inadequate public facilities and a greater reliance on cars. The European Environmental Agency in 2006 expressed the ills as:

> major impacts that are evident in increased energy, land and soil consumption. These impacts threaten both the natural and rural environments, raising greenhouse gas emissions that cause climate change, and elevated air and noise pollution levels which often exceed the agreed human safety limits. Thus, urban sprawl produces many adverse impacts that have direct effects on the quality of life for people living in cities.[79]

The actual problem is not that sprawled, low-density development is necessarily going to be haphazard or will always create spread-out housing with poor facilities, but rather that there is something inherently objectionable about the notion of sprawl. The distaste can perhaps be traced to the extensive 1974 report *The costs of sprawl* prepared for the US Department of Housing and Urban Development as well as other agencies, which condemned sprawl in strong economic and social terms.[80] Aside from increasing car use and destroy-

---

76   Haase, Kabisch and Haase 2013.
77   Howland and Sohn 2007.
78   Lewis, Knapp and Sohn 2009.
79   European Environmental Agency 2006.
80   Real Estate Research Corporation 1974.

ing farmland, the real ill that was identified was the loss of community, leading to isolation and alienation.

The odd voice over the years protested that residents still want to use cars, that farmland was not being destroyed, and that people preferred detached houses on larger blocks of land more than a vague sense of community.[81] Yet sprawl conjured up an urban dystopia, the antithesis of the ideal of blissful suburbia – vast, flat tracks of land with sparse housing, shopping malls abandoned at night with massive open parking areas, where those in need such as the elderly could not find services, and where there was no work, requiring long car rides to other destinations. The juggernaut could not be stopped and the idea of controlling sprawl and having planned and managed growth quickly became an essential part of every state planning agenda, initially in the United States, then Canada, Australia and the United Kingdom, followed by the rest of Europe and Asia.

Growth-management controls are therefore primarily oriented to prevent sprawl and to foster more compact development, according to what are now universally described as 'smart growth principles'. The essence of these principles is the recitation in the negative of any planning idea that might lead to sprawl, as set out in a section of the Vermont *Growth Centers Act* (sect. 13.1), which says that Smart Growth:

> Reflects a settlement pattern that, at full build-out, is not characterised by:
>
> i. scattered development located outside of compact urban and village centers that is excessively land consumptive;
> ii. development that limits transportation options, especially for pedestrians;
> iii. the fragmentation of farm and forest land;
> iv. development that is not serviced by municipal infrastructure or that requires the extension of municipal infrastructure across undeveloped lands in a manner that would extend service to lands located outside compact village and urban centers;
> v. linear development along well-traveled roads and highways that lacks depth, as measured from the highway.

In 2002, the American Planning Association prepared the *Model statutes for planning and the management of change*, which included a 'Smart Growth Act'. That act has as one of its objects to: 'encourage a pattern of compact and contiguous urban growth in locally designated smart growth areas that have been determined to be most ssuitable for growth' (sect. 4-401.2a). It also recognises that the ideal means for carrying it out is to orient state funding to projects for connected facilities and transportation. Under the *Model statutes*, areas suitable for growth are 'certified' only after consultation with the public to determine that they meet the requirements that make them ripe for development.

The phrase 'smart growth' has been expanded beyond compact development to include healthy communities, increased jobs, cohesive neighbourhoods, equitable distribution of the costs and benefits of development, more efficient use of land, and other factors that reflect very high ideals for planning.[82] The European Commission's *Europe 2020* communication uses the concept of 'smart growth' to include an 'economy based on knowledge

---

81 Gordon and Richardson 2000.
82 Ye, Mandpe and Meyer 2005.

and innovation' and a more competitive economy.[83] In fact, it has been suggested that by calling something 'smart growth', any other orientation is by implication 'dumb growth'.[84]

What underlies the move to smart growth are aspirational goals to overcome the perceived ill of sprawl. The measure of what constitutes sprawl is, however, anything but certain and is rarely articulated. This is because the aspirational goals are an aesthetic or philosophical evaluation of low-density patterns based on the perceived lifestyle consequences for the residents. Sprawl also conjures the fear of rapid and uncontrolled expansion of land development that may continuously leapfrog the existing vector of urban growth. However, this may not be the case. A study of the Delhi Urban Agglomeration, a megacity of almost 19 million that is constantly expanding, using the best measures and definitions of what might be sprawl, concluded only a modest increase in sprawl over ten years.[85] The measures of sprawl are not precise and cannot be assessed only by a bird's eye view of a city; Los Angeles is not subject to massive sprawl, for instance, even though it appears spread out and only linked by roads. Nevertheless, the aspirational goals inherent in overcoming sprawl have a basic goodness and reflect a concern for better living, less polluting traffic, healthier walking, and the development of a sense of community.

The effect of smart growth planning controls on restricting sprawl is uncertain. Research has shown that, unless the controls are very restrictive by controlling the details of future development, merely moderate controls based on aspirational goals only lead to greater sprawl.[86] This is probably because the demand for land does not abate and, if one area is not ready for growth, another will be ready, even out of logical sequence, resulting in housing dispersion. There has been, in fact, a greater increase in the United States of detached housing in non-urban areas than multiple dwellings in the urban core.[87] Yet, there is a continuous emphasis on the need to control sprawl in spite of this trend in housing.

In China, development of cities is preferred over suburban growth in fringe areas, highlighting that the ideological and political culture plays a significant part in the attitude to sprawl.[88] It has been pointed out that in Belgium there was, historically, an anti-urban sentiment held by the Belgian elites who enjoyed large, landed, property interests outside the urban centres.[89] As a result, the planning regime allowed development freely, most of which took the form of 'ribbon' development along roads as the state accepted the pre-eminence of private property rights and the resultant privilege to use that land unrestricted by state law (Fig. 2-3). Some have even praised sprawl as facilitating the dream in many cultures of a large home on a big lot;[90] this in fact has been said to be at the core of early patterns of sprawl in the United States.[91] Sprawl may not be an evil as much as a necessity in some cases. In Malaysia, rapid urban growth and an attempt to make urban areas globally competitive by a national economic agenda resulted in greater income separation, forcing lower and middle income families to move out of the expensive city.[92]

---

83 European Commission 2010.
84 Miller and Hoel 2002, 16.
85 Mookherjee and Hoerauf 2015.
86 Paulsen 2013.
87 Laidley 2015.
88 Huang, Lu and Sellers 2007.
89 Halleux, Marcinczak and van der Krabben 2012.
90 Bruegmann 2005.
91 Lewinnek 2014.
92 Abdullah 2012.

Figure 2-3 Ribbon development in Flanders, Belgium. Source: Google Earth.

It is impossible not to see sprawl in every city in every country and, even where there is a concentration on infill, there is nothing to prevent the same problems of dystopia in dense urban areas that face those in the distant suburbs. Alienation, poverty, sterile areas and poor transportation are not confined to sprawling suburbs or to ones that are built according to smart growth principles. However, the idea that something better might be possible than the ills of sprawl is compelling. The smart growth principles have never faltered and were given a boost by the New Urbanism movement. This started with the promise that it could provide improvements in the quality of living in new suburbs by means of architectural controls that created pedestrian-friendly local neighbourhoods with mixed uses and open spaces, resulting in a sense of place.

The New Urbanism movement gained traction because another aspect of smart growth is that the ills of sprawl are synonymous with ugly, modernist architecture laid out in a subdivision pattern that fosters increased car use. It is therefore possible to design areas that improve on design and alter the subdivision pattern. This is accomplished in New Urbanism by the creation of neighbourhoods offering walking distances to facilities, compact mixed-use development, and an attempt at greater wellbeing by specifying the architectural components for all new building. The New Urbanism movement has convinced governments that good design improves the quality of life in all areas. The design is provided in a 'SmartCode' that contains specific requirements as to common zonings, house types in each zone, transportation and pedestrian movements, and even the forms of curbing and public lighting (Fig. 2-4).

2 Planning scale

Figure 2-4 New Urbanist development in Seaside, Florida. Source: Google Earth.

New Urbanism suggests that design can encourage a sense of place and community: a relationship between the inhabitants and the built form that leads to an identification with the benefits and aesthetics of the local setting and consequent wellbeing. The manner in which this occurs is not exactly clear but has that same ring of truth that the Jane Jacob's theory had when it was introduced – the internal, subjective state of an individual is influenced by the external, planned environment. This connection harks back to the what New Urbanism calls 'traditional neighbourhood design' – a return to idealised past patterns that were villages and towns. As such, and if it is true, it is irresistible as a concept and therefore has been adopted in most countries with smart-growth agendas.[93] It is a concept that is seductive because there is something offensive about bland suburbs with cheaply built housing in the middle of nowhere. Smart growth with the benefit of New Urbanism gives a sense of doing something right, of designing to go beyond mere aspirations by tight, form-based codes, and fostering a consensus that community is essential for social cohesion, and that this can be accomplished by providing an interactive environment.

An analysis of smart growth in the Scottish Highlands indicates the manner in which it works in the planning system.[94] New Urbanism ideas have become part of the planning agenda in the United Kingdom and were invoked for the area northeast of Inverness in a town called Tornagrain. The father of New Urbanism, Adreas Duany, went to Tornagrain to conduct a 'charrette', a community participation forum for the purpose of establishing

---

93 Song and Ding 2009.
94 MacLeod 2013.

a shared consensus as to the vision for planning the area. The conclusion reached was to provide for development of almost 5,000 homes on a 140-hectare site according to New Urbanism principles so that no person was further than a ten-minute walk from the central square with its shops and community services. There were, however, concerns about whether retailers would locate in the new area and whether there would be public transport, schools, parks, or jobs.

The approval in Tornagrain is an example of the power of the Jane Jacobs and New Urbanism idea that there is a direct correlation between the quality of life and urban design. The study suggests that the ideas overwhelmed the inhabitants and the council who were swept up in the enthusiasm. It is easy to understand that the New Urbanism ideas are capable of being evangelised and accepted without question. The Queensland *Next generation planning handbook*, for example, is a policy document for the south-east region of that state that is a complete SmartCode for 'making places great for people' and was adopted without any questioning or doubt.

There is, however, no certainty as to the effect of smart growth on the quality of life. In a study of Jacobs' theories as applied to Seoul,[95] it was found that the diversity elements indeed led to more walking over driving. However, this was not true for the New Urbanism idea of having mixed uses: residential and non-residential closeness did not encourage walking, nor did proximity to office areas. Density itself was also not a factor in walking over driving, although density of employment uses was relevant.

The difficulty is not with New Urbanism as a worthwhile concept but rather that it is hard to translate specific design objectives into psychological wellbeing. For a start, it depends on a person's temperament – someone with greater openness may have, the research suggests, a greater connection with the environment.[96] There is probably a clear enhancement of living when a resident is situated closer to nature, but not necessarily from living closer to a civic place or a civic centre, or within a walkable pedestrian area.[97] Whether smart growth will deliver a higher-order place is not conclusive, as what is in the vision of the designer will not necessarily have the same impact on the residents.[98]

Smart growth can certainly give rise to positive planning outcomes. Principles, which appear sound and are an alternative to perceived ills, are addressed. Implementing smart growth by embedding New Urbanism principles in law or policy has the beneficial effect of focusing attention on what is possible, or at least on bringing attention to design. In the Western Australian government's *Liveable neighbourhoods policy*, New Urbanism design principles are expressed in a policy document. This has had the effect of requiring an enhanced discussion of the subdivision design. Even if there is no direct evidence that the quality of life is enhanced by a SmartCode, the attempts to do so are important, despite being symbolic rather than necessarily effective.

The symbolic value of an orientation towards greater attention to design cannot be underestimated. In an evaluation of legislation that is symbolic and not obviously effective, it was concluded that it at least had the effect of integrating part of the legal and political culture with practice by turning the planning culture of the state into a legislative framework.[99] This becomes a 'communicative framework' that explains the hidden goals of the

---

95   Sung, Lee and Cheon 2015.
96   Milfont and Sibley 2012.
97   Scannell and Gifford 2010.
98   Brown and Gifford 2001.

legislation by open revelation of the underlying aspirations. In this sense, no matter what the actual effect, the symbolic significance of a planning regime attempting to create better neighbourhoods is enough to justify smart-growth legislation.

A difficult problem with smart-growth controls is that they must control the sequence of land release for new housing and the choice of infill projects for existing areas. The tight control of sequencing is critical because it inevitably raises the fear of corruption as the returns of rezoning land for housing are the basis of many fortunes. The usual attempt to control corruption in the choice of areas is to provide a special growth commission with members beyond reproach and representative of the various constituent local authorities that can make an informed choice about the order of development in growth areas. The only issue with such a commission is the possible lack of community participation in the process, as the members by their appointment take on a role as the experts on planning issues. The fact that there was participation to identify growth areas in the strategic planning process also means that it may be concluded that those who participated already had their say and sequencing is merely procedural.

As the process of choice is not always clear, public participation in the ultimate choices is still best practice for the outcome to be acceptable to all. However, a review of smart growth practices indicates that participation in choosing the sequence of growth areas among those nominated appears nonexistent. The reason is most likely that the final decision is seen as an 'expert' decision as it depends on a complex equation of agency infrastructure commitments and financing, the vector of previous development, layers of empirical evidence as to housing demand, developer interest, the politics around shortages of housing, and perhaps a policy agenda for what constitutes effective growth.[100]

Smart-growth legislation and place-based codes are, however, best practice because they have symbolic value that accords with aspirational goals. It is probably the case that smart codes and New Urbanism ideas *do not* in fact elevate the quality of life in a new suburb, nor reduce the need to use cars to find work or entertainment. The connection between design elements and subjective states is too amorphous to recognise these devices as the answer to new housing choices. However, they at least open up the examination to the community and government of the social goals being fostered.

2.7.1 Models for determining housing needs

It might appear as a sound proposition that future housing needs of the region or state should be correctly distributed to the constituent local authorities. However, local interests resist increased density on the basis of its effect on the character of nominated areas. The possibility of intense development will always cause anxiety and opposition, even if the effect will ultimately be beneficial.

One model for housing allocation in a regional strategic plan is not to direct density in particular places, but to indicate areas that are suitable for development and encourage local government to decide how to absorb an increase in housing. This is appropriate where there is some doubt that an increase in density will have the necessary effect of absorbing population, especially if housing types are not considered.[101] This is recognised in the

---

99 van Klink 2014.
100 Bengston, Fletcher and Nelsen 2004.
101 Aurand 2010.

Chicago strategic plan *Go to 2040*, which states that increasing density in areas will not necessarily result in take-up.

> Research has found, however, that zoning alone does not determine whether or not developments will result in lower density. Often, suburban subdivisions are not developed to the maximum density allowed by zoning. [A study in 2000] surveyed three single-family developments in Aurora, and found that the developments were only built to between 65 and 86 percent of the maximum allowable density. The research illustrates that regulation does not entirely dictate housing stock, but that market demand and consumer preferences also influence what developers build.

Another model is for the regional plan to go further and set out a clear explanation of the specific needs for housing growth in each area, leaving the specifics to the local land use plan. The 2010 regional growth strategy for Vancouver *Metro Vancouver 2040: shaping our future*, indicates a series of overall principles to be followed: there should be compact cities; an urban containment boundary beyond which development should not occur; the designation of areas suitable for density; and growth should be directed to urban centres. It provides this strategy:

> The role of municipalities is to:
> 1.1.3 Adopt Regional Context Statements which:
>
> a. depict the Urban Containment Boundary on a map, generally consistent with the Regional Land Use Designations map (Map 2);
> b. provide municipal population, dwelling unit and employment projections, with reference to guidelines contained in Appendix Table A.1, and demonstrate how municipal plans will work towards accommodating the projected growth within the Urban Containment Boundary'.

In the *Regional context statement* for North Vancouver, as an example, the statement provides:

> Capacity identified for additional 20,000 population, 10,000 housing units, and 10,000 jobs for year 2030 . . . This meets RGS [Regional Growth Strategy] guidelines provided in Table A.1 up to year 2031.

The regional growth plan provides the reasons for the distribution of future housing and requires a local government, as a condition of its own strategic plan, to indicate how it will accommodate those needs. The *Regional context statement* then becomes part of a local strategy plan: the *Official community* plan.

Research into the Dutch system of planning concluded that designating specific allocations of housing in defined areas does not actually keep track of on-the-ground realities:

> In various regions of the Netherlands the pace of urbanization has been such that whole stretches between the official urban regions have now changed face in light of unplanned piecemeal settlements. This all happened despite the fact that official policies did not allow for such developments. What is more, it could be argued that the developments in many cases took place because of the planning system. There is no built-in check that

2 Planning scale

Figure 2-5 Urban growth boundary in Helvitia, Oregon. Source: Google Earth.

guarantees a selectivity in development. In various regions the planning induced a delay in construction activity leading to building activity elsewhere.[102]

This research suggests that a shorter-term outlook on housing needs is more appropriate than the long-term scale of a strategic plan to allow for flexibility and adaptation to changed circumstances, such as choices of developers outside what is designated, and to have the process constantly under review.[103] San Diego has removed the exact numbers of housing for each local government area from the regional plan on the basis that they should be considered as part of an iterative process that will make sense as it evolves. The system used is the development of a regional housing needs assessment arising from community participation and local government consultation. The regional authority (SANDAG) then requires every local authority to submit its compliance with the housing elements in order to obtain incentive funding based on a scoring system concerned with take-up of a fair share of housing needs.[104] This has the effect of operating the housing needs requirement in a tighter period than that of the strategic plan and tying it to funding, already mentioned as an important lever. More importantly, it allows the assessment not to be fixed indefinitely in either practice or sentiment, and to adapt as developer choices are made and density is provided.

---

102 Hajer and Zonneveld 2000, 348.
103 Balducci 2008.
104 San Diego Association of Governments (2011), policy 033.

The requirement for a 'housing needs assessment' in California has its origin in the California Government Code:

> The Planning and Zoning Law requires the housing element of the general plan of a city, county, or city and county to contain, among other things, an assessment of housing needs, including an inventory of land suitable for residential development, and a program with a 5-year schedule of actions that the local government is undertaking or intends to undertake to implement the goals and objectives of the housing element.[105]

The legislation provides for a reassessment in an eight-year cycle and is clear about the extent of the investigation that must take place, the elements that must be included, and the manner in which it must be carried out in a relatively short timeframe. The last SANDAG reassessment (2013–20) took two years to complete and is for an eight-year period.

The process begins with a housing needs determination, described in the SANDAG regional housing needs assessment as:

> using information from SANDAG's regional growth forecast and the California Department of Finance population estimates, calculates a demographic housing need based on headship and vacancy rates, and household size.

That determination is then used for the fair-share allocation.[106] The San Francisco Association of Bay Area Governments has developed a housing element toolkit based on an earlier document: *Blueprint 2001 for Bay Area housing: housing element ideas and solutions for a sustainable and affordable future* that includes methodologies for ensuring reliable data, population and employment trends, future needs, land inventory, zoning and other matters that lead to a systematic approach to establishing the California housing element.

The effect of this careful interactive approach is to remove the controversial issue of density designation set for the long term by a regional strategic plan and instead to require an ongoing process to reassess and implement the numbers. The advantage of this method is that it offers a chance to combine community participation, affordable housing, an agreed methodology for assessing data, and a tie-in with a regional growth plan. It shifts the responsibility to a co-operative process over a limited time period that is constantly under investigation and discussion rather than an authoritative, fixed determination and allocation. Accordingly, it removes the key factual driver of density placement from controversy and allows it to be dynamic and collaborative.

2.8 Integrated regional transport

There are other agencies that interact with a regional planning agenda. The placement of roads, rail and airports may not be co-ordinated with strategic plans, leading to a situation where the planning system waits on, or is out of sync with, these infrastructure decisions. For instance, a planning authority seeking to increase density in a particular area may not have the road infrastructure in place to support the traffic generated. A state or regional

---

105 California Government Code, chap. 633, SB 2.
106 San Diego Assocaition of Governments 2011, 7.

plan's aspirations and goals may not be part of the transportation authority's agenda. This may occur for the logical reason that future transport agencies' plans are already committed and cannot be altered easily to accommodate a new regional or metropolitan plan when it arises in the middle of a cycle.

Attempts at combining land use planning and transport take two forms. One method is joining planning and transportation in one agency at the state level. This joining of two functions with different orientations is not necessarily a successful approach. In England in 1970, the Department of the Environment was expanded to include transport. In 1976, there was a splitting off of a separate transport department that was then re-joined after 1997, only to be split off again in 2002.

In the United States, the federal government in the *Safe Accountable Efficient Transportation: a Legacy for Users Act 2005* provides innovative methods to obtain private funding for transportation by setting up state infrastructure banks, which gives the states freedom to create their own infrastructure strategy. However, the infrastructure choices are not linked to land use planning. In the Netherlands, the Dutch *Infrastructure Act* gives the ministry in charge of transportation and public works authority that overrides land use plans, although there is support for intertwining the two by having the infrastructure tender process proceed alongside the planning process.[107]

In 2004 the US Association of Metropolitan Planning Organizations (MPO) prepared a report, *Noteworthy MPO practice in transportation–land use integration*, on best practices for integrating infrastructure in plan making. It was recognised that the starting point for planning projects must be an explicit recognition of the need to link infrastructure choices with the plan. This process needs to be initiated by meetings between metropolitan planners and transport planners, who together examine the possible effects of land use on transportation planning. It is reported that the Southern California Association of Governments' Creative Liveable Spaces project, following those meetings, provided that spatial planning include a component of transportation planning by producing maps, growth forecasts, job statistics, information on environmentally sensitive areas, and transportation plans in the same land use plan. In Atlanta, Georgia, the Atlanta Regional Commission provided funds to local authorities to conduct specific studies to integrate land use and transportation.

Some of the integration has been accomplished by the smart growth movement because a major problem of sprawl is increased car usage. The Federal Highway Administration in 2010 produced the *Livability in transportation guidebook*, which adopts smart-growth principles and provides case examples of how transportation can be incorporated into land use decisions. The first example is Charlotte, North Carolina (Fig. 2-6), about which it is explained:

> Over an intensive 9-month period, a series of transit/land use alternatives were tested for each of the five corridors . . . An extensive public outreach process fostered community understanding and consensus around the recommended plan, which called for phased implementation of various transit technologies along the five corridors. Partnerships, such as those with the Charlotte Area Transit System (CATS) and other municipal government agencies, and initiatives, such as the South Corridor Infrastructure Program (SCIP), helped encourage ownership across departments. These efforts helped broaden

---

107 Arts and van Lamoen 2005; Lanferink and Arts 2009.

Figure 2-6 Integrated transport in Charlotte, North Carolina. Source: Google Earth.

the perspective of each department's role and involvement in integrated transportation and land use projects.[108]

All of the other case studies set out in the guidebook include some form of joint 'visioning' of the problems and possible collaborative solutions that embrace public participation. The method proposed in the guidebook is that the transportation agency should be the primary agency that consults with the public and the local authorities, and works in a collaborative design process that leads to concept plans that can be tested. The land use plan then becomes, by definition and name, an 'integrated transport and land use plan.' For example, the Charlotte Plan is called: *The 2025 integrated land use and transit plan*.

The state of Maine formalised the integration by entering into an agreement with the Federal Highway Administration for the preparation of a strategic transportation–land use plan. It lists the responsibilities of the other three stakeholders: a town response panel, made up of representatives of local government; the state Department of Transport; and a steering committee. It documents the purpose of the plan, the roles and responsibilities, and sets out the foundation for implementation.

Inclusion of transportation in the planning process is inevitable because it falls under the rubric of sustainability. The OECD, as early as 1994, initiated the Environmentally Sustainable Project, which made transportation a critical component of sustainability. The United Nations Center for Regional Development conference in 1995 produced the *Aichi*

---

108   Federal Highway Administration 2010.

statement, which said that an integrated approach to planning and transport is essential to sustainability principles. All further documents of the OECD have listed transportation and land use as cornerstones of sustainability.

There is no precise model for integrating planning and transportation as they arise from a planning culture and historical structures of co-operation. Many are mooted, commenced, but abandoned if they are not supported by that culture. As an example, there was an abandoned attempt in New South Wales, Australia, to have a state infrastructure plan take into account the planning system requirements. This was not successful as that planning culture was not based on interagency co-operation and the treasury had effective control of the ultimate decisions on infrastructure.

Integration attempts are fraught with other problems because transport and planning have different methodologies. Transport decisions are not based on community participation or local visions but are directed to more utilitarian concerns, such as construction financing and costs, or geographic distribution of resources. The most sophisticated methods for transportation decisions,[109] based on urban transport modelling, consider variables such as trip generation, traffic distribution, alternative transport modes, and traffic assignment options, and do not dovetail with aspirational planning. The results of infrastructure modelling can only be fed into planning decisions and not integrated with them.

The power of the treasury, as in New South Wales, to control planning agendas through transport and other infrastructure budgeting should not be underestimated. Treasury desires to exact contributions from developers for large developments arising from conditions on development permission to reduce the burden on the public purse. The focus is on revenue and expenditure. The issues of social cohesion or the fabric of a community are not as relevant as encouraging large developments to obtain infrastructure contributions. As the treasury function is relevant to transport and other infrastructure and, as contributions by way of conditions and agreements are required in development control systems, the treasury has a different agenda to the planning authority that may align more closely with the infrastructure agencies.

The most promising methods involve making transportation, land use and environmental impact the subject of models that allow scenario testing. The different orientations of the models mean that it is difficult for coupling the data and outputs. These co-ordinated models are in their infancy but offer a chance to model the effects of transportation decisions and land use decisions on each other.[110]

2.9 Integrated water management

In Nigeria, water resources are plentiful but there are separate federal and state agencies to manage and control the various outputs. This is because water creates different management functions: irrigation, potable water, flood control, drainage, ports, and erosion control.[111] The problem in Nigeria is a lack of institutional depth to respond to all the challenges and therefore there is little emphasis on interagency co-operation. As a result, the various land use planning controls – *Land Use Act 1978*, *Urban Development Policy 1992*,

---

109 Tolley and Turton 2013, sect 8.3.
110 Shahumyan and Moeckel 2016.
111 Stech 2014.

Urban and Regional Planning Act 1992, as well as the *Housing and Urban Development Policy 2002* – have no connection with water management or supply. The *Land Use Act 1978* is typical of a traditional Western approach based on early English legislation that provides for strategic planning and development control with no orientation towards the complexity of water management.

The Nigerian example illustrates that strategic planning does not usually include other activities that are carried out by other agencies. The governance arrangements that make this possible are not prescribed by planning laws and become a matter of shifting alignments. The idea of planning is one-directional: the use of land only and not the use of water or the interaction between land and water.

It can be said that the earliest idea of co-operation between planning and water management came from the Earth Summit of 1992 and later the introduction of Integrated Water Resource Management (IWRM) in 2003 by the Global Water Partnership, which defined the approach as:

> a process which promotes the coordinated development and management of water, land and related resources, in order to maximize the resultant economic and social welfare in an equitable manner without compromising the sustainability of vital ecosystems.

A review of IWRM[112] indicates that, regardless of the attempts at co-ordination, there are conceptual difficulties in linking water and land-based systems. Water issues may demand immediate intervention while strategic planning looks to the future. There are also boundary issues relating to federal, state and local government jurisdictions. The review of IWRM quotes from a report by the Sydney Healthy Rivers Commission of New South Wales that: 'There is a perception that because "everyone" is (apparently) responsible, "no one" can in fact be held responsible.'

The water management cycle is not historically a planning issue and there is little prompting a change in that relationship among the institutions established for that purpose. There is thus a natural degree of exclusion of planning issues and future growth ideas in plans by water agencies who are concerned with investment in stationary infrastructure and, accordingly, it has been said that the field is entrapped in the specialised institutions.[113]

A further difficulty is the lack of hierarchical integration. Water management is often regionalised, offering little possibility of integration with local plans. There are, however, some rare examples of integration. In France, the regional approach to water management is in fact integrated with land use planning. The *Schémas directeurs d'amenagement et de gestion des eaux* (SDAGE) for the broader water basins and *Schémas d'amenagement et de gestion des eaux* (SAGE) for sub-basins, established under the 1992 *Water Act*, led to SDAGE River Basin Committees. These committees are comprised of members of both central and local governments as well as water-user groups, such as industry and farming. Each SAGE is then prepared by a local committee and implemented by local authorities, making water management part of the local agenda, facilitating integration.

---

112   Mitchell 2005.
113   Brown, Ashley and Farrelly 2011.

Certain aspects of water management fit naturally within the realm of land use planning. Flood risk is a common matter that is addressed in allocation of a land use to areas that may be inundated. The UK *National planning policy framework* (para. 100) provides:

> Local Plans should be supported by Strategic Flood Risk Assessment and develop policies to manage flood risk from all sources, taking account of advice from the Environment Agency and other relevant flood risk management bodies, such as lead local flood authorities and internal drainage boards.

Flood risk is a long-term possibility, which may compete with shorter-term planning goals and will limit the use of land. It is, however, often counterintuitive when the risk is not apparent and the land to be utilised appears capable of development or has never been flooded in the past.

There appears to be a general reluctance for planning authorities to examine the influence of water issues outside of flood risk. The impact of a new subdivision on aquifers is one possible exception. This may sometimes be addressed by requiring a developer to produce a groundwater report to examine the impact, but it is hit-and-miss in all countries as there is a lack of clear goals for water quality and aquifer maintenance expressed in planning documents.

The lack of integration of water management with planning most likely arises because of a clash between science and aspirational ideas. Planning is always concerned with the effectuation of a vision and no place has traditionally been found in that vision for water management.

2.10 Best practice

In countries where local governments make planning decisions, there will be some form of regional planning, which will necessarily cause governance issues. These issues complicate the system for stakeholders and delay the implementation of plans due to conflicts that are obvious as well as those that go on behind closed doors arising from the planning culture. Best practice suggests that the governance issues are inevitable but must be the subject of a full explanation to all stakeholders. This fundamental principle is only accomplished where there is an effective, explicit governance model that dictates the relationship of a regional authority with local government and other agencies. The explanation of governance cannot be hidden and left to agency leverage, unofficial deals, professional and personal friendships or economic power. Every aspect of it must be made explicit.

2.10.1 Intervention

Best practice is trending towards increased local autonomy with less interference by the state and regional or metropolitan authorities. This is an impression gained from the rise of a populist sentiment and the way in which that continues to influence planning laws. It can be seen in the devolution of power to local authorities in Kenya and in Pakistan where localism has been strong through all regimes, perhaps to ameliorate the political unrest. Under the martial law of General Zia-ul-Haq, the emphasis was on new local government power. Under the *Devolution of power plan* of 2001, President Musharaf created a new local government system with a push for decentralisation of authority to local governments. These grassroots systems proceed on the basis of returning 'power to the people', although that is often not made explicit, as it is with the UK *Cities and Local Government Devolution Act 2016.*

Devolution to autonomy in planning for local authorities is also a response to the continuous jurisdictional conflict and consequent delay and political battles, rather than as a result of theory. As well, central control has not addressed the problems of urban environments; a speech by the director of the think tank Reform Scotland in 2015 explains it:

> As I see it, the main driver of potential change is an increasing awareness that centralisation, whether at Westminster or Holyrood, has not lived up to its billing. This is despite the fact that it was often implemented with the best of intentions. It was supposed to be the key to tackling social and economic problems, but has not delivered the changes and improvements that people were led to expect or wished to see.[114]

There is a strong logic to this trend, as the governance structure should always be based on the primary premise of respect for local government autonomy because of residents' attachment to a local area. Any claim about local government corruption used as a means to empower regional government must be actual and not implied and have a mechanism to restore autonomy if that blight is corrected.

One of the ways in which this respect can be observed is by the regional authority taking into account local policies and proceeding with full local community participation in every area that is affected. When the need for state intervention is inevitable in local planning, it is best oriented to state or regional issues, accepting that local planning issues are best resolved by local governments.

When the state intervenes in matters of local planning, there should be a clear explanation of the nature of the intervention, of the respective decision-making authorities, and which matters remain exclusively in the jurisdiction of the local government. This should not be left to deduction from reading and interpreting policies and legislation.

For metropolitan government, a governance structure should allow local governments a seat at the metropolitan decision-making level. Best practice is to *elect* representatives from local areas to the metropolitan government. If they are appointed by the metropolitan or state government, there is a degree of distance between local needs and regional needs. The practice of appointing members based on local government nominations creates less distance but removes the community from the appointments, except indirectly.

When there is a regional plan, the local government must indicate the degree to which it conforms to that plan in its own plan. The status of a draft regional plan should not be left to legal interpretation but should be defined by the authorising legislation.

2.10.2 Hierarchy

Where there is a hierarchy of plans, there must be a line of sight through each level; a resident should be able to trace through any regional issue into its treatment in the local plan. This can be done by designating plan elements in legislation or even by an overarching high-level policy that explains the relationships. This is not a trivial best practice but is crit-

---

114   Mawdsley 2015.

ical to the use of large-scale plans that integrate with lower-scale plans. If a regional and local plan can be read with a high degree of consistency, it carries the implication that there is a form of co-operation at work, which leads to confidence in the system and a more orderly system of plan making and amendments.

In all cases, the hierarchy should carry with it the requirement that each authority must justify its functions under the rubric that state issues are for the state, regional issues for the region and, importantly, local issues for the local government. In Poland, the local governments receive a 'superstructure' of federal or state help only when they do not have adequate resources for a problem. The principle of 'subsidiarity' was written into the Polish constitution. In this, the local authority deals with matters an individual cannot handle, the county or *powiat* deals with matters when the local authority is unable, the provinces or *voivodeships* in turn aid the counties, and the state is the ultimate subsidiary.

2.10.3 Co-operative structures

Best practice is to create distinct and public agreements for co-operation between regional and local authorities and not leave it to informal arrangements that exist behind closed doors or are based on historical or personal relationships. This can be effected by an express duty to co-operate in legislation or, at least, designating a defined forum in which co-operation is encouraged. The subject and scope of a regional or metropolitan plan should be restricted by the need for express consultation with the local authority and a full explanation of the manner in which the concerns are addressed. This sets a tone of co-operation and a justification for the outcomes. It is essential to accept that, if there is no co-operation and all details of the plan have to be forced on the local authorities, it is likely to fail. This may not seem to be the case in the beginning, but a local authority has many means at its disposal to stop the implementation of the regional plan by delay, obfuscation and even disobedience, requiring unwanted enforcement actions.

Funding mechanisms, whereby the state rewards local initiatives, are most effective in achieving regional goals and enhancing co-operation. A willingness on the part of the regional planning authority, through co-operation with infrastructure agencies, to supply a train station or a new road is always effective in adding hope to the local governments' carrying out of its own aspirations.

2.10.4 Growth management

Ideally, there should be an agreement reached between the state and local governments as to what level of growth is appropriate for a region.[115] This should not just be a state function or one derived by experts in a bureaucracy based on arguments or theories that are not capable of being challenged. In order to justify intervention and prevent conflict, there should be a clear agreed statement of regional growth predictions, the need for housing allocations, and the manner that they might be absorbed in consultation with the local authority and community.

For growth management, large areas of land that become regional in nature should be removed from local government administration rather than lead to a conflict of views. More particularly, an area that is designated for regional conservation, for instance, should

---

115   Troutman 2004.

fall entirely under the jurisdiction of the regional authority. This does not seem a major problem for obvious regional issues but becomes more complex when the regional authority asserts its power on issues that might appear to be local. Consequently, only those areas that are specifically regional in nature should be removed and the rest left in the local plan with perhaps some regional guidelines.

Smart-growth principles and New Urbanism can be seen as providing the chance to focus on development in an area and are best practice. This does not mean that they are absolutely sound as concepts but they serve the function of requiring a closer examination of the urban environment.

2.10.5 Housing distribution

The areas marked for growth should be allocated and the need for population growth assigned in the regional plan. Using precise numbers that are then forced on a local authority is not the best method. Providing the overall density needed for population should follow a housing needs assessment prepared in co-operation with a local authority for a fixed period of no more than 10 years. A policy on growth should be published for local authorities who then should take responsibility for determining how that growth will be accommodated. If the local authority takes ownership of the process of allocating land for growth in consultation with the community, the imposition on local residents will be less intrusive. The belief that a local area will always resist change is at the core of imposition of density. This arises because of a lack of participation in its fullest sense. When there is full participation in a community, as in the high-rise boom in Seattle, the voices of protest at new development that inevitably follows are not usually raised.

2.10.6 Transport and water integration

Decisions on transport matters should not be left to a transportation authority without integration with the planning process. While combining the functions into one department depends on political alignments, it is not favoured even though it is the most common practice as, for instance, in Spain where the Ministry of Public Works and Transport includes the Secretary of State for Infrastructure and Planning. A planning authority often has to lobby for transport decisions or must convince the Treasury Department, which has no particular desire to co-operate. Even in both formal and informal structures, there is little co-ordination of the different functions because they all have their own methodologies and language.

Best practice may lie in having the infrastructure tender process carried out in conjunction with the planning authority. This will then foster, merely by that structure, early consultation, visioning and closer integration. Attention in the future to integration models and setting up some form of co-operative structure to explore these models, may lead to closer integration.

Water management should become a matter to be taken into account in strategic plans either by its inclusion in a policy or by legislation. It should involve the local authority drawing up a land use plan with provision for water management that goes beyond zoning for flood risk. Water management integration appears most co-ordinated with spatial planning in the Netherlands because of historic necessity. It perhaps will receive greater attention in all countries as the exigencies of climate change become more pressing.

3
Community participation

To have any meaning, the concept of community participation must be that the residents are called upon to present their views because they are acknowledged as having the capacity to offer important input into the planning process. The government carries the responsibility to plan and could do so in the absence of community participation. Therefore, the only logic is that meaning is derived from participation because the residents have something to add that cannot be provided by the professional planners or the elected or appointed officials.

A resident living in a suburb is not, however, likely to have any insight into the placement of, say, employment uses, the effect of transport-oriented design on traffic flow into the central city, the effects of housing density on land prices, or the impact of open space areas on revenue by rates. A resident who is not an expert on land use planning could only have two kinds of input into the planning process. The first is an understanding of what it feels like to live in a particular place: its character and the quality of services. The second is to communicate the community's fears and dreams of what their area might become.

It may be that, with the minor importance of resident input, the main purpose of participation is instead to establish a relationship between the planning agency and the residents so that the subjective experience of individuals then becomes included in government decisions. This appears more important than the actual community input because it offers the hope that there will be less alienation, a sense of community and, perhaps, a better connection between residents. In this way, participation is about pleasing the residents, making the government seem responsive, and suggesting that there will be no autocratic override by a planning bureaucracy.

There are many theories in political science that seek to support community participation as placating democratic functioning; civic engagement and consensus-building among the different stakeholders are the ideals of deliberative democracy. It is, at its highest, a recognition that the planning process is political and that the residents are electors and therefore are entitled to a voice. This adds to the legitimacy of decisions. It also has the effect of providing citizens with information, can be said to add to the continuous need for revitalisation of democracy, will create social relations among those participating, and can theoretically alter the power balance between the planning authority and its residents.

Some commentators, however, have legitimate and considerable doubts about the benefits of participation in the planning process. A common argument against participation is that:

> legally required methods of public participation in government decision making in the USA – public hearings, review and comment procedures in particular – do not work. They do not achieve genuine participation in planning or other decisions; they do not satisfy members of the public that they are being heard; they seldom can be said to improve the decisions that agencies and public officials make; and they do not incorporate a broad spectrum of the public.[1]

This has led to the opinion that traditional forms of participation in planning constitute tokenism and that the only real, effective form is when there is 'radical' participation by group activism and mobilising the community in protest.[2] In a study of participation in two urban areas, Porto in Portugal and Vigo in Spain, it was found that participation itself is not merely a neutral and democratic process but is also a political activity to do with the internecine issues among the urban elites and power structures, and it therefore has a tendency to cause conflict and delays. The study found: 'The most paradoxical conclusion that may be drawn from this research is that the higher the level of participation, the more conflictive the interactions'.[3] In South-East Asia, participation is not effective or perceived as even necessary as the urban governance system is controlled by politicised bureaucracies and patron–client networks for the elite that are used by bureaucrats and politicians for mutual benefits.[4]

As planning decisions create market value through the designation of uses of land, the residents are not merely being given a chance to feel good by making representations, but are exercising a property right to protect their interests. A plan may not directly affect the value of their property but decisions made throughout the planning area have a real, although indirect, effect. A decision to concentrate development along a distant transport corridor, for instance, will have the effect of altering infrastructure expenditure in other places. Putting a library in an adjoining residential area may make that area more popular, reducing other property values. The bundle of rights of a property owner include both tangible and intangible elements that are affected by any decision made in an area, however small.

The realisation of the effect that planning has on the property rights of individuals is probably what stands behind the idea that there should be participation. This is not the case in all countries where land is not privately owned but rather is held by long-term leaseholds, certificates of occupancy, or concessions, where the state retains ownership of the land. For example, in Mozambique, Tanzania, Uganda and Peru, land laws recognise customary tenure regimes and the emphasis is not on private ownership or participation but rather, on community; in Mozambique and Tanzania in particular, the relationship is through *ujamma*: a person is relevant only through the community.

---

1 Innes and Booher 2004, 419.
2 Monno and Khakee 2012.
3 Martinez 2011, 166.
4 Khan and Swapan 2013.

In those countries where there are private rights of land ownership, the sentiment of participation gets stronger from time to time, such as when a desire emerges to compensate those who will suffer a complete loss by a planning decision, but then weakens in the face of economic imperatives for growth. Nevertheless, the primacy of property is very clear in private ownership regimes and understood as a fundamental principle, as in the First Protocol to the 1950 *Convention of Human Rights and Fundamental Freedoms* by the Council of Europe (part 1).

The right to participate is not often expressed in relation to private property interests but rather is promoted as an example of the government doing the right thing. Where a planning decision is made entirely by elected officials, the argument that it is necessary to protect individual rights is somewhat diminished as the councillors are representatives of the residents elected to protect their interests. However, this argument is not substantial as the actual planning is carried out by the professional staff and the elected officials are only stakeholders in reviewing decisions that are made. Accordingly, the importance of involving residents directly in order to have equal input into planning assumptions is a higher-order right.

Planning is a source of hope and fulfilment of aspirations, even though it may not be able to deliver, and it promises that a type of subjective experience may be had. If that experience has to do with feelings of harmony, pleasantness, or some other improved state, the role of the community is greater than normally assumed. Individuals have as much knowledge of these states as planners or elected officials and are entitled to express their views. Planning is not just an expert manipulation of urban objects; it also professes to improve the urban environment and, in that sense, its vision and hopes belong to all.

There is a more subtle basis to the right to participate apparent in the understanding and gathering of the subjective experience that underlies the vision of a plan. As with any social interaction, it is necessary for the participant to be heard, and that is diminished if residents do not receive full attention and respect from the government. This is not an insistence on a legal right or one arising from property but rather is a matter of civility. Every person who has gone to the trouble of preparing a submission, or who has the courage to enter into the dialogue of planning, desires to be heard and acknowledged. This sets the tone for the purpose of planning for a community and, although at best it is a social obligation, as a rationale for the process of participation it overrides concerns about increased delays and expenses.

The connection of an individual with a place and a home arises directly for consideration when land is expropriated or, in relation to refugees, where displacement highlights what they have lost. That connection is profound, and goes beyond property value, and demands dignity and respect at the hands of a governmental authority. Home is said to be 'the beginning of all journeys and that which confers *telos*'.[5] The word *telos* denotes meaning and purpose and a home provides the inner space for that to manifest. A disturbance to a home by a planning proposal stirs opposition and community participation becomes the vital arena where it can be defended and addressed. This extends to anything that is perceived as an aspect of home, so that the loss of a view, for example, is sufficient in legal terms to confer standing on an individual to challenge government action.

The sense of place, the area where one lives, the interactions between neighbours, the juxtaposition of dwellings and services, are all aspects of the underlying social fabric of

---

5   Papadopoulus 2002, 11.

a community. The continuous interaction of individuals in a local setting creates ' social capital', a cohesive bond that provides an identity for residents and promotes a sense of belonging to a social group. The teleological significance of home and the development of social capital both remain unarticulated but are important reasons why the right to participate exists in planning. There is a sense, backed by research, that the formation of support systems, social capital, and religious affiliation, all lead to a 'sense of coherence', which is essential to health and wellbeing.[6] Planning owes its existence to the promise that it can improve the quality of life, that it respects the internal process of individual meaning within a connected community, and therefore the absence of community involvement is anathema.

The value of participation consists of the recognition of importance of all components of the sociological and psychological functions in a community. It can be seen clearly in the case of Peru, which suffered social, political and economic disasters in the 1980s and 1990s. Up until 2000, towards the end of the violent period of the Fujimori regime, there was a tearing of the social fabric.[7] The political theory at that time began to look at community participation as the essential way to rebuild a sense of empowerment and offer hope for social change.

The sense of community is a psychological concept that is said to have four elements.[8] The first is a feeling of being part of a group, the second is a form of empowerment because an individual can influence others in the group, the third is the ability to fulfil needs by being part of a community, and the fourth is a shared emotional connection. Planning assumes it is working to enhance this sense of community but it lacks the levers to control how the social capital will be formed. New Urbanism is a planning device to establish a sense of community by encouraging interactions and walkable neighbourhoods, although its actual effect is not proven. Full participation is the *only* aspect of planning that fully supports the aspirational goals of planning because all of the claims for 'liveability' or 'vitality' are fulfilled when social capital is generated.

A sense of community can only be understood after the fact, when the community is already formed and the interactions have taken place; the possibility of what might happen can only be guessed at in advance. Nevertheless, fostering a sense of community is of sufficient importance to promote full participation in the planning process because only those in the group can explain what has occurred in the locality and what might be the effect of a planning proposal on that social matrix. This is not a minor reason for participation or just another possible layer in why it is important but rather it should stand as the fulcrum for all such discussions in planning.

3.1 Scope of participation

The right of the public to participate is not confined to the opportunity to be heard in respect of the content of a proposed plan. It includes other critical factors, such as the need for the community to understand the planning process and to obtain access to the constant stream of relevant planning information accompanied by explanations. Theoreti-

---

6   Eriksson and Lindstöm 2005.
7   Espinosa and Velazquez 2015.
8   McMillan and Chavis 1986.

cally, this expanded notion of participation includes a fully co-operative relationship with the planning authority where it embraces the principle of being completely helpful and transparent, a concept appropriately named 'communicative planning'.[9] If this concept is accepted in a jurisdiction, it carries with it a clear statement that a resident's role is as important as that of the planning authority.

This form of full participation is illusive. An attempt at expanded participation in the United States is 'ballot-box zoning', in which all re-planning and rezoning questions are determined by a popular vote at a referendum. The US Supreme Court has upheld this method as valid[10] and it has become more popular. It does not, however, allow individuals to make submissions that cover the ambit of possible insights but rather focuses on a 'yes' or 'no' vote. It is actually inconsistent with the concept of being heard or having full communication. The citizens are locked out of the political process that is the nature of planning and relegated to participation in a group that does not promote their individuality.

The UK *Localism Act 2011* provides that citizens can decide by referendum to enter into the market as developers of community assets (the 'community right to build') and that a referendum can also be held to approve a neighbourhood plan. A recognised neighbourhood forum (21 citizens or a group of councillors) can propose a neighbourhood development plan and a neighbourhood development order can be made that allows development without a permit. The neighbourhood development plan is a citizen-led land use plan that is approved by referendum and becomes law as part of the general development plan, granting development permission for projects desired by the community. The effectiveness of these plans has yet to be evaluated, although many are under way (e.g. Sudbury Town, Milton Keynes). This is perhaps closest to full participation, as the right to be heard is included in the right to take over the role of planning.

In the European Union, the standards for participation are derived from the 1998 Aarhus Convention: *The United Nations Economic Commission for Europe on public participation in decision making and access to justice in environmental matters*. This did not immediately create full participation because there was doubt as to whether the rights in the convention apply to plan making rather than just to decisions of an authority when an application is made for development. A ruling was made that it may apply where the plan making is specific about an activity such as a defined project.[11] However, the Aarhus Convention is significant in the search for full participation as it provides for a fundamental right to be heard in relation to environmental decisions that includes the early and complete participation of the community in decision making (art. 6.3). These rights are grouped into a wider framework of what has been called 'environmental justice'. In the South African *National Environmental Management Act 1998* (sect. 2.4.f), the phrase 'environmental justice' is explained:

> The participation of all interested and affected parties in environmental governance must be promoted, and all people must have the opportunity to develop the understanding, skills and capacity necessary for achieving equitable and effective participation, and participation by vulnerable and disadvantaged persons must be ensured.

---

9   Brand and Gaffikin 2007; Purcell 2009.
10 *City of Eastlake v. Forest City Enterprises, Inc.*, 426 US 668 1976.
11 Aarhus Convention Compliance Committee ACCC/C/2005/11.

The concept of environmental justice is an umbrella for ideas about what is necessary for equitable and effective participation. How that is best expressed or implemented is not always straightforward. An example of broad statements of the concepts of effective participation is the Community Local Environment Awareness-raising project in Scotland,[12] which listed these requirements to accomplish the level of environmental justice:

- A wider range of publicity including innovative use of ICT [information and communications technologies]
- Neighbour notification over a wider area for major developments
- Community forums to permit improved community involvement
- Opportunities for earlier community involvement in planning
- Full feedback to the public on relevant factors taken into account in planning decisions
- Role of community planning in producing integrated planning and provision for local communities
- Enhanced use of ICT generally
- Different procedures for different sizes of developments (e.g. bad neighbour developments)
- Adoption of harmonised deadlines for making representations and ensuring that these are very clearly stated on public notices; and
- Use of simpler language in planning documents.

The Awareness-raising Project does not address the issue of the different abilities of members of the community to take advantage of participation opportunities. The US Housing and Urban Development Department (HUD) requires the creation of a citizen participation plan as a condition for cities receiving essential community development block grants and addresses the issue of participation for low and moderate income earners, immigrants and the disabled. The requirements for a citizen participation plan are that it:

> Provides for and encourages citizen participation with particular emphasis on participation by persons of low and moderate income who are residents of slum and blight areas and of areas in which Community Development Block Grant (CDBG) funds are proposed to be used . . .
>
> Provides for public hearings to obtain citizen views and to respond to proposals and questions at all stages of the community development program, including at least the development of needs, the review of proposed activities, and review of program performance, which hearings shall be held after adequate notice at times and locations convenient to potential or actual beneficiaries, and with accommodation for the disabled;
>
> Provides for timely written answers to written complaints and grievances, within 15 working days where practical; and identifies how the needs of non-English speaking residents will be met in the case of public hearings where a significant number of non-English speaking residents can be reasonably expected to participate.

The need to include all residents can be specifically named as it is in the HUD plan or implied as a commonsense approach because of a very broad statement of what is included.

---

12 SEDD 2003.

3 Community participation

The state of Washington is an example of this expansive declaration of citizen participation in growth-management plans:

> Each county and city that is required or chooses to plan . . . shall establish and broadly disseminate to the public a public participation program identifying procedures providing for early and continuous public participation in the development and amendment of comprehensive land use plans and development regulations implementing such plans. The procedures shall provide for broad dissemination of proposals and alternatives, opportunity for written comments, public meetings after effective notice, provision for open discussion, communication programs, information services, and consideration of and response to public comments.[13]

The degree to which stating these principles, or having specific requirements to include those who may have trouble participating, actually create or aid effective participation is, however, unclear. In a study of mandates for public participation in plan making, including the Washington requirements, it was found that they have a positive but not statistically significant effect on the degree of participation.[14] They did, however, at least have a positive influence on increasing staff involvement in the process and, as that increased, participation increased.

The forms of participation and the means of expression or different emphases are, theoretically, open-ended and can provide for any device or requirement that serves the idea of residents becoming an equal partner in planning. The degree to which the planning authority will go to obtain coherent participation is not found in the words but is a measure of the real relationship between citizens and their government. An instance of a strong relationship can be found in Finland.[15] In considering redevelopment of an industrial site by changing to a residential zoning, role playing was employed so that it was possible to experience the new development from the point of view of a teenager, an environmental activist, a housewife and other possible users. As well, a 'fantasy' stage was included to conceive of optimum or utopian solutions.

As the forms of participation can be wide and contain aspirational statements suggesting full participation, it would appear necessary to explain in detail the true nature of the relationship between community and government after participation has occurred as part of the making of the plan. The appropriate place for this detail is the plan itself, adding to the plan's legitimacy, and providing a single source for an explanation of the process and the end result.

The City of Vancouver created and tested an extensive participation model[16] prior to commencing the planning process, including a priority for recruiting a community liaison group to encourage input into the proposals for a plan. At the completion of the plan, the full extent and history of participation was published. Reading the history of participation in the plan provides the reader with a sense that the city was committed to inclusive participation and that the plan represents a synthesis of community views and is a people's plan. The inclusion of the process in the plan itself makes the document appear fair, equitable

---

13 RCW 36.70a 110(1).
14 Brody, Godschalk and Burby 2003.
15 Özer-Kemppainen et al. 2010.
16 CityPlan Community Visions Terms of Reference for Community Participation.

3.2 Implementing participation

In theory it is clear that the factors behind full participation in the planning process are unassailable. The idealistic concepts of good governance, respect, fairness, inclusion and engagement are the touchstones of participation. Yet, in practice, the reasons why there is, in most places, limited participation is not as clear. In places with autocratic rule, in fact and in practice, there is a constant shift in power to the expertise of government with a shared but unarticulated understanding that citizens have the lesser role. In some cases, this may be a function of planning scale: the larger the planning region, the less the relevance of local participants. Portugal and France are examples of the central government devolving planning powers primarily to regions, rather than local governments. The best explanation is perhaps that the subtle relationship an individual or community has to government is based on the degree to which the entrenched development industry and elites are allowed to influence planning authorities. If there is community with corruption, power broking, and authoritarian rule, there is more likely to be top-down planning with limited participation because decisions are made before any participation. In communities such as Portland, Oregon, which prides itself on being an environmentally sensitive community with egalitarian, liberal values, participation is a natural extension and is wide and inclusive.

There is a very clear movement for participation occurring in places where previously it has been nonexistent. Since the first 1958 *Master plan for* Singapore, there has been no form of participation in Singapore. It was not mentioned in the planning legislation and was not even conceived as relevant in the rapid transition that occurred under Lee Kuan Yew. In the mid-1980s, the PAP ruling party introduced a feedback unit to allow a conduit for opposing views, but this was more a gesture than a new direction so it did not have an influence on the planning decisions of the central government. *Singapore 21* and *Remaking of Singapore*, two documents that appeared to create hope that participation would occur, were strong on statements of possibilities but none of it had any real effect. In the major planning issue related to the massive Casino Integrated Resort, there was general public discussion and debate but no community participation process that related to planning. It was clear that the ruling party was not going to allow a universal form of participation in planning and the discomfort of the one-year debate on the resort was probably enough to foreclose any chance of opening up further consultation. However, the need for the community to participate has not abated and the Housing and Development Board along with the National University of Singapore set up the 'Hello Neighbour' program for residents to create design ideas to improve social relations. Although not meeting a level of participation found in Western countries, it has been hailed as the continuation of an unstoppable need for making a community active in its own future.[17]

The underlying assumption of any form of participation is that it not be narrowly construed or limited by mean-spirited tokenism. This implies that there will always be full participation at every step of the planning process, from the earliest inception through to

---

17 Sik and Križnik 2017, chap. 3.

the culmination and implementation of a plan. The earliest inception stage is when there is a realisation that a plan is necessary or desirable. The idea to plan can be prompted by many stimuli, such as a developer seeking approval for a major project or a creeping realisation that the level of anxiety in the community is too great in relation to the environment so that something needs to be done, or by some other factor that triggers a reassessment. There would be a natural reluctance on the part of planners to start participation at this stage as the ideas are incipient. This creates a barrier to early consultation with the public until the ideas are sorted and the experts have had a chance to decide the course of the plan. This may be a reason why full participation is limited in practice.

When the idea that planning should take place is formalised by a resolution or declaration by the planning authority, it implies that there is a premature hypothesis of what is necessary to be done in planning terms. Except where the planning process is triggered by a legislative requirement to plan, or review a plan, there are views of the bureaucracy that already are in place; they are what caused the idea to plan. They may have built up over time or have been discussed behind closed doors. Accordingly, participation should already have commenced to at least address that premature hypothesis.

When looked at from the point of view of participation growing out of property rights, any early constellation of ideas or hypotheses that may affect those rights should be open to analysis and participation. Justification for full participation is not only that it is the manifestation of a property right but also that it is a principle of fair governance: to build a co-operative relationship between the community and government, to strengthen the community by empowering residents, to build trust in government, to allow networks to form, and to bind residents into a tighter-knit community that understands its future.[18] When being fair or communicative is the real touchstone, presenting already-formed but incipient ideas to the community for analysis and discussion appears appropriate. The relative absence of this form of participation in almost all countries suggests that the planning authority cannot be left to its own devices to determine when participation should start and what its content should be. Even when there is an expressed intention for participation, it will be curtailed if planning culture lacks respect for community views at the formative stage.

It is critically important for the state to affirm its commitment to participation but even more important for the planning system to be specific about how and when participation is going to be accomplished. There can be different emphases depending on how the state and planning authority view the reasons for its implementation. If it is perceived as a reinforcement of a right, it will be wider; if it is a question of being fair, the scope may be less if that is not a paramount cultural issue, as has been the case in China.[19] This declaration of commitment and specifying details is particularly necessary because full and wide participation is not an historical tradition in the development of planning, which explains why it is often given then taken away, or is limited. As well, the attitude to participation in planning is tainted perhaps because it grew from environmental and social movements in the 1970s[20] and is therefore often suspected of being a tool of the left or a prelude to community overreaction. If the underlying basis for its implementation is not expressed, its form and substance cannot be understood.

---

18 Binham 2010; Kathi and Cooper 2005; Potney 2005; Fung and Wright 2003.
19 Plummer and Taylor 2013.
20 Midgely et al. 1988.

If there is truly a desire for full participation, there are five models for implementation. The first is to create an enforceable right for individuals to participate in the planning process in the same manner as a human right, such as the right to shelter. This concept of participation being considered a right first arose in the deliberations of the OECD. In 2001, the report, *Engaging citizens in policy-making: information, consultation and public participation*, stated that full participation was an absolute, undeniable requirement.[21] In 2005, the emphasis was no longer on the insistence on a requirement for full participation but on how to evaluate *effective* participation: *Evaluating public participation in policy making*. In 2009, perhaps abandoning the push for a participatory right, the OECD in *Focus on citizens: public engagement for better policy and services*, reported that progress had been made in citizen access to information but not in enshrining rights to participate in legislation.

This method of treating full participation as a right is not expressed in any country because it raises constitutional and international law considerations as to the entrenchment and expression of human rights.[22] The relevant international treaties (the *International Covenant on Civil and Political Rights, First Protocol to the European Convention on Human Rights, American Convention on Human Rights, African Charter on Human and People's Rights*, and *Council on Security and Co-operation in Europe Accords*), do not bring community participation in planning into the realm of a right. Consequently, as constitution and treaties are where rights are accepted and defined, the absence of full participation in that list makes its claim untenable, even though at least it falls neatly into the category of a property right flowing from a proprietary interest in land.

The second method is to include a legislative statement of intent that there will be full community participation in the planning process. As an example of this method, the Vermont planning laws (sect. 4384) state:

> at the outset of the planning process and throughout the process, planning commissions shall solicit the participation of local citizens and organizations by holding informal working sessions that suit the needs of local people.

The international precedent for inclusion of a general statement of purpose for a higher-order principle of full participation is to cast the concept in the widest terms. For example, community participation was codified during the 1992 United Nations Conference on the Environment and Development in Rio de Janeiro as Principle 10, which states:

> Environmental issues are best handled with the participation of all concerned citizens, at the relevant level. At the national level, each individual shall have appropriate access to information concerning the environment that is held by public authorities, including information on hazardous materials and activities in their communities, and the opportunity to participate in decision-making processes. States shall facilitate and encourage public awareness and participation by making information widely available. Effective access to judicial and administrative proceedings, including redress and remedy, shall be provided.

---

21 Organisation for Economic Co-operation and Development 2001b.
22 Bingham 2005.

The third method of inclusion of full participation in legislation is to go beyond a statement of intent and to impose specific legislative duties on the planning authority to provide participation. In the state of Georgia, it is provided that public hearings must be held 'to inform the public about the purpose of the plan and the process to be followed in the preparation of the plan, as well as to elicit community input'.[23]

An example of the imposition of a specific duty is found in the *Local Government in Scotland Act 2003* (sect. 15.1):

> It is the duty of a local authority to initiate and, having done so, to maintain and facilitate a process (in this act, called 'community planning') by which the public services provided in the area of the local authority are provided and the planning of that provision takes place –
>
> a. after consultation –
>   A. among all the public bodies (including the local authority) responsible for providing those services; and
>   B. with such community bodies and other bodies or persons as is appropriate; and
>   C. after and by way of such co-operation among those bodies and persons as is appropriate.

The fourth method is to provide in legislation that the local planning scheme must create a provision for full community participation without being specific as to its content but leaving it to the planning authority to contemplate what is appropriate. For example, the City of New Orleans, Louisiana, provides this requirement for itself:

> The City shall establish by ordinance a system for organized and effective neighborhood participation in land use decisions and other issues that affect quality of life. It shall provide for timely notification to a neighborhood of any proposed Land Use Action affecting the neighborhood; it shall also provide the opportunity for meaningful neighborhood review of and comment on such proposals. In addition, it shall provide the opportunity for meaningful neighborhood participation in the formulation of the Master Plan or any amendment thereto.[24]

The fifth method is a non-legislative approach using a matrix of policies and guidelines backed up by government statements of planning policy. The previous system in the United Kingdom (before the *Localism Act*) was to have a range of policies and guidelines that afforded participation such as the Best Value Scheme, the Comprehensive Performance Assessment, the New Deal for Communities, and the Local Strategic Partnership initiative.

Research has shown that authentic, full participation, if it is not expressly mandated by legislation, is rare because local governments have difficulty sharing power, may not have or want to commit the resources, are sceptical about the effectiveness of participation, and uncertain whether those that participate are indeed representative of community views.[25]

---

23 *GA Comp. Rules and Regulations*, sect. 110-3-2-06.
24 City of New Orleans, *Home Rule Charter*, sect. 5–411.

Accordingly, it appears necessary to at least explain the strong intention of government for full community participation by a specific statement in legislation and also to impose duties on a planning authority to provide participation.

3.3 Phases of participation

It has been suggested that there are three broad phases of community participation in decision making in planning: participation in the plan-making phase, participation in draft planning schemes, and participation for a particular development.[26]

The first and primary phase is participation in the plan-making stage. This appears the most obvious and can be broken down into two sub-phases. The first sub-phase is the very early involvement of the community in identifying the issues before the consideration of any options or goals. The purpose of this sub-phase is to identify that the planning authority has decided to plan and also to expose the issues that motivated the authority, leading to an investigation if there are other issues that affect the area. In practice, it is carried out by a briefing followed by a request to the community to suggest issues the authority may have overlooked. This is the *formative* stage of participation. A good example is the beach town of Narragansett in Rhode Island, which developed a long list of issues, what it called a 'roadmap', after meetings with planning department officials, local commissions, and a public workshop. A *Draft formative issues* paper that was produced from the roadmap states: 'Formative issues are broad in nature and meant to be an umbrella for more detailed objectives and eventually action items.' The paper was distributed to the public and specifically asked: 'Have we forgotten critical issues?'

Another use for formative participation is to test the hypothesis that planning needs to be carried out at all. It is, phrased in this way, a feasibility study to examine if there is a legitimate rationale for commencing any action. This study could raise issues of budget impact, such as the cost of overcoming legal impediments or limitations in personnel. As well, it can establish, given the planning culture and the relative roles and influence of the government agents, whether a new plan is likely to succeed politically. For example, if a local authority is aware that the state has earmarked an area for high-rise development, a proposal to plan for low-rise apartments will be a waste of time.

If formative participation is to take place, it is a qualitative exercise and not concerned with details such as population predictions that may have an effect on the eventual outcome of a plan. It is an exercise in 'what do you think?' and is not diminished because it fails to set goals, objectives, or a vision in a conclusive manner. It is most useful because it makes the existence of a process of planning into a concrete reality for the community and could have the effect of mobilising citizens.

From the viewpoint of participants, they may have little understanding of what is expected of them when they are called to a forum. They are not necessarily given an idea in advance of what is being sought or what form their responses are meant to take. There is no participation system that can be identified where they are provided information before the forum that they can study to formulate a list of issues. The on-the-spot formulation of issues may then result in an impressionistic response, such as 'we don't want high rises.'

---

25 Yetano, Royo and Acerete 2010.
26 O'Leary and Bingham 2003; Brody, Godschalk and Burby 2003.

In formative stage participation, it is preferable to explain in advance what issues are to be discussed. If there are major issues in a location – crime, traffic, poorly maintained open space, or lack of entertainment facilities – these will be self-evident, but for other issues contemplated, some explanation must precede this stage. The best practice is to begin a process of involvement of the community by advance notice of the issues so that the formative stage captures their interest and leads to potential continued engagement. It cannot really be much more than capturing interest as it is only issue identification. Its strength is that it offers the symbolic value of government interaction with the citizenry. This is not to demean the potential contribution of individuals but, at the formative stage, contributions are not likely to be significant.

The next sub-phase is the *visioning* exercise. This can be accomplished in many ways but each method has common characteristics. A formative stage issue or a particular problem becomes the subject of examination in terms of various options or scenarios and a vision for that issue or problem is formulated. The vision is initially in general form, such as 'increase the safety of the area' or a statement that by its nature must be aspirational. The vision then develops and becomes more specific for each issue and can be seen as containing an ultimate solution, even if not expressed in that manner.

The process of visioning can only proceed on the basis that there is sufficient information distributed to the community to make a meaningful contribution. In an ideal form, this is accomplished by offering information sessions in different parts of the city to equip those who might add to the vision at public hearings with the means to address the issues. For instance, in 2004, the City of Montreal held ten information sessions in different parts of the city and attracted around 1,000 participants. A few weeks later, it held public hearings to obtain comments from inhabitants. The city developed various visions, some broad and some specific; in the case of the widest vision, *Objective 1: Improve the quality of existing living environments*, the sub-goals were:

1. Urban revitalisation
2. The maintenance and adaptation of the building stock
3. The development of public and private green spaces
4. The consolidation of commercial streets, strips and centres
5. The improvement of public services and facilities.

None of these sub-goals adequately explain the opportunities and constraints or the nature of these areas. The plan that eventually follows provides the opportunity to indicate the full nature of each goal, such as 'A quality living and urban environment that ensures the safety, wellbeing and tranquillity of residents and promotes individual development and social harmony.' There is then an attempt, through the vision and explanation, to apply these general standards, vague as they are, to different neighbourhoods. In this way, the plan as written has some concordance with the goals and has the ability to create a translation of the vision into action items.

The contribution of the community in the visioning process is more likely to be important than at the formative stage. The community contains experts in various fields among its residents and there will be interests strongly for or against particular issues, leading to a form of collective bargaining, which forms the basis for solutions. The only difficulty in this process is that the balance of power becomes politicised by lobbying, pressure, and influence to obtain an advantage. For better or worse, this is a democratic process and can result in a consensus and, for that reason alone, be deemed successful.[27]

Participation can be envisaged as a simple sequence: the authority indicates that it wants to make a plan, identifies if possible what motivated the desire to begin the process, then works with the community to establish goals for the selected area based on some vision of future options. The vision is the underpinning of the goals and is, by its nature, a series of options, which are then optimised.

The second phase of participation is where the bureaucracy has established a plan and then calls upon the community to comment. The concept is that the complexities of a plan are so great that it is unlikely the community will be able to add anything of significance until the plan is formulated. In regional plans this may be valid, as there is a need to test demographic assumptions as to population movements, employment, and transportation patterns, and to liaise with environmental organisations. Sometimes the evaluation of a scenario may rely on scientific analysis, such as whether to conserve a part of a wetland that does not contribute to the effective functioning of the whole.

The main difficulty of restricting participation to this phase is that the thinking and deliberations that have led the planning authority to make a specific choice may not be apparent. For instance, if a conclusion is to increase density near a transport node and the area is currently single-storey residential, the appearance on a map of a potential for high rise will cause immediate opposition. If it had been explained in a visioning process that the population is rapidly increasing in this area, that traffic has become problematic, that pollution levels are increasing from car exhausts, and that this decision was made after a series of studies, the decision may not be liked but could be more acceptable. Restriction to this after-the-fact phase is perhaps the greatest reason for the discounting of participation as emotions run high if residents fear they are being forced into a situation arising from a completed plan.

Participation after a draft plan is completed is the most used form in planning regimes but appears so obviously as mere tokenism. It is as if the government closes its eyes to the concept of full participation but feels justified in calling this limited form acceptable. It stands for a fundamental distrust of the public, their emotionality or irrationality, and therefore this form is a means to curtail the input to a weak criticism that can then be overcome by the evidence base. Many governments that pride themselves on providing participation stick to this form because any greater participation seems unwieldy and politically embarrassing. It is a paternalistic form of participation that has no theoretical justification, as all it does is limit input, not encourage it.

This form of participation has much to do with the historical view of a government's role in planning. As an example, Ottawa after World War II had Beux Arts architect Jacques Gréber, who was a follower of the French City Beautiful movement, devise the future direction of the city. He was from the modernist school of planners who considered that they were the experts and had little time for community views. The politicians merely accepted his views in laying out the city. This modernist planning movement of constructing a city deliberately from the ideas of a distinguished architect viewed the community as irrelevant and instead relied on grand design. Some post-planning participation was allowed eventually when it became clear that those who sought to shape the city by their own intelligence and power did not succeed in solving the most important urban problems.

---

27   French and Gagne 2010.

The remnants of the modernist approach to participation is still prevalent in most countries, such as Australia: planning is done by experts and the community has its limited say after the ideas are completed. This pattern has changed over the last ten years in other countries, with a move towards localism, which brings with it the relevance of local views. Where decentralisation occurs or there is a desire to seek co-operation, as in Argentina, the idea of participation develops. This change is slow in coming as income inequality and a feeling of helplessness in many communities work against any interest in participating. As well, the community does not understand what is possible. If limited participation has occurred for 40 or 50 years, it becomes part of the form of political engagement and defines how the residents of a community understand how they communicate with government. The idea of full participation is not part of the zeitgeist unless it comes from deprivation, such as has occurred in post-communist countries where the complete loss of participatory rights gave rise to a new demand for full involvement. Research on Serbia's planning system indicates that the volatile political shifts that occurred after the move to a democratic form of government mixed with a newfound desire for capitalist development will not necessarily lead to a stable participation system: 'urban planning legislation followed the moves of a swinging pendulum – from centralized (top-down) model to fully decentralized (participatory bottom-up approach), to yet another re-centralisation and re-decentralisation after (sic) the 1989.'[28]

The third phase of participation arises in systems where there is development control that requires a separate decision on an application for development after the plan is finalised. In many ways, this is not of the same category as formative and visioning participation. Here, individuals who will be affected by a system of development control can make submissions or, in some instances, can be heard. It is an abbreviated form that revolves around self-interest triggered by a projected loss of an amenity, such as a view, or a sense of an area, or by a loss of value. The submissions may, if there is sufficient groundswell by neighbours, have some effect but it depends on the cogency of their objections. This form is not really a contributor to the full exposition of participation but is mentioned as it does involve the affected public in being heard.

3.4 Essential elements of participation

The specific rights or capacities of an individual to participate in the planning process can be vague and difficult to understand. If there is a right to make submissions, can they call expert witnesses to testify? What is to be done if thousands of people want to make submissions? Some form of document, a policy or charter, external to the planning regulations needs to be established that sets out all elements that define what is available. A legalistic set of rules that says a resident can participate by attending and make submissions does not provide sufficient understanding of the nature of the rights and obligations in the process. The scope needs to be explained by a narrative and examples. In the absence of such a policy or charter, it is not possible to clarify the authority's commitment to full participation.

The narrative needs to include a set of principles or rights that serve as the touchstone for action. There is a good model in the City of Portland's *Public involvement principles 2010*:

---

28 Nedović-Budić, Djordjević and Dabović 2011.

1. **Partnership**: Community members have a right to be involved in decisions that affect them. Participants can influence decision-making and receive feedback on how their input was used. The public has the opportunity to recommend projects and issues for government consideration.
2. **Early involvement**: Public involvement is an early and integral part of issue and opportunity identification, concept development, design, and implementation of city policies, programs, and projects.
3. **Building relationships and community capacity**: Public involvement processes invest in and develop long-term, collaborative working relationships and learning opportunities with community partners and stakeholders.
4. **Inclusiveness and equity**: Public dialogue and decision-making processes identify, reach out to, and encourage participation of the community in its full diversity. Processes respect a range of values and interests and the knowledge of those involved. Historically excluded individuals and groups are included authentically in processes, activities, and decision and policy-making. Impacts, including costs and benefits, are identified and distributed fairly.
5. **Good quality process design and implementation**: Public involvement processes and techniques are well-designed to appropriately fit the scope, character, and impact of a policy or project. Processes adapt to changing needs and issues as they move forward.
6. **Transparency**: Public decision-making processes are accessible, open, honest, and understandable. Members of the public receive the information they need, and with enough lead time, to participate effectively.
7. **Accountability**: City leaders and staff are accountable for ensuring meaningful public involvement in the work of city government.

The principles are an explanation of what an individual can expect. It is possible to read these and be able to assert that the city is accountable to the public and there should be participation from the earliest stage. This is explicit and not subject to doubt as the language is not expressed in legal form but rather in a manner that provides a full explanation of the scope of participation. It suggests, by the clarity of the wording, that any processes that will be followed are bound to this approach of full participation.

Portland can be said to be enlightened in this regard but is certainly not typical. Very few systems impose standards or principles for communication and resort to only second-phase participation: comments after the plan is created. In that case, it is not as fruitful to explain the *full* scope of participation because it does not exist: the government is presenting ideas that have been developed with the help of professionals and are essentially selling the ideas to the public. As plans are complicated, the full implications of what is proposed may never come to the surface and any document explaining the process other than in a procedural way will not be able to ameliorate disputes and disappointments.

A study of participation in South Africa explains the various abuses that have occurred in the name of participation, such as governments offering resources to the poor in return for support.[29] It suggests, as a reaction to these problems, that participation should work to include respect for the indigenous community, to listen to all people and not just community leaders and interest groups, to include the less vocal and marginalised groups, to

---

29   Botes and van Rensburg 2000.

guard against domination by particular interest groups, and to empower the community to understand how to share in the benefits of what is proposed.

One factor highlighted in the study is particularly interesting: 'Acknowledge that process-related soft issues are as important as product-related hard issues.' The concept behind this is to include a social scientist as part of the team to help develop the soft issues of community cohesion, helping individuals to find a voice, encouraging the benefits of social networks, accepting the effect of the government reaching out to disadvantaged groups, and creating social capital, which may be as important as the project itself.

The role of social capital created by involvement in community participation is not a mere by-product but rather a central force of social change. That voice of the disadvantaged and poor fosters involvement in wider political issues and creates community-based organisations that may have a stronger voice in future planning issues. In Manila, the social capital created through reforms of decentralisation and civil society involvement in politics worked in creating organised involvement in urban policy and planning.[30] It was a sense of belonging among the disadvantaged that encouraged community involvement in the planning process.

Social capital requires local participation in issues that affect the community even where there are limitations on the benefits of participation for wider metropolitan or regional issues. It is clear, however, that community participation may be more readily accepted where there are specific local problems that can create a particular focus. This was managed in the planning process in a town in Norway by separating the wider, strategic questions from the immediacy of critical, local decisions.[31] In Pakistan, as an example of participation in a particular issue, community groups are integral to the development of local sewerage systems.[32]

This concept of dividing the issues so as to focus on those where local participation will be most helpful is not one that has been embraced in theory by strategic planning. However, it exists as a matter of practice as planners are more likely to be open minded in respect of submissions or ideas as to smaller, local issues than in relation to more regional matters, such as shopping centre policy or housing distribution. The importance of local opinion can be found, for instance, in assessing the impact of tourist development, for government investment in local infrastructure, for local roads, and for climate change adaptation.

There is an important dimension, often overlooked, as to why a planning authority should consult with the local community over local matters in the planning process. The involvement of local residents offers some symmetry in terms of knowledge and aspirations: on local issues, the residents are experts and hold insights not necessarily available to planners. This emphasis creates meaning for residents and encourages them to take an active part in the entirety of the process.

Local issues are also a chance for emotionality. Emotions in a participatory environment are too often perceived as outside the boundaries of the enquiry. The venting of emotions is consistent with theories that, for there to be a true communicative interaction, there must be irrationality as well as rational argument.[33] It is only when the local commu-

---

30 Shatkin 2007.
31 Amdam 2014.
32 Ahmad et al. 2012.
33 Kiisel 2013.

nity is fully engaged that the process becomes one of mutual discovery, and participation goes beyond a mere formality.

The paradigm for which there is no effective counter-argument and is the right focus for the participation process is that of *collaborative* planning. This differs from the second phase of participation where residents are asked to react to a draft plan. In that phase, those with views are more likely to experience that they are battling against entrenched forces, and to suspect influence peddling and back-room deals. Perhaps the only argument against full stakeholder involvement in planning decisions is that full participation will delay the planning process, especially where developers have land-holding costs. In a rising market, this argument makes little sense as the land value increases over time. In a falling or uncertain market, this argument has cogency, but in the context of a plan succeeding as a product of consensus, it is not sufficient to place limitations on the kinds of participation that are possible.

One proven forum where residents have participated in a collaborative way is in local budgeting and allocation of funds according to local priorities. Case studies have indicated that collaborative discussions with local engagement have been useful in a variety of ways,[34] such as a ten-year financial plan in Melbourne, Australia, created with the use of citizen juries to collaborate and advise on the spending of a $5-billion dollar budget. Citizen juries consist of representatives chosen at random from the community and overcome the difficulty of the reluctance of some residents to participate because of a reticence about speaking at forums. They offer a chance to streamline the full complement of participatory processes but do not give those who were not chosen as much of a say about the range of options or aspirations. They are particularly useful, however, in single-issue matters.

3.5 Access to information

Information is the touchstone of effective and full participation, and a policy or schema for participation cannot logically propose methods of participation until this issue is made clear. To fully participate in a discussion of the future of an area, each participant must be informed of the issues that confront the community, existing solutions, policies, the opportunities and constraints (such as open space, conservation, and infrastructure), and all other public records that form the background against which choices must be made.

Making all information available has been found to have a secondary, positive effect because citizens are more likely, by their new-found understanding, to accept the bureaucratic process, increasing the likelihood that their submissions will be well considered and have an impact. This in turn increases the bureaucratic tolerance for participation as the input is helpful, not merely argumentative or ill informed.[35]

The concept of full access to information for effective participation, as opposed to full participation itself, has a recognised human rights dimension. For instance, the 2001 *Declaration of principles on freedom of expression of the inter-American commission on human rights* asserts a fundamental right to access public information. The right is not specific to the planning process but has the more general effect of members of the community being able to seek and receive information that is necessary to make an informed submission.

---

34 Innes and Booher 2004.
35 Kweit and Kweit 1980.

However, there is no systematic treatment in any jurisdiction of the scope of this right and the extent of information that is required to be effective for participation. This is probably because it is not possible to indicate what mix of information should be available as there are myriad forms that it may take.

The information that can be provided is of three basic types, all of which overlap.[36] The first is historical information: the result of previous participations on any related subject, any unpublished policies or discussion documents, or any statements made by officials about the future of the locality. Secondly, process information gives the ability to understand how policies and plans are to be made, including timelines. Substantive information, the widest form, includes all documentation, which encompasses any and all of the information that is available to the decision maker, including technical and scientific information.

There must be, ideally, some method by which an individual can seek help to understand what is presented. Studies in Venezuela found that offering training to individuals in the use of information and the operation of electronic databases increased the participation of individuals as they became more committed to the process.[37] However, the fact remains that some of the information will be difficult to understand and an issue arises as to the duties of the planning authority to explain through experts what it means. As this is not employed in planning systems, it increases the tendency for experts to rely on a point of view uninformed by local input. There is no doubt that the expert has a greater influence than the residents resulting in what the philosopher Jürgen Habermas calls 'distorted communication'[38] as there are then different levels of understanding: residents use facts and experts offer nuanced opinions.

Although it is not possible to list all the information that is necessary for a planning authority to communicate with the community, it is possible to show that the planning authority has a duty to produce all information that is necessary to enable the process to be effective and to prepare some documentation explaining what is being produced and the issues that are to be addressed. The *Planning, etc (Scotland) Act* of 2006 (sect. 9) contains some provisions that indicate this approach:

1. With a view to facilitating and informing their work in preparing a strategic development plan, a strategic development planning authority are to compile a report (a 'main issues report').
2. A main issues report compiled under this section is a report in which are set out –
   A. general proposals by the authority for development in the strategic development plan area and in particular proposals as regards where the development should be carried out (and where it should not), and
   B. general proposals which constitute a reasonable alternative (or reasonable alternatives) to those mentioned in paragraph (a).
3. The report is also –
   A. to include information sufficient to secure

---

36 Hadden 1981.
37 Pena, Olivar and Primera 2008.
38 Habermas 1970.

a. that what is proposed can readily be understood by those persons who may be expected to desire an opportunity of making representations to the authority with respect to the report, and
b. that such representations can be meaningful, and

B. to draw attention to any differences between the proposals for development mentioned in paragraphs (a) and (b) of subsection (2) and the spatial strategy set out in the authority's strategic development plan (if any such plan is for the time being current).

The concept of producing a 'main issues report' before the visioning process as well as the requirement that information and participation be the duty of planning authorities, appears to be an effective means to both create recognised rights and duties and to reassure the community that they are entitled to obtain that information.

The consequence of breaching a duty by not supplying effective information is to possibly render the process invalid, thereby reinforcing the importance of full disclosure. This concept of invalidity has been applied to other forms of consultation where it has been found that meaningful participation cannot take place unless information is adequate to allow an understanding of the issues.[39] This makes the enunciation of the need for information sufficient to understand that it is essential to the nature of participation, as is the corresponding duty of the planning authority to provide that information.

The use of web-based information technology and communications (ICT) fundamentally alters the possibilities for participation.[40] It allows the community to have ready access to current information to build its knowledge base of the operation of the planning system and to allow it to be a collaborator in plan making and decision making. The underlying basis for effective use of ICT is to put content online that, at a minimum, must include all relevant factual data, all other information that is available, but also, to be effective, a guide for its use. However, it is capable of more. As an example, the Televote system is a deliberative poll that can be used for voting on issues arising in planning,[41] while the 'deliberative polling' system[42] is used to test if the effect of increased information on an issue can change attitudes, allowing participation to be tailored for discrete issues. Electronic town meetings are another example of what is possible. They have been tested in Belfast, in Palermo, Italy, and in Cyprus, but are still in an experimental stage.

3.6 Methods of full participation

One study evaluated the different methods of participation: a citizen advisory committee, citizen panels, citizen juries, citizen initiatives, negotiated rule making, mediation, and other ideas. It was concluded that no one method was preferred over another as each had advantages and disadvantages. It was, however, perceived that a combination of methods was more effective than just one.[43]

---

39 *Cheslatta Carrier First Nation v. British Columbia* 1999. BCJ No. 2639, affd [2000] BCJ No. 2030.
40 Brabham 2009.
41 Slaton 1992.
42 Fishkin 2009.
43 Renn, Webber and Weidemann 1995.

All possible methods are directed towards eliciting the views of those participating, either by free-form discussion, led discussion, voting, consensus building, formation of groups, and other means to weigh and evaluate the manner in which the community views its locality. It is not possible to set a precise regulatory form for the process, as all of the methods are cogent. It is therefore appropriate to name the process a 'vision' process, the function of which is to produce a community vision statement that encapsulates and expresses the views of the community about the locality. The expression of the end product indicates the nature of the exploration by the community but not the particular method.

It appears appropriate, given the different possibilities of approach, that the options be placed in a policy or participation plan to explain the methods to be used to formulate a vision and the expression of that vision in a written form as a vision statement. Oregon has a requirement in its legislation that a participation plan be prepared by each local authority. It states:

> Each city and county governing body shall submit to the commission, on a periodic basis established by commission rule, a program for citizen involvement in preparing, adopting and amending comprehensive plans and land use regulations within the respective city and county.[44]

This provision expresses that there must be a participation plan approved by a central body, which will establish the parameters of the process that will be followed. Its advantage is to provide an agenda, timelines, and the manner in which the various alternative methods of participation are to be employed. It offers the chance to evaluate the fairness of the procedures, the manner in which participants are informed of meetings and encouraged to attend, the information that is to be supplied, and whether the structure of the discourse will be effective.[45]

An example of a successful participation plan can be found in Kent, Ohio. The local authority initially formed a 45-member steering committee with residents and organisations. The steering group, with the help of council staff, set up meetings for the entirety of the community in four rounds at convenient times in familiar local places. The fact that the invitations came from the community members of the group and not from the council was seen as effective in generating high meeting attendance. The first meetings were for brainstorming what the residents valued about the area and how they saw the future. The second was to prioritise the issues from the first meeting. The third was to focus on individual sites that needed planning and to elicit views on what would be best for those areas. The fourth used a focus-group approach where the council staff had drawn up a draft plan and the residents were asked if it reflected the vision.

The Portland Housing Bureau's citizen participation plan is another example of the extent of participation that is possible. It starts with a definition of all terms that are to be used (e.g. 'moderate income household') and an explanation of all the government participants that have a role in the process. It then explains that there is a responsibility on the planning authority to encourage individuals who might otherwise not be motivated, to participate. This is accomplished by holding various types of community meetings, by consulting with lay advisory groups, by meeting with service providers to these communities,

---

44 Oregon Revised Statutes, chap. 197.1601b.
45 Webler and Tuler 2000.

by providing technical assistance to groups representing these individuals, by using networks that pre-exist and web-based notifications, by making translation services available, by broadcasting on ethnic and local radio, by publishing in ethnic and local newspapers, by conducting meetings in languages other than English, and by using focus groups. This is a genuine attempt at being inclusive, making the recruitment of individuals to participate a fundamental aspect of the plan. It also makes separate provision for including people with a disability. As to access to information, it states: 'Each jurisdiction shall ensure full public access to program information provided such information does not infringe upon any individual's rights.'

Given the range of methods that can be used, the plan does not explain what will happen at specific meetings but sets out the number of meetings and what the notice of meetings must contain. It is an attempt to analyse every aspect of the process and the form and substance conveys that there is a real and substantive desire for full participation by the entire community.

These plans include the first process phase of formative participation and the subphase of visioning. The examples given of Kent and Portland are not, however, the norm. Participation might be required in a jurisdiction but it is more likely to be in relation to a top-down plan, with only a chance for comments: the second phase form of participation. An interesting case study in Zagreb, Croatia, explains the prevalence of such a second-phase system even though the intention for participation was wider. From the 1950s, the socialist government restricted the use of foreign experts. When Croatia declared independence from Yugoslavia in 1991, it retained a legacy of Soviet-style housing estates: long blocks of apartments with little architectural finesse. The contrast in building forms is great, as the medieval town has historic buildings, Le Corbusier-style boulevards, and concentrated development because of the mountains to the north. In 1993, master planning began to bring diverse elements together in some development harmony. The legislative requirements for planning in this process included specific rules for participation in the *Regulation of public debate in the process of spatial plan approval*, which was a roadmap for establishing a formative and substantive citizen involvement. It has been said in relation to the regulation:

> It should be noted that although the plan stresses the importance of public participation, it still supports a classic system of planning dominated by the preparation of detailed technical plans by trained professionals only.[46]

The Zagreb process is indicative of the planning process in most countries where the strategic and spatial plans reflect more of the professional input into land use decisions and less of community aspirations. This is not from lack of knowledge of what is possible by way of participation, as the regulation of public debate in Croatia was intended to widen the scope to full participation. Serbia, another former Yugoslavian country, started its planning process with Western ideas of participation in 2003. The legislation, calling for participation and transparency, reflected the concept of participation drawn from the *European spatial development perspective*, which had its origins in the *Urban communications* of the European Union in the late 1990s, which provided that it was 'becoming more important to engage the participation of local participants to ensure their needs are addressed

---

46   Cavrić and Nedović-Budić 2007.

in implementing legislation or programmes.'[47] A study has concluded that there is, however, very little participation that takes place in Serbia unless there is a controversial issue where the citizenry is activated and rise up in protest.[48]

There are two resultant contrary arguments. The first is that full participation is always a necessary aspect of the planning process because the community has local knowledge and has property rights, and because it is fundamental to democracy to allow stakeholder involvement in planning decisions. The other argument is that this is not an absolute requirement in planning because it has more to do with the planning culture, which includes the historic relationship of the community with government. However, when there is a full system of participation in legislation and policy, the possibility that it will be used increases and may become a focal point for claims of increased involvement of the community and greater legitimacy of planning decisons.

3.7 Advisory panels

In addition to the classic forms of participation, where the community is seen as owners and tenants who are to have a say in planning decisions, another form is that of a citizen advisory panel. The concept was developed in the United States and in Europe in the 1960s, mainly to establish panels to collaborate on urban renewal projects.[49] It was perceived at that time that these citizen bodies were useful politically as rubber stamps for planning authorities, adding legitimacy to controversial planning decisions.[50] Their purpose has since grown to include the function of offering more general advice as the non-political voice of the community and are an adjunct to full participation, guaranteeing the voice of the community does not disappear after a town meeting.

The existence of continuing, long-term panels, rather than issue-based participation, encourages individuals who have the time and ability to contribute to the deliberative process. It creates a standing body of participants who, over time, develop an expertise in planning issues and a relationship with the planning authority and can also communicate back to the community. This backwards communication is not catered for in the usual form of participation as the community ceases to be involved when the plan is finished, leaving no accountability for the successful implementation of the vision.

The apparent advantages are many.[51] A paper advocating for citizen advisory groups in planning in Vermont states:

> A citizen advisory group is a good way to let citizens shoulder some of the burden of the municipal planning process (without shirking your duties of course). The advisory group can get the job done while incorporating citizen input every step of the way. While not as indepth as a community-wide visioning event may be, a citizen advisory group allows your planning commission to gain insight into important preferences as determined by a

---

47 Commission of the European Communities 1997
48 Nedović-Budić, Djordević and Dabović 2011.
49 Lynn and Busenberg 1995; MacCallum 2010.
50 Arnstein 1969; Susskind and Elliot 1981.
51 Harless 1992.

sample of your community's experience and expertise. Whenever a group of people converge to discuss a planning topic, you are likely to observe community-held opinions.[52]

To a larger degree than community participation, citizen advisory groups suggest a form of governance in planning that is inherently transparent and inclusive. However, they do not change the manner in which planning is implemented or envisaged as the groups become embedded as part of the system rather than being an independent voice that offers a different viewpoint. As they are perceived as part of the existing systems, the groups may find that they are co-opted and marginalised and the only way to be heard by the professionals on important issues is to be disruptive. In a classic study of some failures of San Diego planning, it was stated:

> Even when locals participate in the citizen advisory groups and are thereby able to influence the negotiation process, they tend to use disruption as a primary tactic, relying, as one city official suggested, on the recitation of horror stories and demands for some type of action. Consequently, they tend to get preempted, even when they have already been co-opted.[53]

Advisory groups are also employed in making recommendations on applications for development and amendments to legislative instruments that implement a strategic plan. For instance, in Victoria, Australia, planning panels consist of experts to whom individuals can make submissions and the panels then have the duty to advise on planning scheme amendments. In Nova Scotia, Canada, *The Municipal Government Act 1998* (chap. 18) provides for citizen advisory committees as well as forms of planning panels that are involved in making recommendations.

The appointment of such groups makes irrefutable sense in seeking best practice because they account for representation of community members who are not able to come forward for a variety of reasons and do not have the time or inclination to be committed to participation. They also offer continuous monitoring of the derived vision. Accordingly, to carry out this representative function, a citizens' advisory group should be drawn from as many neighbourhoods as possible, not be a spokesperson for particular interest groups and its members, and have a commitment to engagement with the community and planning authority, demonstrated by past actions or simply by their enthusiasm. These panels or groups could be elected by the community to make them truly representative or chosen by the local council. As elections are time consuming and expensive, the most common form is appointment by the local council on the application of individuals after scrutiny of their qualifications and interest.

Ideally the function of a planning advisory group would be to liaise with the planning authority and to make recommendations on every planning issue, and at the formative stages to be involved with fostering community participation in the vision process. The planning authority must have regard to the recommendations made by the group for it to be functional. As the concept is sound, and can perhaps avoid some of the lacunae in full participation and consultation on every planning issue, it is an open question why they are not created in every jurisdiction. It may be because of a lack of knowledge of the concept,

---

52 Sawyer and Schmidt 2004.
53 Hogan 2003.

lack of interest in expanding participation, or a planning culture where the claims for participation are muted. Reports on participation in Malaysia do not mention these forms of citizen involvement[54] probably because of a shared national understanding that rights to participate are weak as they have been diminished by the courts and discounted by planning authorities.[55]

3.8 Choosing stakeholders

Participation is acceptable for residents and local stakeholders, such as mortgagees and potential buyers, and is not extended to those with no apparent direct interest in an area. There is an argument to be made that passers-by may have some stake in the future planning of an area, but that argument does not coincide with the reasons for participation: representative democracy and the assertion of accrued rights.

There are many organisations that have legitimate interests in planning outcomes even though not resident, such as environmental associations, business associations and social welfare groups. In many cases, their interests overlap but all can make a case to participate within their own agenda. They are excluded perhaps because they are perceived by planning authorities as politicised and therefore having entrenched, one-sided views. However, studies have shown that as they provide a useful input into planning, their views, however polarised, are helpful and sustaining as offering different insights and expertise.[56] Their organisation and history of working with government also improves communication and relationships with planning authorities where that may not previously have been the case.

The importance of organisational stakeholder participation in planning is echoed in successful experiments of involvement in environmental decision making. Here the issues are often complex and raise difficult scientific questions. Input from organisations that have a continuing, professional understanding and viewpoint leads to a greater refinement of the issues and solutions. Organisational participation also has the advantage of ameliorating concerns about hidden external influences by donations or patronage, as well as conferring the residual benefits of new relationships between stakeholders, perceptions of fairness and trust, increasing the legitimacy of decisions, and anticipating and analysing negative consequences.[57]

There are different techniques that are used to identify relevant stakeholders in the community participation process. For example, the 'snowballing' technique provides for a list of known stakeholders to be sent to other identified groups in order for them to recommend still others that might be interested.[58] Of course, a problem in stakeholder identification is that casting the net widely may increase the complexity of the participation because of ideological conflicts, the presence of lobbying groups formed just for participation as stakeholders, the fact that well-funded interest groups may have a stronger presence than those with less funds, and the risk of attracting those who have no stake in the local vision but are interested in a particular perspective. As a consequence, there have

---

54   Chee and Paang 1992.
55   Maidin 2011.
56   Curry 2012.
57   Reed 2008.
58   Stanghellini and Collentine 2008.

been attempts to limit stakeholder involvement to those groups that have a legitimate, established interest having regard to qualitative evaluations conducted by the authority.[59]

It is too costly and time consuming to identify every stakeholder. One convenient method for identification is to allow formal registration of stakeholders as a requirement to participate in the visioning process and then to supply information during that process to all other participants of the views of registered stakeholders as they emerge. This has the effect of reducing suspicion of the power of certain stakeholders in the process.

As there may be many stakeholders with conflicting ideologies and agendas that could cause delay in the participation process, it is useful to have stakeholder workshops before the main visioning workshops to attempt to reach some consensus. It is also possible for stakeholder groups to meet separately to provide material into the visioning process, as was done in Alexandria, Virginia, for the Glebe Park Redevelopment Project.

3.9 Regional planning participation

Participants in the process usually derive their interest from local concerns rather than those that are distant, even though the outcomes of a regional or sub-regional planning process may dictate the local planning outcomes. It is important that the community be able to understand the impact of regional and sub-regional issues on their local area and how that constrains local options and opportunities. In addition to the visioning process for local planning, the community must be involved in the larger visioning process with some awareness of what issues may be of concern to them.

The community participation visioning process for regional or sub-regional planning is theoretically the same as that for local visioning. As an example, the public participation process in Sacramento, California, includes these steps in its regional visioning process:[60]

- Base case regional futures and indicators study
- Education in smart-growth principles
- 29 neighborhood-level workshops
- County-level scenario development
- County-wide workshops – select county scenarios
- Regional scenario development
- Elected officials briefings
- Tall Order Regional Forum – preferred regional scenario
- Public opinion survey
- Elected officials summit.

The main purpose of the regional and sub-regional visioning process is to expand the local visioning process to incorporate a wider geographical context, while remaining aware that the regional setting dictates many of the local choices. Information needs are thus wider and must take into account regional transport issues and other infrastructure decisions.

As there is a distance between the goals for the region and an individual's local concerns, it is natural that there will be resident reluctance to contribute to the wider context.

---

59 Luyet et al. 2012.
60 Lurcott 2005.

3 Community participation

For the regional authority to be inclusive, the need for a participation plan or policy that engages the community in *formative* participation in all aspects of the planning process, such as making plans and policies, appears critically important to engage early interest before the issues become overwhelming. The UK *Local Democracy, Economic Development and Construction Act 2009* (sect. 75) provides, in respect of regional planning:

Community involvement

1. For the purposes of the exercise of their functions in relation to the revision of the regional strategy for their region, the responsible regional authorities must prepare and publish a statement of their policies as to the involvement of persons who appear to them to have an interest in the exercise of those functions.

One of the difficulties with the regional participation process is that the issues are more complex and technical, such as the calculation of the need for land use for schools given population projections over time. This requires a greater explanation briefing for participants, leading to a longer, more involved process. In the overload of information, it is possible that the participants will be reduced only to those who have the time and interest to stay with the process, thus diluting the possible scope of participation. An answer may lie in organising workshops around specific issues rather than a general region-wide participation process.

3.10 Input to draft plans

This has been described as the second stage of participation: where a draft plan that was subject to a visioning process has reached a regulatory form, such as: a draft local land use plan; a draft sub-regional delivery plan; or a planning instrument developed by the state for overarching purposes, such as a state or national planning policy. If this has been part of a full participation process and is not the only form of participation, it is a necessary step to align the vision with the draft plan. At this point, it is appropriate to bring the plan back to the participants for a 're-visioning' to analyse and discuss as an extension of the visioning process.

It may be that some instruments or policies that have come out of the strategic process are not now appropriate for a re-visioning process. For example, the making of state-wide policy in respect of natural resources or transport, suggested by the strategic plan, may be unsuitable for a further collaborative exercise because the planning content has become part of other agency agendas or is now a national or state imperative – or even a government policy platform.

Making written submissions is the traditional manner in which participation has taken place for draft plans or policies. Submitting these by electronic means has streamlined that process[61] and has the advantage of providing relevant information on a web portal so that it can be assumed the submission will be made with knowledge of all relevant matters. Written submissions are not the only form. When there is a vision statement in place and where formative participation has been part of the process, it may be that further

---

61 Conroy and Evans-Cowley 2006.

participation in meetings should take place with the same participants, refining the document. As some matters are appropriate for further meetings and some are not, it may be that a choice has to be made by the authority. The UK *Local Democracy, Economic Development and Construction Act 2009* (sect. 23) provides:

> Duty of public authorities to secure involvement:
> 1. Where an authority to which this section applies considers it appropriate for representatives of interested persons (or of interested persons of a particular description) to be involved in the exercise of any of its relevant functions by being
>   A. provided with information about the exercise of the function,
>   B. consulted about the exercise of the function, or
>   C. involved in another way,
>   it must take such steps as it considers appropriate to secure that such representatives are involved in the exercise of the function in that way.

This act followed on from the 2008 white paper, *Communities in control: real people, real power*, which emphasised the efficacy of participation but did not specify the extent of that consultation. A recent examination of participation techniques at the draft plan stage found that more active participation was relevant and useful for this aspect of planning, not just for the visioning process.[62]

What is apparent is that there is no specific code or set of procedures to apply to draft planning documents and all that can be provided is some guidance for the planning authority as to what might be useful, leaving the techniques to be developed by experimentation and evaluation. However, there should always be a presumption that there must be public meetings unless there is an exemption granted. Exemptions are appropriate in some cases as indicated in the UK *Local Democracy Act* (sect. 76) in relation to revisions of regional strategies:

> Examination in public
> 1. The responsible regional authorities may when preparing a draft revision of their regional strategy arrange for an examination in public to be held.
> 2. In deciding whether or not to arrange for an examination in public to be held the responsible regional authorities must have regard to
>   A. the extent of the revisions proposed by the draft revision,
>   B. the level of interest shown in the draft revision, and
>   C. such other matters as the responsible regional authorities consider appropriate.

3.11 Best practice

Best practice in community participation is grounded on the concept that full participation is effective in the planning process because it recognises private rights, it creates social capital, it is consistent with the democratic function of government, and the outcome of the process is understood to have been reached by consensus. This relies on the political

---

62 Cooper and Smith 2012.

will and a methodology to achieve this goal. There appears to be no counter-argument to full participation in Western countries where the idea of participatory democracy is espoused. With respect to the planning cultures of other countries, participation may not exist because of the disconnected relationship of government to citizens. However, it still bears scrutiny, as the eventual outcome of strategic planning with participation will refine the issues, test assumptions, and result in a plan that is appreciated.

The literature and best practice suggests that the basic principles for full community participation are the following:

1. Have a statement of legislative intent for full participation;
2. Create a basic right to a hearing in planning matters by law or at least by policy;
3. Impose duties on a planning authority to carry out full participation;
4. Establish a model charter or policy of public participation that establishes the principles to be followed, explains the formative and visioning process, and sets out the procedure for participation, including stakeholder registration;
5. Require that the planning authority establish a participation plan based on the charter or policy to be approved by the state before it is implemented;
6. Refer to the charter or policy in the legislation to connect the practice with the legislative intent;
7. Impose a duty on a planning authority to provide sufficient information to allow participation;
8. Establish a web based portal to be a source of information;
9. Create local planning panels or citizen advisory groups in the legislation;
10. Impose a duty on the planning authority to take into account the submissions of the local planning panel or citizen advisory group;
11. Prepare guidelines that set out the mechanism for acceptable visioning techniques;
12. Set up a system of monitoring and evaluating community participation.

3.11.1 Model policies

As the models vary, it is necessary for a planning authority to set out a complete policy in order to explain the scope and operation of such a critical aspect of planning. Accordingly, Appendix 1 contains an attempt at establishing the essential elements that should be in a policy or charter on full community participation. Appendix 2 is a model policy having regard to best practice with all elements addressed.

2
Implementing the plan

4
The bases of regulatory controls

A strategic plan derived from a process of community participation most accurately describes the present and desired future state of land use for all stakeholders. This is because the strategic plan is a narrative explanation that requires no complex interpretation and is imbued with the idea that it is providing the vision of the community upon which it is based. As it has this critical function, the modern view of planning is to include a relevant strategic planning component of a vision or goals in all planning documents: in regulations that control the use of land, in policies, and in the plans for individual projects. By itself, however, a strategic plan does not have the effect of controlling the use of land and needs legal enforcement mechanisms.

'Command-and-control' is the phrase used to describe the regulatory process of implementing the strategic vision by legal controls. It takes the common form of a combination of a spatial plan that illustrates on a map the uses that are possible and legal provisions for compliance and permissions. The strategic plan remains the underlying basis for the spatial plan and regulations. In the United States, as the prime example, legal controls in the form of the legal instrument of an ordinance and a map (the spatial plan) are both required to be in accordance with, or consistent with, a comprehensive plan, which is a strategic plan. As one example, the City of Seattle Comprehensive Plan, *A plan for managing growth 2004–2024*, is the basis for regulatory provisions: the *Seattle municipal code*, which sets out the uses that are permitted and the controls for building (Title 23: Land Use Code). The code states: 'The purpose of this Land Use Code is to protect and promote public health, safety and general welfare through a set of regulations and procedures for the use of land which are consistent with and implement the Comprehensive Plan' (sect. 23.02.020).

It is the strategic planning process that offers a vision of how land should be used for the benefit of the community. The vision is translated into how land is actually to be used. For example, a vision of residential peace and quiet in a strategic plan requires that incompatible uses such as an industrial activity cannot be carried on near residential housing. The spatial plan, be it local or regional, merely reflects that vision of the strategic plan on a map.

The operative planning controls consist of laws to implement the carrying-out of the land uses that are designated on the spatial plan. Land use *policies* are created to interpret or refine the laws or to provide a justification for the planning controls. Ideally, planning controls in the form of laws and policy establish a cogent means by which to translate the strategic plan. This is to enable the realisation of the goals for an area, which are then, because of the more precise legal form, commonly understood.

These legal controls consist of three parts: the spatial plan in the form of a map showing the land uses; a set of regulatory provisions as to what can and cannot be developed in each area on the map; and policies that provide more detail or explanation of what development is appropriate. The regulatory provisions usually incorporate the spatial plan, which are considered together as one instrument. The combined spatial plan and regulatory provisions has many names: master plan, comprehensive plan, zoning plan, zoning ordinance, zoning by-law, development plan, or environmental plan.

In some countries, such as the United States and Canada, the predominant form of planning control is a zoning plan that establishes the details of the future use of land by designating uses on a map according to zones of uses with common characteristics. It also indicates which uses are permitted and which prohibited in each zone. Reliance on the zoning map and permitted and prohibited uses is referred to as a 'plan-led' system, as the decisions about appropriate land use are derived from the spatial plan. In other countries, such as England, Malaysia, Nigeria, and Sri Lanka, there is less emphasis on strategic planning and more on a case-by-case determination of what is an appropriate use at the time an application is made. This system is referred to as 'development control'. An early statement about development control is that it 'involves regulation of the detailed aspects of development, about which precise guidance cannot be given by the development plan.'

There are also hybrid systems, such as in Australia, where the zones set out what is prohibited but all other uses (aside from perhaps single-family dwellings) require development permission. In terms of forms, as it is most congruent with the notion of futurity, a plan-led system appears to be at the heart of all systems, even in development control regimes to a greater or lesser extent, as it has the most cogency. In the United Kingdom, which has a development control system, the 2006 *Barker review of land use planning* recommended a shift to a plan-led system because: 'It provides business with a greater degree of certainty about likely development than would otherwise be the case and enables communities to engage in developing a vision of the future of their area.'[1]

There is no best system, even though a plan-led system seems more logical and structured. Development control systems have the advantage of forcing a detailed analysis of a particular area that might not have been undertaken in a strategic plan. The choice of system is a matter of historical development and the planning culture, so that the efficacy of a system must be examined in the context of planning outcomes rather than of form.

4.1 Relationship of strategic plans to controls

A strategic plan should not offer directions as to how controls are to be implemented because to do so would confuse the role of the strategic plan as a document reporting the vision and direction for urban growth. Accordingly, the regulatory provisions are separate but they must be read together to understand what the planning system is trying to accomplish. In practice, there are many different forms for deriving insight into the relationship between strategic plans and regulatory provisions. On the one hand, there may be no for-

---

[1] HM Treasury 2006, 7.

mal link: the zoning by-laws of the boroughs of Montreal, for example, make no reference to the strategic plan, the *Metropolitan land use and development plan*. On the other hand, there may be a more direct linking: the City of Johannesburg's *Consolidated town planning scheme* includes the goals of the strategic plan within the regulatory scheme.

As there is no universal formulation, a strategic plan may contain or suggest controls or the controls may contain strategic planning policies. The strategic plan is not fundamentally, by its nature and process, a legal document, but as the zoning and development laws must be in accordance with that plan, it is most often the case that the visions of the strategic plan are incorporated somehow into the legal structure. The result in any form, regardless of a specific linking, is that all decisions are made according to the strategic plan as well as the regulatory system that zones and provides land use classifications.

Many goals of a strategic plan, such as the expressed aspiration to 'create more vibrant cities' or 'increase the liveability of the area', cannot be *directly* translated into the formal language of a legal restriction. There is therefore much in a strategic vision that is not able to be guided by legal regulation because these controls are based on restriction and permission and do not directly encourage or discourage development. If, for instance, the strategic plan calls for 'vitality' in a neighbourhood, the legal controls may permit mixed commercial and residential uses or prohibit high-rise buildings or light industrial uses. These regulatory provisions hint at an outcome but do not contain the mechanisms required to fulfil the aspiration.

This point of contact between the regulatory controls and the strategic plan – the ability to translate strategic ideas into legal structures – is a difficult issue in evaluating the effectiveness of planning. It appears at times that the two are speaking a different language. In recognition of this lack of fit, from the legal point of view, the concerns have been reduced to whether regulatory controls are *consistent with* the strategic plan and whether the regulatory controls will not defeat the plan. The requirement is only for a general consistency between them and not a direct matching.

The cause of the mismatching is that the goals of a strategic plan are vague, aspirational, and general, a logical consequence of imagining future states. The factors that yield success, such as developer interest, buyer interest, and service-provider plans, are out of the reach of a strategic plan. The plan therefore sets up the preconditions that will allow the goals to be reached. The legal controls of prohibiting and permitting will not necessarily provide for fulfilling those preconditions. They offer simply an indirect interpretation of the aspiration, understood by deduction from what is allowed and what is prohibited. If there were no strategic plan or one that is not comprehensive, it would be very difficult to deduce what the legal controls are attempting to promote in terms of aspirations.

Land use regulation cannot always control the future of an area no matter how consistent with a strategic plan, as there are unforeseen consequences brought about by many factors in the planning culture. This can be observed in the failed attempt in Mexico City to prevent expansion to the south in the preservation zone by a strategic policy. The possibility of high levels of illegal settlement was not foreseen and therefore not taken into account by the land use regulations.[2] With a population of over 20 million, Mexico City is in the category of a megacity, where strict compliance with a plan's intent becomes more difficult. In another example in India, restrictive land use regulations to control the quality of neighbourhoods by providing minimum floor-area ratios have raised the cost of own-

---

2   Guillermo Aguilar 2008.

ership and have had the effect of creating inner-city homelessness and increased suburban expansion.[3] In these situations, the policy pronouncements in the strategic plan have had no effect because the legal controls were not capable of executing the vision or anticipating the consequences.

Nevertheless, the rational view is that having done all the hard work of strategic planning, the stakeholders must comply with the legal controls as the only possible manifestation and practical implementation of the plan. It is assumed that, because such complex thinking and diligence has contributed to the strategy, the legal controls must become the single best enunciation of the urban future. Cities are thus bound by the logic of the process and the relationship of the regulatory instruments to the strategic plan, or the spatial map to the strategic plan is not questioned. It is, in fact, universally accepted that regulatory controls, although incapable of delivering the aspirations of the plan, are the only means by which a plan can be implemented and so, in practice, take a higher role than the strategic plan. Mere policy statements around the strategic plan, or the weight given by government to the plan, are not sufficient and require laws, even though the vision may be lost in this process.

As they are an amalgam of complex issues and decisions arising from the strategic planning process, spatial plans that set out the uses on a map take years to develop. Upon completion, the maps remain static for many years, hardening those variables, eventually and inevitably becoming inconsistent with market trends and governmental objectives. As it is not possible for a spatial plan to anticipate the more distant future, some form of development control is introduced to allow flexibility.

Development control as a device for flexibility takes many forms, such as: separate decisions to amend a spatial plan at the behest of a landowner; allowing a variance to the strict requirements of a plan from time to time; or employing a permit system where certain uses and development must be the subject of an application.

A plan-led system is based on a strategic plan but may incorporate some type of development control. A strategic plan and development control, usually with different emphases, are the two essential forms of planning controls that exist in all systems no matter the different governance or institutional arrangements. When China enacted the *City Planning Law 1990*, for instance, it provided that all cities must have a first-tier strategic, master plan to determine the nature and direction of development in a spatial layout and also a second-tier regulatory control plan, providing details of allowable development for each area.[4] The City of Shenzhen, in creating the regulatory control plan, introduced a development-control permit system for some uses because of a lack of certainty as to the appropriate development, while referencing the master plan as the basis for land use choices.

In all systems, a spatial plan is a concrete end product of the strategic planning process. It has, by its simplicity, the ability specifically to address planning issues by designations on a map. These planning issues include, for example, reducing environmental damage through the restriction of harmful uses, or providing areas for public good, such as recreation or schools. The spatial plan is well understood and easy to grasp. This allows it to have a role equal to, or more important than, the vaguer strategic plan and complex legal requirements as the essential component that declares land use.

---

3   Sridhar 2010.
4   Tian and Shen 2011.

4 The bases of regulatory controls

4.2 The reasons behind planning controls

Planning controls spring from the strategic planning process as the only effective means to carry out the vision and goals. However, the spatial plan and legal restrictions soon become the planning process, as the strategic planning exercise is historic and falls into the background as the origin of the controls. A landowner will look to the legal controls to decide the possible uses to which their land can be put. As the controls continue year after year, the original, underlying vision may be lost and any amendment to the planning controls may proceed in the absence of a new vision.

Planning controls derive their force from creating predictability, not because they advance the original vision or strategic goals. Uncertainty and the resultant anxiety arising from lack of predictability is a psychological problem. However explained, such anxiety is indeed the driver for the establishment of and changes to all planning controls: to make the rules governing property certain. For example, anxiety arises when residents of a quiet residential area face a proposed strategic plan that hints at the possibility of an intrusion of a high-rise building. This anxiety then pressures the planning system to react by attempting to offer some regulatory countermeasure to the community, such as increasing the rights of residents to object or to prepare a rational set of required guidelines to determine how the intrusion can take place.

An absence of planning controls would mean that anything could happen in the name of a strategic vision. A developer might take advantage of a strategic statement to 'enhance tourism' by seeking to build an incongruent hotel in a residential area. Not knowing what is permitted and what is prohibited would engender fear and anxiety in all residents. It is not just residents who become anxious. Lack of certainty in the creation of rules through planning controls affects other stakeholders. When a developer makes an investment in farmland on the basis that it will eventually be allocated for housing according to the spatial plan, the inability of the system to deliver an outcome because of delay or bad decision making causes anxiety. If the decision to change land use is perceived to be made by a decision maker who may be subject to corruption, or the rules are so complex that they are hard to navigate, this will put pressure on the system to establish an independent body or a set of policies to reduce stakeholders' anxiety.

Anxiety resulting from lack of predictability is, in fact, the basis for the introduction of and amendment to planning controls. Anxiety can arise from every aspect of land use and planning controls, even at the simplest of levels. Excessive red tape and form filling, for example, will cause anxiety and a demand for streamlining. However, the anxiety that drives planning is not always warranted. A higher-density development in a residential area may, in fact, be beneficial as it could attract more retail or government services for the existing population. It could open up new transportation routes, existing properties could increase in value, entertainment uses may be attracted to the area, and the high rise looking down on the streets below could reduce crime. The anxiety then is often irrational or at least not completely countered by rational argument.

The source of the anxiety is primarily a fear that threatens the stability of the individuals in the community. The fear is of the unknown, conjuring images of a future that will destroy some of the basic expectations of residential life: privacy, safety, protection from invasion by those who are alien to the values of the area, and maintenance of wealth, which is a fundamental element of security. As the psychoanalyst Alfred Adler puts it, anxiety moves an individual to desire a previous state where there was security and thus pushes that person to assert some form of control to retain that state.⁵

The assertion of some form of control to overcome the fear moves governments and leads to the idea that a strict set of planning controls can provide predictability, or at least relieve anxiety. When this is not realised, planning controls are amended or new ones are invented to better manage the anxiety. An obvious example is when planning controls allow an institutional use in a residential area, such as a halfway house. The lofty ideal of a community supporting drug rehabilitation can give way to anxiety and, ultimately, opposition. A 1995 publication of the US Department of Health and Human Services explains it well:

> The opening of an alcohol or other drug treatment program, regardless of treatment modality, is often met by community resistance. Neighborhood opposition has delayed or prevented the siting of many treatment programs and even disrupted the relocation of existing programs. Unfortunately, even if a program ultimately prevails, the fight can be costly, not only in terms of resources, but in its effects on the clients as well. In one instance, a New Jersey town's campaign of harassment against a recovery home caused each of the home's residents to relapse.⁶

Some planning regimes appear more efficient than others in providing relief from anxiety. However, the reasons for the existence or evolution of a specific planning control or device to offer predictability and relief from anxiety are not, however, always clear. There is a multitude of alternative ways to solve the same problem. For instance, to provide some relief from a rigid land use classification, the power to vary can be assigned alternatively to local residents, a panel of experts, an independent decision maker or a court, all of which provide sufficient justification for the same task: an easing of restrictions. Sometimes the reason for a practice, whether rigid or flexible, may be a result of an historical accident or subtle, cumulative changes over decades of trial and error. There may also be shifts in political alignments, such as pro-development or anti-development, or the emergence of a particular personality that has sway over the planning agenda.

The argument that the real purpose of planning controls is not to relieve anxiety, but rather to focus on making a city more 'liveable', is ultimately a statement that bears no historical relationship to how cities develop. Planning controls, even where liveability is expressed as a goal, depend less on their ability to provide greater resident wellbeing, as that is a very uncertain possibility, and more on relieving tension caused by anxiety. For example, take a cautious walk down the forbidding streets of East Cleveland, the poorest area of the poorest city in the United States, and see how the 2003 *City of East Cleveland master plan* goal to 'revitalize neighborhoods' has no possibility.

Jane Jacobs' theory of vital, diverse neighbourhoods was a vision of planning that suggested it could deliver a form of pleasure and sustained interest. Such a vision cannot be translated into a unitary or singular planning solution through planning controls, which leads to the sound argument that the importance of master planning with lofty goals is overrated.⁷ The problem has been that her theories have been overwhelmingly accepted

---

5   Adler 1930.
6   Weber, Cowie and the Center for Substance Abuse Treatment 1995.
7   Morgan 2012.

because they had an 'apple pie' feeling about them: diversity and interest sound like what everyone needs. This is not to discredit the idea that diversity and interest may result from mixed-use development and urban design patterns, but these factors, and all planning based on lofty ideals, do not alleviate anxiety and have made planning controls work too hard to accomplish what is not possible.

The supposition that planning controls should reflect the aspirations and vision for a community may not be relevant. The vision, when examined, is a projection of what is missing into an unknown future. The formation of the vision starts from a lack: we are missing vitality in this area; that patch of nature is not protected; the neighbourhood is decaying; or some other lament or fear. It is indicated by very broad statements as an unknown future cannot be tethered. The aspirations are so amorphous yet planners jump on this bandwagon as it suggests an answer.

It is not therefore a vision or abstract goals that lie behind planning controls, but rather it is the tension in the system arising from anxiety on the part of the stakeholders, including government, that dictates the forms that the controls take. Predictability is essential to all individuals and the mixture of strategic planning and controls are the crude ways this is accomplished to provide perceived certainty in the ownership and use of property.

When a system creates planning controls because of this anxiety, rather than a vision or aspiration, it takes the form, as it must, of a set of compromises due to the different interests and anxieties of stakeholders. An example of that compromise is allowing greater participation of land owners in decisions, but making sure this occurs in a fixed period so that the developer has predictability. Another might be allowing the local council to decide an application for development but giving the applicant an appeal to a higher decision maker based on the anxiety that the council might get it wrong.

The anxiety is never described as such in planning strategies or resulting controls and is masked in terms of economic growth, sustainability, maintenance of property values, or residents' rights. These terms are in fact all measures of anxiety. Sustainability, as one instance, is a statement that there is a shared anxiety about the impact of a development on the environment for present and future generations. Anxiety is often diffuse and difficult to describe, but it is evident. As a result, those who create the planning controls are constantly having to monitor a build-up of anxiety and how it should be managed by planning controls. Significant pressure by vocal residents will not go unnoticed by a local council when it reaches a certain strident level.

It is not possible to measure when the level of anxiety is such that a solution is required and a planning control introduced. What constitutes anxiety may be clear in one country, such as the importance of maintaining rights for residents to participate in the planning process, but this might not arise in all countries because of the particular culture. The lack of community participation in China, for example, is an accepted part of the planning culture.[8]

If it is realised that anxiety is the driver of planning controls, it leads to an understanding that the visions and goals are less important than conflicts and tensions. If there is a concern for high-rise buildings in a residential area, the planning controls need to address that issue and not rely upon some unreachable goal of 'vital neighbourhoods'. This would also allow the planning scheme to be less rigid and more adaptable to issues as they arise. Amendments to this framework should be made as needed and not according to some vi-

---

8 Wu 2015.

sion that is vague and unreachable. What works against this analysis of flexibility is the need for predictability so that the planning controls are solid, fixed, and not likely to upset property decisions. A desire for rigidity, however, is behind many planning failures.

4.3 Planning aspirations and controls

As it is assumed that controls exist to carry out aspirational goals, it remains important to examine whether the controls do in fact reflect the visions in a strategic plan. There are aspirational goals in all strategic plans and the argument follows naturally that the controls that support these goals are beneficial and efficacious. The Ontario *Planning Act 1990* provides that the purpose of the planning controls is 'to promote sustainable economic development in a healthy natural environment within the policy and by the means provided under this Act' (c.P.13, s1.1). Alternatively, strategic plans are framed in a manner that lauds the existing character of an area, pointing out its uniqueness and making planning controls serve that purpose. The City of Berkeley *General plan: a guide for public decision-making* (2003) illustrates this goal:

> Berkeley is a unique place. It has a population that is ethnically, culturally, and economically diverse and its citizens value that diversity. Its citizens care deeply about their community and many participate actively in its civic affairs.

These statements do little to explain how the controls should work or how they were conceived in relation to the aspirations or even what underlying tensions led to their formation. The result is an inference that it was the vision that informed and shaped the regulatory scheme. This disconnect between the true reason for controls as providing predictability and relieving anxiety and not instead to further the lofty goals of a strategic plan perhaps accounts for the honesty in the Singapore *Planning Act 1998* and the Singapore *Master plan 2014*, as neither offer a purpose or goal for the planning controls.

On closer examination, aspirational goals are primarily about relieving anxiety. As an example, New Hampshire, offering a realistic statement that land use regulation 'often fails to deliver goals', suggests four general criteria to be used as the reasons that dictate the types of planning controls: prosperity (economic development); sustainability (care of the environment); liveability (to maximise public benefit and contribute to the quality of life; and mobility (a good transportation system).[9] It assumes that these four criteria will continue to be referenced as the reasons for the restrictions on land use. Prosperity and sustainability have already been visited as the two aspects of the more general concept of sustainability. 'Sustainability' has its historical roots in anxiety arising out of concerns for the environment, originating in the environmental movement from the late 1970s. 'Economic growth' has a similar basis as it was championed in the post-industrial period since the 1990s so that cities did not fall behind and could remain 'competitive'. Of these, the environmental concern offers the greatest underlying natural anxiety associated with the loss of nature as the awful consequence of industrialisation, linked to loss of meaning. This anxiety is so great that it is the reason that it sometimes overrides all other factors in the application of controls. In the case of a Vancouver waterfront development with different

---

9   New Hampshire Department of Environmental Services 2008.

4 The bases of regulatory controls

Figure 4-1 Telegraph Avenue in Berkeley, California. Source: Wikimedia Commons, CC BY-SA 3.0.

interacting forces, such as strong citizen representation, a pro-development stance of the local government, and an attempt to create an elite demographic, the environmental issues forced a compromise in the name of the common public good.[10]

What is being proposed in phrases such as 'common public good' and the process of balancing sustainability and growth as the basis for planning controls is not anxiety but rather a utopian view that residents will make 'good choices' to form a good society, based on self-improvement, neighbourliness, and social cohesion: 'This new therapeutic paradigm effectively seeks to create new subjectivities able to cultivate self-competencies leading to a "better life" and a "better city."'[11]

If the common public good stands as a reason for the planning goals, reflected in the New Hampshire criteria, the test is whether that reason can be implemented by restrictions on the use of land. If it can, then anxiety reduction is only one factor in forming planning controls and another may, in fact, be creation of a better life.

The 2013 OECD *Better life index,* although not related to land use planning, is useful to explain what is meant by the elements of a better life. The index contains a 'Life Satisfaction' index that measures a person's evaluation of their life and the more objective 'How's Life?' index that examines such matters as household net income, employment rate,

---

10   Holden and Scerri 2015.
11   Gunder and Hillier 2009.

and similar statistical measures. There is also a qualitative measure of the social support network and the degree of community consultation on rule making. The Federation of Canadian Municipalities *Quality of life reporting system* has indicators for affordable housing, civic engagement, community and social infrastructure, education, the local economy, the natural environment, health, financial security, and personal safety.

The criteria in these indices relate to levels of satisfaction of an individual derived from public choices of built form, community services, governance and safety. The supposition is that if these are provided to a certain level they will necessarily have a positive effect on residents. They do not measure the relationship of these public choices to the complex web of emotions, feelings, life-altering situations, loneliness, anxiety, drug dependencies and similar urban issues but postulates that the criteria chosen will advance the quality of life. They are, when addressed in planning, the planners' views of what constitutes a good life.

None of these measures are actually used in making planning choices, although some planning issues, such as community engagement and the provision of infrastructure, are used. They are kept vague and general in a strategic plan but are not used directly in the formation of the operative planning controls. The reason is that legal, regulatory planning controls regulate the height and size of the built form of an urban area; the interaction of uses; the density of buildings and areas; the relationship of services to residents, such as community services and shopping; the availability of open space; and other matters that relate to the way land is used. Out of the choices made, such as increasing density, other potential externalities flow that need control. These include lack of light from overshadowing, lack of privacy, long commuting distances, and noise. The OECD measures and the Canadian measures may incorporate some issues but do not establish a direct link between the planning choices for allocation of land use and building controls to a better life.

It is, of course, not possible to underestimate the effect of the built form on the subjective psyche and the quality of life indices. The idea of shelter is an extension of identity and persona, so every form of housing in a particular culture is a reflection of that shared idea. Many of the indices hark back to a generational idea of a quieter, more integrated life, based on the small town or neighbourhood. One study from an Australian coastal town concluded that the elements that formed that view of a shared ideal were the natural landscape, beauty, pleasantness, distinctiveness, charm, familiarity, openness, liveliness and safety.[12]

This aspect, the subjective effect of the built form on the individual, is what is being sought as the common public good or the goal of planning. It should be and is, however, in practice rejected as the basis of planning controls in all countries because the individual and collective impact of what might yield a better life is not clear. The Florida *Comprehensive Planning Act* (sect. 163.3177, part II), as a common example of a reaction to the vagaries of subjective impacts, requires very concrete resolution of land use issues, disconnected from the subjective aspects of quality-of-life concepts:

> future general distribution, location, and extent of the uses of land for residential uses, commercial uses, industry, agriculture, recreation, conservation, education, public buildings and grounds, other public facilities, and other categories of the public and private uses of land, traffic circulation, waste disposal, conservation, open space, and the provision of housing.

---

12 Green 1999.

None of these elements are concerned with the subjective experience of traffic circulation or the effect of public facilities. Instead they are concentrated on the more solid pattern of uses and their interaction. Although it is clear that the built form influences subjective states, the exact manner in which this occurs is not understood and therefore cannot serve as the basis for planning controls. Striving for a better life or the common public good, to the extent that it is aimed at producing subjective states in residents, is not a basis for regulatory controls. In a study analysing the consequences of built form on the mental health of older men, it was found that greater access to community health resources improved outcomes.[13] The same result was true for terraced housing, as bringing neighbours closer encouraged the build-up of social capital. The results suggest that social cohesion can be enhanced by the built form, because it increases a sense of neighbourhood satisfaction and thereby alleviates alienation and isolation.[14] However, the only true manner in which the subjective effect of the built form, such as social cohesion, can be accurately assessed and used as the basis of planning controls is by evaluating a normative future scenario, as each area is different in terms of housing, demographics and social makeup. The method is called 'backcasting' or developing the land use model of how the future scenario will operate and to see if it will, within the goals it supports, succeed.[15] A future scenario is used to distil, to the extent that is possible, the subjective reaction of experts and residents to what is missing from the existing built environment and, therefore, what is envisaged as an idealised state. This is an uncommon practice and is only used rarely in all counties surveyed and then only experimentally for environmental issues and testing urban resilience, such as occurred in Helsinki.[16]

As a matter of planning practice, as the measures of quality of living and the content of a future state are unclear, planning controls both in drafting and execution reject the subjective aspects, even though they were the basis of the vision and goals in the strategic plan. They are focused instead on the lifting of anxiety and other ideological issues, such as neoliberal forms of capitalist accumulation. To claim that planning controls serve liveability or wellbeing is to mock these subjective and ideological values, as they do not register quantifiable or understandable concerns that can be translated into regulatory forms. If they are too complex and amorphous, they cannot really be addressed.[17] They should not be set out in planning instruments as they cannot be understood, much less are they capable of being described in a way that gives them priority or efficacy.

The disconnect between the subjective quality of life and planning controls is often obvious, facilitating the argument that they are not the basis for regulation. A good example of this is Vancouver, which refers to its concern for quality of life as 'Vancouverism'. The public website for Vancouver states:

> That means creating a city of neighbourhoods where people can work, play, and shop. It also means creating urban environments where residents feel supported and engaged, and can enjoy a vibrant street life and their fellow residents.

---

13 Sarkar, Gallacher and Webster 2013.
14 Dassopoulos and Monnat 2011.
15 Haslauer, Biberacher and Blaschke 2015.
16 Neuvonen and Ache 2017.
17 Dissart and Deller 2000.

The planning controls for Vancouver do not provide any guidelines on how the controls can be used to assist residents to be supported and engaged, but remain solely legalistic, technical and functional. A study has argued, in a review of 25 United States cities where there has been an emphasis on creating specific goals under the wide rubric of sustainability, that little has changed and the goals have not been accomplished.[18]

The idea of 'mixed use' areas is often expressed as providing an altruistic goal that fulfils a social purpose by encouraging walkable neighbourhoods, following the principles of New Urbanism and the legacy of Jane Jacobs. It is also based on the idea that walking improves health and so suggests distribution of public services and shops in the same catchment. The public health aspect has been praised on the basis that the more uses, the greater the walking, leading to the reduction of obesity and heart disease.[19] The connection assumes that more people will walk for sufficient time and exertion that some benefit will accrue. It is difficult to understand whether the consequential effect of walking is a goal of land use planning at all and, if it is, whether it justifies its own zoning form. It seems more of a response to correct the United States pattern of zoning residential land cut off from commercial shopping and recreational activities.

The purpose of mixed-use controls is clearly aspirational but is concerned also with relieving anxiety in terms of areas that create isolation, alienation and lack of social relationships. The aspirational goals are based on assumptions that the variety of uses, most notably coffee shops, will bring out the citizenry and provide them with a chance to interact. It perhaps will give them an opportunity to feel that they are part of a bustling, interesting metropolis. This exercise in social engineering is based clearly on relieving the opposite – dead, lifeless areas that are unpopulated. It is difficult to be specific about the goal that is to be delivered except to phrase it in the negative as to what it is relieving. In any case, anxiety as the basis of planning controls is just as germane to mixed-use areas as it is to every aspect of the planning system.

If anxiety is recognised as a legitimate cause of planning controls, it is easier for a strategic plan to be explicit about this reason and better shape the controls. If it were said, for example, that there is a fear that the residents of an area will be dwarfed by high-rise buildings and that will cause them anxiety, then a planning control that says the area should retain its single-family residential homes makes sense. It makes more sense than expressing the aspirational goal of liveability or vibrancy.

4.4 Best practice

The lack of connection between strategic planning goals, when they are expressed as hopes for the future, and the legal controls expressed in operational language, is a barrier to the ultimate implementation of a plan. The reason is that the legal controls, such as zones, permitted uses, building size, height restrictions, and setbacks, are rough attempts at producing an aspiration, leaving no explanation of how the two are linked. This is inevitable because the nature of strategic planning is to think ahead to an imagined future and the nature of planning controls is to restrict or permit.

---

18 Hirt 2013.
19 Ashe et al. 2009.

This problem can be addressed by a more specific linking of the aspirations with the controls. The best example is a brochure that accompanies the *Berlin land use plan: Contents and conventional signs* (*Erläuterung der Darstellungen*), which explains in a separate narrative the purpose of each zone and the rationale behind the listed restrictions. For example, for 'Mixed Building Land', comprising more intense developments in city centres and major district centres, the choice of the zone is explained:

> The building block shown here is located in the eastern city centre. It comprises mainly offices, but also a hotel, shops and a number of flats for city dwellers. Density and intensity of use are high: GFZ 4.5; GRZ 0.8; 120 inhabitants/ha; 900 jobs/ha.

GFZ and GRZ are respectively the floor-space ratio (ratio of gross floor area to land size), and the ground space ratio (ratio of area covered by building to lot size). Combined with the number of inhabitants and jobs, this is a measure of the densities it is hoped to reach. This explains the zoning map and creates a tie-in with the strategic plan, *Berlin land use plan 2015* (*Flächennutzungsplan Berlin 2015*), which sets out priorities for urban centres.

This is a simple solution. It is an explanation of each zone that is set out on the spatial map in language that reflects the strategic plan and then links the separate requirements of the legal controls. It is a statement that the strategic plan has highlighted future directions that need to be addressed, the zoning map has indicated where those future directions are going to occur, and the brochure explains the link to the restrictions.

4.4.1 Anxiety

Emotionality expressed by residents is met by rational arguments from the planning authority. There is no other response possible that accords with a bureaucracy's operation to deliver a fact-based, rational response. Emotionality has the effect of polarising stakeholders and creating the risk that the emotional arguments will be discounted or not understood. The anxiety behind the emotionality is not usually confined to individual views but is a socially constructed assessment or expression of perceived risk. Nevertheless, it is emotionality and anxiety that lead to planning controls.

The New South Wales Department of Primary Industries published a fact sheet in 2011, *Land use conflict risk assessment guide*, to address potential land use conflicts in rural areas. It proposed that where there may be a conflict, information should be gathered about the potential change, the risk of the new activity should be assessed on a uniform measure of risk ranking, and risk reduction management should take place. This risk assessment has been applied to rural and mining areas where the conflicts between activities on land and natural resources is obvious, as has occurred between farming and limited water resources in Kenya.

The strength of a risk assessment system is to develop a uniform measure of risk and to build a dataset of the effect of potential conflicts and a means to resolve the ensuing anxiety. It underlines that anxiety about risk is responsible for land-use conflicts and leads to planning changes. Best practice that follows is to examine strategic choices and to assess development proposals with the understanding that the planning system fundamentally is based on relieving anxiety. If this is understood, then providing full explanations, establishing risk assessments for choices and consequences, being open and not defensive to community fears, and listening to the community input, will make the system more truly responsive. The planning controls that follow such a change in attitude will then be understood in the proper context of resolving the anxiety surrounding land-use conflicts.

5
Zoning

The concept behind spatial planning is that the future state of an area resolved in the strategic plan can be implemented by indicating a range of land uses on a map. The explication and arrangement of land uses on a map have controlled the layout of many cities since the earliest planning schemas, such as the early grid pattern of the Corp of Engineers in 1682 in Philadelphia or the spatial grid of the Eixample district of Barcelona. This spatial designation of land uses has cogency because it fosters an argument that it creates a sense of order and fairness and, most importantly, that residential property values can be preserved by discouraging and separating out deleterious uses.

The Polish *Act on Spatial Planning and Management 2003* lists the issues to be absorbed in a spatial plan:

- requirements of spatial order, including those of urban science and
- architecture
- architectural and landscape qualities
- environmental requirements, including water management and protection of cultivable soils and forests
- requirements of preservation of cultural heritage and modern cultural achievements
- requirements of health care, safety of people and property, and also needs of the disabled
- economic qualities of space
- ownership title
- security and defence needs of the state
- public purpose needs.

The strategic plan contains the vision, goal and priorities and the spatial plan converts these by use of a map to the physical space on the ground, such as providing for buffers around heavy industry or creating recreational open space. The objects are placed in juxtaposition to each other, so a commercial area can be put close to a residential area or a polluting industry can be separated from a conservation area. Spatial planning addresses the uses to which land can be put for areas that have common characteristics or are delineated by topographical restrictions, such as a river, mountain, highways, and conservation areas with associated buffers. Each area must be defined in some way to distinguish it from

Figure 5-1 Industrial zones separated from residential areas. Source: Google Earth.

other areas and a determination made as to its boundaries. This division into parts or areas allows separate visions for different zones.

The setting of a boundary for a zone may be as arbitrary as drawing a line on a map without a clear reason. Indicating where high-rise buildings can be built on the fringe of a single-family residential area or setting an exact rural-urban boundary is not usually based on technical information, even though the change in land value on one side or the other is significant. Zone boundaries are ideally chosen by expert opinion with community participation and negotiation with stakeholders. Some attempts have been made to use a spatial decision support system where quantitative models of visualisation are used that can analyse terrain, hydrology, vegetation, industry output, urban growth rates, hospital beds, and numerous other factors that are scored and distinguished from other areas.[1]

When a boundary is set between zones, there may be little understanding of transborder interactions or how one zone integrates with another. This lack of precision occurs because the division into parts is based on disparity and separation, discouraging linking, even though it has planning consequences. The classic example is the historical practice of widely separating employment and residential zones, thereby increasing the trip to work.

As the boundaries between zones are not precise, aside from topographical restrictions, there is a possibility of introducing a transition zone as an area moves from one predominant use to a mix of uses. A 'commercial transition zone' in the *Charleston County,*

---

1   Arciniegas and Janssen 2012.

South Carolina comprehensive plan provides this zoning between existing commercial and residential areas, allowing residential uses in a commercial zone.

The land uses on the map are grouped into zones that reflect their basic overall character: residential, commercial, industrial. It is theoretically possible to assign each property with a separate designated use to encourage diversity within an area but this would create difficulties in monitoring and enforcement. It would also confuse the question of what is appropriate for future development. As a consequence, zoning for an area or district is directed at creating a primary or overarching use, although there is usually an attempt to make some gradations. The industrial zoning for Rio de Janeiro, for instance, is divided into three zones: Areas of Strictly Industrial Use, Areas of Mainly Industrial Use, and Areas with Diversified Use.[2]

Of all possible uses, residential zones constitute the highest in the hierarchy of uses and the fulcrum around which planning occurs. It is this to which we give the greatest value.[3] Accordingly, other uses flow from their relationship to residential areas, such as shopping, places of work or worship, recreation areas, and public open space. This is particularly the case in the United States with its prevalence of detached single-family homes and its tendency towards exclusionary enclaves that eventually forced local governments to provide a fair share of lower-cost housing. It is also the case in Australia, where 75 per cent of the population live in single-family dwellings. This insistence on single-family enclaves is not as prevalent in much of Western Europe,[4] but the importance of the home as the key to spatial allocation remains.

It is probably the case that zoning has actually caused residential exclusivity as it became a tool for resolving unexpressed fears of racial and socio-economic infiltration. The European structure of ancient towns with historic cardinal points and pre-existing designations of social structures may have taken some pressure off zoning to be used as a means of protection. In the German and Austrian systems, the zones are more broad and are mandated at a federal level: residential, mixed, commercial and special, further divided into 11 more general classes, such as general residential, village-type, and so on, but without any single dwelling zones.[5] All detailed development plans are required to follow the federal land use classifications.

The importance of zoning to protect residential land values is formalised in Western countries and is obvious in a land use plan but is not always apparent in developing countries. In these places, a lack of emphasis on residential land values arises from deficient or confusing land tenure systems, an unstable constitutional order, inter-group conflicts, divides between caste, race and ethnicity, and economic and social disparities. Consequently, any attempt to plan for residential exclusivity in developing countries cannot be hidden and instead highlights the social disparities.[6] It is accurate to say, however, that the tendency towards using land use planning to protect residential exclusivity is prevalent in any culture where there are middle-class aspirations of social status, as can be seen by the emergence of residential enclaves in Delhi.[7]

---

2 *Law No. 466 on the industrial zoning in the Metropolitan Region of Rio de Janeiro.*
3 Mallet 2004.
4 Hirt 2014a.
5 Hirt 2014b.
6 Yiftachel 2006.
7 Dupont 2015.

For each zone, there are legal controls that provide for three basic options for the use and development of land: that certain uses and buildings are prohibited as being inconsistent with the purpose of the zone; that listed preferred uses are permitted; and that some uses do not fit neatly into the zone, thus requiring separate consideration at the time they are to be so used. Vietnam differs from this model and provides positive ways in which land is to be used to conform to the hierarchy of strategic plans: national, regional, cities, districts or projects. The difference in emphasis is significant in that a capacity to prohibit a use and the existence of discretionary uses that need approval requires an understanding of the vision by deduction as to what was intended; a list of what can and should be done in the area as in Vietnam is a restatement of the vision.

To give a working example of a common system, a single-family dwelling will be a permitted use in a residential zone, a factory will be a prohibited use, and a wine store may be permitted in a residential area only with approval. It can be seen that the definition of a use in a planning scheme such as a 'shop' becomes critical, as a wine store may or may not fall within the definition and this makes the application of the planning controls very precise and legalistic. Fortunes can be made and lost by developers because a definition can be either wide or narrow. Some places suggest a uniform set of definitions so that a shop in one place is at least considered a shop in another. However, the need to separate out inconsistent uses gives rise to a requirement for definitions and, in turn, takes a broad and aspirational vision and reduces it to the meaning and interpretation of use definitions.

For each use that is permitted directly or allowed with approval, there are building standards as to height (e.g. only one storey in a residential zone), minimum lot size or the ratio of height to lot size, and other controls relating to the placement of the building on the lot. These ' development standards', as they are called, are usually technical and fixed. The maximum that is allowed in a zone dictates the form that buildings take because the natural tendency for a developer is to obtain the greatest advantage. In some places, such as New York, the unused parts of the maximum height, the 'air rights', can be sold to a nearby developer, preventing a uniform skyline.

The minutia of detail of development standards is the most complicated part of zoning laws. In large cities, it requires a gruelling effort to establish what is possible and demands expert help; in New York, as an example, one paragraph of the *Zoning resolution* for measuring the bulk for a mixed commercial/residential building in commercial zones states:

> In the districts listed in paragraph (a), without a letter suffix, and in C5-2, C5-3, C5-4, C5-5, C6-1, C6-1A, C6-5, C6-6, C6-7, C6-8 or C6-9 Districts, the bulk regulations applicable to Quality Housing buildings may, as an alternative, be applied to the residential portion of a building under the same conditions set forth in Sections 23-011, 35-22 and 35-23 . . .

These controls are contained in a formal legal instrument: a by-law, ordinance, or some regulatory document that enforces the manner in which land uses can occur in different zones. The legal instrument makes reference to the zoning map that is either included in the document or referenced. In larger cities, the maps are plentiful and are incorporated by reference.

The source of the designation of a zone and its rightful place in the spatial plan is based on an assessment of the nature and character of the area as it is and will be. It therefore draws its legitimacy as an expression of the strategic plan even in the absence of a narrative explaining its purpose or the fact that it does not have a direct concordance with the goals and aspirations. The decision to zone an area is not perceived as random and is understood as being influenced by significant, measurable factors such as population forecasts and transport routes. Existing transportation routes are often a key factor in establishing credibility for the choice of zones, as shown in a study for Spain where the location of highways was the major reason for rezoning land for urban, rather than rural use.[8]

Land use designations for a zone do not need to be achieved only by a generalised view of the character of an area, its potential, or the placement of transportation routes. Mathematical models have been developed that attempt to refine the decision about the appropriate zoning and take into account population forecasting, patterns or vectors of existing development, and ecological issues. The ecological issues, as found in a study of northern China, have a high priority in the operation of these models, as these issues have a particular intensity due to the nature of the multiple environmental variables addressed in the equations and ensuing interrelationships.[9]

There are policy choices that must be made in respect of conflicting interests that are not reflected in models, such as the effect of a decision to allow zoning for retail shopping in one area on the existing shops in a nearby area. These land use conflicts are resolved by historical rules, such as that competition should not be a relevant land use consideration, or that there should be different forms of shopping (large retail centres as well as llocal shops) in proximity to every resident.

As a matter of practice, the choice of forms for residential zoning is not derived from mathematical modelling but is influenced by a subjective assessment of the character of the area and the unarticulated goal of residential exclusiveness. The assessment that relies on the character of the area and includes exclusivity is also the basis for development standards for that zone. In this sense, the zoning is self-selecting for residential areas as it is congruent with the operation of the land market where the factors of character and exclusivity are critical to land transactions.

In Houston, Texas, there is no zoning code and therefore there is a greater reliance on an intelligent market, deed restrictions, and the common law of nuisance. This is a recognition that the assessment of value is what establishes the efficacy of a market. It is interesting that the lack of zoning does not resolve the problem of land-use conflicts in residential areas as Houston was faced with the attempt to develop a 21-storey high-rise in the Southampton area, which came into conflict with the residents of an affluent, single-family enclave. The mayor announced a movement towards a 'general plan' as a means to prevent loss of exclusivity in order to reduce future controversies.

The assessment of the character of an area has a methodology referred to as 'urban morphology' or 'urban tissue'. This is a survey of the typology of the existing buildings, which then forms the basis for a determination of the character for the area. However, this characterisation is not always easy, as when there is a mix of largely single-storey and some double-storey development, it must then be determined if it is a single-storey zone with aberrant double-storey buildings or an existing mix. Another similar method is to determine the urban form and character by the interrelationship of streets and blocks, land size and proportion of coverage, buildings, rooms or built spaces, structures such as walls

---

8   Garcia-Lopez, Sole-Olle and Viladecans-Marsal 2015.
9   Chen et al. 2008.

or roofs, and materials. This yields an impression of the underlying sense of a particular area that is its character. An application of this method to the streets and buildings of the French town of Mennecy indicated that its character was one of distinction: one street that is different from another, and areas that are unique because of building size.[10]

In the United Kingdom, zoning maps are not used, but each local plan contains policies for areas that become material considerations in the system of development control where permission must be given for development. It is a zoning system by another name as it attempts to explain the character of an area in order to assist in determining appropriate development. As an example, the 2015 *City of London local plan* provides that in the Financial and Business Centre area, there must be 'robust evidence' to support the loss of existing office accommodation because it no longer is viable. This classification is based on a perceived need for office space, not justified in the plan.

The *London local plan* for the Financial and Business Centre highlights the difficulty with the practice of establishing a zone (or a policy) based on a perceived need. The zoning gets fixed even though the need is no longer important. There are studies of the development pipeline for London that indicate that there is an increase in office space and that no shortage exists.[11] If this is the case, the policy is a burden on the city, unrelated to changing circumstances. In fact, certain areas in that centre may be appropriate for residential use instead of office, allowing closer connections between home and work and adding to the longer-term viability of the area.

The ideas of spatial planning and zoning are universal because their absence leads to rampant speculation, corruption and use conflicts. Therefore, the need to be definitive in setting out zones is essential and it does not matter perhaps if the zoning designations are based entirely on non-enduring factors. The zoning is creating the market and the markets are essential for city growth and functioning. Ironically, it is also the case that a spatial plan itself creates speculation, encourages corruption to get uses changed, and engenders land-use conflicts. Speculation is strongest at the urban fringe as the so-called 'up-zoning' of farm land to residential will yield the highest profit. Obtaining rezonings is not merely of interest to local investors as, over the last decade, the profit has attracted out-of-area private equity funds.[12] As a result, the stakes are so high that the decision to rezone land is perhaps the largest cause of pressure on planners and governments and the one decision that has many secondary consequences, such as fostering wealth inequality, creating a rise in rates for an entire zone, and making land unaffordable. The positive and negative effects of zoning are relatively balanced and arise equally because planning requires that an attempt be made for predictability yet it is not possible to foresee the factors that will combine to suggest a different land use.

The response of government to the perceived negative effects of zoning has usually been to centralise decision making to move it away from local government, who are assumed to be more vulnerable to corruption. This leads to a lack of citizen participation and fosters top-down planning. This is in spite of the strong argument that zoning decisions made at the local level *with increased community involvement* are in fact the best form to prevent subtle political influences and biases in zoning choices.[13]

---

10   Kropf 1996.
11   Deloitte Real Estate 2015.
12   Daniel 2012.
13   Shah 2014.

5 Zoning

Figure 5-2 The Meadowhall Regional Shopping Centre in Sheffield. Source: Google Earth.

The decisions made in a plan cannot be easily reversed once they are laid down on a map as zones. As a result, the reasons why a particular zoning choice was historically conceived can be lost over time and new designations may become too hard to implement. For this reason, zoning is often referred to as a 'dead hand', freezing the choices for land use for long periods of time. A good example is the Meadowhall Regional Shopping Centre in the Lower Don Valley of Sheffield, opened in 1990, and having had the effect of drawing shopping away from the high street to a central mall (Fig. 5-2). The Sheffield plan, *Citywide options for growth to 2034*, refers to a plan to attract retail shopping back into the city centre by setting up special retail zones but with no definite ideas of what effect this would have on the pull of Meadowhall or how it might work, simply referring instead to a 'series of challenges' (par. 17). No thought was given to differentiating shopping needs from the start in the original plan even though research shows that city centre shopping areas and remote shopping can co-exist when there is a differentiation of goods being sold.[14]

The vision in a strategic plan and the controls in a zoning ordinance are best seen as a funnel, wide at the top for the vision, but narrow at the end for the controls. A developer looks at the zoning ordinance to ask what can be built where and is not interested in the strategic vision or the greater good of the community that is the basis for the vision and strategy. The vision sits as a vague background of what is a good idea and is not used by the developer unless it will give an advantage when seeking a rezoning or development

---

14   Ozuduru, Varol and Ercoskun 2014.

permission. This is not a theoretical distinction because, as a matter of practice, it is understood that the visions are never implemented through zoning controls as ideas at the higher abstract level do not translate well into zoning or building controls. A study of the zoning ordinances of 32 cities in the United States found that only one third had even attempted to use zoning to implement sustainability goals.[15]

There is a natural reluctance for local governments to venture outside the traditional tools of zoning as they are oriented towards preserving values and separating discordant uses in order to support higher aspirations about what may be good for the future. The power of preserving property values should accordingly not be underestimated and is the primary and most important influence on the prevalence of zoning. Aside from the economic need for a secure land tenure system and land markets, maintenance of property values is also important for governments as a means of assessing land values in a taxation system where there is a mature market. If the market is not robust, as a study has shown in the Ukraine, it is difficult to establish land value and zoning may take on the role entirely of creating that value.[16]

5.1 Zoning and property rights

The effect of zoning is to confer a bundle of property rights on a landowner. The construct of a 'bundle' is a recognition that property is more than tangible real estate and carries with it certain intangible rights. As classically expressed: 'We may speak of a person owning land and using it as a factor of production but what the landowner in fact possesses is the right to carry out a circumscribed list of actions.'[17]

The equation to determine the scope of the rights is to first postulate the ability to use a property unfettered and deduct from that the restrictions placed on the property by legal instruments. In the case of zoning, the property right is what is left over as the potential of the land for development. Thus, if the land is restricted for no use other than a public use, the owner has lost all potential and should obtain compensation for the loss of that property right. In the United States, this is called a 'regulatory taking' in that the property rights are taken away by the state through zoning regulation. In Austria, this right to compensation is so firmly established that if the land was able to be used for development anytime in the last 25 years, a change to allow only a public use attracts compensation.'[18]

Cuba offers useful proof that zoning exists to create property markets, rather than merely to regulate the use of property. There have been no private property rights in Cuba since 1959; the Marxist doctrine is that productive property that can be used for social wealth is to be owned by a co-operative, not a person:

> The foundational principle is that under Cuba's Marxist-Leninist economic organization, only the people, organized through the state sector and directed by the CCP [Cuban Communist Party], can aggregate the means of production and engage in collective activities for social rather than individual profit.[19]

---

15 Jepson and Haines 2014.
16 Kryvobokov 2004.
17 Coase 1960.
18 Hiltgartner 2007.

Without the need to protect proprietary interests and where the central decision making is for the good of the state, the emphasis shifts away from zoning as the way to control land use to a flexible project-by-project evaluation of what is appropriate development and the realisation of the goals of the strategic plan.

> That a particular project does not conform exactly with the general plan does not seem as important to Cuban planners as the implementation of the general vision formulated by planners for a city or region.[20]

The Environmental Licence System in Cuba is essentially a development control system requiring an emphasis on a case-by-case determination of the congruence of a proposal with the general vision contained in a strategic plan. If there is a case-by-case determination, the need for a zoning ordinance diminishes and the importance of the strategic plan increases. This is regardless of the land tenure arrangements.

The purpose and effect of zoning is therefore to confer property rights for the operation of an effective land market. A land market is essential, especially in developing countries, as it creates tenure security and encourages investment, as found in Africa.[21] The value of land for land sales and rental is essentially determined by the zoning laws. This embraces all of the common devices that lead to a potential for development within a particular zoning designation, such as urban containment policies, housing distribution and growth management, height restrictions and plot ratios, and the difficulty and resultant cost in obtaining final approval for a development project.

In respect of obtaining development approval, it is argued to be axiomatic that the stricter the zoning laws, the more expensive property becomes.[22] There is a convincing argument that fewer restrictions in zoning laws reduce the cost of land and housing. In a study in Israel,[23] it was suggested that there is greater compliance with a plan when the requirements are seen as flexible, rather than weak or less restrictive. This may appear to be anathema to planners as the prevailing idea is that, after the years of preparation of the general strategic plan, it is to be enforced strictly as it is the shining conclusion of the community vision. However, the test is not the strictness or restrictions in the wording of the zoning laws themselves but rather the manner in which they are implemented to be effective.

The difficulty with strict systems is that there is always pressure to amend the zoning, seek a variance, find some way to extract a favourable decision or even proceed under the radar, such as an informal system of building housing in areas of Indonesia.[24] The result is further costs of development, insecurity in the administration of the system, and the possibility of corruption and political influence.

---

19   Backer 2013.
20   Yates 2003.
21   Holden and Otsuka 2014.
22   Hilber and Vermeulen 2010.
23   Alterman 1976.
24   Monkkonen 2013.

5.2 Up-zoning and value capture

When zoning is changed to allow a more valuable use, an 'up-zoning', it is moving up the ladder of preferable uses. Examples are the zoning of farm land to allow residential development or increasing the allowable height or density of buildings within a zone. The value is in the potential profit to a developer and thus the sale price of the land. The increase also may occur by government expenditure in many ways, such as the provision of new roads or a railway station. The two are different in kind: when land is up-zoned, the value is created by a government permission, but when there is new infrastructure provided, the government is contributing an asset that increases the value of land.

Up-zoning creates obvious wealth potential for those who can exploit the increase but also to existing residents who find their property has increased in value. They have been 'bettered' by the decision to up-zone while others may have been affected injuriously. An example would be a museum placed in a residential area: those properties next to the museum would find their property reduced in value but those a street away would see an increase in value. The English *Uthwatt report* of 1942, from the Expert Committee on Compensation and Betterment, suggested that every planning decision caused a 100 per cent shift in value, so that for every gain, there was a corresponding loss.

Historically, schemes that tried to balance compensation for injurious affection with levies for betterment have failed because of the difficulty of valuation and administration of the rise and fall, but the idea that government decisions lead to an unearned increased wealth for developers has never faded. The schemes have relied on the theory of the 19th century economist Henry George that these unearned profits should be made available for public use.

The increase in value also arises where the government provides an infrastructure asset. Having a sewerage system put into a rural area will facilitate a higher use for residential development. In 1977, the economist Joseph Steiglitz stated that land values increase at least as much as government infrastructure investment and that a tax on this increase is the most efficient means to finance public expenditure.[25] The latter is not referred to as the recovery of betterment as it does not relate to an up-zoning but rather to an infrastructure contribution from those who benefit. The two get confused when land is up-zoned and there is also infrastructure.

The idea of capturing this value was not at the forefront of financing public infrastructure expenditure until the cost of works began to exceed government budgets. Public–private partnerships were used throughout the world and became a primary source of infrastructure funding, especially in relation to toll roads. A study of their use in Canada in 2016 highlighted some important deficiencies, which could be said to be the reasons why value capture has become the current, viable alternative.[26] The cost of financing fell on the private sector and, with large and long projects, high gearing becomes burdensome, there are high transaction costs in preparing projects, the barriers to entry require government to give up profit to the private sector, and there is continued uncertainty, inflexibility, and difficult contract-management requirements. The government takes the ultimate risk, which can arise if the private party goes bankrupt.

---

25 Arnott and Steiglitz 1979.
26 Boardman, Siemiatycki and Vining 2016.

Where there is no legislative power for governments to collect value capture, there is 'silent' capture, where the developer is offered an up-zoning or development permission in return for a private agreement to provide funds for infrastructure. Where there is a legislative scheme, legal systems for value capture vary greatly. In the United States, the designation of Benefit Assessment Districts allows legal capture of value around areas of mass transit, and tax increment financing is used to raise property taxes according to the aggregated benefits of infrastructure. This use of property taxes is not necessarily available to other countries, which have different planning cultures and regulatory structures.[27]

5.3 Zoning amendments

In some countries, a strategic plan and a spatial plan do not attempt to cover an entire urban area but designate areas for future development and leaves it to a further plan to determine the details. In Israel, for instance, there are two forms of plan. The 'outline plan' is prepared by the local council as a wider, strategic plan and establishes the zones, the densities in those zones, and the consequent road network for the entire municipal area. 'Detailed plans' are made for particular sites or areas and indicate the specific land uses that are permitted on the initiative of the developer. When a developer seeks a building permit, the congruence of the application with the detailed plan and the outline plan is examined. Japan and Norway are other examples, cast in a different manner, of wider zoning leading to more detailed plans. In Tokyo, the *Act on Special Measures Concerning Urban Reconstruction 2002* allowed areas to be specially designated Special Urban Renaissance Districts, outside the master plan, which requires detailed development plans and zoning for each. In Norway, there are 'area zoning plans' for the larger areas and also 'detailed zoning plans' proposed by developers for smaller areas or particular projects.

Amending a spatial plan to allow new projects is perhaps the most common aspect of zoning administration. It is a statement that to reach the vision of the strategic plan, some areas require more thought and detailed proposals. *Miami 21* is a zoning scheme based on New Urbanism principles that has been amended 55 times from 2010 to 2016 to add new projects and specific requirements. The strategic plan, by providing for new projects, still requires that its vision for that area be maintained.

Project plans for particular developments, when completed, ideally need to find a place in the strategic plan but it is not so easily amended; it is often left as is. As the strategic plan is the culmination of years of research, community involvement and political infighting and lobbying, once it is complete, it is not usually challenged or its contents changed, even though there may be gaps in the plan.[28] It takes on a monolithic role in defining the area and it is rarely rethought from basics but undergoes changes indirectly by amendments to the spatial plan and zoning scheme.

The amendment of the spatial plan for particular projects in areas marked for future development may, at first, be seen as a refinement of the strategic plan, within the same vision and consistent with goals and aspirations. However, as the vision is fixed, amendments to spatial plans that carry a new vision or direction add great complexity as they find no natural place. The major initiative of the New York mayor, 'mandatory inclusionary

---

27   Root, van der Krabben and Spit 2015.
28   Berke and Goodschalk 2008.

Figure 5-3 Shinjuku renaissance district, Tokyo. Source: Google Earth.

housing', was derived from a political agenda requiring a share of all housing to be affordable. The agenda was implemented by an amendment to the *New York Zoning Resolution* in 2016. As it was not accounted for in the current comprehensive plan, it offered a new vision. As this new vision must be explained in theory and in practice, the amendment is over 50 pages and is difficult to understand.

Amendments to the zoning plan are, in fact, to be encouraged and considered to be good practice. They enforce the idea that, as market needs and political agendas change, there must be flexibility in zoning. These amendments, however, are considered on an ad hoc basis and are not part of the initial visioning or goals of strategic planning, which seek to create and promote a unitary vision of a community's future. The statement is made explicitly in the initial strategic plan that it and what follows in the zoning plan can be relied upon and has finality.

A problem is that the finality of the vision in the plan is stated in absolute terms, making its amendment uninviting. The *Portland, Oregon comprehensive plan*, for example, alludes to having fully met future needs by a vision statement setting out 'where the city aspires to be' and pronouncing goals and policies that 'provide the long-range planning direction for the development and redevelopment of the city.' The Comprehensive Plan Map is said to be a 'planning guide for spatially defining the desired land uses and development in Portland.' The future state shown on the plan map for Portland is presented as providing the best outcome for an area and therefore is offered as a conclusion and does not hint that it is subject to re-evaluation. When it reached this final form, it was meant to represent a consensus of the stakeholders' competing claims for what is best. As it took so long to produce, it is accepted by the community as the right planning answer and becomes fixed in the minds of all participants as the way forward.

This sense of finality is enhanced by the continued use and operation of the plan, as planners and elected officials develop the capacity to understand and digest its contents as the structure within which they work. There are other subtle factors that cement the concept that the strategic plan is fixed, such as its conformity with ingrained cultural ideals and the ethos of the community; the Australian idea that each family should have a quarter acre of land (known as the 'Australian dream') is not articulated but can be seen in the plans for strategic growth areas in every major city. The concentration on authority and order in Singapore creates that highly structured urban setting. The obvious emphasis in Shanghai on economic growth can be seen in the imposed and grand land-use plans.

It is important to realise that, although the spatial plan and zoning scheme are easily amended, the strategic plan is not easily amended and the vision becomes rigid and outdated. This affects the scope of any future amendment of the spatial plan and zoning requirements. This rigidity of the strategic plan encourages the belief that having a fixed vision is in fact conducive to the future of urban living and should only be amended if necessary. At first glance, it appears useful to have a fixed view because property values can be determined, predictability is necessary, and the system has to be clear and able to be understood. The consequence, however, is that the vision of the strategic plan becomes further removed from the actuality of what is happening in the city.

Historically the changing patterns of social problems are not reflected in strategic plans derived from a vision. As it is so difficult to amend the vision of a strategic plan, these problems are therefore not addressed in future plans. The issues plaguing urban areas are then addressed by reconstruction or gentrification or by removing them from the planning agenda and handing them to other agencies. For example, it is clear that public housing developments in many US cities are major areas of crime, but the strategic plans cannot address these issues, which resulted from bad visions and choices in housing development, transportation and associated employment areas. The *East Los Angeles community plan* did not address the poverty and crime of that area in 1978 and has never been changed to deal with extreme problems that threaten the fabric of those communities.

The inability to challenge the limited and entrenched vision of the historic strategic plan is not just a technical issue, creating a limited scope for zoning amendment, but rather it creates a social impediment that prevents cities from changing. The fixed vision imposes rigidity and holds back amendments that may be appropriate but vary from the original ideas. The lack of amendment to strategies in a strategic plan makes the plan a political and ideological statement rather than a dynamic document open to change. It is possible to contrast this with post-communist regimes that have had to tackle ideological and social issues in strategic planning, as there were no previous visions. In the Czech Republic, after the collapse of communism in 1989, there was an immediate move to devolve planning to local authorities.[29] The initial effect has been fragmented strategic plans and constant change.[30] However, this change has allowed the cities to be in transition, to develop and unfold in form and function. The needs and dimensions of social change are ongoing and should allow the strategic plan and spatial plan to move with what is necessary, such as the

---

29 Simpson and Chapman 1999.
30 Maier 2000.

desire of some countries to mix neoliberalism with socialism as the aspirations for urban growth,[31] or to use the planning system to address inequality as in South Africa.

This suggests that strategic plans should be able to be amended more easily and there needs to be new ways to open the scope for zoning amendments to deal with market changes, pressing urban issues, and new points of view. Flexibility in the vision as well as in the instruments is necessary for cities to adapt and for the planning process to have a meaningful role in social issues. However, this rarely occurs.

Conceptually, the problem lies in the strategic plan being linked with high goals and aspirations. It does not matter if these are the right visions for contemporary problems because the plan has made its mark on the community and decisions are made because of it. If a vision is that the waterfront should have high-rise buildings as an entry statement to a city, investment decisions, property prices, political alliances, council elections, infrastructure plans – all have been solidified around this vision. If, in ten years, the high-rise buildings have led to crime, alienation, ugly development and lack of light and space, the failure of the vision is greeted by new ways to enforce the original vision, rather than a new vision. Amendments follow the original vision, which has imprinted the city with its aspirations.

This is not a phenomenon that can be reversed, meaning that amendments to a spatial plan must indeed retain the original vision even if it is no longer sound. A new imposed vision will always appear suspect and controversial as it does not have the advantage of a well-worn vision. The Lahore, Pakistan Development Authority moved outside the strategic plan in 2015 to widen the beautiful tree-lined Canal Bank Road for a third lane, destroying the trees. The *Master plan for Lahore* had no mention of this project and the Supreme Court initially ordered the project be stayed as it had no inherent public purpose and then allowed it, forcing the court to evaluate the merits of the project as if it was the planning authority.[32]

5.4 Merging of policies in spatial plans

In the United States, the notion of the 'comprehensive plan', the name given to a combined strategic, spatial and regulatory plan, is that it is both a policy document that sets out the relevant visions, goals and considerations in non-legal language, as well as a more formal zoning ordinance to implement the spatial plan. There are therefore no policies external to the comprehensive plan. In New York State, the statute defines a 'comprehensive plan' as:

> the materials, written and/or graphic, including but not limited to maps, charts, studies, resolutions, reports and other descriptive material that identify the goals, objectives, principles, guidelines, policies, standards, devices and instruments for the immediate and long-range protection, enhancement, growth and development of the city. (*General Law*, sect. 27, 3a)

The *Standard State Zoning Enabling Act* in use in many parts of the United States, and followed in state legislation that authorises zoning, provides that the zoning ordinance (the

---

31 Hatcher and Thieme 2016.
32 *Lahore Bachao Tehrik v. Dr Iqbal Muhammad Chauhan, etc.*, CMA 3221/2012.

implementing plan) be 'in accordance with the comprehensive plan'. In one key decision, *Udell v. Haas*,[33] the New York Court of Appeals stated that 'one of the key factors' to be used by the courts in determining whether zoning is 'in accordance with a comprehensive plan' is whether forethought has been given to the community's land use problems. The court stated:

> Where a community, after a careful and deliberate review of 'the present and reasonably foreseeable needs of the community', adopts a general developmental policy for the community as a whole and amends its zoning law in accordance with that plan, courts can have some confidence that the public interest is being served.

The effect is that all policies, citizen participation, and long-range planning is in the comprehensive plan, and the zoning ordinance, being one part of the that grouping, gives effect to this plan. This has the positive effect of allowing a policy document (the comprehensive plan) to have legislative force and to restrict a planning scheme to what is necessary to enforce the policy. It allows a more refined understanding of the relationship of the strategic and spatial plan to the regulatory controls.

This concept is also prevalent in Canada, where, for example, the *Official plan* under the *Ontario Planning Act*[34] consists of one document that contains all of the planning options, the policies that are relevant, and also the land use standards and restrictions. A zoning by-law is then passed that must comply with the official plan; the by-law is merely the regulatory provisions and it is the official plan that is the focus of attention. The *Toronto official plan 2002* has five chapters: the first outlines the structure of the plan, the second the goals for the city (e.g. vital neighbourhoods), the third what is necessary to accomplish these goals, the fourth the land use designations and policies, and the fifth contains the development criteria.

This is also the system in Germany, where the spatial plan reflects state and federal policy and the local plan carries out the regulatory needs of the spatial plan but does not itself attempt to describe the goals and policies that are relevant. It is also the system across Scandinavia, where the comprehensive plan is not binding but dictates the development plan that contains the regulatory provisions, which must then strictly accord with the comprehensive plan.[35] This type of regime creates a direct link between the plan, the relevant policies and the regulatory provisions. It differs from those systems where the zoning ordinance or planning scheme is the sole legal instrument (as in Australia) and is divorced from the strategic plan.

The most complex aspect of the relationship of plans and policies is when policies are unofficial. This is an ethical issue related to the acceptability of controls used by the planning authority through an agenda decided behind closed doors. This is more deleterious than is apparent as the consistency and transparency of open decision making accounts for much of the trust that is placed in the planning process. An important study of planning in Indonesia explained that it is primarily leadership, in the sense of an authority pursuing a clear articulated planning policy agenda, that fosters co-operation and trust.[36] If there is

---

33   *Udell v. Haas*, 21 N.Y.2d 463, 470 (1968).
34   *Ontario Planning Act*, RSO 1990, c.p.13.
35   BSR Interreg III B Project, 'Promoting Spatial Development by Creating Common Mindscapes', for Sweden, Finland and Norway: http://commin.org/en/commin/.

little trust in the openness of government, the leadership of the planning authority is weakened. As there are so many stakeholders involved in planning, the presence of unofficial policies outside the plan or prevailing sentiments that emerge in council meetings but are not shared, take away faith in the planning regime.

The existence of a set of policies outside the plan, even though official, creates difficulties for those who seek to understand the regime. A state policy for lot sizes may dictate the process for those seeking to subdivide but there may be no guide in the local planning scheme that explains how the policy is to be interpreted. In many countries the system is only understood by those who are planning experts, or 'statutory planners' as they are called, who know how the pieces of the puzzle fit. It is incumbent on policy makers to fully explain the path that an interested developer should follow to navigate the policies and plans but this does not appear to exist. At most, it is stated, as in the *Berlin plan*, that there are multiple documents that must be examined, and there is a brochure that explains in general terms how they are related. If no guide or roadmap can be found, the system is only understandable by those who are experts.

5.5 Zoning goals

The goals for zones for a named purpose are not self-evident from the name given. A 'mixed-use zone' or a 'Residential B zone' require deductive reasoning as to the purpose, having regard to what uses are meant to occur. As a consequence, the original, underlying goals of a zone are often forgotten.

In the United States, many zoning ordinances (the regulatory part of the comprehensive plan) explain in narrative form the reason for the zone and the goals that are to be achieved, drawing from a summary of the comprehensive, strategic plan or elaborating on specifics for particular districts. An example is in the Little Rock, Arkansas zoning ordinance:

> The West Little Rock District is a stable area with much of the land developed. The current zoning patterns in most cases have been established for many years. The plan does not anticipate dramatic changes in the future . . .

Another approach to explaining the goals of the zoning controls is in the Netherlands (through the *Vijfde Nota plan: the fifth memorandum on spatial planning*) to show maps with layers oriented to the various urban flows: traffic flows, ecological flows, water flows, and infrastructure networks. This gives a better picture of the spatial orientation that underlies the choices made and the goals enunciated. It also contains scenarios in map form, which allows an understanding of what is possible and the effect of different alternatives.

Since sustainability has become the major platform for the choice of goals in a strategic plan, the issue arises of how to express that as a goal as the basis in whole or in part for a specific zone in the spatial plan. The UK *Planning policy statement no. 1* provided for the delivery of sustainable development in the making of plans as well as in deciding applications for development permission. It related the concept of sustainability to social cohesion and personal wellbeing, thereby expanding the range of relevant considerations

---

36   Fahmi et al. 2016.

to any planning issue that touched on quality of life matters but making it difficult to be clear about why areas are considered in a particular way in a development plan.

What is significant about that policy statement is that it contained a detailed enunciation of the principles relating to sustainable development that became an underlying layer and a set of general guidelines in the making of spatial plans, with the idea that all of the following would be somehow behind the purpose of the land use designations:[37]

1. Recognise the needs and broader interests of the community to secure a better quality of life for the community as a whole.
2. Ensure that plans are drawn up over appropriate time scales, and do not focus on the short term or ignore longer-term impacts and the needs of communities in the future. Planning authorities should consider both whether policies have short term benefits which may have long-term costs, but also whether short-term detriments (which are capable of being mitigated) may be offset by longer-term benefits which are realistically achievable.
3. Not impose disproportionate costs, in terms of environmental and social impacts, or by unnecessarily constraining otherwise beneficial economic or social development.
4. Have regard to the resources likely to be available for implementation and the costs likely to be incurred, and be realistic about what can be implemented over the period of the plan.
5. Take account of the range of effects (both negative and positive) on the environment, as well as the positive effects of development in terms of economic benefits and social wellbeing. Effects should be properly identified and assessed through the sustainability appraisal process, taking account of the current quality of the environment in the area and any existing environmental issues relevant to the plan.
6. Ensure that plans and policies are properly based on analysis and evidence. Where the outcome of that analysis and evidence remains uncertain, makers should exercise and demonstrate soundly based judgement, taking account of the other principles set out in this paragraph. Where justifiable on the basis of the evidence available, a precautionary approach to proposals for development may be necessary.
7. Take full account of the need for transparency, information and participation.
8. Recognise that the impact of proposed development may adversely affect people who do not benefit directly. Local planning authorities can use planning conditions or obligations to ameliorate such impacts.

This policy statement was replaced in March 2012 by the *National planning policy framework* and, for the purpose of simplifying the policy statements, the detailed concepts were replaced by more general words that divided sustainability into three functional parts: an economic role, a social role, and an environmental role:[38]

- **an economic role**: contributing to building a strong, responsive and competitive economy, by ensuring that sufficient land of the right type is available in the right places and at the right time to support growth and innovation; and by identifying and co-ordinating development requirements, including the provision of infrastructure;

---

37 Office of the Deputy Prime Minister 2005, 10–11.
38 Communities and Local Government Committee 2012.

- **a social role**: supporting strong, vibrant and healthy communities, by providing the supply of housing required to meet the needs of present and future generations; and by creating a high quality built environment, with accessible local services that reflect the community's needs and support its health, social and cultural wellbeing; and
- **an environmental role**: contributing to protecting and enhancing our natural, built and historic environment; and, as part of this, helping to improve biodiversity, use natural resources prudently, minimise waste and pollution, and mitigate and adapt to climate change including moving to a low carbon economy.

As sustainability is the basic rubric for modern planning, it needs to be explained generally for all spatial plans, as it has in the United Kingdom, but also *specifically* in zoning systems as to how these principles apply to zones or areas: which are designated because of an economic role or a social role. The various definitions and principles in the UK policies, although explicating sustainability, do not explain the treatment of a particular area. By creating the general goals that any local plan must follow, they excuse enunciation of goals for specific areas, thereby making only a weak connection between the spatial plan and the explanation of what it is trying to achieve.

The general trend is to place sustainability goals outside the actual regulatory instrument in a separate document and accordingly it is likely that it will be decided that there is no need for explanation in the strategic or regulatory plan. When this is the case, a specific statement of the effect of this goal for each relevant zone is lacking and the relationship of sustainability to planning cannot be determined.

Instead of having a wide concept of sustainability, more specificity can be achieved by extracting particular goals for certain areas or by setting out measures that indicate the sustainability benchmarks for the zoning or area chosen. In some cases, where zones are based on specific, enunciated principles, the connections may be obvious, as in Florida, where there are sustainability measures for discouraging urban sprawl, supporting energy-efficient development patterns, and reducing greenhouse emissions in specific zones.[39]

In Portland, Oregon, the Bureau of Planning and Sustainability assigns a sustainability expert to each district to advise and provide that component of the planning process to local councils that are responsible for zones and regulations. The bureau has other responsibilities, but the liaison between a sustainability bureau and a district planning process can prevent that process being too general about sustainability. It can also provide specific goals that define the purpose of the zones for individual areas.

The difficulty is that all attempts to link sustainability to zones, although aiming at the same general goals, change the emphasis and meaning of sustainability for its particular purpose. As well, these definitions are vague and not able to be measured, so there is no method to understand if the goals are met by the zoning designation. The UK goal of 'supporting strong, vibrant and healthy communities' is unlikely to be understood as the basis for an area in a spatial plan.

A better definition that can be applied to particular zones may be that contained in the 'Natural Step' measure of sustainability[40], which provides that all development and activities have to be measured and explained against these four conditions:

---

39 Fla. Statt. Ann., sect. 163.3177(6)(a) (West Supp. 2009); Salkin 2009.
40 James and Lahti 2004.

- nature is not subject to systematically increasing concentrations of substances extracted from the Earth's crust;
- nature is not subject to systematically increasing concentrations of substances produced as a byproduct of society;
- nature is not subject to systematically increasing degradation by physical means;
- people are not subject to conditions that systematically undermine their capacity to meet their needs.

The Natural Step criteria, placing nature or ecological considerations as the centrepiece of sustainability goals for spatial planning, are in use in plan making in Sweden (where it was developed) for 70 cities and towns and is also used in Whistler, British Columbia (*Whistler 2020: moving towards a sustainable future*). It appears to be the only system that creates an evidence-based, working definition of sustainability that can be applied as a goal for specified areas and measured for qualitative assessment.

5.6 Strategic environmental assessment of the spatial plan

As sustainability and triple bottom line (or quadruple bottom line) assessment underlies the making of a plan and the choice of areas, there needs to be a means to examine the efficacy of their application in the spatial plan and legal standards. This is difficult as the sustainability measures are worded in general terms, quantitative tools for assessment are not available, and the concluded balance of economic growth and ecological issues is too vague to be expressed with any certainty. The concept has developed of a 'strategic environmental assessment' (SEA) to at least measure the cumulative effects of a plan, including its zoning designations, on the environment. This avoids the question of explaining the TBL balance as the basis for a zone and focuses only on the environmental impact of what is proposed. It has the effect of bringing cumulative environmental impacts, an aspect of sustainability, into practical focus before a spatial plan is implemented. As it requires an evidence base and rigorous testing, it becomes a quantitative method of assessing the implications of the zoning choices.

The need for assessment of a wider plan at the plan-making stage by an SEA, rather than just an environmental assessment of a particular project, is traceable to the 1969 US *National Environmental Policy Act*. The idea was advanced in the 2003 *Kyiv (SEA) Protocol* on the use of an SEA in plan making that came into effect in 2010 and was ratified in 2016 by 28 countries. The protocol specifically requires consideration of an SEA in the making of a plan or program, defined as (art. 6):

> 'Strategic environmental assessment' means the evaluation of the likely environmental, including health effects, which comprises the determination of the scope of an environmental report and its preparation, the carrying-out of public participation and consultations, and the taking into account of the environmental report and the results of the public participation and consultations in a plan or programme.

However, the purpose and possible scope of analysing the cumulative effects of a special plan by an SEA have not been applied consistently. The European Union has a directive that an SEA is automatically required for plans and programs.[41] However, the directive is limited to the effects on certain sensitive industries such as waste-water management and tourism for certain types of land use plans (art. 3b), and for specific projects listed in Annexes I and II of another directive.[42] Other plans and programs, which set the framework for future development consents for projects, are subject to assessment if an examination, according to the complex criteria laid down in Annex II to the directive, shows that they are liable to have significant effects on the environment.

The European Union Directive for an SEA applies 'upstream' to certain public plans, while the longstanding Environmental Impact Assessment (EIA) Directive that calls for environmental assessment of development projects applies 'downstream' to public and private projects. The objectives of the SEA for the limited set of public plans are expressed in terms of 'sustainable development', whereas the aims of the EIA are purely an environmental assessment of new development.

The relationship between the SEA and an EIA is not completely clear. An assessment of the SEA process in 2009 found that there was confusion as to which project needed an EIA and which an SEA. It was concluded as to the relevance of an SEA for designated projects in a plan:

> A majority of MS [member states] particularly mentioned the contribution of the SEA to an improved organisation and structure of the whole planning procedure, regarding this as a positive element. In particular, the formal requirements of consultation with environmental authorities and the public have led to increased transparency in the planning procedures.[43]

The Danish *Planning Act*[44] requires that significant projects must be pre-identified in the plan as requiring an EIA, thus combining the SEA with the EIA. This would mean that an area zoned where there is vulnerable land can include a requirement that there be an EIA. The Danish act states:

> Projects that are likely to have significant effects on the environment shall not be initiated before guidelines are produced in the municipal plan on the location and design of the project with an accompanying environmental impact assessment (sect. 11g).

This is in keeping with the EU Directive on EIA Screening of 2011.[45] That directive requires member states to identify certain named projects in advance to be assessed, but it also incorporates the more ad hoc test of whether the project is likely to have significant effects on the environment. It is clear that this remains a complicated process.

A German evaluation of the SEA process[46] indicated that it would be useful at the spatial plan-making stage because it is necessary to understand cumulative impacts and an EIA is only suitable for single projects. The SEA also has the advantage of focusing a

---

41 2001/42/EC9 (Strategic Environmental Assessment).
42 85/337/EEC.
43 Commission of the European Communities 1997, 9.
44 *Consolidated Act No. 812 of 21 June 2007.*
45 Directive 2011/92/EU of the European Parliament.
46 Joint paper of 18 Central European Countries (CADSES), *Best practice handbook for strategic environmental assessment (SEA)*; 'isoteia' model, July 2006.

plan-making authority on what areas are vulnerable, allowing zones to be created to reflect that vulnerability, providing a wider forum for citizen participation than just the planning process, encouraging the consideration of sustainability issues, and suggesting consideration of land use alternatives that cannot be considered at the EIA stage.

A distinct benefit of an SEA for a spatial plan is the ability to assess its cumulative aspects resulting from zone designations and land use controls rather than having to wait for the environmental impact of a future project. It prompts a wider examination of alternatives and an assessment of whether individual development possibilities will have an impact over time as that is not always readily apparent when a strategic plan opens possibilities for longer-range development. The cause-effect relationships of decisions can also be evaluated as well as its impact on resources and the environment.

There are multiple methods that can be used for a determination of the cumulative impacts of a spatial plan.[47] One method is to establish baselines for valued components of the environment, then predict the cumulative impacts of potential development and compare the potential to the baselines; this will suggest mitigation measures and restrict the planning choices for a zone. Another method is to identify possible cumulative impacts based on sustainability principles that are wider than ecosystem impingement. A further method is to examine what are the likely development possibilities over time and the sequence of development in order to determine the manner in which the cumulative impacts will progress.

The scale of an SEA determines what can be included in observing the cumulative impacts. However, there is a case that the wider the area covered by an SEA, 'the less likely a particular effect is to be identified as being significant, because more other sources of effect get captured in the analysis.'[48] It is also the case that generalised assessment of the impact of policies will probably be ignored when the direct effects of a plan are considered. There is also the problem that, if the SEA is for a narrow area, it might not be undertaken as it is such a complicated process. A study has shown that, at least in California, an SEA is neglected at the level of a local plan because of a lack of environmental goals, no specific commitments to assessing cumulative impacts, no specific tools to provide assessment, and the absence of any monitoring programs to examine the effect of implementation following assessment.[49]

The zoning of land is the expression of all future development possibilities and failure to assess the cumulative impact means that sustainability goals can never effectively be analysed. An SEA is the means of assessment because it must be in accordance with sustainability principles. The International Association for Impact Assessment has prepared the *Strategic environment assessment performance criteria*.[50] It emphasises the nature of the connection of land use with sustainability as a means to measure the impact of zoning and thus development choices. It also suggests that it be carried out with full participation of all government bodies and communities affected.

---

47 Bragagnolo and Geneletti 2012.
48 Bragagnolo and Geneletti 2012, 44.
49 Tang 2009.
50 International Association for Impact Assessment 2002.

5.7 Best practice

Zoning has existed in one form or another in all planning systems from ancient times. It is a natural extension of the desire to separate incompatible uses and will always be part of any regime. The drivers for best practice are to make the choices for a zone or area understood, to be flexible, and to accord with sustainability principles.

5.7.1 Explanations

It is best to enunciate the patent and hidden goals of a spatial plan in all aspects for a user of the system to understand why choices have been made. If this is found in the strategic plan and not the spatial plan, references should be made as to where a reader can find that link. A successful spatial plan will explain the basis for zoning fully, honestly and frankly. The method that can be used is to have a short narrative of the vision for the zone and indicate how the density controls reflect that vision. As with the *Berlin plan*, this does not need to be in the spatial plan, which is merely a map with land use designations, or in the regulations that permit or restrict, but in an external document for the public.

Although it is convenient to provide for a common set of zone names, it would be useful if each zone name was accompanied in the spatial plan itself with a short explanation of what that zone name conveys. There are no instances that can be found where a spatial plan indicates why the zone boundaries have been created. Therefore, if it is possible to explain the reason for the scale of the zone, such as 'this zone is a protected area because it has unique flora and fauna and that uniqueness ends at the highway and a new zone allowing residential development begins', this will enhance the understanding of the spatial plan.

It is important that an individual be able to ascertain into what zone their land falls. This might seem fundamental, yet there are many spatial plans for large cities, such as New York, where it is very difficult to discover the zoning of a particular parcel. To accomplish this, it is necessary to have a single map designed just for that purpose or an online service where that information is provided. Often spatial plans have many markings in zones to indicate overlays or other controls that require observance. A map that gives an initial zoning picture can then direct the user to further maps that contain additional restrictions, such as heritage protection or height restrictions. These comments support the principle that a spatial plan and accompanying regulations should not be created for experts but for the community. This is difficult as the eventual plan will be complicated because of development and new policies over time, but ideally the basic question of the origin and nature of the zoning should be able to be answered.

5.7.2 Positive uses

In prescribing uses in zones, it is best to elaborate the positive ways that land can be employed in a zone, further refining the purpose of a zoning choice. It is important that some methodology is applied to determine the urban morphology of an existing area to better indicate why the proposed positive uses are encouraged. This may not be covered by a narrative for a zone or a spatial plan as that is usually accompanied by restrictions that require a deduction as to what is required, such as a high-rise building not exceeding a certain plot ratio and of only so many stories. Providing examples of what is sought in a spatial plan, or in a strategic plan that is referenced, will better explain the zone and encourage compliance.

5.7.3 Amendments

Best practice is to apply the full measure of community participation to significant changes of zoning in the strategic plan or in the spatial plan. This prevents the original vision in the strategic plan limiting the changes. This review of the vision usually awaits a periodic examination of the strategic plan, but when there is a significant change in the spatial plan, or where the zoning leaves further consideration of a project possible, it is time to re-examine the vision.

The spatial plan must be seen as flexible and the amendment or variation process be accepted as part of the plan by explaining that amendments are part of the regime. An amendment should not be seen as an exception to the vision but rather a re-examination of the aspirations and goals. Treating it as rigid means that the amendment process is cumbersome, time consuming and political. It is only rigid because it is captured by a historic vision that has, by continued compliance, become inflexible.

For there to be flexibility, it is essential to understand that the zoning plan, based on a vision or goal, is indeed not final and is subject to market forces and changes in the community. Therefore, within the strategic plan it is best to state that it was made at a specific point in time and should not be regarded as rigid and incapable of change. It should also be stated that the planning authority is open to amendments to the spatial plan to adjust for changes to the market, or for other circumstances, such as social issues. If this statement is not made, the strategic plan provisions restrict change and innovation.

In countries where there is development control, it is often the case that an appeal is available to an applicant who has been refused permission to develop; in Malaysia there is the Appeal Board, in Hong Kong there is the Planning Appeal Board Panel. Appeals against a refusal to obtain a rezoning are not allowed in the same manner because the decision on zoning affects the entire community and not just the applicant. There is technically no reason why the decision on zoning should not be subject to an appeal by the applicant. A development project that is subject to an appeal may have a greater effect than a rezoning of an area. The consequence of not allowing such appeals are protracted, emotion-laden law suits where the community, or a part of it, is frustrated and loses faith in the planning process. There are many cases where the fight against a rezoning by environmental groups seeking to protect an area have long, bitter histories, such as the battle to preserve the extraordinary tropical rainforest site of Gunung Leuser National Park in Aceh, Indonesia. There is no basis in law or planning practice not to extend appeals to rezonings where the vision can be re-examined.

5.7.4 Policies

All policies, official or unofficial, that may be used in determining the interpretation of an amendment to a spatial plan must be fully available. It is incumbent on the planning authority to explain how to navigate the policies, their nature, and their application. It is not enough to merely publish a list of policies or to direct the community to planning experts; there must be a guide to their use and how they interact with the spatial plan.

It is not enough to draw on general sustainability policies to justify a zoning designation, even when they might be able to be deduced for specific areas. All of the principles of sustainability that apply must be explained for each zone so that they can be considered explicitly for a zoning amendment. This does not need to be in the spatial plan, complicating assessment of designations of areas on a map, but best practice requires an external document, such as a policy, that explains the manner in which the principles have been applied to a specific area. If this does not appear, then merely having a principle of balancing the environment with economic development makes no sense as the basis for an economic zone in which areas are protected.

Ideally, unofficial policies should not be allowed to form the basis for a zoning or planning decision. If the policy is not published, it should not be taken into account in a decision to rezone. However, once it has been published, it should be accepted regardless of its history.

5.7.5 Value capture

As value capture appears to be an intrusion into property rights, it must be explained fully. The reasons for its use and the exact methods of exaction must also be completely justified. The greatest difficulty is that betterment levies based on an up-zoning are often confused with contributions that are sought because of the provision of infrastructure. Land that is up-zoned may benefit from that infrastructure, or land may be up-zoned because infrastructure is already provided, and this is the true basis for the levy. The value should not be captured twice by betterment and infrastructure contribution and it is best practice to specify the reason for any levy in terms of betterment and contribution.

5.7.6 Strategic environmental assessment (SEA)

An SEA is the only method to justify the allocation of land uses. It should be made mandatory and subject to the full measure of community participation. The SEA has the advantage of justifying all zones by examining the cumulative impact of a spatial plan. It serves the function of proving all claims in relation to sustainability as the basis for a plan as it examines carefully whether the outcome has struck a balance between environmental issues and economic growth. For example, rezoning of farmland may, in fact, decrease the capacity of sustainable farming. Although the SEA is not directly related to every consequence of a plan, in practice, the full range of uses and their collective impact brings up many of these issues that otherwise might not be analysed.

The SEA process presents an opportunity for the community to participate in the evaluation of zone choices and provides the means for community engagement in the *spatial* plan rather than just the strategic plan. The SEA process can also reflect back deficiencies in the strategic plan and offer alternatives to be considered when that plan is addressed. It has the effect of having the vision re-examined, which can have an influence on zoning amendments.

The role of the SEA is to inform decisions that are to be made. It does this by pointing out the positive and negative aspects of proposals, such as zones on a map and restrictions in those zones. It can predict what the consequence of a spatial plan may be in terms of the environment and can suggest alternatives to mitigate any negative outcomes. The time and expense involved is the only perceivable disadvantage of the process. However, best practice is to have an SEA for spatial plans.

The OECD Development Assessment Committee in 2006 produced guidelines for the effective application of an SEA. These conclude that pilot projects should be undertaken initially to establish precedents and practices and that SEA processes be introduced gradually.[51] Best practice is said to be, among other factors, integrating the SEA with existing policy and planning structures and encouraging stakeholder participation, while recognising that its success depends on the capacity of the planning authority to carry out the process and act on the results.

---

51   Organisation for Economic Co-operation and Development 2006.

6
Development control

'Development control' is the phrase applied to a form of planning control where a planning authority makes an individual determination on a case-by-case basis of an application by a developer for the use and development of land. It is, by definition, concerned with the process of the making of an application for development on land and the determination of that application by a planning authority.

Development control is a system for the individual, one-at-a-time determination of the suitability of the application for the intended site as opposed to the creation of an earlier strategic, spatial plan that determines land use rights and opportunities in advance. When the emphasis in a regime is on development control, the importance of a land use plan is therefore diminished and any plan is viewed as a guide. The land use plan in a system of development control is then only tone factor in the determination along with other considerations that relate to the effect of the use on the area where it will be situated. These other factors include the impact of the proposal on the amenity of the existing area, the resulting externalities caused by the use such as traffic and noise, and the congruence of what is proposed with policies of the state or local authority enunciated from time to time.

In contrast to development control, strategic planning implies that all the decisions about the suitability of a particular use in a defined area are pre-determined by a community vision. This is achieved by extensive community participation, subsequent goal setting, evolved strategies, and specific targets. This is why planning practice uses the term 'plan-led' to refer to the primacy of strategic planning in setting the uses and development of land. In a plan-led system, the emphasis on development control is reduced because decisions have already been made – they are the essence of the planning process that should not be disturbed by exemptions and ad hoc decisions.

As the system of development control reacts to an application, accepting input only from immediate neighbours, it lacks the larger consultation brought about by full community participation in the strategic plan. The advantage of a larger consultation process that leads to a vision that is manifested in a plan is that it is the balancing of different stakeholder interests in a negotiated outcome. The benefit of development control, in terms of consultation, is a focus on the immediately affected community and the impact of a specific application, thereby refining the vision for that area. It also creates a sense of empowerment by its immediacy in those who object to a proposal that is not available for participation in more general planning ideas, such as choosing growth areas.

The English land use system is recognised as a prime example of development control and is a planning tradition that has found its way into other countries that have drawn on that structure through adoption of English law. The English system of development control is a consequence of a specific turning point in English planning and developed from a series of cumulative historical developments.[1] The starting point was the Elizabethan Poor Laws in the late 1600s, which provided for improved standards of health. When health reform was formulated into law, it included a system of zoning to separate out discordant, harmful uses. This plan-led system remained as the principal form of control until 1947. The government of the day became focused on the financial effects of planning decisions following a war-time appraisal by the Uthwatt Committee that those who were affected negatively by planning should receive compensation and those who benefited should pay a percentage of that increase. This occurred, as revealed by the terms of reference, to stabilise the value of land for the reconstruction effort. The committee highlighted that the zoning system created a 'purely individualistic approach to land ownership' and that planning 'must advance within the condition of the society it is designed to serve'.[2] Accordingly, seen from a societal point of view and establishing the real value of land, it was apparent from Uthwatt that every time a decision was made granting the right to develop, one landowner was benefited and another suffered loss. As these development decisions had a financial effect on individuals, it was recommended that they should be made by the central government. In consequence, the right to develop or use land was no longer permitted as of right or part of the bundle of rights granted by property ownership. Instead, those rights were nationalised by the state, which was required to make the critical decisions that resulted in compensation or betterment levies. This is the system that persists: a case-by-case development control system in which rights are not granted by the plan but rather by the granting of permission by the state.

The English development control system does not exist in a vacuum in whicha every decision is totally ad hoc. The 1990 *Town and Country Planning Act* provided that each local authority in metropolitan areas should produce a 'unitary development plan', which is a strategic plan with two parts. The first is a statement of the local planning authorities' policies and the second 'a written statement formulating in such detail as the authority think appropriate . . . their proposals for development and other use of land in their area' as well as a map 'showing the proposals on a geographic basis' (sect. 12.4). This is very much the product and basis of a plan-led system. However, the act also provides (sect. 57.1) that 'planning permission is required for the carrying out of any development of land', where development is defined as the carrying out of building works or a material change in use. The planning permission conveys the right, not the development plan, as it is provided (sect. 75.1) that the permission, once obtained, 'runs with the land' for the benefit of future owners.

When considering the application for planning permission, the planning authority considers the development plan (sect. 70.2) and other material considerations. The plan is only one of the considerations to which the authority must have 'regard'. The strategic plan is therefore secondary to the case-by-case determination of an application for development.

---

1 Booth 2003, chap. 2.
2 Uthwatt 1942.

Planning in the City of Sheffield illustrates how the development control system operates in relation to a spatial plan. There is a 2009 *Core strategy,* which is a spatial plan. It is clear in that strategy, as it would be in any plan-led system, that certain areas are suitable for particular uses, such as employment lands, new housing, and offices. The 'key diagram' accompanying the core strategy shows wide areas that appear as zones, but there is lack of specificity as to boundaries and activities for specific properties. The differences with zoning are twofold: the spatial vision in the core strategy is to be achieved through policies rather than a zoning map and regulations that prohibit uses, and the map is broad-pbrush and not specific as to properties.

The *Town and Country Planning (General Permitted Development) (England) Order 2015* exempts some uses from the need for permission, essentially conferring a right. There is a category of 'permitted development' for which planning permission is granted; for instance, the enlargement, improvement or other alteration of a dwelling house. The order also provides for 'development not permitted' for each such use class, as for instance, creating a higher roof through alterations.

The allocation of areas for different uses in this system of development control is a form of zoning created as a matter of policy rather than a spatial plan, and is a relevant consideration in the determination of an application for development. Since this policy is a relevant consideration in granting planning permission, the result is very similar to a plan-led system but without rigid zone boundaries. As one commentator has put it: 'although separation between land uses is embedded in the system, the legal boundaries around residential uses (especially single family) seem more porous than in America.'[3]

Development control with some underlying plan-led strategic planning is a common form of planning control. It arises directly as the essential structure of a planning system or when a plan-led system leaves growth centres or activity areas subect to future approvals. However, it is rare that there is a pure system of development control where a case-by-case analysis is the only method and approach. In all Australian states there is a zoning plan categorising each use but also, in most local authorities, the system makes almost every use and development subject to permission, creating a mix of development control and plan-led control. In New South Wales, the City of Blacktown *Local environmental plan 2015,* for example, has 20 different zones and for each zone the plan indicates what uses are permitted without consent, the narrow use for which the zone is contemplated, those that are prohibited, and a very large range of uses that require development permission. In some zones, such as the High Density Residential Zone or Neighbourhood Centre Zone, no development is permitted as of right, turning this into a development control system. For High Density Residential Zones, for example, the plan states:

Zone R4: High Density Residential

1. Objectives of Zone

    - To provide for the housing needs of the community within a high density residential environment.
    - To provide a variety of housing types within a high density residential environment.

---

3   Hirt 2012.

- To enable other land uses that provide facilities or services to meet the day to day needs of residents.
- To enable certain activities to be carried out within the zone that do not adversely affect the amenity of the neighbourhood.
- To permit residential flat buildings in locations close to public transport hubs and centres.

2. Permitted without consent

- Nil.

3. Permitted with consent

- Boarding houses; Building identification signs; Business identification signs; Child care centres; Community facilities; Dwelling houses; Emergency service facilities; Environmental facilities; Environmental protection works; Exhibition homes; Exhibition villages; Flood mitigation works; Home occupations; Hotel or motel accomodation; Information and education facilities; Neighbourhood shops; Places of public worship; Public administration buildings; Recreation areas; Recreation facilities (indoor); Recreation facilities (outdoor); Residential flat buildings; Respite day care centres; Restaurants or cafes; Roads; Seniors housing; Serviced apartments; Shop top housing; Take away food and drink premises; Water reticulation systems.

4. Prohibited

- Any development not specified in item 2 or 3.

There are countries that have based their planning systems on the English model and therefore mimic that development control regime. Sri Lanka and India, as examples, have followed a development control model. As with the English legislation, the *Maharastra Regional and Town Planning Act 1966* in India provides for the creation of development plans but contains the critical section (sect. 43.1), which states that no person can carry out development or change a use without permission and (sect. 46) that the planning authority shall have due regard to the development plan.

The disadvantages of a system that relies primarily on development control is obvious. An individual has no way of knowing in advance the ultimate outcome of an application to develop, except in cases where the use or development is allowed by a permissive device such as a use-classes order. It could be said that,th although a right to use and develop land is not defined or granted in the development plan, the importance of the development plan as a relevant consideration grants an inchoate right. This arises because of the inevitable link between a development control decision and the plan as the legislative provisions require that any planning permission decision be in accordance with the development plan, unless material conditions indicate otherwise.[4] As well, in England, the *National planning policy framework* (para. 14) suggests that applications should be approved without delay when there is compliance with the development plan.

---

4 Hardwicke Parish Council 2013.

The basis for a comprehensive plan in the United States, a plan-led system, conveys a series of rights which must be exercised for the good of the community because of the legal doctrine that legislative power must be exercised for overall community benefit and not for one individual more than others.[5] Accordingly, the emphasis is on the entire community and not on single applications. This is the test that is applied when a developer seeks to create a special zoning for an individual block: the benefit that accrues to a single owner has to be justified as advancing community interest.

It became apparent in planning practice in the United States in the 1970s[6] that a zoning ordinance should be considered ineffective unless the quality of the strategic plan fully supported the community interest. This investment in good planning for the entire community,s and the legislative requirement for comprehensive planning, strengthened the reliance on the strategic plan as the basis for any exemption, such as a spot rezoning for a particular project.[7] It was a realisation that there can be a consistent approach only where exemptions stood on the firm base of a comprehensive plan. The consequence of the exemptions relying on the comprehensive plan is that they are considered only a 'variance' from the plan and are to be made with regard to, or consistent with, the plan. Accordingly, it is stated that variances had only a practical effect to:

> afford a [safety valve] against individual hardships, to provide relief against unnecessary and unjust invasions of the right of private property, to provide a flexibility of procedure necessary to the protection of constitutional rights, and to keep the law 'running on an even keel'.[8]

A variance, a form of development control, is therefore designed to operate only when there is hardship in complying with the comprehensive plan and not as a general system of development control. Accordingly, variances historically were used sparingly throughout the United States.[9] It has been observed that, beginning in the 1970s, the safety valve developed a 'steady leak'[10] and that variances are now not only commonplace but, where they are sought, they are frequently granted.[11] In all of these exceptions, the comprehensive plan has a major role in guiding variance decisions. Exceptions have increased over the last decade to the point that the US system now has characteristics of a development control system but the existence of the plan remains the cornerstone of evaluating the efficacy of decision making.'[12]

There are two types of variance. The first is referred to as a 'use variance'. As an example, the Summit, New Jersey, development rto egulations provide that an application can be made to a zoning board of aardjustment for variation to 'a use or principal structure in a district restricted against such use or principal structure'. The other type of variance is

---

5 Kiefer 1960.
6 Rogers 1979.
7 Sullivan 1997.
8 McQuillin 1983.
9 Sampson 2007.
10 Weaver and Babcock 1979.
11 Ownes 2004.
12 Sullivan 2010.

in terms of building standards such as height and open space and is accordingly called an 'area variance' or a 'minor variance'.

A use variance is effectively a rezoning. It is a necessary safety valve where a zoning system is relatively rigid, which is the nature of legal instruments that are inherently prescriptive. Many tests for the granting of use variances have emerged. In the *New York Town Law*, it is provided that a variance is possible '[w]here there are practical difficulties or unnecessary hardships in the way of carrying out tlhe strict letter of [local] ordinances', provided that 'the spirit of the ordinance shall be observed, public safety and welfare secured and substantial justice done.' In 2006, this was amended to add more specific criteria:[13]

1. No such use variance shall be granted by a board of appeals without a showing by the applicant that applicable zoning regulations and restrictions have caused unnecessary hardship. In order to prove such unnecessary hardship the applicant shall demonstrate to the board of appeals that for each and every permitted use under the zoning regulations for the particular district where the property is located,
   A. the applicant cannot realize a reasonable return, provided that lack of return is substantial as demonstrated by competent financial evidence;
   B. that the alleged hardship relating to the property in question is unique, and does not apply to a substantial portion of the district or neighborhood;
   C. that the requested use variance, if granted, will not alter the essential character of the neighborhood; and
   D. that the alleged hardship has not been self-created.

The Canadian system, modelled on the US notion of a comprehensive plan, made spot zonings, where a rezoning was given for particular parcels of land, the safety valve, creating a de facto system of development control.[14] This has evolved in the last tenspe years to allow greater flexibility, and a 'minor variance' has been interpreted as having a flexible meaning, expanding the scope of exemptions.[15]

The use of the system of 'aspecial permits' in the United States is similar to a system of development control. Unlike an amendment to a zoning ordinance or a minor variance from a zoning restriction, a special use permit requires an adjudication by a planning authority of an application.[16] The City of Phoenix, Arizona, for example, requires special permits for such uses as a religious retreat facility, quarrying, car yards, trailer parks, or the conversion of apartments to a motel. Accordingly, the development control aspect is employed when there is a higher level of scrutiny required for a use.

Special permits are not anomalies and arise directly from the historical development of zoning. The US splanning system grew out of the *New York Zoning Ordinance 1916*, which was concerned primarily with the effect of shadowing from large buildings. It employed a set of standards similar to a building code. From that concept, development was allowed as of right if the building complied with the code. It was realised in 1961 that conformity with building codes led to areas with uniform height and bulk and the zon-

---

13 *New York Town Law*, sect. 267b 2.
14 Kumar 2005.
15 2008 *CanLII* 52618 (Ont. Div. Ct).
16 *Arnel Dev. Co. v. City of Costa Mesa* 620 P.2d 565 (Cal. 1980).

ing ordinance was amended that year to create 'special districts' that offered flexibility, especially if low-income housing was provided or other benefits, such as theatres, were supplied.

The difference is one of emphasis: in development control there is a paternal, government hand over land use decisions and in plan-led systems there is an emphasis on individual property rights. There is, however, no reason why both cannot be employed in a single system. The Indonesian *Spatial Planning Law 26/2007*, which is an attempt to modernise planning after Suharto's New Order regime, suggests a de-emphasis on single tools so that development control and zoning are deliberately intermixed (along with other devices such as tax incentives) to accomplish planning goals.

The essence of plan-led systems is that where the full, strategic planning process has been undertaken, there is less of a need for broad-scale development control. This, however, makes the improper assumption that the strategic planning process will necessarily deliver all planning outcomes. It is impossible to predict how a projected future for an area will occur and therefore putting complete faith in the strategic plan is misplaced. As a result, there will always be development control in some form in all planning systems as a safety valve but not always as the focal point.

The advantage of reliance on strategic planning, both as the basis for land use allocation and development control, is that it offers a higher degree of certainty as to expected outcomes. Development control appears as a vote of no confidence in the community vision but is acceptable because it allows the actual impact of a development to be brought to light, giving neighbours a more focused connection to the planning process.

It is difficult to investigate the efficacy of development control compared to zoning as a land use technique. In a 2003 study comparing the US and UK systems in terms of their effects on housing costs, it was pointed out, surprisingly, that the UK system focuses more detail on a project and area and effectively had greater control over development than the US zoning system and is, in practice, more dependent on a strategic plan: 'The UK can essentially be characterised as "plan-led", whereas the US could be described as "market-led".'[17] The reference to market-led means that planning is dictated by the needs of market stakeholders – developers and the community – as opposed to the UK system where the development plan is ultimately more important.

Examining the efficacy of development control is especially difficult in developing countries, where many buildings are constructed and uses are carried out without permission (as in Tanzania). One study of the effect of development control in a town north of Nairobi states that 80 per cent of development in Nairobi, and 75 per cent of development in Dar es Salaam, was undertaken without permission.[18] The Kenya *Physical Planning Act* (cap. 286) provides that there can be no development without prior permission having been obtained. The study suggests that there is lack of compliance because of the:

> high cost of designs, processing and approval, inordinate delays, bureaucratic ambience, lack of awareness of urban development control instruments, insecure land tenure, nature and type of development whether semi-permanent or permanent developments, precedents, and impunity as it relates to others [who] are also doing it.

---

17 White and Allmendinger 2003.
18 Ngetich, Opata and Mulongo 2014.

Another reason given for the inability to examine the efficacy of development control in other regimes is that there usually is not just one authority and one simple decision that is required. There may be a multiplicity of authorities who have policies or standards that apply to a development. This occurs because in a system of development control with less emphasis on emphatic zoning, there is a tendency for various regulatory authorities to create policies to account for specific situations in order to have their say when an application for development is made. Policies are also made by the state to ensure that local planning authorities consider matters of state interest or considerations that are seen to be essential to the planning process, such as sustainability criteria. *Planning policy Wales*, for example, is a 231-page document that then annexes another 23 technical notes, and a nine-page list of other policies, all of which apply to a development application. In this matrix, it is not possible to say if development control is more efficient than the lengthy process of strategic planning.

In development control, the strategic plan takes on the characteristics of a policy, although it has higher precedence than policies made for a general or subsidiary purpose. The advantage of this approach is that there is no need to translate the strategic planning policy into tight legal restrictions as with spatial plans and regulatory provisions, and the narrative can become more useful in understanding appropriate development. However, the proliferation of policy in all development control systems creates a professional class of planners whose job is to decode the policies and determine the approach of an application. The result is that an individual can only know the extent of their rights and obligations in respect of their land by making use of a professional layer between them and government.

6.1 Interactions between policies and decisions

It is essential that the strategic planning process produce more than just general goals for an area in order for the decision makers in the development control process to be properly informed. A vague goal, such as increasing the amenity of the area, does little to inform a decision maker when a development application is to be considered. What is necessary in a strategic plan that is an adjunct to development control is that policy scenarios are set out and the reasons for each goal established fully, using a narrative form through which the true intention of the goal can be expressed. As well, the priorities among the various goals and strategies must be made clear.

There are two forms of goals that are relevant to the creation of a strategic plan that are useful in informing the development control process. The first is where goals that arise from the priorities and strategies in the strategic plan are made concrete and understandable for the development control system. An example would be the explanation of the need to maintain a maximum height of two storeys in a residential area with views to a body of water. The second is where the plan provides indicators for how it is possible to test the goals. Research on the indicators of sustainability[19] as one example of such a goal suggests that a choice of measures is helpful as there is a multiplicity of variables that may be considered in assessing an application for development permission in relation to sustainability principles. The multiplicity arises because it is necessary to examine the effect of the proposal on other systems, such as the environment or transportation, now and in the future,

---

19 Bossel 1997; Pinter and Hardi 1995.

in addition to drawing conclusions on the viability of the area and its capacity to absorb the impact of a new use.

There cannot be a direct and complete concordance between the goals and strategies in a comprehensive, strategic plan and a decision made in development control. The plan cannot fully inform the making of the decision as development control will raise considerations that were not apparent or contemplated at the time of the making of a strategic plan. If development control is to have a profound relationship to the comprehensive plan, the critical elements that underlie a decision, such as development standards and the important sustainability indices, should be developed at the same time as the strategic plan, made the subject of a community vision, and therefore reflect, as far as possible, the goals and strategies. Unfortunately, this is not often the case as the strategic plan does not concern itself directly with decision making outcomes under development control: the strategic plan sets the vision and the spatial plan and legal instrument set the permissions.

Where there is strategic planning resulting from a community vision, development control theoretically is really an exception and not the rule, especially when the development standards and other details are made part of the community participation process. The strategic plan, especially if created after community engagement, suggests an ideal solution has been reached, and flexibility has no real place. Various devices that introduce flexibility in zoning had their origins in the United States, not to add flexibility for its own sake to a comprehensive strategic plan, but, it has been suggested, rather as a response to what was perceived as rigid, homogeneous zones and a lack of mixed-use diversity.[20] The need for flexibility to respond to rigidity makes sense but the idea that the need for mixed uses led to increased flexibility may not be convincing. An interesting study found that mixed uses are not likely to be sought as exceptions in homogeneous zones because the natural market favours consistency in order to protect property values.[21] Some proof can be found in Houston, Texas, where the separation of discordant uses and concentration of similar uses in other areas mimics zoning even though there are no zoning laws.[22] As a consequence, promoting flexibility by introduction of development controls to accomplish diverse forms of development is not as effective an argument as the need to have flexibility because the strategic planning process fixes the designation of appropriate uses as an idealised solution, discouraging variations.

There is, however, an alternative body of research[23] that suggests that, as a general proposition, allowing development control in a plan-led strategic planning regime is to be preferred because it is not possible to adequately predict all land use patterns by strategic planning. A critique of a rigid, strategic planning approach is that the push to be comprehensive causes too detailed or prescriptive regulations as there is a tendency to enforce a complex vision. The idealised quality of the strategic plan is responsible for more rigid controls as there is a tendency to seize on a consensus as the complete solution.

The balance appears to be to allow and incorporate development control deliberately in a plan-led system but to use it for specific discretion for particular uses in stated circumstances. As an example, it has been argued that the Hong Kong planning system provides a balanced mixture by use of the outline zoning plan, also called a development permission

---

20 Talen 2012.
21 Grant 2002.
22 Buitelaar 2009.
23 Faludi 1987.

Uses always permitted	Uses that may be permitted with or without conditions on application to the Town Planning Board
• Agricultural use • Government use (police reporting centre, post office only) • House (new territories exempted house only) • On-farm domestic structure • Religious institution (ancestral hall only) • Rural committee/village office	• Eating place • Government refuse collection point • Government use (not elsewhere specified) • House (not elsewhere specified) • Institutional use (not elsewhere specified) • Place of recreation, sports or culture • Public clinic • Public convenience • Public utility installation • Religious institution (not elsewhere specified) • Residential institution • School • Shop and services • Social welfare facility • Utility installation for private project

Table 6-1 A list of permitted uses in an outline zoning plan from Hong Kong.

area plan, which identifies as-of-right development in one column and uses that might be permitted in specific, defined circumstances (see Table 6-1).[24] The emphasis in this system is on the strategic plan but with development control a subset of the plan in situations where the disposition of various uses is not clear or requires special consideration.

There is a strong argument that the place of development control is not only an exception to, or a subset of, a strategic comprehensive plan but is of equal importance in any planning system. No matter how thorough the strategic planning, there will be constant pressure by developers to change the plan by any means and eventually, as the plan becomes dated, that pressure increases so that development control will become inevitable and thus equally as important as the plan.[25] Development control is therefore a natural evolution that must be considered as part of a plan-led system. The French experience has shown that any attempt at complete legal certainty by use of a strategic plan without development control will eventually be eroded by continuous applications for rezoning.[26] It has been stated that this erosion alters the manner in which planning is carried out:

> The continuous elaboration of rules to cover unforeseen eventualities results in the rules becoming more complex and difficult to apply. Inevitably, developers resort to negotiations in advance of a formal application.[27]

In order for the development control aspect to be congruent with the strategic planning, it must fall out of, or evolve from, the planning exercise and the community vision so that the ambiguities or concerns are made patent and the circumstances for its exercise and the standards to be applied are made clear. The consequence is that all the flexibility

---

24 Booth 1995.
25 Arnold 2007.
26 Booth 1995.
27 Cullingworth 1994.

mechanisms, including zoning amendment procedures, should be built into the plan and recognised as aspects of the planning process.

The method to achieve congruence between the development control aspects and the comprehensive plan is by requiring that development control provisions, be they exemptions or development standards, be consistent with the strategic plan. The degree of consistency is not always going to be clear or useful unless there is a complete explanation of the nature of the congruence. As an example, in 1994 in Ontario the planning legislation provided that all decision making be 'consistent with' provincial policies but, in 1996, this was altered to require that local authorities 'have regard to' policies, and in 2004 the legislation changed the emphasis back to 'consistent with', aware of the need for greater alignment. What is important in any form is, at a minimum, the express recognition of the nexus and of the fact that the hierarchical relationship of plan and development control needs to be explained.

6.2 Changing systems

There is little change in systems from plan-led to development control for several reasons. The first is that the system in use reflects the planning culture and change may be incongruent with those factors. Examples were given in the Introduction of New South Wales and the Netherlands. The second is that the existing system arose because of historical and political ideology as in the case of war-time concerns for stabilising property values in England. The third is that every system is striving for certainty and will be invested in the belief that it has delivered the best planning controls; the systems are too entrenched to be questioned.

The most important reason for altering a plan-led system is when there is inadequate translation of strategic goals into the zoning. This is because, in reality, a sense of place is created by the regulatory provisions, not by the strategic plan.[28] Understanding that this is the case has led to increased use of detailed, form-based codes, inspired by New Urbanism in the United States, and apparent in the comprehensive plan for Miami, *Miami 21*, in order to define the essence of an area by regulations. The concept is that controlling the fine details of development, such as setbacks, variety of housing, paving, and of boundaries between uses, creates a closer alignment with strategic goals. This is atypical of planning systems: a study of 25 US cities has found that, although there is an interest in reform, there have been few attempts at changing the structure of traditional zoning.[29]

No matter how desirable it would be to move away from a dysfunctional system, the planning culture has created an integrated web of participants in the planning and developer community who have established complex interactions and paths into the system. The desire for change, no matter what the weakness of a particular system, only comes about as a political statement, such as the changes that occurred in the planning system in Poland after 1989, reasserting private rights after decades of a system that weakened those rights and the power of citizens. The *Act on Spatial Management 1994* moved the planning function from central government to local communes and de-emphasised the need to make spatial plans in all instances.

---

28 Eran 2005.
29 Hirt 2013.

The reluctance to change has been overcome in certain instances, such as in the Netherlands, always a forerunner on matters of planning.[30] In 2008, as discussed in the Introduction, the Netherlands changed from a development control system to a plan-led system. Research[31] has examined the effect of the new system on the existing institutional structures for planning and measured the quantitative data on effective planning outcomes. It is worth repeating that the 2008 Dutch legislation, at its inception, only allowed exemptions to the strategic plan when the planning authority agreed to adjust that plan to reflect changes. In 2010, because of a backlog of requested exemptions, this requirement was eased to allow for exemptions even if the planning authority did not agree to adjust the plan. The consequence was that exemptions became the rule and there were three or four times more exemptions than adjustments to the plan. The demand for exemptions naturally increased because the plans became static as they could be ten years old without amendment. The study concluded that there must be flexibility and that a plan-led system cannot dominate to the extent that it becomes rigid, as the plans become outmoded, freeze the system, and are counterproductive to effective land use outcomes. To effect a balance for this system, the form of exemption was altered to allow a plan for a particular project to become, when approved, an exemption. The study concludes that land use plans should have a dominant, steering function but cannot be the sole basis of planning:

> Not only is it considered difficult to prescribe or allow for future developments without creating an inflexible regime for these developments, even when this is done in a rather broad way, there are also various formal institutions at the local level which hamper the adoption of this type of plan and consequently require more detailed plans.[32]

The Dutch system required flexibility and, as one commentator put it, 'the Dutch system, in attempting to provide certainty through the requirement of commitment to a rigidly preconceived plan, is too inflexible to be useful in practice'. It was further stated that the English system of development control 'allows for far greater flexibility as decisions can be made in light of current thinking, rather than by reference to possibly out-dated proposals.'[33]

In the United Kingdom in the 1990s, for a variety of reasons, changes did occur that led to the development plan becoming more important in the development control process. In 1990, the government adopted a direction towards 'sustainability', requiring that the broad goals inherent in that concept be embedded in plans. This had the effect of creating a desire for more plan-led development that incorporated these goals and less ad hoc development control where sustainability received cursory attention. In 1991, a new section was added to the planning legislation that provided:

> Where, in making any determination under the planning Acts, regard is to be had to the development plan, the determination shall be made in accordance with the plan unless material considerations indicate otherwise.

---

30 Pojani and Stead 2015.
31 Buitelaar, Galle and Sorel 2011.
32 Buitelaar, Galle and Sorel 2011, 939.
33 Thomas 1983.

Several interpretations of the effect of this provision were given,[34] one being that this created only a presumption in favour of the plan that could be overcome by other material considerations. This was correct because an historically strong system of development control in Britain and the existence of a system of appeals arising solely from development control meant that the system was not able to be oriented towards plan-led control of planning. In 2004, the planning system was changed to provide for more top-down control through regional assemblies to give guidance to local authorities in the form of principles and policies. The effect of this was to strengthen the application of policy in the making of a decision rather than incorporating policy in a strategic plan, thereby weakening a plan-led system. In 2007, the policy task was given to regional development agencies that were focused on incorporating these principles and policies in regional economic strategies. Local development frameworks were then introduced, not as a plan-led imperative, but rather to reflect the emphasis on policy making as a 'folder' of policy documents, maps, strategy descriptions, statements of community involvement and monitoring reports.

A reflective study[35] indicates that the importance of the plan was effectively downgraded in that system and became only one factor in decision making and that other 'material considerations' had an equal role as criteria for consideration of a development application. The changes in the planning system were meant to represent a shift away from development control to greater strategic planning[36] but had the effect of downgrading the role of the plan to that of a guide rather than as the focal point for allocation and development of land uses. However, a later analysis of this system[37] concluded that the degree of its success lay not in the plan-led or development control emphasis but in a close alignment of local government goals with larger government strategic visions. An important example of this is where a planning objective is the supply of housing and the methods of either plan-led or development control become largely irrelevant to the task:

> Arming regional planning bodies with evidence of market signals would give them a stronger hand in dealing with more parochial interests. This is an approach dominated by strategic thinking with regions setting affordability targets (measured in terms of a supply-and-demand equilibrium) with the aim, over the long term, of achieving a better balance between housing demand and supply.[38]

The UK political agenda of 2010 abolished the regional devolution of power and created a move to localism, the consequences of which (especially in areas that used to function as regions[39]) are still unclear, but the plan-led provisions in the planning legislation have remained. What emerges from an analysis of the British system and its attempts at reform are that the strong, historical culture of development control, which has its roots in a local, political milieu in which citizens feel part of the decision-making process,[40] is not easily replaced by community involvement in wider strategic planning or a belief that local interests need to be overridden for the community good.

---

34 MacGregor and Ross 1995.
35 Bingham 1998.
36 Doak and Parker 2005.
37 Gallent 2008.
38 Gallent 2008, 316
39 Shaw and Robinson 2012.
40 Othengrafen 2010.

The *English local development plan*, which was previously called the *Local development framework*, still remains in the current system as a series of documents including the evidence base for planning decisions, a core strategy, and various supplementary planning documents, such as an affordable housing plan. The significance of strategic planning cannot be denied in the United Kingdom but is not the focal point of development, and the plan component is fundamentally designed to contain the policies, directions and background to inform a development application.

Change is not likely to occur in the form of planning systems but there may be, as in the examples given, a continuous shift in emphasis as to the importance of the underlying plan in development control. This indicates that best practice changes will also follow along the lines of the existing system and a wholesale reorganisation is not likely.

An examination of development control and plan-led systems does not indicate that one is particularly better at achieving the goals of sustainability or ameliorating urban ills. Some plan or set of policies will always emerge under the name of forward planning, but there is no plan that does not require careful consideration of particular developments, especially if they are intrusive in an area.

6.3 Localism and development control

'Localism' is the term used to describe a devolution of power to local communities and a corresponding decrease in the power of the central authority. In planning terms, it represents a move towards local communities being unbound by state or federal planning requirements. Local planning is far less complicated than regional or sub-regional planning as it is possible to develop a future scenario that is capable of being implemented because of the scale. However, even the move to localism does not change the relationship of development control to a strategic plan.

The source of localism is perhaps David Cameron's July 2010 announcement in the United Kingdom of a retreat from big government and its regulatory framework in favour of small communities that thereby develop social capital by empowerment.[41] The radical changes in the UK *Localism Act 2011* did not alter the principles of development control but decentralised decision making to local neighbourhoods. The only significant change to encourage forward planning is in the *National planning policy framework*, which provides (sect. 15):

> Policies in Local Plans should follow the approach of the presumption in favour of sustainable development so that it is clear that development which is sustainable can be approved without delay. All plans should be based upon and reflect the presumption in favour of sustainable development, with clear policies that will guide how the presumption should be applied locally.

The *Localism Act 2011* essentially leaves the process of development control intact but makes the considerations of sustainability local in nature and subject to a plan. The retention of development control was not strictly necessary as a plan based on sustainability could, in fact, dictate future development. As well, there remains a backdrop of consistent

---

41   Holman and Rydin 2013.

criticism of the development control system as slow and impeding the market economy.[42] The effect has been that, although plan making has been returned to a local level and is critical, the plan still remains only one relevant consideration that is taken into account in decision making.

Unlike systems where there is a regional or municipal plan and the local government decides applications for development, in the case of localism the plan-making authority becomes the decision maker. There are no clear guidelines as to how the two functions should be exercised together. The Government Consultation Paper on the *Neighbourhood Planning Regulations* of October 2011 stated:

> We do not propose to prescribe exactly how the local authority should make key decisions – for example whether by delegated officer, a full meeting of the Full Council or via the Council's Executive, or whether there must be a majority vote at those council meetings in order for the decision to be valid. We believe this is for local planning authorities to decide.

The trend internationally is, in fact, to make plan-making authorities the decision-making authorities because this creates a direct link between the making of the plan and decisions under the plan, thus aligning the localism agenda to effective planning. The advantage of the linking is that, over time, the vision in the plan becomes entrenched and is able to be understood in relation to a development application. This traditional form of localism may however be displaced where there are alternative choices for governance, as where diverse areas are treated as a specific economic unit. In Brazil,[43] as an example, there is an emphasis on a 'microaxis' of development, identifying those areas that have an economic link rather than those based on geography or historic classifications. The government identifies strategic municipalities that are given specific rules for urban management, sometimes resulting in a loss of local political autonomy to meet the economic goals. Brazil is an exception and the practice of other Latin American countries where there are traditional local governments is that decision making remains in the hands of those governments, allowing the linking.[44]

In the United States, there appears to be a trend towards linking plan making with decision making through the relaxation of a zoning ordinance and the increased use of special permits, which amount to a form of development control in specific instances.[45] This is implicit recognition that the system of area variances and special permits is a de facto development control regime that is constantly being expanded and should be exercised as part of, or consistent with, the plan making. This has resulted in a decrease in the need for congruence with the strategic, comprehensive plan in recognition that the permit decision will be thorough and take into account all relevant matters. In Wisconsin, for example, a 2010 amendment to the planning laws[46] provides that, instead of the zoning ordinance having to be in strict compliance with the comprehensive plan, the phrase

---

42 Booth 2002.
43 Farret 2001.
44 Irazabal 2009.
45 Martin, Puentes and Pendall 2006.
46 *2009 Wisconsin Act 372.*

'consistent with the comprehensive plan' only means 'furthers or does not contradict the objectives, goals, and policies contained in the comprehensive plan'.

The move to localism reflects disenchantment with regional government's overbearing power, such as using prescriptive methods to curb urban sprawl,[47] as well as a desire for local autonomy in times of global confusion. In planning terms, it is reflected in a greater concentration of development control to assert the direct power of the local government. This can be seen in Canada.[48] In Ontario,[49] local authorities are able to make development permit by-laws, a development control imperative, rather than just using zoning amendments and variances.

Decentralisation or localism as a trend may be occurring for two reasons. The first is the emergence of economically driven and oriented land use plans that are a consequence of the World Bank LED (Local Economic Development) incentives for local government, making local decision making more important. These incentives are responsible for a range of local autonomous plans in Bulgaria, Lithuania, Poland, Russia, Slovakia, the Balkans, Columbia, Peru, and Yemen.[50] The second reason has been labelled the 'new political culture'[51] and is a consequence of local sustainability concerns, as higher-educated citizens seek a greater role in decisions that affect the environment. As a consequence, it is observable that regional authorities or municipal commissions are now being established more for particular purposes, such as integrating land use with transport, as with the California Regional Transportation Planning Agencies, or the North Central Pennsylvania Regional Planning and Development Commission. There are few new authorities that have emerged of a regional nature and the movement increases towards localism.

The move to localism is contradicted when the decision-making function in development control is separated from the plan-making function. In most states of the United States, for instance, a use variance and area variance, both of which require the exercise of discretion, are decided by a separate Zoning Board of Adjustment. The board is either appointed by the council or elected and consequently removes the final decision on variances from the local authority. This is a result of the historical development of zoning boards but there is, perhaps as a result of that separation, no evidence that there is an attempt to widen the use of variances.

It could be argued that splitting the two roles is theoretically sound because they are fulfilling different roles: plan making is an administrative task and decision making has the quality of adjudication; a 'quasi-judicial' role, as it is called. The justification for this split is also that it allows planning to concentrate on the wider, strategic role, rather than diminish that role in the context of a discretionary exercise.[52] However, it is hard to escape the idea that independent or separate decision making on development control arises because of fears of corruption; it is said that 'corruption is unfortunately endemic in the land-use planning field.'[53] The World Bank's yearly *Doing business* report highlights that corruption in obtaining building permits or development permission is rife in many countries, such as Italy.[54]

---

47 Litman 2016.
48 Grant 2009b.
49 *Ontario Planning and Conservation Land Statute Law Amendment Act 2006*.
50 Capkova 2005.
51 Paterson and Saha 2010.
52 Albrechts 2004.
53 Chiodelli and Moroni 2015.

The notion of corruption as the basis for splitting the decision-making function from the plan-making function can be questioned. The perception of corruption in the planning system is measured by a comparison to a completely perfect decision. It is stated:

> often such a view of corruption is built on the model of the Weberian bureaucrat, that is, the role fulfilling, disinterested professional occupying a particular location in an organizational structure based solely on professional competence and merit.[55]

It may be that there are no disinterested professionals without an established point of view who can make a development control decision. Independent decision makers are chosen from the ranks of those who have planning knowledge with their own historic biases and career aspirations. These decision makers are not judges and do not necessarily have a professional dispassion. The most that can be implied is that they will work to a somewhat higher ethical standard. The San Francisco Bay Conservation and Development Commission has a policy that provides:

> It is Commission policy that Commissioners and their alternates avoid discussion of permit application matters with individuals or groups on any side of an issue outside of the formal public hearing process and record. If such discussions or contacts occur, at a public meeting the Commission member involved will disclose the name or names of those involved and the substance of the contact. An opportunity will then be provided for rebuttal of the information disclosed.

The quasi-judicial role of a zoning board may also be tainted by political nepotism or influence.[56] Perhaps as a result of this fear, the zoning board is given limited jurisdiction, which results in a distribution of decision-making powers: a small-scale subdivision may go to council, a larger one to the locally appointed Planning and Zoning Commission, all zoning amendments to the council, and variances left to the Zoning Board of Adjustment.

The most significant difficulty arising from an independent decision-making authority is clearly the consequence of separating out the local authority plan making from the development control decision making. The decisions of the independent authority for development permission or for a variance have a profound long-term effect on the local area but do not have the same connection with the entirety of the planning process that was undertaken. It has been argued strongly[57] that the emergence of this split in the United States is not because of the efficacy of separate decision making but is a matter of culture and history and it is not useful to compare different regimes for best practice. There is a long history of the emergence of boards as separate entities and this cultural claim may be valid. However, the fact that the decision makers are not as conversant with the local culture, and are not responsible to the electorate, appears to be contrary to the image of a local planning system that reflects community aspirations.

There is clearly no perfect model for decision making in development control. It has been said:

---

54 World Bank 2013.
55 Gupta 2012.
56 Sampson 2007.
57 Booth 1993.

Emphasise certainty as the key attribute of a system of control and you find that the subterfuges used to surmount constraints threaten the very legitimacy of the system. Elevate flexibility as the touchstone of the effective planning systems and you may find yourself enmeshed in impenetrable ambiguities which do not serve anyone very well.[58]

6.4 Development control and delay

The most significant issue for development control is its effect on the housing supply. The UK *Barker review of housing supply* in 2004 and *Land use planning* in 2006 indicate that delays in the development control process directly affect the ability to deliver housing. A thorough study of the UK system determined that the delay varies depending on the local authority but that in any event 'development control is a lengthy process with a considerable degree of variability and uncertainty over how long it will take.'[59]

One of the significant causes of delay is the myriad policies that must be understood and applied in a development control system both by the developer in putting forward a plan and by the decision-making authority in determining the application. The task of the UK *National planning policy framework* was to reduce 1300 pages of policy statements into 58 pages of text. It accomplished this by establishing core planning principles in general terms that serve as a guide to development. For example, one core planning principle expressed in the framework is that planning 'not simply be about scrutiny, but instead be a creative exercise in finding ways to enhance and improve the places in which people live their lives.' By making the policies less prescriptive, they are easier to understand and apply as the spirit of the guidance is clearer than by deducing the purpose of technical restrictions.

A method used in New York to decrease delay for major projects is to establish special districts for larger projects and then specify with great detail the standards to be applied and those that are discretionary, which are subject to negotiation or special permits. For example, the Special Hudson Yards District contains 91 sections of detailed requirements and ten maps. It therefore places emphasis on planning before this large development opportunity and leaves open only some matters for a discretionary decision. It is essentially a guided, precise master plan that reduces the amount of discretion and provides for special permits only where necessary.

The Planning Officers' Society in Wales circulated a *Handbook for development control identifying good and best practice* in 2005 that concentrated on efficient practices to avoid delay. A report for the Wales Audit Office in 2010 reported increased efficiency in adopting a systems approach of examining all aspects of the application when it is put forward and indicated that this was successful in reducing delay in one case study.[60]

The Department of Communities and Local Government in the UK issues guidance documents, such as the *Guidance on the pre-application process: Consultation* (2012). Guidance documents are also a common characteristic of environmental assessment and permitting. The US *Environment Protection Act* (EPA) issues 'Significant guidance documents' on almost all matters of concern and does so under rules for preparation of guidance doc-

---

58 Booth 2003, 8.
59 Ball 2011.
60 Zokai et al. 2010.

Information item and location requirement	National policy driver	Types of application that require this information	What information is required and links to further advice
Impact assessment: city-wide	PPS 4: Planning for sustainable economic growth	The impact tests consist of two sets of assessments: one applying to all forms of economic development and the other required for all retail developments not in a town centre and not in accordance with an up to date development plan.	Further advice: Policy EC10 and EC16 of PPS 4, Planning for sustainable economic growth, prescribe the tests which this authority will need to assess the application.

uments issued by the President's Office of Management and Budget (the 'Final Bulletin for Agency Good Guidance Practices') that constitute best practice in guidance statements.

A key method of reducing delay is to make particular forms of non-controversial development subject to exemptions. Allowing these forms to be certified by a qualified person rather than the planning authority relieves some of the accusations of delay for development control. In the United Kingdom and Australia, these exemptions or 'complying development', as they are often called, are restricted to single- or double-storey residential homes that comply with a detailed code.

The delay caused by development control can be addressed by various means related to deadlines for a planning authority to make a decision, enforceable by a right of appeal, but the most important approach is to streamline the process of making an application and coming to a decision. This is an administrative issue and an occasion to consider best practice.

6.5 Applications

The preparation of an application for development permission must take into account and consider the various matters that will be relevant to the decision maker. In the case of a comprehensive plan in the United States and Canada, all policies and strategies are contained within that plan so an applicant for a variance or spot zoning need not go further afield. However, there are always ad hoc policies, policies in preparation or in draft form, unofficial policies, and policies that are still in existence but no longer used. It is important that an applicant be able to ascertain exactly what policies must be taken into account.

In the United Kingdom, a 'tick-box' approach to applications is required, providing a guide to relevant policies to inform the applicant of the necessary emphasis and information.[61] As an example, in respect of one criteria:

A mistake that is made in providing a list of policies that are relevant is, as in the Western Australian *State planning framework*,[62] to list the relevant policies but then allow other policies and strategies not listed to also have effect. As policies can proliferate, it makes it difficult for an applicant to be sure of what policies to address and in what detail.

In the United Kingdom, as the strategic plans are in fact the policy guidelines and therefore have a different purpose than the comprehensive plan in the United States, there

---

61 Communities and Local Government 2012.
62 Western Australian Planning Commission 2006.

has been an attempt to have policies be more consistent and understandable. This is reflected in an experiment in Scotland to create model policies, similar in wording and effect on a prescribed range of topics for each local authority.[63]

Another method to inform the applicant of what is required is by conversations with, and advice from, the planning authority staff. In the City of Vancouver, before an application for rezoning is made, an individual contacts the zoning centre, speaks with council staff and obtains a briefing on what policies and plans apply. Most importantly, the council staff explain whether the application is likely to be supported and any issues that need to be addressed in the application. It is explained that, if staff feel that council might support it, an enquiry is made to the director of planning and the staff assist in the making of the enquiry.[64] At that stage, the director of planning will indicate whether there is a positive response and, if so, an application can then be made. Prior to the application, a 'pre-application' meeting is held where a council planner will review the contents of the application and recommend meetings with other staff members who can refine the information provided.

These steps in the City of Vancouver do not apply to development applications, only rezoning, but are illustrative of an attempt at pre-application consultation. In the United Kingdom, the new *Localism Act* requires a developer to consult with the community before making an application. Various local governments in the United Kingdom have put together options for pre-application advice but impose differing charges for whether the advice is provided in writing or in person.[65]

Another alternative to aid the application process is for the applicant to test the views of the planning authority and obtain preliminary approval or what is called 'approval in principle'. The *Singapore Planning Act* provides:

1. An application for outline permission shall be determined on the same basis as an application for planning permission or conservation permission except that the competent authority shall have regard only to matters relating to land use, intensity, type, form and height of the proposed development or works.
2. Outline permission shall constitute approval in principle for the proposed development or works, but shall not authorise the carrying out of that development or works or any other development or works . . .
3. Where subsequent to the grant of outline permission an application for planning permission or conservation permission is made during the validity period of the outline permission, the application shall be determined on the basis of the further details supplied on that subsequent application.[66]

That system has proven to be a major factor in investment decisions made by developers who have come to rely on outline planning permission to test various proposals before advancing with the one that is most beneficial.[67] The concept of 'outline planning permission'

---

63   Lloyd and Peel 2007.
64   City of Vancouver website, 'Enquire about and apply for rezoning', http://vancouver.ca/home-property-development/enquire-about-and-apply-for-rezoning.aspx.
65   South Cambridgeshire District Council website, 'Pre-application advice', https://www.scambs.gov.uk/content/pre-application-advice.
66   Chapt. 232, sect. 18.
67   Woodhead 2000.

is a means to refine the development contemplated before making a full application or can be used when details are to be left to further applications. In France, it has another function, explained as:

> a means of establishing initial contacts between developers and controllers, ensuring that land can be acquired with some security, and providing basic guidance for the preparation of an application for a *permis de construire*. It also serves as a declaration of intention on the part of the developer and the local authority.[68]

The important aspects in the making of an application are that the developer be made aware of all information that is relevant, have a chance to understand the form and content of the application by discussions with the planning authority, be able to receive advice if the application is outside the bounds of what might be contemplated and, finally, have some means of negotiation to correct the application.

Many of these goals of clarity in the application process and appropriate, negotiated development, have been achieved by 'contract zoning' where the parties enter into a formal contract for development. This is consistent with the contemporary move to so-called 'new governance' where the emphasis is more in favour of public and private participants linked by agreements rather than top-down government imposition of control.[69] There are difficulties, however, that arise from failed negotiations, the length of time necessary for completing the contract, and the phenomenon of the planning authority and the developer seeking more than is otherwise possible in a development application. In the United States, the placing of onerous conditions on agreements has been a major source of litigation.[70] Although there are difficulties in turning a permit power into a negotiating power, the concept of contracting is a modern and acceptable approach to land use planning.

Contract zoning has the negative consequence of excluding the public from participating and, even if public hearings are held after the contract is in draft form, the parties are too entrenched in their positions to be moved by submissions. One solution offered is to allow a member of a community group an opportunity to be present and make submissions in the negotiation process,[71] although this may have little effect as the parties do not need to accept those submissions. The use of contracts and bargaining is inevitable for large projects but the difficulties of altering the accepted structure of conventional decision making means that they should be used cautiously and not as the primary means of development control.

Much of the handling of applications depends on the planning culture and the attitude of individuals towards government. When there is a distrust and a fear that the system is adversarial, developers and planning authorities fight for their positions and negotiations are a matter of state power and developer concessions. To correct this, it is necessary to have a carefully worded process in place to balance the rights of stakeholders in advance, such as an opportunity for a developer to move from failed negotiatons with the planning authority to an independent decision.

---

68 Punter 1988.
69 Delmi 2012.
70 Hall 2007.
71 Ryan 2002.

Santiago, Chile, offers a different perspective. Planning in Chile, because of the political history, is aimed at achieving social transformation by means, in part, of 'planning without a plan'.[72] As an example, private companies are encouraged to participate in the supply of infrastructure outside the scope of normal processes by a 'concessions' system, where the state auctions off public works projects without retaining a promise of return on investment. This gives the private sector a rewarding role in the planning system and encourages the secondary benefits of collaboration, transparency and accountability.[73] This imaginative arrangement with the private sector contrasts with the usual planning system, which is fundamentally rigid, focused on process rather than results, and maintaining the same power structure.

6.6 Tested procedures on application

The Idaho *Local Land Use Planning Act* is considered a leader in procedural matters for those seeking special permits. It provides that, upon application, any person can request to be heard on the determination of a permit. It also provides that:

> The procedure established for the processing of applications by this chapter or by local ordinance shall include the option of mediation upon the written request of the applicant, an affected person, the zoning or planning and zoning commission or the governing board. Mediation may occur at any point during the decision-making process or after a final decision has been made. If mediation occurs after a final decision, any resolution of differences through mediation must be the subject of another public hearing before the decision-making body.[74]

Mediation has the effect of making the process one of a conversation between interested parties. The usefulness depends on whether there can be resolution of the application before it proceeds further. Vermont has an Environmental Court and a study[75] examined both mediation at the permit application stage as well as in the court. It was concluded:

> At all levels, there were high settlement rates for cases that were evaluated to be appropriate for mediation, due to a combination of factors including willingness of parties to engage in mediation and explore settlement options, the nature of a case and the number of settlement options that are possible.

The best practice is any device or concept that gets the developer and planning authority having a discussion about the development application. Singapore, as mentioned, as well as Malaysia and the United Kingdom, offer the capacity for an 'outline application' and allow the submission of a broad proposal to test the allowable land use, plot ratio, building height and form. The testing means that there is an opportunity to negotiate, discuss, modify, and refine an applicaton. A decision under the Singapore *Planning Act* is an 'approval

---

72 Silva 2011, 41.
73 Silva 2011, 40.
74 *Local Land Use Planning Act* , sect. 67–6510.
75 Field, Harvey and Strassberg 2009.

in principle' that does not give authorisation to develop but allows the developer to then refine the application with some confidence. The City of Hillsboro, Oregon, is an example of a local authority that has a detailed system of 'concept development plan approval' that is a prelude to making a final application for large projects.[76] That approval is an approval in principle but is binding as to density and uses.

This notion of providing flexibility in the early stages of the application, combined with mediation, brings the stakeholders together to form a consensus. The essence of these systems is that they provide an alternative to a formal application and decision, which brings with it conflict and confrontation.

The real delay in an application occurs where the potential development causes anxiety among neighbours as a perceived imposition on their property interests. A large project next door that can affect the sense of community or a high-rise building that exceeds the height of others leads to conflicts that are then addressed only in a formal setting. In that setting, the planning authority may waiver, seek official and unofficial reactions, consult with the community, and delay will accordingly occur. A system of early mediation, consensus building, and full exposition of the nature of what is proposed may have an ameliorating effect. It will still be the case that mediation and concept plans may not resolve a planning application but the path to settlement is capable of reducing delay.

6.7 Time to determine applications

The American Planning Association has developed a guidebook of model procedures in planning statutes.[77] It offers two possible alternatives for a permit system to reduce the time in which a decision must be made in development control. The first is that if the application is not considered within the time set out in the zoning ordinance or guideline, then the application is deemed approved. The second is that, when the time expires, the applicant receives back their application fee, which could be substantial, and they can commence proceedings unless:

> within that period the local government has identified in writing some specific land development regulation provision with which the application does not comply, and that prohibits the development of the property.[78]

The California *Permit Streamlining Act of 1977* established the Office of Permit Assistance for the benefit of promoting a quicker resolution of permit applications under the California *Environmental Quality Act*. The act's important contribution is that it divides the process into three stages. The pre-application phase is where scoping meetings are held with relevant agencies in order to discuss how the rules apply. The second application phase includes the agency determining if the application is complete and, if incomplete, the applicant is told where the deficiencies lie. When complete, a failure to decide in time leads to a deemed approval.[79] The third is the review phase in which the application is con-

---

76 Zoning Ordinance no. 1945, sect. 136B (VII) (6).
77 American Planning Association 2002.
78 American Planning Association 2002, sect. 10-210(1).
79 California Government Code §65956(b).

sidered. Dividing the approval down into specific phases, with steps explained for each, gives the applicant a clear view of what must be done.

The City of Winnipeg, Manitoba, introduced a *Building permit strategy and action plan* in 2012 that has some relevance. That strategy suggests that there be an audit approach so that:

> Based on a statistically weighted sampling plan, applicants with a performance history of code-compliant permit applications and inspections will be audited, at both the plan examination and inspections stages, less often than those whose performance shows a history of non-code-compliant plan submissions and/or deficiencies on inspection.[80]

This audit system has the effect of placing greater reliance on applications from developers or consultants who have previously been shown to comply and, consequently, their applications are more rapidly processed. This is also accomplished by the use of private certifiers, so that a certificate of compliance by a certifier will have the same effect and will not require further examination. The Winnipeg strategy also encourages training sessions for consultants to explain what is expected for applications and it offers greater communication with professionals as to what information is required, leading to what it calls 'lean process improvement'.

Various attempts have been made to monitor the times it takes for approval of a development application under different circumstances and to adjust those times according to different variables.[81] Timeframes alone are not indicative of the success of the process as that is dependent on the relationship of the decision to the strategic plan and its vision. Accordingly, when the application is made under a plan-led system, it may require considerations that may not have been accessible at the time of the creation of the plan.[82] This may be an occasion to not rush the system and to consider the new vision created by the application. This is especially true if the development is to be resolved by agreement that involves negotiation, where the conditions can go beyond the matters envisaged in the strategic plan. Consequently, in a plan-led system, times should be imposed for processing an application but there may not be justification for a 'deemed to comply' system when time limits are exceeded.

Another alternative to speed up the determination of development applications is to concentrate on expediting particularly important projects. An experiment in Florida in 1997 for speeding up projects deemed to be for the economic benefit of the state required extensive pre-application discussions directed at providing guidance to the developer and creating, by agreement, a 90-day timetable to set the goals necessary for completion. Each participating agency in this process was given 30 days to identify any significant issues. This was not binding but served as guidance for the completion of the application by the developer so that adjustments were made in relation to a time goal. If there were objections when the application was made, expedited hearings by a judge were provided to clear roadblocks to completion of the project.[83]

---

80 *Builidng permit strategy and action plan*, http://winnipeg.ca/ppd/PermitsXpress/PDFs/.
81 Musil 2007.
82 Norton 2011.
83 Raepple 1997.

6.8 Relevant considerations

The concept of 'sustainability' is so open-ended and includes all manner of social and economic considerations that it is difficult to assert that any issue relating to land use is irrelevant. The task of considering what factors arise or should be considered in a determination of a development application is thus made more complicated. The social effect of a decision or the economic consequences of allowing a development[84] are, in modern practice, contained within the definition of sustainability that takes into account the broad effect of a decision on future generations.

It has been the case historically in all jurisdictions that the economic consequences of a development on other uses are only taken into account when there is an effect on an existing community service, such as a large shopping centre or office building.[85] These economic issues have been excluded as irrelevant to the choice made by a developer to risk a development that will be in competition with others or to build a project that is unsustainable from an economic point of view. However, this discounting of the economic impact of a use is no longer clear as the lines are now blurred between economic effect and land use choices because of the scope of sustainability.

The difficulty with a planning authority crossing over into economic analysis is that assessing the relevance of the risk to a developer requires a complex, economic analysis and is not suited to making land use decisions based on planning concepts or to planning authorities that are ill equipped to make economic decisions.[86] In addition, there is a range of different pricing models to examine the viability or impact of a development because of exogenous factors.[87] In carrying out that analysis, or when considered by a planning authority, it is very difficult to predict the effect on the use because of competition by other uses, or the effect caused by the project on any uses, other than very large commercial sites.[88]

There is, however, a natural tendency to want to examine a development in the context of the effect in relation to existing uses and thus competition from these uses. This leads to the explicit or implicit assessment of the potential viability and impact of what is proposed. It is therefore important for a planning authority to explain that it is specifically excluding economic considerations related to competition and viability from the range of relevant considerations it is taking into account in assessing an application. The width of sustainability, and its adoption in planning, requires this specific explanation.

There may be some exceptions where assessment of competition is relevant, such as as a backdrop to regulating specific uses where completion may change the character of the area. The *San Francisco Planning Code* uses this approach in respect of the ability to restrict 'formula' retail uses or chain stores:

> The increase of formula retail businesses in the City's neighborhood commercial areas, if not monitored and regulated, will hamper the City's goal of a diverse retail base with distinct neighborhood retailing personalities comprised of a mix of businesses. Specifically,

---

84 Foy 1990; Robinson 2004.
85 Doring, Knappitsch and Aigner 2010; Tang and Choy 2000.
86 Buttimer, Clark and Ott 2008.
87 Henderson and Thisse 2000.
88 Davis 2006.

the unregulated and unmonitored establishment of additional formula retail uses may unduly limit or eliminate business establishment opportunities for smaller or medium-sized businesses, many of which tend to be non-traditional or unique, and unduly skew the mix of businesses towards national retailers in lieu of local or regional retailers, thereby decreasing the diversity of merchandise available to residents and visitors and the diversity of purveyors of merchandise.[89]

As the range of relevant considerations in the determination of a development application is large and has been increased by the widely defined concept of sustainability, it is important that the reasons behind a decision are explained in full to understand which considerations have priority. The experience in the United States[90] is that reasons are not often clear when a variance is allowed, especially when there is a negotiated outcome or a compromise made to the applicant's proposal.

The expanding areas of relevancy after the rapid rise of sustainability requires that the reasons given by a decision maker must be drafted in such a manner so that the relevance of various factors becomes known, both for the sake of informing the applicant and allowing an appeal, but also to inform future applicants in that locality of what factors have crept in and which are excluded.

6.9 Issues relating to the decision maker

In the United States, there is a constitutional imperative that there be procedural due process in decision making and this applies, accordingly, to the making of land use decisions for variances, special permits and other exemptions. The due process requirement requires that a person whose property is affected has a right to be heard, requiring an oral hearing in all instances.[91] This has an effect on the role of the decision maker and the manner in which decisions are made.

For many decisions, the planning authority delegates the power to another body. Delegation of decision-making power in planning has historic precedents in the United States as the *Standard State Zoning Enabling Act* in 1922 divided the plan function (to be carried out by the council) and the administrative or implementation function (to be carried out by a zoning administrator, who was often the building inspector). At that time, granting exceptions to the comprehensive plan was historically given to two agencies: the Planning Commission, which would consider rezonings in line with the planning function, and the Zoning Board of Adjustments, which considered variances and special permits in accordance with the administrative function.[92] Thus, there is a system in the United States, based on legal underpinnings and the development of the planning system, for the delegation to non-council boards and a confidence in that process as decisions are subject to judicial review.

---

89 *San Francisco Planning Code*, sect. 703.3(9).
90 Sampson 2007, note 14.
91 See Rocky Point Plaza Corp., 621 N.E.2d 566, 572 (Ohio Ct. App. 1993).
92 Mandelker 1963; Anderson, Brees and Reninger 2008.

The OECD in its report *Cities for citizens*[93] suggested that in the governance of cities, there is no ideal model of decision making but that there are certain basic principles of metropolitan governance. One principle, as an example, is the concept of 'coherency', which proposes that it is always to be made clear exactly who is responsible for the multiplicity of actions that constitute a decision. Another is the principle of 'competitiveness' that requires that each local government be operated efficiently and therefore all decisions occur in a manner that improves the economic success of the area. Underlying these are the more fundamental, *a priori* principles of local decision making, including: '[to] introduce greater transparency and accountability in decision making processes'. The OECD suggests:

> The transparency, accountability, integrity and legitimacy of the rules, institutions, values and practices upon which a society functions are essential determinants of the quality of decision-making interpreted at the metropolitan level.[94]

The issue for decision making is therefore whether biases, interests and individual proclivities weigh against local governments making decisions in respect of planning applications. The extent of those biases or interests is not readily apparent in most instances because the courts have allowed local governments to maintain set views because of the necessity that local governments have already made decisions of a similar nature. As well, there is an acceptance by the courts that the wheels of democracy mean that views might change. As an example of the latter, in the English case of *R (Island Farm Development Ltd) v. Bridgend County Borough Council*, the applicants had been granted permission to develop a site adjoining a local government property. For the development to be realised, it required that the land of the local government be sold to the applicants. There was an election in the council after the permission was granted but before the decision to sell. Members opposed to the development were elected, including the person who was a member of a community group that had fought against the decision. The new council refused the sale of the land, making the development impossible. The judge stated:

> [They were] entitled to have regard to and apply policies in which they believe, particularly if those policies have been part of their manifestos. The present regime believed that the development . . . was wrong and they made it clear that that was their approach. In those circumstances, they were entitled to consider whether the development could lawfully be prevented.[95]

Although correct in law, it directly raises the issue of prejudices, political views, and biases that should be irrelevant to decision making in a development control system. It is not possible to end these biases because they are subtle aspects of the decision-making process in planning, such as a tendency to opt for the status quo, or putting greater emphasis on the loss of an old use rather than the gain of a new one, or applying a hidden bias formed from

---

93 Organisation for Economic Co-operation and Development 2001.
94 Organisation for Economic Co-operation and Development 2001, 41.
95 *Island Farm Development Ltd, Regina (on the Application of) v. Bridgend County Borough Council* [2006] EWHC 2189 (Admin.).

local knowledge by the establishment of a 'bright line' – a standard or issue that received local attention and that is then the unarticulated benchmark for future decisions.[96]

The benefit of having independent decision makers is then obvious because of these hidden biases. It does, however, run counter to the inherent benefit derived from elected officials being possessed of local knowledge so that their decisions most likely reflect the interests of the community. The balance in favour of independent decision makers arises because the details of the local knowledge and interests are unarticulated and a cloud hangs over the reasons for decisions of elected officials. This is particularly true if their decisions lack consistency and are unable to be clearly factored into the result by an applicant. It is also the case that communications outside council are not monitored, nor are moral or personal views explained. The result is that governments, to maintain the local council as decision maker, have shifted the emphasis to independent decision makers or drafting of ethics codes to prevent unseen bias.[97]

The use of independent decision making has been crystallised by the Smart Growth movement, which requires regional authorities to override local interests for the purpose of housing density distribution.[98] This has arisen from the patent difficulty of trusting councils to make effective land use decisions that support the regions over local concerns and this one factor has changed the approach to requiring accountability and transparency in local decision making. As an example, decision making by councils in the United Kingdom is now subject to the 'overview and scrutiny provisions' of the *Local Government Act 2000*, which holds decision makers responsible to an Overview and Scrutiny Committee that can call in decisions and have them reconsidered.[99]

The move to localism brings consideration back to local stakeholders and away from independent decision makers or regional planning authorities. It is a statement that the local area residents are best able to understand the fabric and future of their communities. The problem of unexpressed bias is endemic to all authorities and therefore should not rule out local councils on this basis, as it is in the nature of democratic functioning and can never be effectively eradicated. An independent decision maker may, in fact, follow a government agenda, mindful of being reappointed, or may have had a work history where the views of that agenda were paramount. It is therefore not possible to compare the quality of planning decisions made by local authorities with those of independent decision makers on the basis that one or the other has less bias. As planning decisions are not precise and can be influenced by so many factors, the answer lies in a governance structure that is derived from community engagement so that there is faith in the process, even though there may be unarticulated biases. If this is the best compromise, local decision making is most reflective of those aspirations in a way that is not possible for independent decision making.

No reason can be given, where there are no historical precedents for independent decision makers as there is in the United States, to move away from localism and to appoint independent panels. The use of the word 'independent' suggests that it is independent of the local politics and is without bias or a possibility of being influenced. It is meant to convey that the decision will be better and based on more rational approaches. Although it has

---

96   Pratt and Zeckhouser 2000.
97   Salkin 2011.
98   Bollens 1993; Carruthers 2002.
99   Coulson 2011.

symbolic value, the notion of independence with perfect cognitive capability that is completely rational and neutral does not realistically apply. The best model is a body that makes continuous decisions that display a consistency over time, and that arises in planning in the context of local decision making where the decision makers are the same, compared with independent bodies whose members are chosen from a panel.[100]

Sometimes too much knowledge is contrary to the planning process. An independent decision maker will be appointed because of decades of work in the planning area, in whatever capacity. In that time, the decision maker will have built up ideas on how the system should work, what is a good project, and which members of the planning fraternity can be trusted. Local decision makers are not usually planners and bring an approach to do with community expectations and the desire to accord with what is popular to be re-elected. This often makes their decision-making appear naïve compared to that of the independent expert. However, since planning is not precise and there is no perfect decision, it is possible that aligning with the community expectations outweighs a so-called expert opinion. There is a certain dynamic quality to local decision making that best reflects an interaction between the community and government and offers the chance for better governance through community involvement.

The on-the-ground operation of participation, even protest, of the local community in controversial projects with local decision makers brings a new element into the interaction of neighbours. It is a common purpose or alignment of beliefs that takes away the isolation of living in urban environments. When there is an independent decision maker, that element is suppressed as the views are often reduced by those who have no stake in the community.

6.10 Conditions and agreements

When a permit for development is granted, conditions can be imposed, requiring the developer to provide more than was offered in the application. This occurs in all development control regimes as the conditions are said to flow from the permit as a way to refine or shape the approval. Contributions to infrastructure, as it reflects the effects of of the development on the locality is an example of a condition that can be imposed. As planning has no fixed boundaries, it is possible these conditions could include matters that are outside the direct purview of the utilitarian goals of harmony and order by design. The extent of the conditions is not usually questioned when they are obtained by requiring that the developer enter into an agreement with the authority to set the conditions; the developer in this case is content to supply whatever is needed to carry out their project.

An example of using conditions to provide for requirements outside the application is that of provision of affordable housing. In many countries, conditions can be imposed that offer a bonus in density in return for the developer providing affordable housing. As the requirement is so far outside what is sought by planning conditions, it is justified by offering the bonus. This concept, however implemented, is called 'inclusionary zoning'; the *Seattle Municipal Code* provides:

---

100   Lai 2016.

'Bonus development' means floor area allowed in stories wholly or in part above the base height limit on condition that low-income housing be provided, or that a payment in lieu thereof be made, under this section.[101]

It is termed 'inclusionary' because it provides social inclusion for low-income residents. The proposition supporting it as a relevant condition is that social inequality in a community is a planning issue that can addressed by the development control process. It falls into the melting pot of planning because it is framed as social inclusion for the enhancement of a diverse population and therefore has to do with the quality of life that planning claims to enhance. It appears that at the time of its emergence in the 1970s, social inclusion was a reaction against the use of exclusionary zoning in the United States, where zoning was used to keep areas exclusive by restricting lot size and therefore the cost of entry. However, it is now justified in terms of diversity of population and also as a response to the inequality resulting from neoliberalism.

A comparative analysis of the use of inclusionary zoning in Europe, the United States, and several other countries indicates that there are two standard methods used for social housing.[102] The first is for the government to insert public housing into existing communities as a commitment and an aspect of the strategic planning process, and the second is to require new private developments to have a mix of development types, including housing for low-income buyers. This can occur by different forms of planning control: by a spatial plan mandating inclusionary housing in an area, by granting the power for a planning authority to seek an agreement with a developer, or by providing a condition of development consent for affordable housing.

Studies have concluded that inclusionary zoning has a positive effect on the successful delivery of affordable housing and does not impede the profitability of private development.[103] As a concept, it is now too well established to question whether it falls properly within the umbrella of planning and the current interpretation, used in Britain, is that it derives its legitimacy as an aspect of 'planning gain': that a developer has the benefit of permission and therefore it is acceptable to seek something back for the community by way of affordable housing.[104]

The imposition of planning conditions to carry out a planning agenda not addressed in the strategic planning process is common. For instance, where there is a general legislative requirement for sustainable development but the details are not set out in the strategic plan, conditions can be imposed for every element of sustainability through conditions for particular developments, as has occurred in Malaysia.[105]

This wide use of conditions raises the issue of whether developers of land should have a burden imposed by way of condition that serves a wider governmental agenda such as affordable housing or infrastructure spending that is not related directly to the development itself. The UK *National planning framework* has six tests to determine when conditions should be imposed: whether the condition is necessary, related to planning and to the development, enforceable, precise, and reasonable in all aspects. The scope of

---

101 *Seattle Municipal Code*, sect. 23.48.011.
102 Calavita and Mallach 2010
103 Brunick 2003; Schuetz, Meltzer and Been 2007.
104 Crook, Henneberry and Whitehead 2016.
105 Johar 2007.

6 Development control

Figure 6-1 Affordable housing in Edinburgh. Source: Google Street View.

what is 'related to planning' depends on what is considered relevant in the strategic plan. The Nairobi *Integrated development plan* 2014 makes the following subject matters important: 'the promotion of gender equity, youth empowerment and the interests of vulnerable groups'. Concerning gender inequality as a planning issue, it is statemd (para 1.5): 'Improving equity in gender issues and reducing gender disparities will benefit all sectors and thus contribute to sustainable economic growth, poverty reduction and social injustices'.

The United Kingdom appears to be unique in trying to examine whether the effect of conditions on a developer is so great that it no longer makes the development viable. Circular 05/2005 provides that when a developer is required to enter into an agreement to carry out conditions, including making financial payments, the developer should submit its financial information as the basis for negotiations. In 2008, *Planning policy statement 12* introduced the notion that viability considerations should be part of the range of relevant considerations in assessing planning agreements. The development viability models used identify the revenues and costs for the development, predict the financial inflows and outflows, and thereby the profitability by the resultant increase in land value.[106] Revenue will be lower if there is a need to supply, say, affordable housing, anna this is factored into the model. It is pointed out that these models are not necessarily complete as there are uncertainties in inputs and outputs.[107]

The financial modelling, to the extent that it has some accuracy, at least acknowledges that the rights of the developer, upon whom the urban environmespent relies, are accom-

---

106 Crosby, McAllister and Wyatt 2013.
107 Crosby, McAllister and Wyatt 2013, 9–19.

modated through acceptance of the profit motive and provide for impingement to a level where the development is still viable. However, since the range of matters is so vast and can include almost all economic and social issues that become a burden on the developer, there must be some way to address those conditions that are at the fringe of planning. When they are at the edge of what might be included in planning, they are often offered by way of bonuses, such as for financing a public entertainment facility or providing more open space than required. This seems the most appropriate means for these elements. The *Los Angeles City Code* provides that every developer of commercial or industrial development must pay an 'arts fee'.[108] The Arts and Cultural Facilities Trust Fund provides that, if facilities, services and community amenities for cultural and artistic purposes are provided in a development, then the developer will get a dollar-for-dollar contribution from the city.[109]

Offering bonuses to a developer to advance the public interest does not always result in benefit. It has been found that providing open space in New York in return for a bonus led to unusable spaces as developers minimised costs in terms of upkeep or presentation and made the areas uninviting.[110] The obligation then follows that to reduce the tension between developer and planning authority, a financial assessment of the impact of conditions should be carried out to complete a negotiated set of conditions that are not just an onerous exaction, but are for the benefit of the developer and community.

6.11 Standards for development control

It is possible that the outcome of strategic planning will result in the conclusion that a particular area should have special treatment to be imposed by restrictions on uses. These include, for example, limiting the form of development in an historic district or requiring the maintenance of a unique residential or landscape character. In such cases, permitted uses will be strictly limited and expressed as such in the strategic plan. The nature of the built form of the uses is not, however, usually considered in the strategic plan; its exact parameters are left to the regulatory scheme where the standards for development for each use are set out.

Criticisms have been levelled at the English system where there are no fixed development standards and much is left to discretion in the process of development control. It has been stated that the consequences of weak criteria for development are a lack of certainty, increased political influence, and the lessening of legitimacy due to a lack of accountability to a standard.[111] As well, in the absence of third-party rights of appeal where neighbours can take their case to a higher authority and there is a lack of community participation in the application process, it is doubtful if it could be said that a decision is necessarily in the best interests of residents where there are no standards to be used as a benchmark.

A further problem in using general restrictions or open-ended standards for development is that there is no ability to measure outcomes for the community. Ad hoc decision making, or even a decision that looks to the strategic plan, will not be able to be measured in terms of the effect on the market and services that it influences. The only certainty for

---

108 *Los Angeles City Code*, sect. 91.107.4.6.
109 Established under the *Los Angeles Municipal Administrative Code*, art. 21.
110 Smithsimon 2008.
111 Booth 2009.

the community in a system of development control is that delays in the processing of applications drive up costs and prices.[112]

The *Barker report* in the United Kingdom found that a single method or set of standards for evaluating applications is not possible because uses differ: the handling of large infrastructure projects by development control, for instance, should not proceed along the same lines as standard household applications. It was suggested in the Killian Pretty Review of 2008 that building requirements in development control should instead depend on the goal they are serving and not be a set of standards determined in advance.[113]

Accordingly, the most effective means of providing standards for development control is that which is linked back to the goals and strategies of the strategic plan. For example, if a goal is to have greater density around transportation nodes, standards that can fulfil that goal and are specifically directed are more effective than general, unexplained restrictions, such as building height, setback or density.

Standards related to specific goals can be either general or specific. For example, the state of Maine *Subdivision performance standards* state:

> Except in areas of the municipality designated by the comprehensive plan as growth areas, the subdivision shall be designed to minimize the visibility of buildings from existing public roads. Outside of designated growth areas, a subdivision in which the land cover type at the time of application is forested, shall maintain a wooded buffer strip no less than fifty feet in width along all existing public roads. The buffer may be broken only for driveways and streets.

Performance standards for development that are related to goals and strategies, as in Maine, have been in existence for decades. They appear to have their origins in the placement of industrial uses with the resulting goals of preventing dust, smoke and other externalities.[114] This concept of 'use performance' is the ability of a use to fit various standards of compatibility at a particular site, rather than to comply with generalised standards for a type of use. As conceived in the United States, use performance was originally an alternative to zoning and not an adjunct but, historically, it was not embraced because it was contrary to the planning culture and meant that ordinances had to be rewritten.[115]

In 2000, the creation of 'smart codes' shifted the emphasis away from use performance to matters such as social, health, and design criteria that encouraged a high quality of the built form and integration of development for the creation of social cohesion. This was a movement away from general standards to providing for a type of social structure in a specific location. Smart codes are derived from New Urbanism, which is directed to the creation of compact, socially connected neighbourhoods with mixed uses and walkable dimensions. In this model, higher density development can be accommodated in lower density areas if it conforms to design criteria and social coherence. The first smart code of Duany-Plater Zyberk & Co, said to be the originators of the concept, emphasised the need for appropriate standards to fulfil the higher-order design and social goals of New Urbanism.[116] It therefore contains provisions satisfying the specific needs of New Urbanism by

---

112 Barker 2004.
113 Killian Pretty Review 2008.
114 Rose 1969.
115 Marwedel 1998.

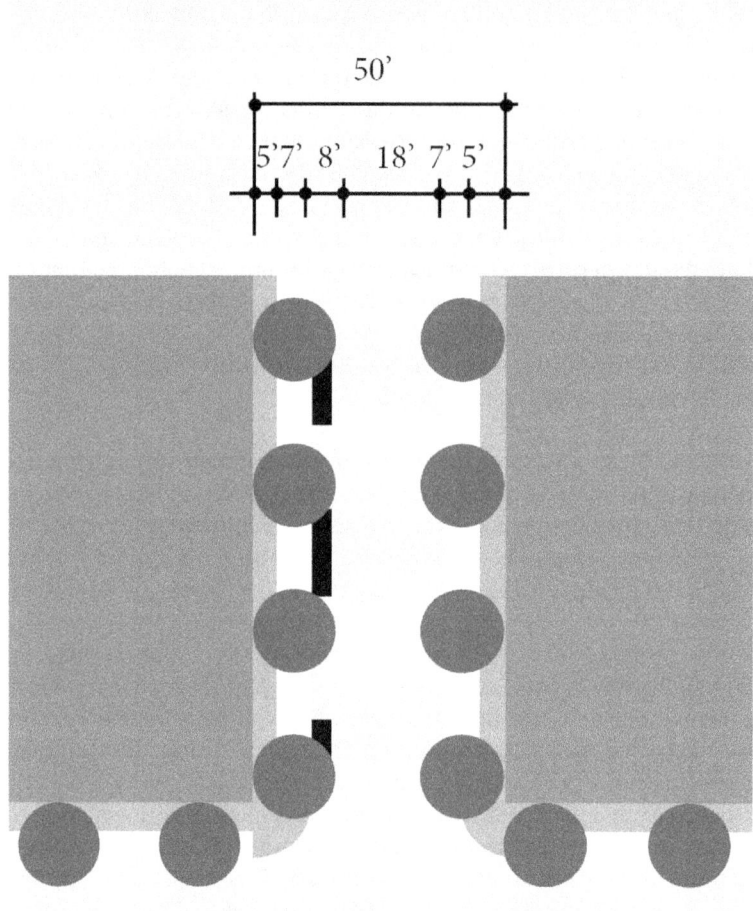

Figure 6-2 Diagram of a 50-foot thoroughfare, dapted from the smart code of Lauderhill, Florida.

creating a traditional town like environment. However, because it is the codes that are in a sense creating the specific forms of social interaction, they are, in practice, tightly restrictive. Specific controls are needed rather than the generalised requirements of building standards as they orient to create a community arising with compact, walkable neighbourhoods with different housing types. Accordingly, they are precise in building design and use-placement; they are not directed at flexibility or to rapid assessment of applications.

---

116 Duany 2002.

An exemption to standardised development criteria in the United States is 'planned unit development', which employs the concept of master planning for a discrete area in which the design elements and the standards are incorporated into specific zoning controls. This is necessary because the achievement of variety in design is not possible by strict regulation or even by performance standards. The master planning process indicates the manner in which design can be accomplished:

> Ideally, there should be either a limited number of indeterminate standards counterbalanced by a strong and publicly visible review process that can add specificity, or fixed design standards with mostly administrative approvals on the assumption that the fixed standards protect the public interest. The first alternative is appropriate for larger projects where flexibility in providing design opportunities is important, while the second alternative can be used for more limited projects, such as cluster housing.[117]

Planned unit development is simply the carrying out of planning for a particular project and designing the development criteria that are appropriate. This can be combined with performance standards, which contain a full explanation of what is sought, around which the standards gather. An example is one of the first performance standards, the Bucks County, Pennsylvania, *Performance zoning model ordinance*, which states:

> A performance standard subdivision is a type of cluster development in which the developer may choose to develop a variety of housing types subject to the regulations stated below and all other applicable requirements of this ordinance. Performance standard subdivisions allow the grouping or clustering of dwelling units, permitting a variety of housing types to encourage better, more flexible designs. The subdivision as a whole must meet prescribed standards for open space, density, and impervious surfaces.

The advantage of this mixed form is that it explains the underlying goals of the performance standards and directs that the requirements follow an understandable context. This points, as a matter of best practice, to the need to include performance standards, in whatever form, in the visioning process for strategic planning. This inclusion arises because the purpose of performance standards is to adjust the use to the site rather than to have a set of standards for a particular use. Thus, the relationship of the site to the overall strategic plan requires that its content and dimensions be examined at this early stage.

An assessment of performance-based standards indicates that there have been significant difficulties in administration in the United States, New Zealand, and the Australian state of Queensland.[118] This is because they require complicated qualitative assessment of the degree of compliance as it is much easier administratively to resort to prescriptive standards. However, performance standards are appropriate when examined in light of strategic planning where they are manifestations of a community vision for particular areas or projects and are not imposed standards that have no context. In strategic planning, examining how a particular area should develop and evaluating the relevant goals and strategies presupposes that decisions will be made at this stage that influence how that area is to be controlled. Performance-based standards have the effect of reflecting that vision

---

117   Mandelker 2010.
118   Baker, Sipe and Gleeson 2006.

and giving logical justification, especially when an application for development permission is made.

6.12 Best practice

The UK system is the regime most copied in other countries that have adopted development control, both because of historical connections for those countries that adopted English law and also because, as a 70-year-old system, it contains the most refined aspects. There have been many reviews of the system and how to make it more efficient. However, the UK system has worked through most of the issues of having an effective development control system. In other countries where development control has been adopted, such as for special permits in the United States, the issues are largely the same with different emphases and, interestingly, the conclusions and practices are very similar to the current UK system.

An historical examination of the UK system shows a constant desire to make the development control system more effective and efficient. The delays in the system have largely been the cause of these reviews and the analysis is of streamlining procedures. The purpose of these best practice suggestions is to address some of the issues overlooked by the reviews and those that might have universal application to all systems of development control.

The needs of a development control system can be summarised as having the qualities of some relationship to a spatial, strategic plan, an ability to analyse each application in light of relevant material considerations at the time, and making a decision in the context of policies that inform the applicant of what is relevant for the state or local government.

6.12.1 Range of considerations

If strategic plans contain aspirations and hopes that are in language that is merely aspirational and difficult to understand, such as promoting a 'vibrant city', this should not be a licence to open up considerations in development control relating to social issues. The effect of an application on 'quality of life', diversity of population or weight gain are not matters that should be considered as they are outside the framework of planning and are too vague for implementation in development control.

The concept of sustainability when used in relation to development control should not be given a wide reading to encompass any manner of issue that adds to the social and economic development of an area. How a use might impact an area economically by adding jobs or the viability of the project are not relevant considerations as they too are uncertain; they arenot the responsibility of the planning authority and are outside of its capacity for evaluation. It is common to tout a development as fulfilling employment needs or being consistent with a government's economic agenda. However, the degree to which the project will create jobs is highly speculative as workers may not live in the area and, more importantly, the use might cease, to be replaced by another use that provides less employment.

It is tempting to think that all manner of criteria that have to do with urban living are relevant but when an application is made for development, the applicant should be confined to proving the impact of the use on the strategic plan and the local character and amenity. To go beyond those limitations means that the decision will be made on grounds that are not capable of supporting a particular use.

Applicants are unsure of what criteria will affect the application and it is best practice for a statement or document to set out the relevant considerations that are to be taken into account. For instance, it may be that buildings should have windows that overlook the street for crime prevention, or that a shop selling cigarettes should not be too close to a school. This could have arisen from past decisions or earlier policy statements. These policies and the range of relevant or material considerations are only known to experts because they rely on interpretations of local policies, practices and ideas. If a council is anti-development, for instance, and that is not articulated, it is difficult for an applicant to understand that sentiment. Informing an applicant and the community of what considerations may be considered should be presented by way of an explanatory document. An example could be:

> Competition: The council will not consider the economic impact on other uses as a barrier to your application. Exceptions to this consideration may be entertained where the impact is so great as to cause the actual loss of an important, existing local amenity, such as a local shopping centre.

6.12.2 Decision makers

Decision makers must know the intention of the plan makers explicitly instead of by interpretation of the regulatory instruments and policies. As the regulatory instruments or policies are fundamentally ones of restriction and control, they do not provide a complete explanation of what is sought for a locality. The best practice is to provide as much information for the decision makers as possible about the reasons for the regulatory controls and the relationship of the controls to the vision for the area and, as well, how it reflects regional issues. The only means to do this is to make the planning process and its outcomes part of decision making. In terms of operation, this requires that the plan-making authority be the decision-making authority for development control.

There is a tendency to create independent decision makers to decide development applications to avoid concerns about local government councillors being lobbied or corrupt. If there is no recognised case of bias or corruption that appears, the move to local decision making in development control is the best practice. It is possible, at least for an applicant, to understand the previous affiliations and interests of a local decision maker who has an historical relationship with an area. It is not possible to understand how an independent decision maker views an area where they are not resident or may have developed an unexpressed poinwht of view that cannot be scrutinised by the residents. In the absence of historical governance structures that require independent decision makers, the establishment of such an independent system is an unnecessary degradation of local government power.

6.12.3 Plan-led systems in development control

If there is a strategic plan, it is important for a decision maker to refer to the vision, policies, and goals for an area in making a decision. The effect of this is to have the strategic plan itself create a proper structure for variances and exceptions under the plan-led system to establish that link.

In order for a plan to have legitimacy in decision making, there must be community participation in the formation of the plan itself. This will give greater effect to a decision made that is congruent with the strategic plan. The extent of the participation that has taken place should be included in the plan so it is perceived as a community plan and has greater influence than a top-down plan. There should be substantially more development as of right hightlighted in the strategic plan to guide the drafting of the regulatory provisions, as well as a list of positive uses, so that the purpose of an area is thereby clarified for the decision maker and it becomes clear that there are areas that need further planning as the true basis for development control.

The details of a strategic plan that are necessary to inform proper decision making should at least contain the following aspects (extracted from the *Comprehensive plan for the City of Greensboro, North Carolina*,[119] often proposed as an exemplary plan):

- Vision statement
- Area types: areas that are distinguished by broad patterns
- Factors that signal change: conditions and influences that will cause change
- Growth scenarios: A conceptual depiction of future conditions and development patterns
- Community character
- Relevant considerations
- Sustainability concepts
- Comparison of vision to trend in growth
- Growth strategy
- Parks, open space and natural resources
- Man-made environment (historic and scenic places)
- Housing and neighbourhoods
- Policies for existing neighborhoods
- Housing density requirements
- Economic development
- Goals and policies to enhance economic development
- Transportation
- Goals and policies to enhance transportation issues
- Community services and infrastructure.

This long list of matters in a strategic plan provides an opportunity to fully understand the concept of a zone's designation and restrictions that are the subject of a development application. Each of these goals and topics can then be applied to analyse the efficacy of what is proposed. The plan in this form does much of the work for the decision maker, including a section on relevant considerations that have been used in formulation of the goals and policies. In the absence of a strategic plan, the decision maker is forced into a deductive process, examining what is prohibited and what is permitted in order to see what might be the fate of the proposal and makes a decision by surmising the goals and intent. At that point, the applicant will resort to study documents or speeches of government officials to say what the area is meant to become. This means that the decision on an application is not resolved in light of the highest and best use that was derived from a consensus of the community and agencies.

6.12.4 Region-state interactions

A requirement for best practice in development control is to understand the relative roles of the state, region, other authorities, and local governments in navigating an application and decision. This needs to be fully explained in a guidance statement so an applicant is aware of the relevant policies and restrictions contained in all documents. As a result, all regional or state policies that are relevant, both official and unofficial, need to be consolidated in an outline document similar to the UK *National planning policy framework* that establishes goals, planning principles, and presumptions (including sustainability) for use in decision making. It should be the case that any policy not listed is thereby *not* a relevant consideration.

It would be useful to provide specific indicators in these guidelines as to how to measure compliance with the goals in the metropolitan or regional spatial plans and against which an application can be benchmarked. This will allow the applicant to go beyond making statements that it complies with a general goal and to be able to prove that compliance as a matter of evidence.

6.12.5 Processing

For efficiency, the system should provide an applicant with multiple options in the making and processing of a single development application. The decision maker could then analyse the different development scenarios and decide which they prefer. If no preference is determined, the decision maker should be able to go back to the applicant and suggest what might be necessary. The developer should be able at some point, if no options are deemed worthy, to initiate mediation to work through with the decision maker what is the best use of the site and how an application may proceed. This sequence is useful as a positive indication of developer–decision maker co-operation as opposed to the current situation where the developer sees the decision maker as obstructionist. This removes the negative view of developers and serves to create an atmosphere where the planning authority may have a better chance of obtaining development that is desired under the strategic plan.

3
Planning and climate change

7
Planning and greenhouse gas mitigation

The translation of an international obligation of a climate change treaty, such as the *Kyoto protocol* or the *Paris climate agreement*, into national legislation that authorises an emissions trading scheme, a carbon tax, or regulatory control of industry, is referred to as a 'top-down' approach; that is, the legal structure of domestic legislation takes its shape from the higher-order obligation under the treaty. This top-down approach was favoured by the UK *Stern report* of 2005 in suggesting an emissions trading system as the preferred legislative solution to address an equitable obligation for developed countries to reduce greenhouse gas emissions (GHGE).[1]

There are many who have doubted this headlong rush into the acceptance of a national scheme based on emissions trading or a carbon tax to solve the global warming crises.[2] The doubt arises because these instruments, to be effective in terms of their theoretical goals of economic efficiency and distributive justice, must apply equally to all countries and be carried out in domestic legislation. This has not occurred.

Therefore, an individual country cannot rely entirely on the mechanisms decided in Kyoto or Paris and, in fact, developed countries must supplement the international regime with domestic solutions. Using domestic action has been referred to as a 'bottom-up' approach. However, there is no agreement on the form that these bottom-up mechanisms should take. A 'strawman' assessment to come up with ideas from scientists and lawmakers created dozens of possible solutions, such as a tax to be used for research and development on abatement technologies and automobile emission restrictions.[3] That assessment also suggested a 'pledge and review' system where countries and industries would try out new ideas and report back to a central registry. The difficulty with most solutions for climate change, be they top-down or bottom-up approaches, is that they cannot rely upon existing legislative models for implementation and require new legal structures.

---

1 Stein 2010.
2 Pizer 2006.
3 Bodansky, Diringer and Wang 2004.

7.1 The relationship of planning to GHGE

Land use planning is concerned with regulating activities that take place on land in order, in part, to separate discordant uses. It is not concerned with activities that take place in the atmosphere or, more importantly, are not local or regional in nature. There is, accordingly, no natural fit between GHGE abatement and land use planning. However, as the *Stern report*[4] stated:

> ... their design and implementation can have important implications for mitigating climate change and also has the potential to influence the resilience to the impacts of climate change, for example, in the management of flood risks or water scarcity.

This statement views planning as a participant in both mitigation of GHGE and the abatement of impacts from climate change. The report considers planning as only a contributor to mitigation and abatement but not as the major driver; that was left to an emissions trading scheme. This is due to the fact that the *Stern report* was specifically an economic analysis of global warming and therefore economic instruments were the prime methods of abatement and the comments on planning were contained in a section of 'other' mitigating possibilities.

There are two questions that Stern left unanswered about planning assisting in mitigation and abatement. Are the issues relating to GHGE mitigation and abatement consistent with land use planning? And can land use planning be of equal importance to economic instruments in mitigating GHGE?

GHGE have a possible relationship to land use planning in four ways: first, as a planning externality; secondly, on the basis that the amelioration of GHGE is in the public interest; thirdly, GHGE mitigation is an aspect of 'sustainability' and its key relationship to planning; and fourthly, as an extension of pollution controls. All of these are the bases by which there can be explicit recognition of GHGE mitigation and adaptation in policy documents related to planning.

7.2 GHGE as a planning externality

The first approach to incorporate GHGE issues in planning is that they are an 'externality' or consequence of land use; emissions result from the manner in which an activity on an individual parcel of land is conducted.

In all land use issues, the manner in which land is used can result in proximate and remote externalities. The use of the term 'externality' here is not a reference to economic externalities but rather, as it is used in planning, to the effect of the proposed use of land on adjoining parcels of land and on the community more generally. For example, a new high-rise dwelling has a direct, proximate effect on adjoining land in terms of overlooking or shadowing, but it also has more remote effects, such as increased traffic on regional routes from more residents and ensuing car trips.

A proximate or remote externality in planning is conceived of as imposing a cost burden on the developer, not on the community, because it arises from the consequence of the

---

4 HM Treasury 2006.

approval or carrying out of the development. If a cost burden by way of a levy or charge was placed on a developer that did not arise from the development itself, it would be considered a form of taxation that requires separate legislative authorisation outside planning legislation. If it is an aspect of the consequence of development or, as the term is used, there is a 'nexus' with the development, it is considered as a price that the developer must pay for the privilege of receiving permission to develop. This extends to other externalities such as noise or smoke resulting from the use and its effect on other properties.

The cost imposed on a developer is that of removing or moderating the externality. The usual forms of imposing a cost are either by requiring a payment of a contribution towards services or requiring the developer, at their expense, to ameliorate the impact of the proposed use. That amelioration of impact may be achieved by limiting the operation of the use (thereby requiring a reduction in the intensity of the use) or by the developer expending money to limit the impact on adjoining uses. The attempt in both of these forms is to normalise the externality by private contribution so it does not fall to the public purse.

The externality effect of a development on adjoining private land is also extended to public land, such as a wetland or conservation area, and it is here that the link with GHGE may be most relevant. A natural asset such as public or conservation land in planning terms is a 'public good' to be enjoyed by the public either actively or passively. The public good that is to be protected in planning terms is the enjoyment of the natural asset in a manner that leaves it undisturbed; using wetlands as an example, by preservation of a functioning habitat corridor or protection of a pristine listed wetland. The amelioration of impact on a public good is accomplished by limiting the operation of the use or by requiring the developer to take steps to preserve the public good, such as providing land for a buffer between the development and the natural asset.

In all these instances of ameliorating the impact of a public good by imposing a cost on the developer, it is usually for a good that is adjoining or suffering an observable and direct impact from the development. The public good of *clean air*, or protection of the community from bad air, is in one sense contiguous as it affects adjoining properties but in another is far removed, as the effect of the emissions are not necessarily localised. To embrace the remote consequence of a development, it is necessary to take a conceptual step that the preservation of a public good is in the 'public interest'.

The 'public interest' in planning is an acknowledgement that private rights must give way to a larger framework. This could be a scenic view or the overriding need for a public use, such as a hospital, that outweighs local amenity issues. It is the very essence of planning, and encompasses all manner of criteria that serve a greater community interest.[5] As a consequence, the reduction of impacts from GHGE are a matter of public interest and so appear as an aspect of relevant planning considerations.

The relevance of public interest in planning is not, however, altogether clear. It has legitimacy as an extension of state control over land use, as the basis for citizen participation, and as the overt criterion of the success of a plan. However, it loses clarity because it is really an aggregation of subjective experiences of the population based on the aspirational concept that the plan must somehow improve the lives of the citizenry. The concept then must rely on broad utilitarian principles that are the basis for welfare economics and unitary concepts that the public interest transcends individual interests. The only true test of the public interest is whether the plan benefits the residents *in the planning area*, as this is a

---

5   Alexander 2002.

measure that can be tested. This is a strong test because the essential ideological issue with planning is whether the bundle of rights accompanying land ownership can be restricted for the common good. It is only when that good can be somehow measured, as it can be for a smaller area, that the balance can be achieved.

The use of the public interest criteria as the basis for regulating the worldwide phenomenon of GHGE does not carry technical weight. Public interest can be relied upon as a generalised norm on the basis that planning should do good or, as a state instrument, should be for the welfare of the populace. It does not, however, fit neatly into the concept of strategic or spatial planning and does not fully support the use of planning to mitigate GHGE.

7.3 GHGE as pollutant

GHGE are, in terms of an externality, also within the definition of an 'air pollutant'. They are, therefore, subject to the historical recognition that matters of pollution are recognised issues in planning. The recognition perhaps first occurred in the United Kingdom in the 1970s[6] in relation to smoke and other visible emissions and, since then, there has been no question that control of pollution is within the planning agenda. This is because pollution in visible form is an obvious externality of land use and its inclusion is an aspect of passing the cost burden to the developer as a condition of approval.

The issue of whether GHGE are a form of pollution arose in the United States Supreme Court in *Massachusetts v. Environmental Protection Agency* in respect of a statute that referred to 'any' air pollutant.[7] It was held that GHGE are within the definition of 'any'. The reach of planning considerations to include pollution and the inclusion of GHGE within the definition of pollution means that there is little doubt that GHGE are an aspect of consideration in planning decisions. However, some level of proof must be advanced that there would indeed be a contribution of a project to GHGE and that is still very imprecise even by precautionary principle standards.[8]

7.4 GHGE as an aspect of sustainability

The third link between GHGE and planning is contained within the notion of 'sustainability' that is the contemporary expression of the public interest. Sustainability is the essential basis for arguments that press planning into action for climate change.[9] Sustainability is indeed a convenient peg on which to hang all claims that planning has a role in mitigation of GHGE.

The *National planning policy framework* in the UK makes a link between planning and climate change by indicating that the environmental dimension of sustainable development includes the need to mitigate and adapt to climate change. It therefore becomes a 'material consideration' in deciding an application for development permission.[10]

---

6   Wood 1996.
7   *Massachusetts v. Environmental Protection Agency* 549 US 497 [2007], 127 S.Ct. 1438.
8   McKain et al. 2012.
9   Wilson and Piper 2010.

In Australia, under their system of development control, the New South Wales Land and Environment Court[11] has found that sustainability includes the precautionary principle where scientific uncertainty is resolved against the proposal and that this is applicable to GHGE. The court referred to Principle 4 of the *Rio declaration*, which states:

> In order to achieve sustainable development, environmental protection shall constitute an integral part of the development process and cannot be considered in isolation from it.

The *Rio declaration* arose from the 1992 United Nations Conference on Environment and Development, also known as the Earth Summit. At this conference, the *United Nations framework convention for climate change* (UNFCCC) was also signed. The two are often wrongly assumed to be related. They are not directly connected as the negotiations for the UNFCCC did not take place at the Earth Summit and followed a different path.[12] Nevertheless, sustainability and control of GHGE and its impacts are now considered to be aspects of the same phenomenon and, as planning is to be carried out sustainably, the inclusion of mitigation of GHGE is a necessary consequence.

The EU created the 'Covenant of Mayors' to meet reductions of GHGE. The covenant relies upon the *Leipzig charter on sustainable cities 2007*. That charter includes various goals for cities, including developing energy-efficient buildings to combat climate change. The essence of the charter is sustainable development according to the balancing of the triple bottom line. This requires 'integrated urban development' defined widely as: 'a process in which the spatial, sectoral and temporal aspects of key areas of urban policy are coordinated'. The covenant also relies on the *Aalborg commitments of 2011*, which developed themes for sustainability, including reducing energy consumption, greater reliance on renewables, and a commitment to 'deliver integrated management towards sustainability, based on the precautionary principle':

5. Planning and Design
We are committed to a strategic role for urban planning and design in addressing environmental, social, economic, health and cultural issues for the benefit of all.
We will therefore work to:

1. re-use and regenerate derelict or disadvantaged areas.
2. avoid urban sprawl by achieving appropriate urban densities and prioritising brownfield site over greenfield site development.
3. ensure the mixed use of buildings and developments with a good balance of jobs, housing and services, giving priority to residential use in city centres.
4. ensure appropriate conservation, renovation and use/re-use of our urban cultural heritage.
5. apply requirements for sustainable design and construction and promote high quality architecture and building technologies.

---

10   *EC Gransden & Co. and Falkbridge Ltd v. Secretary of State for the Environment*: QBD (1986), JPL 519.
11   *Walker v. the Minister for Planning and Ors* [2007] NSWLEC 741.
12   Parson, Haas and Levy 1992.

The applicability of the precautionary principle is the most important aspect of sustainability in relation to GHGE – it provides that the unresolved science of global warming is relevant in planning decisions. This is because there is a natural connection between the principle and the uncertain quality of climate change science. The principle was expressed in the *Rio declaration* as:

> Where there are threats of serious or irreversible damage, lack of full scientific certainty shall not be used as a reason for postponing cost-effective measures to prevent environmental degradation. (Principle 15)

The principle developed historically[13] to deal with the difficulty of detecting pollution where it was not visible, yet could possibly be a significant health risk. The main problem with the principle is that it allows for consideration of speculative, unclear risks. It does not offer a risk-management approach but instead requires precautions arising specifically from uncertainty. There is, however, a direct fit with climate change where, as the *Stern report* illustrated, the gaps in the data are secondary to the evidentiary link between GHGE and global warming. The precautionary principle has its origins in the prevention of pollution so is an overriding framework for all activities that bear on the environment. It must therefore take into account issues relating to GHGE. As it is an overriding framework, it includes an assessment of planning issues and, in this way, GHGE issues and planning issues dovetail.

There has been no attempt to actually balance the triple bottom line in respect of GHGE but rather it is the use of sustainable development as an overarching concept under which GHGE mitigation and abatement can find a place. The concept is not made explicit in sustainability definitions, but it carries with it an idea that it is a positive statement of a concern for the environment, and so it naturally concerns efforts to reduce GHGE.

7.5 Explicit recognition in planning

The main connection between GHGE and planning is now found in many explicit statements. A 2007 white paper in the United Kingdom, *Planning for a sustainable future*,[14] mentioned that the planning process could aid GHGE mitigation in this single sentence: 'Crucially, planning can help speed up the shift to renewable and low carbon forms of energy.' At the same time as the white paper was being prepared, a draft supplement to *Planning policy statement 1 on sustainable development* called *Planning policy statement: planning and climate change* was issued.[15] That statement suggested that planning could be responsible for mitigation of GHGE in terms of assessing the carbon impact of regional strategies. The key to regional spatial strategies was said to be for the local government to:

> consider how the region's activities contribute to climate change and provide a framework for integrating policies for the development and use of land with other policies and programmes that influence the nature of places and how they function.

---

13 Whiteside 2006.
14 Department of Communities and Local Government 2007a.
15 Department of Communities and Local Government 2007b.

Another example of this direct link is an initiative by the International Council for Local Government Initiatives, Local Governments for Sustainability, an organisation of local governments in the United States, taken up most prominently in Massachusetts, mandating local governments to create climate change programs. These programs, as in the Cambridge, Massachusetts, *Climate protection plan 2002*, contain land use recommendations that meld the climate change initiative with zoning issues.

California created a GHGE statute that requires a state cap on emissions and a plan of action that began in 2009.[16] Most significantly for this analysis, a concomitant bill requires all transport planning to take into account methods to reduce vehicle emissions, including: 'The relationship between land use density and household vehicle ownership and vehicle miles travelled in a way that is consistent with statistical research.'[17] The bill places emphasis on transportation modelling:

> Current planning models and analytical techniques used for making transportation infrastructure decisions and for air quality planning should be able to assess the effects of policy choices, such as residential development patterns, expanded transit service and accessibility, the walkability of communities, and the use of economic incentives and disincentives.

The bill also provides that each local government shall prepare a 'sustainable communities strategy' including the mitigation of GHGE resulting from new development, although it specifically excludes that the strategy would interfere with the zoning ordinances. Finally, it provides that environmental impact statements for significant projects include GHGE information. An indirect relationship between planning and GHGE thus arises by the inclusion of GHGE issues in environmental legislation, as in Washington and Massachusetts,[18] which is taken into account in the planning process in respect of reviewable projects.

In all cases, except where the consideration involves obvious emitters, the manner in which planning should encompass GHGE is not clear. Where there is an attempt as in the planning policy in the United Kingdom and the California bill, the burden is shifted to other agencies to come up with plans on how to reduce GHGE in the context of planning. This is because planning is looked at as offering limited possibilities for dealing with GHGE compared with economic instruments, such as cap and trade.

The wording of the 2015 *Paris agreement* does not establish a link between spatial planning and climate change. After the *Paris agreement* and before the formation of the *New urban agenda*, an issue paper was prepared in 2015 by a UN team: *Urban planning and spatial design*. The paper was fed into the Habitat III conference that developed the *New urban agenda*. It essentially makes one relevant connection that infill rather than growth on the urban fringes reduces GHGE. The *New urban agenda* has general statements and one specific recommendation supporting compact cities to create economies of scale. No specific link is made to the means by which the goal is able to be created by planning structures or legislation.

---

16 *California Global Warming Solutions Act 2006*.
17 Senate Bill 375 2008.
18 *State Environmental Policy Act*, Washington, chapt. 43-21C RCW; *Environmental Policy Act*, Massachusetts, chapt. 30.

7.6 Effectiveness of mitigation as planning policy

The most comprehensive policy to use planning as a means to reduce GHGE was the supplement to the UK *Planning policy statement 1: planning and climate change*. It is useful to understand whether the contents of this best effort were effective in suggesting how planning could assist mitigation of GHGE. That policy was replaced by the *National planning policy framework*, which did not contain the same details as the previous policy.

The first statement in *Policy statement 1* is that a regional planning strategy employing a spatial plan should integrate climate change issues and should:

> pay particular attention to the location of major generators of travel, the effect of differing patterns of urban growth on the movement of goods and supply chains and the potential to build into new and existing development more efficient means of energy supply and increasing contributions from renewable and low-carbon energy sources.

The connection is developed through reducing car emissions and promoting energy efficiency. The wording creates an important sentiment but is not effective in providing any means of implementation. Inclusion of 'location of major generators of travel' is a difficult idea to comprehend as these uses must be located somewhere and will cause traffic generation no matter where they are placed. Placing them near existing residential areas in the name of infill may, in fact, cause more problems of traffic congestion on busy roads.

It is also not possible to understand how to implement the effect of 'patterns of urban growth on the movement of goods and supply chains'. Freight routes are to do with efficiency lines between rail and supply depots and retail outlets. It is not a subject matter that can have as its guiding principles the reduction of GHGE because it would impact on economic matters relating to the cost of goods.

The second strategy is stated to be:

> focus substantial new development on locations with good accessibility by means other than the private car and where it can readily and viably draw its energy supply from decentralised energy supply systems based on renewable and low-carbon forms of energy supply, or where there is clear potential for this to be realised . . .

The desire to focus new development on public transport areas is consistent with the theory of what is referred to as transport-oriented design. Decentralised or distributed energy is a concept that encourages local energy supply through the use of individual solar panels, small-scale wind turbines, micro hydro where there is a source of flowing water, and other technologies to generate heating.[19] Putting them in the policy has no effect as a principle to be followed. The only example perhaps of connecting planning policy and distributed energy is in the Ontario *Green Energy Act 2009*, which provides that renewable energy projects will be exempt from planning laws.

The next two statements of the now defunct UK *Planning policy* provide for increased renewable energy, a factor not really part of the planning process, and then:

---

19 McCormick et al. 2008.

- recognise the potential of, and encourage, those land uses and land management practices that help secure carbon sinks;
- consider the potential for carbon capture and storage, and the need for supporting infrastructure, and help realise this potential...

The location of a particular carbon sink, such as in a forest or in patches of open space, cannot be analysed in terms of effectiveness.[20] To what extent, for instance, does a public park reduce GHGE?[21] The potential for carbon capture and storage is again not a factor of allocation of uses through the planning process but of finding suitable areas for sequestration when that technology is proved effective.

These examples highlight the problems of the use of planning policy to mitigate GHGE. Planning theory and practice are primarily concerned with spatial design, the separation of land uses, and efficiencies that can be achieved in that process. When GHGE are added to this theory, it is possible that the tool of spatial design by means of transport planning or manipulation of the uses of land to aid GHGE mitigation can be envisaged as benefits that can be delivered. However, the complex forces that create land use decisions are not easily changed to focus on the externality of GHGE. Introducing the entire GHGE agenda in planning policy may have no practical benefit but at least creates the idea that when a decision is to be made about the allocation of uses, the fact of the need for mitigation of GHGE is a relevant consideration.

7.7 Planning solutions for GHGE mitigation

The Intergovernmental Panel on Climate Change prepared a report, *Climate change 2014: mitigation of climate change*, to assess current efforts including land use planning.[22] The report (sect. 12.5) indicates that the reduction of sprawl and thus energy consumption is the primary spatial planning effect to mitigate GHGE. This is accomplished by compact cities created by urban boundaries and smart growth, infill of existing areas, reducing the distance between residential areas and employment centres, creating self-contained communities, and emphasising transport-oriented design.

In summary, there are possibly only three relevant areas that can yield GHGE mitigation when planning is examined for specific implementation possibilities. First, there is the increased efficiency of dwellings in terms of reduced energy consumption; second, by a planning process that reduces the number of vehicle trips and, third, by control of specific development, such as factories that will emit GHGE. There are other variations on these three[23] but they remain the main focus of planning's input into mitigation.

---

20 van Mitten et al. 2008.
21 Kirschbaum 2003.
22 Intergovernmental Panel on Climate Change 2014.
23 Fitzgerald and Lenhart 2016.

Figure 7-1 Toyama Prefecture compact city, Japan. Source: Google Earth

Historically, planning is not oriented towards the use of any of these methods. The origin of planning controls is, in part, founded on the need to separate incompatible uses by establishing zones for the aggregation of related uses and prohibiting uses that are incompatible. Accordingly, by its very nature, zoning separates commercial and industrial uses from residential uses and creates the need to increase vehicle trips to work. As a result, planning, in its historical context, did not tend naturally to reduce vehicle trips. As well, building efficiency was never seen as an aspect of land use planning but was the subject matter of another regime of building controls.

Movements in planning theory towards smart growth, more infill, transport-oriented design, New Urbanism, and energy-efficient design have occurred without a direct connection to GHGE mitigation. These movements have internal cogency as consistent with planning theories in relation to reducing road congestion, creating more 'liveable' areas, and lowering the cost of building maintenance. It indicates that as cities grow, traffic, treated as creating pollution, has reached sufficient levels that these movements are relevant and necessary for efficient cities.

The connection between planning and GHGE mitigation is actually occurring, in spite of the lack of a natural fit. The creation of a policy as in *Statement 1* or the specific linking of GHGE mitigation with planning is useful to create a focus for the decisions, even though that focus does not appear to be part of the general body of planning theory.

7.8 Building efficiency

Building efficiency as one aspect of GHGE mitigation is not usually considered part of the spatial planning process but is included in linkages such as *Statement 1* as an aspect of planning. The concept behind building efficiency as a form of mitigation is that buildings are responsible for GHGE because of design imperfections that can be improved to prevent energy wastage and so require less output from power stations.

Building efficiency is proffered as a means of GHGE mitigation even though there are only speculative projections about the degree of savings. The GHGE mitigation arising from building efficiency is not known for several reasons.[24] Efficiency measures only apply to new buildings or those that are subject to extensive renovation and not existing stock, meaning the overall effect cannot be clearly evaluated. Another reason is that attempts to alleviate demand for electricity by 'demand management' programs have not proven successful because consumer behaviour is independent of these programs. The most significant reason could be that the efficiency of buildings will not necessarily lead to lower demand for electricity because, if the cost of using electricity is reduced by efficient technology, it may prompt increased usage.

The possible effect of efficiency is seen, however, as beneficial even though the precise effect is not known.[25] This is because modelling of efficiency measures is possible so that it can be concluded that energy consumption can be reduced theoretically by efficiency.

An example of the modelling of building efficiency is the 'DOE-2,' a computer program for building energy analyses, which can break down the efficiency of every building component such as the effect of the thickness, order and type of materials, and the orientation of exterior walls and roofs. Ten thousand runs of the program created the ASHRAE-90.2 standard that is used in the USA for efficiency measures for low-rise residential buildings. The US Green Building Council developed the *Leadership in energy and environmental design* (LEED) that provides a rating system based on this standard for the evaluation of energy performance. The efficiency modelled by the program is also analysed according to 'time-dependent valuation' that examines the cost effectiveness of measures having regard to different times of day, different seasons, and varying energy usage.

The essence of residential efficiency is the ability to reduce the use of heating and air conditioning that draws power. Ideally, the building will be airtight, insulated, and all electrical equipment will operate efficiently and run for less time. Voluntary reductions beyond that may not occur for a variety of reasons: consumer confusion about GHGE; mortgage lending practices that treat energy savings as just another cost; income levels that make reductions less attractive to some; and a doubt about the relative worth of energy efficiency in relation to its expense. Attempts at using 'programmable communicating thermostats' that provide wireless signals and can be controlled centrally have been less than popular.

Commercial activities require a wide variety of building types, making a single code of building efficiency difficult. As well, the energy 'load' varies according to the specific use made of building elements, such as lighting, heating, refrigeration, air conditioning, hours of operation and work efficiency. The industrial sector, the most obvious emitters, can make improvements in building use, for example, by downsizing the motors used to

---

24 Taylor 1999.
25 California Environmental Protection Agency 2008.

match the load. Individual solutions by industry, such as improved water-removing techniques in a pulp mill, are also a possibility.

These building efficiency concepts are not really planning solutions. They are concerned with building and use efficiency, but not the nature of that use. Neither are they concerned with the creation of a spatial plan, or a plan shaping a community that, somehow, by its sophistication, reduces GHGE. They are mechanical solutions that are directed to reducing energy consumption and are thus useful in the desire to reduce GHGE. However, even though they are not part of the historic nature of spatial allocation of land use, they can be included in the planning regime as development standards, as shown by the UK *Planning and Energy Act 2008* that provides:

> A local planning authority in England may in their development plan documents ... include policies imposing reasonable requirements for:
>
> a. a proportion of energy used in development in their area to be energy from renewable sources in the locality of the development;
> b. a proportion of energy used in development in their area to be low carbon energy from sources in the locality of the development;
> c. development in their area to comply with energy efficiency standards that exceed the energy requirements of building regulations.[26]

7.9 Transportation planning

With GHGE mitigation as a relevant consideration, planning can address the issue by allocating uses in a manner that reduces vehicle trips and so yields decreases in vehicle emissions. This is perhaps the most direct way that planning can aid GHGE mitigation.

Vehicle emissions are a significant source of GHGE. For instance, in 2005 in the EU, they accounted for 21 per cent of all GHGE[27] and in Australia they account for 13.5 per cent.[28] If planning could somehow, by the placement of uses, reduce the number of trips to work, the distance travelled, non-work related excursions, and freight journeys, it might result in a reduction of vehicle emissions.

A study by the US National Research Council[29] found that one clear use of planning for mitigation of GHGE is more compact development, which reduces the number of trips by 5 per cent to 12 per cent and cuts fuel. It was postulated that if 75 per cent of new development were made more compact, there would be a 7 to 8 per cent decline in GHGE by 2050.

The planning process can help reduce the number of vehicle trips in four ways that may serve to ameliorate GHGE. The first is 'transport-oriented design' (TOD), the concept that orients increased density of housing near public transportation nodes thus reducing the use of cars. The second, often working with TOD, is the planning for mixed-use areas that include local services and commercial uses joined with residential uses, shortening the distance residents need to travel to go shopping. The third is, either in the absence of or in

---

26 *Planning and Energy Act 2008*, sect. 1(1).
27 European Environmental Agency 2007.
28 http://www.environment.gov.au/climate-change/greenhouse-gas-measurement/tracking-emissions.
29 Transportation Research Board 2009.

conjunction with TOD, to use transport demand modelling to optimise the transportation options for new communities. The fourth is designing new communities to provide for desired destinations within walking distance.

It is worth repeating that these GHGE mitigation techniques run counter to the themes that underlie the planning process. The traditional concept behind zoning is to maintain property values by exclusive residential areas that do not have commercial intrusions or high density. As a consequence, the separation of commercial uses from low-density residential uses is a precept of zoning. If an area is zoned for a use more intense than single-family residential use, it is said there is a 'down-zoning'. It is partially for this reason, but also for economy of scale for developers, that retail shopping policy concentrates commercial uses, such as big box shopping centres, in a single area that requires access by road, causing increased traffic. The economic justification for centrality of shopping is that concentration of compatible uses will be beneficial overall for all shops and that there is a single destination that provides convenience and recognition for consumers. Concentration of uses is also consistent with the provision of services as an aspect of 'central place theory', which postulates that a central location for services can best serve regions, and shopping centre size can be adjusted to population.

Mixed-use development is not consistent with the American, Canadian and Australian planning ethos and its use varies in different countries in Europe.[30] The theoretical underpinning for mixed uses has always been that boring, homogeneous areas are anathema to the social life of a community. However, the desire for mixed uses is rarely found in suburban areas because it is difficult to negate the purpose of zoning, which is to maintain property values and the rateable base. Where there have been changes, it is usually as part of the cultural life of an existing urban area where compatible uses are seen as adding vibrancy to the metropolitan fabric. However, as a means to change existing suburbs by reducing the number of trips, mixing uses it is not likely to be a prime tool of GHGE mitigation.

The main method suggested for reducing trips to work is the adoption of TOD: concentrating residential density at public transport routes, theoretically reducing commuters' use of private vehicles. Although the exact contribution of TOD to reduction of GHGE cannot be calculated for an individual site, it is clear that increasing density without access to public transportation would result in a greater number of trips than providing public transport convenience. TOD can take many shapes, from increasing densities around existing public transit nodes, creating a specific project in a new area, using light rail or bus extensions for distribution of density, providing permissive zonings in areas near transit but with no specific projects, and other attempts to move development closer to nodes.[31] A variant of TOD is to take advantage of density along travel routes rather than concentrate major density at transport nodes. For example, in Marin County, California, the *Marin plan*, which is highly cognisant in its contents of GHGE provides specifically that the area along US Highway 101, already developed, be the focus for future development by this mandate: 'Concentrate urban development in the City-Centered Corridor, where infrastructure and facilities can be made available most efficiently.'[32]

---

30   Kasanko et al. 2006.
31   Transportation Research Board 2004.
32   *Marin countrywide plan* 2007, http://www.future-marin.org.

Figure 7-2 Transport-oriented design (TOD) in Emerson Park East, St Louis, Illinois. Source: Google Earth.

Setting aside an area for increased density near a transportation route or node does not assure it will necessarily be used in that way as development opportunity is primarily a business decision. If an area is zoned for increased density, the land values rise immediately and for a developer to locate a new project in that area means that profits will be diminished because the cost of land acquisition is higher. It is only when development options are restricted elsewhere that developers are forced into one location because large development companies must continue to make investments and take up any decent opportunity even if there is a low return.

In one of the few studies analysing developer and community reactions to higher densities in Vancouver, British Columbia, it was found that as local authorities required the developer to obtain a permit to increase density, this discouraged development. It forced the developer to make a large initial expenditure to prove the project. The community, when faced with increased density, became concerned with design issues and the perceived loss of lifestyle and focused on opposition, discouraging small developers from taking up the options. The consequence is that there is not necessarily an immediate take-up of higher density opportunities for TOD because of these barriers.[33]

TOD has the effect of reducing vehicle trips and is a clear, positive step to reduce emissions. In the case of existing communities, the increase in density near transport nodes is obvious. However, the most important connection between planning and emissions is in

---

33 Coriolis Consulting Corporation 2007.

respect of new suburban communities on the urban fringe in which TOD may not be appropriate. A submission by the Land Use Subgroup of the California Climate Action Team, a multi-agency group set up to provide recommendations to the California Air Resources Board, analysed 'urban sprawl' as the land use factor that has most led to vehicle emissions; in California's case, 30 per cent of GHGE in 2004. The underlying reason was that population increases drove the distribution of that population into new communities away from urban centres with link roads back to urban amenities and other new communities, as well as separation from employment opportunities. All of these led directly to increased vehicle trips and emissions.[34]

It would seem that there should be public transport options built into the planning of new communities. How to accomplish this is not easily resolved. The planning process and the provision of new infrastructure, such as new rail lines, are not directly linked, as has been explained. The examples of difficult linkages are easy to find: the Victorian Department of Transport, Planning and Local Infrastructure, where the three were joined administratively, appeared to be the answer, but these functions were split off into three separate departments in 2015, indicating just how difficult co-ordination of these activities can be.

Infrastructure spending is most often a *response* to a regional plan that allocates land for new housing. The link is then made after the plan, as with *Connect SEQ 2031: an integrated regional transport plan for South East Queensland* that amended the previous transport plan to accord with the completion of the *South East Queensland regional plan 2009–2031*. The problem is that the regional plan, or metropolitan strategy only dictates areas that may be developed, so the actual location of new communities is suggested and not fixed. As well, budgets for large infrastructure agencies, such as for roads and hospitals, get funded in the interim and the money to complete transportation nodes for new development is not always there when the time comes, shifting the burden to developer contributions.

When an analysis is made of transport requirements for new greenfield areas that are not concentrated on public transport nodes, the method by which transportation solutions are optimised is through 'transport demand models'. These methods calculate the manner in which people travel and therefore the infrastructure required to meet that demand. The fundamentals of all models are the same: the origin of trips is stated and then the distribution of possible trips is determined, the available modes of transport are analysed, and the number of trips is calculated. These transport demand models do not address GHGE but are based on economic efficiency of infrastructure expenditure thus theoretically sharpening the transportation options to reduce trips. However, they cannot be worked too hard as the fact of distance to work and facilities are a consequence of establishing new communities. Accordingly, a California legislative bill to link planning to GHGE stated that what is required is more of a sentiment: 'alternative development patterns or additional transportation measures.'[35]

It is the case that a degree of GHGE mitigation can occur by optimising the transport options available to new communities and in the building of infrastructure with a substantial focus on the GHGE agenda. This is accomplished theoretically by the use of transportation models that can calculate the GHGE scenarios presented by different op-

---

34   Land Use Subgroup of the California Climate Action Team 2008.
35   Senate Bill no. 375, 12.

tions. More general models for the calculation of transport options existed before GHGE issues and were made relevant to GHGE effects because they allow for pollutants in their formulation.[36] These general models are necessary because the issue in transport modelling is not just vehicle emissions but also the potential for future fuel efficiency, impacts of decreased use of diesel, and other variables.

The combination of these factors is the most important basis for mitigation attempts: decreasing distance between services and residential development, refining transportation options having regard to GHGE, and employing New Urbanism tools of walkable neighbourhoods and integrated services in new communities. This strong belief that vehicle trips can be reduced by effective planning will slowly begin to be part of the planning process so that projects that accord with smart growth will be given precedence over those that ignore such issues.

7.10 Specific GHGE emitters

Planning has another role to play in GHGE abatement that can have a more immediate effect. Development control is a regulatory system that requires permission to undertake development. This discretionary allocation of land use is the primary means by which planning can take into account GHGE abatement because, at the time of making an application to commence a development, the GHGE implications of a specific use may be analysed.

To analyse GHGE consequences for all uses would be impossible. Stern was content to go after 'obvious' emitters and, in the same way, planning can identify the targets that are important. A starting point is that such uses would be most clearly identified in legislation required of a participant in the *Paris agreement*. Identification compels reporting of GHGE levels, which is then accomplished by the legislation requiring specific industries to disclose their GHGE if they are over a certain level of emissions.[37]

Having identified the possible targets, the question is how to gauge the mitigation that is possible. Signatories of Kyoto and now Paris have accepted GHGE mitigation targets on the basis of a national total. It is not possible to say to an industry that is seeking a development permit that it must accord with this total as its contribution is unclear. It is also not possible to merely say that there must be a reduction when the effect cannot be measured. It is possible to require a wholesale mitigation, but the requirement is meaningless without some idea, even if not precise, of the contributory effect of the industry at a particular location.

The UK *Planning policy statement 1* contained a provision that each region establish GHGE trajectories having regard to the emission carbon rate for new dwellings and commercial buildings, the expected energy reduction from building efficiency measures, the possible use of renewable energy technology, and the transport demand of new developments. This could lead to planning documents that, in turn, are relevant for determining planning applications as the effect of a proposal on the trajectory can be analysed. It is not suggested that developments be conditioned to cut a certain percentage of GHGE, but the

---

36   Chien 2005.
37   *National Greenhouse and Energy Reporting Act 2007*, sect. 13.

consistency of the proposal with a policy based on regional assessment of GHGE mitigation will be relevant.

The *National planning policy framework* changed the emphasis to creating a low-carbon future by use of renewable energy and then suggested guidelines to enhance that choice through development control (para. 98):

> When determining planning applications, local planning authorities should:
> - not require applicants for energy development to demonstrate the overall need for renewable or low carbon energy and also recognise that even small-scale projects provide a valuable contribution to cutting greenhouse gas emissions; and
> - approve the application if its impacts are (or can be made) acceptable. Once suitable areas for renewable and low carbon energy have been identified in plans, local planning authorities should also expect subsequent applications for commercial scale projects outside these areas to demonstrate that the proposed location meets the criteria used in identifying suitable areas.

The system of development control is in place in most countries in some form, meaning that no new mechanisms need be established, such as an emission trading scheme requires. Most buildings, at one time or another, because of renovations or changes of use, require permission, bringing the housing and commercial stock into consideration. The UK statement is defective in terms of proposing goals that are easily expressed but difficult to deliver. However, the combination of regional assessment of GHGE trajectories with planning goals brings the two closer together and makes for a useful filter for development applications to mitigate GHGE.

7.11 Governance for climate change mitigation

The mitigation of greenhouse gases arising from international treaties is primarily a national issue. As a result, there are national incentives that do not take into account local issues or governance structures. To take the example of the US efforts to reduce carbon emissions, there is a complex national and state structure, with little attempt at co-ordinating with local government. At the federal level there is the *Clean Air Act*, a command-and-control system for carbon emissions derived from inclusion of greenhouse gases as pollutants, the subject matter of that act, by a decision, already mentioned, in the Supreme Court in *Massachusetts v. EPA*. Since that decision in 2007, the Environmental Protection Agency has established an evolving regulatory scheme for stationary source GHGE and, with the National Highway and Traffic Safety Administration, vehicle emissions. The EPA has stepped into the regulation of GHGE after the defeat of the Waxman-Markey Bill that would have introduced a cap and trade system for the United States.

The EPA rules consist of two essential forms. The rules for vehicle emissions are supplemented by the *Energy Independence and Security Act 2007*, which requires annual improvements in fuel efficiency of 5 per cent per year. The regulatory scheme for stationary sources of GHGE includes the 2009 *Greenhouse Gas Reporting Rule* that requires GHGE for 10,000 facilities. The facilities include direct greenhouse gas emitters, fossil fuel suppliers, industrial gas suppliers, and facilities that inject CO_2 underground for sequestration.

The EPA also requires pre-construction permitting for major new and modified stationary sources and applies operating performance standards. On 27 March 2012, the EPA proposed a *Carbon pollution standard for new power plants*.

Control of GHGE also arises indirectly by legislation and rules directed at other activities. On 27 January 2010, the US Security and Exchange Commission (SEC) published *Commission guidance regarding disclosure related to climate change* that requires all publically traded companies to disclose risks arising from climate change developments. A 2011 report from Ceres, a non-profit coalition of institutional investors, environmental organisations and other public interest groups, concluded that corporate filers must gain experience in communicating the risks associated with climate change under the guidelines. The *Sarbanes-Oxley Act* increases the general level of disclosure for public companies and, because of the classic Supreme Court decision in *TSC Industries Inc. v. Northway Inc.*, any material element must be disclosed that raises the level of corporate exposure on carbon-related issues.

In 2012, PNC Bank, a lender to listed companies, sought a 'no-action' letter from the SEC so that it could exclude a shareholder proposal that:

> [PNC] report to shareholders by September 2013, at reasonable cost and omitting proprietary information, PNC's assessment of the greenhouse gas emissions resulting from its lending portfolio and its exposure to climate change risk in its lending, investing, and financing activities.

In 2013 the SEC refused to issue PNC Bank with a no-action letter, forcing PNC to comply with the shareholder request. This places a burden on financial institutions that deal with listed companies to disclose GHG emissions.

Carbon regulation also arises in general environmental legislation. The *National Environmental Policy Act* contains requirements for an environmental impact statement (EIS) for major federal actions that impact the environment. The same applies for state acts (SEPA). The Council on Environmental Quality's 2010 guidance on the inclusion of climate change is non-binding but has become an aspect of an environmental impact statement in many federal agencies, such as the Department of the Interior and the US Forest Service.

The most direct regulation in respect of GHGE is by administrative rules put forward by the EPA and the Council on Environmental Quality. The EPA is committed to expanding its rule-making power after it made a scientific determination that GHGE are harmful. The EPA rules are in constant change because of continued attempts at blocking the EPA rule-making power by litigation and in the House and Senate.[38]

In New York, performance standards by the Department of Environmental Conservation provide carbon emission standards for electricity facilities. This is only one of the many programs for the State of New York where the mitigation attempts blend into the state functions of planning and infrastructure. The programs of the state are not mandatory but affect every development, as they are official policy. They are derived from *Executive Order No. 24* of 2009, *Establishing a goal to reduce greenhouse gas emissions eighty*

---

[38] This chapter was revised in January 2017, after the US presidential election of November 2016 but before any decisions had been made affecting the rule-making power of the Environmental Protection Agency.

percent by the year 2050 and preparing a climate action plan. They include *Climate smart communities*, the 2013 *State energy plan*, the 2011 *ClimAID* study on adaptation, and the 2010 *Interim report on the sate climate action plan*. The planning policy to reduce emissions are contained as to infrastructure in the *State Smart Growth Infrastructure Policy Act* and the New York Energy Efficient Portfolio Standard. The New York *Environmental Quality Review Act* requires all decision makers to consider environmental impacts. In 2012, DEC published new rules for EIS assessment that now include the taking into account of climate change.

At the international climate meetings in Copenhagen in December 2009, President Barack Obama pledged that, by 2020, the United States would achieve reductions in GHGE emissions of 17 per cent from 2005 levels. In 2015 the EPA issued the *Clean power plan,* which required reductions from the power sector of 32 per cent below 2005 levels. The *Tailoring Rule* of 2010 brought the largest stationary sources of GHGE under a permitting system. This implies the need for the continuous monitoring of proposed regulatory schemes and investment laws that relate to the monetising of carbon.

Attempts at regulation are constant and it does not appear to matter whether the source is linked to planning or is in separate pronouncements or legislation. There have also been many unsuccessful attempts at legislation to regulate carbon such as the American *Clean Air and Security Act 2009*, the *Black Carbon Emissions Reduction Act 2009*, the *Clean Energy Jobs and American Power Act 2009*, the Waxman-Markey proposals, the *Liberman-Warner Climate Security Act 2008*, the *Low Carbon Economy Act 2007*, and the *Climate Stewardship and Innovation Act 2007*.

California's *Global Warming Solutions Act 2006* proposed a state-wide GHGE limit to be achieved by 2020. Senate Bill X1-2 became law in 2012 to codify this limit by directing the Public Utilities Commission to increase the amount of electricity generated by renewable energy resources each year. In early 2012, California introduced a cap and trade system. Under the ARB (Air Resources Board) *Regulation for the Mandatory Reporting of Greenhouse Gas Emissions*, there are specific requirements for greenhouse gas reporting and verification from facilities, fuel suppliers and retail electricity providers.

In an accompanying memorandum to the 2013 statement by President Obama releasing his *Climate action plan*, there is an aggressive timeline for the EPA to adopt, and for the states to implement, 'carbon pollution standards, regulations or guidelines, as appropriate, for modified, reconstructed and existing power plants.' The plan also establishes the goal of doubling renewable electricity generation in the United States by 2020. This may have been an important pronouncement as it took the issue of mitigation out of the hands of local government that proceeded slowly on planning changes to a federal directive that could move more quickly. If there is a decrease in these rules and regulations, the emphasis will again fall back on local government.

As the focus shifted to federal mitigation attempts and away from planning, the critical issue became the scope of rule making by the EPA under section 111(d) of the *Clean Air Act*. The EPA may introduce measures for target-setting of GHGE. This target can be 'mass-based', which prescribes a total tonnage for each state, or a 'rate-based' system that works by pound/megawatt hour. With a mass-based system, cap and trade will be a likely consequence and with rate-based, there would be considerably more regulatory compliance required. If this rule-making power is lessened or destroyed, the reallocation of these issues will fall on the states, who do not have the same restrictions in place either directly or through planning. It may have the effect of encouraging the use of planning devices as a means of mitigation. However, the historical development of planning in the United States as regulating known and visible externalities will not mean rapid amendment of local planning systems.

Into this complex mix are added city governance structures that have to find devices to co-ordinate with national and state agencies. Cities have responded in an ad hoc way with transportation ideas, increasing greenbelts, and flood-risk zones. It has been argued that stand-alone policies for mitigation of GHGE are unlikely to be successful because of the difficulties of jurisdictional complexities and have not accordingly been part of the land use planning system,[39] especially after reliance on the EPA rule-making power.

Cities have other more immediate issues than GHGE, especially in developing countries. GHGE mitigation ideas are popular but are not always turned into regulatory forms. In an analysis of 200 European cities across 11 countries that have some form of climate change mitigation and adaptation control, it was argued that, if all the planned actions were implemented, even though many of them are merely ideas, there would be a 37 per cent reduction in emissions, far short of the 80 per cent required to avoid warming of 2°C above pre-industrial levels.[40]

Nevertheless, land is where the GHGE emerge and planning must have a contributory part to play. The only means by which this can occur is by the planning system and the larger GHGE regimes having a coincidence of agendas. A clarifying study makes the case that only when the local agenda and that of GHGE mitigation are aligned can there be any effective use of planning.[41] This is accomplished by greater densities in existing areas near transport nodes to reduce vehicle emissions, retrofitting buildings for greater efficiency, and encouraging renewable energy, to name but three broad possibilities. These possibilities exist but need to be more focused and measurable if there is going to be a concentration of mitigation initiatives.

It can be said that the incentive for using local regulation to combat GHGE is diminished where the issue of climate change is not made the first priority in urban areas. This is for many reasons, such as a belief that it falls under national initiatives and a general ignoring of the threat that the world faces, probably for psychological reasons.[42] However, there are some possible ways to mitigate GHGE that are practical and can be made part of a planning system.

7.12 Best practice

The national efforts for mitigation must be combined with local efforts and not be seen as separate. The national agendas are top-down approaches and do not take into account local needs or agendas. This co-ordination occurs when there is some local or regional awareness of the need for mitigation of GHGE, in part as an aspect of the planning agenda. This can be accomplished primarily by some explicit statement that mitigation is important in the strategic plan or in the relevant considerations for development control. If this occurs,

---

39 Viguie and Hallegatte 2012.
40 Reckien et al. 2014.
41 Dulal and Akbar 2013.
42 Stein 2015.

there is then an impetus for co-operative arrangements and absorption of top-down policy by local authorities.

The sustainability agenda stands as the basis for mitigation of GHGE in planning and this should be highlighted in strategic plans, if not in a separate overarching document as suggested. Planning, through a description of the scope of sustainability, must recognise the importance of mitigation as a relevant consideration. When it is recognised, it will have an effect. If it is not made specific, it will be entirely left to top-down approaches. As mitigation appears to go against the traditional bases of strategic and spatial planning, the regional and local authorities need to be re-educated in the devices that can be used to mitigate GHGE. Merely providing a regional requirement for TOD or compact areas does not provide the guidance needed. A guidance statement of techniques is essential to bring the devices into popularity.

The place of mitigation in planning has not been helped by vague statements about encouraging compact cities developed according to TOD or infill. There is always a push by inner-city residents to shift new housing to the urban fringe, thereby reducing the loss of their amenity by increased density in established neighbourhoods. It is therefore important to give mitigation a wider definition not restricted to compact cities and reducing trips. It may be that public transport options can be made available to new suburbs so that a compact city approach is not needed. If there is a definition that is set out with a description of the goals of mitigation and how they will be applied in the exercise of discretion in the case of the original plan as well as for rezonings and development control, this will make the linkage patent.

The need to be explicit is necessary because the actual effect of a use on GHGE in a particular locality is not always clear. A stationary emitter could be near a forest and it might be said that there is an offset by that being a carbon sink. Therefore, although a planning scheme might not be able to apply specific restrictions, it could indicate the relevance of mitigation, allowing a developer to address that issue in an attempt to satisfy the planning authority. If this is established as a practice, then mitigation will make its way more firmly into the planning agenda.

The device of what is called 'shared socioeconomic pathways' perhaps highlights the real possible influence of planning on mitigation. The pathways are narrative storylines of the future, examining demographics, economics, technology, and other socio-economic indicators to determine what will happen and its effect on mitigation and adaptation of GHGE. Inputs, such as increased use of renewable energy, crop yield improvement, use of nuclear power, population increases, urbanisation, and other factors, are all brought into the assessment of what might happen to GHGE. One analysis has argued that the future will bring resource efficiency, more emphasis on sustainability of agriculture, and that these societal trends create a pathway to be able to argue that there will be less GHGE in the future.[43]

Planning has the capacity to create a pathway for the future of mitigation of GHGE because of its connection with sustainability. By recognition of mitigation as an aspect of GHGE, it is possible to explain transportation issues in these terms as well as offering bonus density for energy efficiency. It does not need to prove its case in terms of measuring the GHGE of a prospective use but rather can assert mitigation as a backdrop to elements

---

43 Van Vuurnen et al. 2016.

in the strategic plan. This will then add to it becoming a societal trend and to having influence on future planning scenarios.

8
Adaptation for climate change

Revised from Stein 2014.

Adaptationaccepts that global warming exists and seeks strategies to ameliorate its effects. Unlike mitigation of GHGE to lessen the threat of potential effects, the nature of adaptation is to adapt to the consequences as they occur. Strategies for adaptation are not confined to those produced by national governments and solutions are promoted by regional planning authorities, voluntary alliances, local government associations, and metropolitan and local governments. In practice, the adaptation attempts at the regional or local government level are largely ad hoc and planning is given only a minor role.

The relationship of adaptation to planning, to be fully explained, requires traversing its evolution and the manner in which it has developed as a consequence of a national framework that is insufficient. This involves a complex assessment of national failuresbecause local attempts at adaptation have grown out of national failures, delays, and unresolved governance issues. It is the insufficiency of national approaches to adaptation that has opened the possibility of adaptation becoming a planning matter. This is because adaptation itself does not follow naturally as a planning or local government policy issue because the ultimate effects are speculative both in terms of timing and impact.

The approaches to adaptation fall into these two broad typologies. A top-down approachto adaptation, as with mitigation, is where a national government follows and interprets international climate change agendas to yield an adaptation strategy that becomes a national policy, referred to universally as a National adaptation strategy NAS). The bottom-up approachis where adaptation solutions to specific climate change vulnerabilities are proposed by regional, metropolitan or local governments.

A 2010 study for the Netherlands Commission for Environmental Assessment *Knowledge for climate* series[1] explains that the difference is largely based on the scope of risk assessment. An NAS or a top-down approach examines the risks arising from global climate change projections scaled down to a national level. Accordingly, the NAS assesses vulnerabilities and therefore adaptation for a nation. The bottom-up approach, in contrast, assesses vulnerabilities at a local level. As it is a local scale, it is also distinguished by the availability of local input through community participation. The Netherlands assessment states:

---

1   Ludwig and Swart 2010.

The bottom-up approach for developing adaptation options and making choices can be considered as a guided societal consultation process between stakeholders, in order to arrive at preferred and socially accepted risk-management policies, strategies and adaptation actions.

The top-down approach makes adaptation a subset of world climate change modalities and offers physical solutions that do not take into account the social or political consequences of adaptation as it is removed from the local stakeholders and institutions. The bottom-up approach draws on existing institutions and local or regional sentiments to create policies that are derived from social and shared imperatives. This of course is not always the case, but characterises many of the forms of adaptation strategies that have emerged.

The Netherlands report does not suggest that the two are mutually exclusive and proposes forms that are a mix of the two. The first mixed form is the development of a national policy framework that incorporates international goals but also analyses local risks, vulnerabilities, and capacity to adapt. The second is the inclusion of national adaptation goals into existing local decision frameworks, such as EIA or water management. In the second instance, adaptation strategies become an element or relevant consideration in an existing decision-making process in both plan-led and development control systems.

8.1 Immaturity of top-down approaches

A review of adaptation reveals that most are in the process of being prepared and are not complete strategies. In a 2010 report, the OECD commented:

> OECD analysis shows progress across all developed countries in terms of understanding climate projections and its impacts, and in identifying adaptation options. Less progress has been made on establishing institutional mechanisms and explicitly incorporating climate change risks in projects and policies.[2]

Many of the NAS documents that have been put forward are partial, incomplete, and do not offer details of implementation and are therefore immature. Italy provides an example of an adaptation strategy with the implementation still in progress as of 2016. The slow progress is for several, common reasons, including only recent acceptance of adaptation as an aspect of climate change, lack of methodologies for assessment of risk, uncertain capacity to adapt, and complex governance issues.

There are historical examples of national strategies for adaptation to climatic events, such as the control of inundation in low-lying areas in the Netherlands,[3] but the need for long-term planning for adaptation as a global phenomenon arising from climate change is relatively recent; there is no reported NAS until 2007, which was in France (*Stratégie nationale d'adaptation au changement climatique*).

The development of national strategies is a consequence of recent acceptance of adaptation rather than just mitigation as a possible focal point for climate change. Before 2001, there was little attention given to the concept of adaptation in any country. The World Bank

---

2   Organisation for Economic Cooperation and Development 2010.
3   Colijn and Binnendijk 1998.

briefly mentioned it in 1999.[4] The United Nations Framework Convention on Climate Change (UNFCCC) in 1997 makes reference to the need for parties to have adaptation measures in Article 4.1(e):

> Co-operate in preparing for adaptation to the impacts of climate change; develop and elaborate appropriate and integrated plans for coastal zone management, water resources and agriculture, and for the protection and rehabilitation of areas, particularly in Africa, affected by drought and desertification, as well as floods.

It is argued that because this article also dealt with the effects of climate change on oil exporting countries (art. 4.10), the adaptation provisions, occupying a minor place in the convention compared with mitigation, received little attention initially.[5] The argument continued that *The Delhi declaration on climate change and sustainable development* in 2002 is therefore the first document that suggests that adaptation should be a significant component of climate change policy. It is the Delhi Declaration, not the UNFCCC, that invites all developing countries to develop and implementnational adaptation programmes of action (NAPA).[6] The guidelines for NAPAs were put forward in 2001[7] – there was no substantive action until that time.

The continued delay in national adaptation planning can also be attributed to the lack of methodologies to assess the impact of climate change in terms of risk and vulnerabilities, which is the precursor to discovering solutions. The methodologies for assessing environmental impacts more generally first emerged in the early 1990s to address aspects of the environment included within the overarching concept of sustainability.[8] However, as these methodologies developed, it was unclear which tools could be employed to assess climate change as opposed to more specific or proximate environmental issues. The 1994 Intergovernmental Panel on Climate Change (IPPC) report on *Technical guidelines for assessing climate change impacts and adaptations* provided a preliminary series of steps that were called a 'study framework'.[9] However, these steps were criticised as being focused on searching for a single solution when adaptation was a more complex, iterative process.[10] The United Nations Environment Programme (UNEP) in 1998 presented a more detailed discussion of these guidelines that reduced the process to a defined set of steps (Scoping, Select Methods, Data-sets and Baselines, Test Methods, Develop Scenarios, Examine Future Impacts, Identify Adaptation Options, Integrate & Synthesise), but did not provide guidance as to their content, leaving them difficult to apply.[11]

In 2007, new detailed methodologies for assessing climate change impacts were put forward by the IPCC.[12] The 2007 advances were explained as:

---

4 Burton and van Aalst 1999.
5 O'Keefe et al. 2008.
6 Decision 8/CP.8 FCCC/CP/2002/7/Add. 1.
7 COP, Marrakesh, decision 28/CP.7.
8 Dalal-Clayton 1992; Donnelly, Dalal-Clayton and Hughes 1998.
9 Carter et al. 1994.
10 Klein, Nicholls and Mimura 1999.
11 Feenstra et al. 1998; Benioff, Guill and Lee 1996.
12 Intergovernmental Panel on Climate Change 2007.

Significant advances in adaptation assessment have occurred, shifting its emphasis from a research-driven activity to one where stakeholders participate in order to improve decision-making. The key advance is the incorporation of adaptation to past and present climate. This has the advantage of anchoring the assessment in what is already known, and can be used to explore adaptation to climate variability and extremes, especially if scenarios of future variability are uncertain or unavailable.

To be effective, adaptation strategies also require an assessment of disaster risk and risk reduction for isolated events, and that imperative first appeared in the December 2007 *Bali action plan* that sought strategies for both risk management and risk reduction strategies. In a specific context dealing with Nairobi, the UNFCCC Subsidiary Bodies meeting in Bonn in June 2008 requested information from parties on the inclusion of disaster-risk programs in national policies and programs.[13]

The *IPCC fourth assessment report* indicated that there must be a reduction in vulnerability to risk.[14] This 2007 report set out some possible adaptation strategies but did not indicate which were successful and so was not suitable as a basis for guidance on adaptation strategies. This guidance was left to the *IPCC fifth assessment report* of 2013, which produced, as part of that cycle, the 2012 *IPCC special report on managing risks of extreme events and disasters to advance climate change adaptation*.

This special report emphasised that 'resilience' was one of the factors necessary for adaptation, defined as:

> The ability of a system and its component parts to anticipate, absorb, accommodate, or recover from the effects of a hazardous event in a timely and efficient manner, including through ensuring the preservation, restoration, or improvement of its essential basic structures and functions.

The concept of a resilient city then became part of the planning agenda for many cities. In 2014, Los Angeles appointed a resilience officer to plan for dealing with disasters. The London *Managing risks and increasing resilience* document is linked as a climate change adaptation strategy. The *Paris agreement* uses the term 'resilient' as does the *New urban agenda* in 2016, and it is now an accepted term for adaptation for buildings and infrastructure.

8.2 Unaddressed goals of a national adaptation strategy

The UK *Climate impacts programme* developed various tools to assist in the steps for climate change adaptation planning. The *Climate change adaptation wizard*[15] sets out the potential coverage of an NAS:

- Building adaptive capacity
- Gathering and sharing information

---

13 United Nations Framework Convention on Climate Change 2008.
14 Intergovernmental Panel on Climate Change 2007.
15 Willows et al. 2003.

- Creating a supportive institutional framework
- Creating supportive social structures
- Delivering adaptation actions
- Bearing the risks
- Sharing or spreading the risks
- Avoiding or reducing the risks
- Exploiting new opportunities

A survey examined adaptation strategies of the United States, the United Kingdom and Australia and discovered disparities between the coverage that is possible in this model and what actually is attempted. It was found that there is less attention paid to the second part, the *Delivering adaptation actions*, in that it:

> treats the management of such consequences as a consideration of the tail-end of the assessment process, rather than an issue to be considered throughout.[16]

These two broad categories of 'building capacity' and 'delivering options' are theoretically distinct, thus allowing the first to pass for an NAS as it is less difficult to understand adaptation as a form of impact assessment for which there are methodologies. The delivery of on-the-ground adaptation options is a more difficult process, leading most NAS to settle initially for the first aspect and not the delivery of action plans. A study of NAS development in Europe concluded:

> the strategies themselves remain largely focused on the improvement, provision and dissemination of knowledge on climate change impacts and adaptation options, particularly to lower tiers of administration.[17]

This phenomenon occurs because it is easier to prepare a section on building capacity on a national level than to deliver options on that scale. In preparing a section on building capacity, climate change details can be acquired across a nation as there are existing methodologies. As it is important to express common problems, such as coastal erosion on a country or regional basis, a national direction without specific actions follows. A national approach does not, however, identify particular nuances between areas at this level because the issues are general risk and national capacity building. The delivery options for implementation also depend on the use of regulatory tools that are available at the particular governance level that is necessary for implementation and are not necessarily part of a national approach. Floodplain management has, for example, been traditionally a matter of land use controls and actions taken under local ordinances even though it can be assessed for risk and vulnerabilities across regions or on a national level.[18]

---

16 Preston, Westaway and Yuen 2011.
17 Westerhoff et al. 2010.
18 Nunes et al. 1999.

8.3 Governance failures in national adaptation strategies

The OECD evaluation of *National communications for annex 1 countries* in 2006[19] indicated that there was, at that time, relatively little attention to adaptation reporting and progress in the preparation of an NAS. A survey of the United States, United Kingdom and Australia as to first generation adaptation strategies concluded that, because this process is so slow, lacking in institutional investment and caught in governance conflicts, there was an 'adaptation deficit' and it is thus argued:

> The prevalence of adaptation deficits casts significant doubt on the capacity of institutions to develop and implement robust strategies for adaptation to both current and future risks.[20]

An assessment of adaptation strategies in 2009 of EU member countries found weaknesses in NAS primarily because of a lack of co-ordination in governance arrangements.[21] These governance issues arise from two sources. The first is confusion about what is required from different agencies in terms of capacity building, the first component of an NAS. A Netherlands study stated:

> However, in most applications of this framework for evaluation of vulnerability and adaptation options, adaptive capacity is not included in practice because commonly agreed methods to quantify adaptive capacity do not exist.[22]

The second is a belief that adaptation can be driven from national policies that will trickle down to lower levels, the so-called 'mainstreaming' approach. The *IPCC special report* states:

> There is *high agreement* and *robust evidence* to demonstrate that the mainstreaming of disaster risk management processes into development planning and practice leads to more resilient development pathways.[23]

The need for a national approach and mainstreaming as the preferred method of adaptation was perhaps fortified by the establishment of the Least Developed Countries Expert Group at the 2007 Bali conference that set out a work program for a national adaptation program of actions (NAPA for these countries, reliant on mainstreaming. By April 2010, 44 NAPAs were developed and a further guide, the *Step-by-step guide for implementing national adaptation programmes of action* was produced. The supposition in the guide was that adaptation policy would be effectuated by mainstreaming. The Least Developed Countries Fund as of 2016 has raised almost a billion dollars to assist in implementing adaptation. Analysis of the use of these funds has shown that they have had success in increasing adaptive capacity but have been unable to mainstream adaptation and, instead,

---

19 Gagnon-Lebrun and Agrawala 2006.
20 International Panel on Climate Change 2012, 410.
21 Biesbroeck et al. 2009.
22 International Panel on Climate Change 2012, 380.
23 Ludwig and Swart 2010, 380.

efforts have been fragmented and ad hoc. The reason given is the lack of capacity in these countries to make the investments work.[24]

There has been a tendency to look at mainstreaming as the means to justify nations obtaining additional funding for developing adaptation strategies and also because of the National Communication requirement of the UNFCCC. As an example, the Global Environment Facility (GEF) funded the Pacific Island Climate Change Assistance Program,[25] which was one of the first forums to report to the UNFCCC under the national communications requirement to consider adaptation. This dovetailed the vulnerability and adaptation strategies with the need for the national communication reporting and made the strategies the basis for further GEF funding.[26] The emphasis on 'national' continued the emphasis on top-down, mainstreaming approaches.

In 2008, the UNFCCC published the *Compendium on methods and tools to evaluate impacts of, and vulnerability and adaptation to, climate change*, as a 'second-generation' approach. More sophisticated analyses of vulnerabilities and adaptation needs were developed for national programs and a means of mainstreaming was again suggested. This fostered a renewed reliance on a national, mainstreaming approach that often ignored subnational or local programs except perhaps to use them as illustrations.

The governance problems from an NAS arise because of the conflicting agendas of state and local government agencies. As described for water management in Canada:

> In Canada, introducing adaptation measures can be challenging, simply due to the fact that many different levels of government administer water management activities. Even within one level of government, several separate agencies are often involved in water legislation.[27]

In 2007, Canada introduced regional adaptation co-operatives to co-ordinate adaptation governance issues, among other matters. The governance conflicts in all jurisdictions also arise because state agencies plan in 10–15 year cycles and cannot easily absorb national policies that may require their agendas to be altered. The result is that lip service is paid in many instances and ignored in others where the integration is not easily understood. A 2016 study by the OECD[28] found that successful mainstreaming was uncommon, perhaps due to the complexity of linking with existing policies that go beyond adaptation, such as poverty reduction, biodiversity, and the economic development of cities. A study of mainstreaming in Sweden found that it conflicted with legal norms as to the precautionary principle and free trade and was unsuccessful because of lack of competencies at the national level.[29]

---

24 Sovacool, Linner and Klein 2017.
25 Pacific Island Climate Change Assistance Programme 1999.
26 Warrick 2000.
27 Lemmen and Warren 2004.
28 Organisation for Economic Co-operation and Development 2016.
29 Carina, Keskitalo and Pettersson, 2016.

8.4 Other top-down approaches

There are five essential forms of top-down approaches to adaptation that are not restricted to the publication of an NAS. The first is an overarching policy or policies, not amounting to an NAS, that are meant to mainstream into other non-adaptation policies in a seamless manner. The second is where there is policy integration because of a political system that provides for integrated decision making. The third is where only some of the multiple themes of adaptation are dealt with in an NAS or national policy due to their complexity and others develop separately. The fourth is where the difficulty in developing an NAS leads to an amalgam of disparate policies, and the fifth is where individual projects are presented as the proof of a unified national policy and are essentially a substitute for an NAS.

A 2009 European Union Commission white paper[30] proposed a framework to align with Article 4 of the UNFCCC's call for national adaptation strategies. The objective of the EU *Adaptation framework* was to prepare, during 2009–12, a comprehensive EU adaptation strategy that would be commenced in 2013. The concept is that adaptation could then be mainstreamed into other EU policies. A working paper attached to the white paper[31] identified relevant EU policies and the manner in which adaptation issues could be integrated. The EU *Water framework directive* that was adopted in December 2000[32] was presented as an example of a model. This directive requires a river basin management plan to be prepared by December 2009 by EU members in line with the directive. The EU enforcement mechanism could then be used to take non-complying member states to the European Union Court of Justice to enforce compliance.

The EU directives do not offer specific adaptation strategies and leave the details to member states. As an example, Article 10 of the EU Commission *Decision on criteria and methodological standards on good environmental status of marine waters* provides:

> Progress towards good environmental status is taking place in the context of continuous broader changes in the marine environment. Climate change is already having an impact on the marine environment, including on ecosystem processes and functions. In developing their respective marine strategies, Member States need to specify, where appropriate, any evidence of climate change impacts. Adaptive management on the basis of the ecosystem-based approach includes the regular update of the determination of good environmental status.[33]

As of 2016 there is no evidence that there has been any integration or co-ordination of adaptation with EU development policy. This could be a result of the difficulty of achieving what has been called policy 'coherence' in the EU. The complexity of 'vertical coherence' between EU policy and that of member states has led to it being called 'mission impossible'.[34]

In China, policy integration takes two forms: co-ordination of policy making between different bureaucracies and integrating different policies into one single consensus policy.

---

30 Commission of the European Communities 2009.
31 European Commission working document SEC/2009/0386.
32 European Commission directive 2000/60/EC.
33 European Commission decision 2010/477/EU.
34 Carbone 2009.

There is a specific emphasis on policy co-ordination in respect of climate change.[35] It arises in all policy settings when China accepts international norms that then motivate the bureaucracies to bargain for their interests within the framework of those norms to reach consensus. In the case of climate change, this was enhanced by the United Nations Environment Programme advice and foreign expert opinion where there was previously little knowledge. This overcame the Chinese 'authoritarian fragmented model' of policy making where it can be disjointed and fragmented. The *National climate change programme* of China of 2007, as revised in 2015, sets out the goals of adaptation in general terms. In 2009, a joint project of China, the United Kingdom and Switzerland called *Adapting to climate change in China* concentrated on adaptation needs generally and in three provinces, and has produced an adaptation policy for Guangdong.

Adaptation is applicable to many sectors and programs of different agencies and is not a singular process. The adaptation problems such as sea-level rise, loss of marine biodiversity and drought, brought about by climate change, cut across different sectors of an economy such as forestry, fishing, tourism and recreation. Due to this wide diversity of issues, an adaptation strategy can either combine the multiplicity of needs into a single document under one banner of adaptation or deal with each of the many issues separately. The diversity of issues means that there is no uniform approach or solution for adaptation and it is impossible for a single policy to be drafted that does more than highlight the issues and suggest some form of action. A prime example is the Canadian NAS, *From impacts to adaptation: Canada in a changing climate 2007* that outlines every aspect of adaptation by sector and also by region and gives examples, but not specific solutions to adaptation. The more recent *Federal adaptation policy framework* of 2016 is more general, perhaps in recognition that an NAS is not capable of enunciating all relevant issues.

The recognition of multiplicity seems to discourage rather than encourage action plans, or at least changes their focus to a set of principles and not actions. Even though the 2007 Canadian NAS is comprehensive in its list of issues, it is often ignored in practical solutions. An example is the operation of the Canadian *Environmental Assessment Act* that requires agencies to carry out an *Environmental impact assessment* for all projects.[36] That act does not require adaptation considerations to be taken into account nor does the relevant policy document, *The cabinet directive on the environmental assessment of policy, plan and program proposals*. Instead, there is a reference back in the directive to examine if the project promotes the *Federal sustainable development strategy*, which is another climate change policy but which does not address adaptation. As a consequence, adaptation is not part of the governance structures of Canadian federal agencies and adaptation appears directed to local initiatives as shown in the *Adapting to climate change: a risk based guide for local government and changing climate, changing communities: guide for municipal climate adaptation* publication of the federal government and in the 2015 *Implementation framework for climate change adaptation planning at a watershed scale* of the Canadian Council of Ministers of the Environment.

Another example of the diversity of issues discouraging national action plans for implementation can be found in India. India's *National action plan on climate change* was announced in 2008 by the Prime Minister's Council on Climate Change and provides for eight broad 'national missions'. These include sustaining the Himalayan ecosystem, sus-

---

35 Yu 2004.
36 Smith 2010.

tainable agriculture, sustainable habitat, and enhanced energy efficiency. It was proposed that mission documents for the implementation of each of the eight topics be submitted on each area by 2008. The eight, however, do not include pressing practical issues such as the need for adaptation due to sea-level rise that is a major concern for urban areas in India.[37] Due to the lack of integration with the mission documents and the complexity of the topics outlined in the missions, the pressing issue of sea-level rise has been dealt with outside the NAS. New coastal rules establishing coastal zones under the *Coastal Regulation Zone Notification 2011*[38] were made under existing environmental legislation that set up Coastal Management Authorities in 1998 for purposes unrelated to climate change sea-level rises.[39]

8.5 Arrangements due to difficulty in implementing an NAS

Germany is an example of arrangements being made for adaptation because of delays caused in implementation of an NAS. This arises by virtue of a governance paradigm that has made policy integration difficult but has yielded other forms for adaptation. Following major flooding in the low-lying Wadden Sea, an initial flooding plan was created in the early 1960s. A new plan, the *Schleswig-Holstein coastal defence strategy*, prepared in 2001, contains the first consideration in Germany of adaptation to climate change. It is a policy document that was to be applied even in the face of reports that there were going to be no sea-level rises and that even the risk of storm surges was low.[40] It is based on the principle of 'integrated coastal defence management', which considers coastal defence as part of a spatial land use planning process and not just a 'hold the line' response. This is significant because the existing defences are sea dykes and this was a shift away from reliance on dykes into spatial planning.

The *German strategy for adaptation to climate change* (*Deutsche Anpassungsstrategie an den Klimawandel*) was adopted in 2008. It is expressed to be a general framework and suggests that an adaptation action plan be created by March 2011 between the federal government and the Länder; it states:

> The targeted adaptation process coordinated between the federal and Länder levels calls for a systematic approach with the creation of a common base of methods, knowledge and data on the impacts of climate change, the expected consequences and the effects that can already be observed.

However, it indicates that most of the Länder have carried out studies on the effect of climate change and that their adaptation strategies were under way. The 2011 *National adaptation action plan* contains a summary of the Länder projects for adaptation and those to be carried out with Federal and Länder co-operation.

The complex interaction between layers of government that led to an incongruity in national and local policy, such as illustrated in Germany, is said to arise for four reasons, in addition to the delays in the preparation of an NAS.[41] The first is a lack of clarity about the

---

37 Revi 2008.
38 Latha and Prasad 2010.
39 Environmental Protection Agency 1986.
40 Hofstede 2008.

potential ambit of an adaptation strategy. There is a narrow definition of climate change of the UNFCCC arising exclusively from human activity and there is the wider IPCCC view that it is a change arising from any source. On the narrow definition, adaptation is restricted to the solutions arising from the failure of mitigation.[42] On a wider view, the existing environmental risk issues are absorbed into the wider framework. A greater emphasis on one or the other can lead to a lack of policy coherence. The second is that adaptation must go beyond immediate responses and require changes in production and consumption processes, meaning that they are meaningless unless they are supported by other policies. This confusion leads to an absence of implementation, a lack of financial commitments, and no monitoring and evaluation, as the consistency between policies is not addressed. The third is that adaptation strategies have used a top-down approach as scaled-down models from global climate models. As mentioned, this has ignored societal processes of adaptation that include issues such as the socio-economic effect of droughts on marginalised social groups. Not including such analyses weakens the national adaptation policies and invites other analyses, the nature of which is unclear. Finally, although mitigation is a matter of national government and international negotiations, adaptation is sometimes seen as a local or regional issue, and therefore not readily suited to an overall national response.

8.6 Bottom-up approaches

Many adaptation strategies and concepts can be labelled bottom-up because they are unconcerned with national climate change issues and are not dependent upon an NAS. They arise from regional agreements, NGO action,[43] local initiatives, national focus on a particular problem, and private initiatives in anticipation of climate events. The main typologies are those that are regional in approach or arise from local initiatives through metropolitan or local governments.

The vulnerabilities in Europe are identified as the mountains that will undergo geomorphological and ecological changes resulting from temperature increase, coastal areas affected by sea-level rises, especially on the Baltic, Mediterranean, and Black Seas, and potential destruction of habitats and ecosystems.[44] These risks, spread throughout Europe, transcend individual boundaries and are regional in nature.

National strategies discount regional or local initiatives and try to solve these issues by a top-down approach. Concerning the Alps, for example, the Austrian *National adaptation strategy*[45] and the Belgium *National climate change adaptation strategy* of December 2010,[46] which were to be a prelude to developing a national adaptation plan, do not deal with adaptation for these mountains. In fact, the Belgium strategy specifically discounts the local and regional adaptation initiatives as being a result of a 'bottom-up approach' and therefore not 'easily recognisable in international inventories'.[47] It should be pointed out

---

41 Görg 2010.
42 Pielke 2005.
43 Obermaier et al. 2009.
44 Medri et al. 2008.
45 Westerhoff et al. 2010, 278.
46 National Climate Commission 2010.
47 National Climate Commission 2010, 7.

that the National Climate Committee maintained the primacy of its top-down approach by assigning federal entities to reduce emissions in the Flemish, Walloon Forest, and Brussels regions in 2004 and the Belgian strategy in 2016 added regional adaptation strategies for the Flemish and Walloon regions as national objectives.

The Bulgarian *Second national action plan on climate change 2005–2008*, updated in 2014 after the Fukushima nuclear disaster, requires research and analysis of adaptation techniques for future implementation, as does that of Hungary.[48] The *Hungarian strategy*, however, concentrates on the effect of drought and mitigation rather than adaptation, as do most other European Union countries. In all these forms of developing strategies, there is concern about the difficult governance issues that arise between adaptation as a regional issue and national concerns. The reasons for the concerns are best explained in a review of adaptation attempts by Nordic countries, where it was concluded:

> Placing adaptation on local agendas requires networks that cut across governance levels, including regional capacity and responsibility. National adaptation policy initiatives are necessary but not sufficient for local adaptation responses. In Nordic peripheral regions, local adaptive capacity is often linked to the ability to compete in market-based systems, including economic resources, technology, and infrastructure.[49]

The complete strategies that successfully link regional concerns with an NAS are few. In France, the *French national adaptation strategy* was adopted by parliament in 2006 and the *National adaptation plan* in 2011.[50] The strategy had a progressive list of adaptation steps to be taken, starting with developing greater knowledge on vulnerabilities, updating observation systems and exchanging information, convincing regions of the need for adaptation to be worked into departmental, regional and local plans, and utilising legislative and regulatory instruments by reviewing laws and texts so that climate change is taken into account. There are, however, no specific actions or legislative amendments suggested. A report to the French prime minister and parliament in November 2009 indicated 'identified lines of adaptation' that included sector solutions such as alternative agricultural systems, water sector robustness, and a building and urban framework that reduces the demands on energy, particularly that of air conditioning.[51] The adaptation plan contains various action recommendations, including a 'governance action sheet', which indicates some of the difficulties. For regional government, the basis of planning in France, it states:

> In the field of regional governance, the complexity of the system, especially as regards the distribution of skills, responsibilities and resources, has been perceived as a potential source of difficulties for the implementation of adaptation policies.[52]

The answer it gives is to mainstream national policy and to continue to evaluate regional and national approaches to seek consistency. However, most of the actual initiatives in this form of adaptation in Europe are not progressed under an NAS. Two European Environ-

---

48 Diossy 2009.
49 Nilsson 2009.
50 National Observatory for the Impacts of Global Warming 2007.
51 National Observatory for the Impacts of Global Warming 2009.
52 National Observatory for the Impacts of Global Warming 2007, 62.

mental Agency reports in 2014 and 2015[53] confirmed that it appears difficult for an NAS to incorporate the myriad of local adaptation needs. There are, however, individual projects assisted by NGOs, such as the Climate Alliance, made up of 1500 member cities and districts,[54] where the NAS is merely a framework and concrete projects are at a regional, metropolitan or local level.

Cities have unique adaptation issues that are not necessarily related to national or more generalised objectives. This is particularly true of mitigation attempts, such as bicycle plans, organic waste, green buildings, electric-hybrid buses, green roofs, and the myriad other issues that can be addressed across a metropolitan area. Storm drainage, green roofs to absorb heat, health planning, and local risk assessment are examples of adaptation possibilities across a metropolitan area. A survey in Portugal found that the national climate change plans and European strategies hold minor importance for municipalities. A realisation of the future impacts expected for the region was the greatest driver of local adaptation ideas but was hampered by a lack of capacity to understand the potential impacts.[55]

In Toronto, short-term measures for adaptation were approved by council in 2008 to improve emergency responses and to produce better adaptation responses by a more accurate risk assessment. They included specific measures, such as better drainage for storm water. In 2008, a comprehensive program for full adaptation planning was suggested and that year it was recommended:

> In order to adapt to the long-lasting change in weather patterns due to climate change, City Council direct that climate change mitigation measures and explicit goals for adaptation of infrastructure and buildings be incorporated into Toronto's Official Plan and request that the Chief Planner report on the amendments appropriate to the Official Plan incorporating such measures.[56]

It was also proposed that all departments include adaptation in their planning, yet it was reported in 2009 that adaptation goals were not put in some departmental budgets nor have they been specifically related to climate change projections.[57] In 2014, the council adopted the report *Resilient city: preparing for a changing climate*. That report stated the need:

> to establish a process to manage across City Divisions and Agencies the interdependencies of infrastructure and services identified as being at risk to a changing climate; and to explore partnership opportunities with the private sector and broader public sector, such as telecommunication, private utility, healthcare, banking and insurance, in the implementation of collective action that increases Toronto's resilience to a changing climate and extreme weather.[58]

---

53   European Environmental Agency 2014 and 2015.
54   Garrelts and Lange 2011.
55   Campos et al. 2017.
56   Toronto Environment Office 2008.
57   Penney, Dickinson and Ligeti 2009.
58   Toronto Environment Office 2014.

The problem with municipal imperatives is that, as the timeline of necessary changes is not fixed, the budget requirements of agencies affect existing commitments and there is uncertainty on the content of the collaboration. The assessment of risk to climate change is a long, expensive process and is especially difficult over a large municipality. It consists of identification of hazards, consequent vulnerability and adaptation capacity, requiring an assessment of the ability to respond, and the possibility of a solution. This makes the process highly intensive and a strain on local finances. When the problems are found, the tools are not always clear as the framework of laws may not be sufficient to provide solutions.

It appears that local initiatives are most likely to follow a climate event where the realisation of a significant problem becomes apparent. Local authorities do not appear to model the effects of climate change, such as the extent of sea-level rise or the occurrence of drought, because these remain national or global issues. It is more likely therefore that an event prompts action. The 'Dry Line', a 12-kilometre high-water barrier for southern Manhattan, arose from the devastation of Hurricane Sandy in 2012 and construction is set for 2017.

8.7 Adaptation and the planning process

The hazards facing a local community by the effects of climate change are best understood by the residents. It is difficult for an entire adaptation plan at a national or regional level to embrace all the possible effects that depend upon nuances of topography, wind exposure, housing materials, and transportation patterns. The adaptation needs to be analysed at a local level:

> Adaptation to climate change is highly local, and its effectiveness depends on local and extralocal institutions through which incentives for individual and collective action are structured.[59]

There is room for adaptation initiatives in the planning process because the effects are on uses conducted on land. This can be accomplished by making the goals of a wider area, metropolitan or regional strategic plan express the general idea of adaptation, leaving local plans to fill in the detail for specific areas when they come to be zoned or developed. Local plans can explain those areas that are at risk, such as flood-prone lands, and provide conditions for building, such as a required setback. A plan-led system is one way that the overall capacity of the land can be understood and explained in terms of risk and possible solutions.

In making this risk assessment as part of the planning process, the planning authority must establish the degree of sea-level rise, and the impact such as erosion, flooding, storm surge, drought, the vulnerabilities of particular areas, and the land uses that may be affected. Inclusion in a plan does not in itself lead to a positive set of actions for the future. This requires steps to be taken to prepare for, or adapt to, possible events. In this way, planning is limited in its effect on adaptation to identifying areas at risk. It would likely be seen as unreasonable for a developer to carry out works to prepare land for all climate change

---

59 Agrawal, Kononen and Perrin 2009, 177–78.

eventualities and therefore planning's role is to assess the risk of future events and prohibit or restrict development.

It is straightforward for a strategic plan to address the need for resilience and flood risks but it is not easy to make those ideas operational. This is not only because adaptation requires positive steps that are usually outside planning, but also, as it has been pointed out in a study of Sydney,[60] because there are constraints in carrying out local adaptation requirements to do with leadership, institutional governance arrangements, and competing planning agendas. The complexities of adaptation methods also suggests that it take place outside the planning process. An example is the strategic plan for Rio di Janeiro 2013–2016 that acknowledges adaptation needs and suggests the further development of an adaptation strategy.

More effective integration of adaptation with local decision making arises where an application for development is made and adaptation issues can be considered. Where there is a system of development control generally, or development in a particular area requires a permit, considerations of adaptation actions are a natural occurrence of risk assessment and can be a relevant planning issue. It does not matter if the work is carried out or addressed outside a strategic plan as long as there is some mention of a connection or that these issues are a relevant consideration.

Adaptation can be considered a relevant consideration of an application for development if it exits either in a policy document or is considered as within the scope of land use planning. In the New South Wales Land and Environment Court, the effect of climate-change-induced beach erosion was considered a relevant consideration.[61] In the United Kingdom, adaptation arose in *Planning policy statement: planning and climate change*, which provided for adaptation to be a relevant consideration in planning and decision making. The same is true of its successor, the *National planning policy framework*. The framework provides that local authorities should take into account mitigation and adaptation strategies 'taking full account of flood risk, coastal change and water supply-and-demand considerations'. In addition, it is also indicated that:

> Planning plays a key role in helping shape places to secure radical reductions in greenhouse gas emissions, minimising vulnerability and providing resilience to the impacts of climate change, and supporting the delivery of renewable. Achieving sustainable development and low carbon energy and associated infrastructure. This is central to the economic, social and environmental dimensions of sustainable development.

The idea in the United Kingdom is to deliver adaptation both through local decision making and spatial land use planning. An assessment of UK adaptation efforts highlighted this viewpoint:

> Adaptation is not an objective or process that should be considered in isolation. Adaptation is one part of broader decision making, for example it is an integral part of sustainable development, land use planning, resource and risk management, and environmental sustainability.[62]

---

60 Measham et al. 2011.
61 *Aldous v. Greater Taree City Council* [2009] NSWLEC 17.
62 Ranger et al. 2010.

There are instances where local land use planning has been used as the primary method of adaptation.[63] In Faenza, Italy, for example, an incentive program has been created for developers to locate in specific 'bio-neighborhoods'. In Stuttgart, Germany, the *Climate atlas*, which indicates particular vulnerabilities, is referenced in a *Climate booklet* that in turn informs the *Building code* that regulates development and requires climate impacts to be considered.

The difficulty with acceptance of adaptation in land use planning is that planning laws are entrenched and have a certain internal culture of administration and structure. Introducing adaptation as a planning issue requires amendment to planning instruments or policies that may be contrary to the principles for various zones. In some cases, restrictions on a use because of identified risks may amount to a compulsory acquisition of land and require compensation that an authority may not have included in its budget.

There are two methods by which adaptation can be absorbed more easily into planning regimes. The first applies to developing countries where the planning system is not yet fully entrenched as in Ho Chi Minh City (HCMC).[64] It is recognised in that city that the impact of sea-level rise will affect the built environment, reducing the areas that are available for housing. This is significant in HCMC as 50 per cent of suburban districts are in flood-prone areas or areas where long-term development is not indicated. As the use of planning is relatively new in HCMC, the use of planning tools was not entrenched and lent itself to a 'green agenda' that could be introduced without modifications and made sea-level rise a relevant development consideration. As a consequence, detailed arrangements for adaptation are made for all levels of development.

An appendix to the annotated UNEP 1998 guidelines for the preparation of NAPAs emphasises the need for integration of the NAPA into existing development plans and therefore into the land use process.[65] A model is expressed by reference to the *South Pacific regional environment program*:[66]

> 1. For each development proposal, determine if modifications are necessary following an analysis of:
>   a. the effects of climate change on the proposal itself;
>   b. the effects of the proposal on key ecosystems, resources and environments that are sensitive to climate change; and
>   c. the effects of the proposal on the ability of communities to cope with climate change impacts.
> 2. Develop options for how the proposal may be modified in light of this analysis.
> 3. Evaluate the modification options.
> 4. Integrate approved modifications into a revised development proposal.

This is a recognition that a NAPA must be implemented through the planning and policy development cycles, leading to the conclusion that:

---

63 Green and Blue Space Adaptation for Urban Areas and Eco-Towns project in Europe: http://climate-adapt.eea.europa.eu/metadata/projects/green-and-blue-space-adaptation-for-urban-areas-and-eco-towns.
64 Eckert, Voigt and Kien 2009.
65 Feenstra et al. 1998; Benioff, Guill and Lee 1996.
66 Feenstra et al. 1998, Appendix B, 27.

A system for integrated land and resource planning and management is critical to translating synergies between adaptation needs and national development planning goals into practice.[67]

A second method arises from the positive tie-in of sustainable development and adaptation.[68] Sustainable development has the consequence of promoting the resilience of communities to climate change and the wider goals of social benefits that accrue. Sustainability as a concept has the capacity to recognise adaptation and disaster reduction. In any event, sustainability is an aspect of land use planning and therefore inherently contains many of the goals of adaptation.

In some areas, the linking of land use planning and adaptation is ineffectual because of more systemic problems requiring different adjustments. For example, slum dwellers in informal settlements in developing countries are not necessarily considered in flood mitigation strategies and the land use laws serve only the more established social structures.[69] This reflects the theory that, when social and ecological scales are out of step, adaptation is difficult.[70]

The relationship between land use and NAPAs for developing countries has not been obvious. It has been argued that NAPAs in developing countries have concentrated on rural areas and not urban areas:

> Even fewer of the NAPAs consider the specific question of how urban planning and urban governance need to be modified in order to address climate change adaptation more effectively.[71]

This is perhaps best understood because adaptation turns on the application of local knowledge to vulnerability issues, such as: the precise effect of various tipping points; demographic predictions; social stratification issues; political realities; governance arrangements; the fear of disasters or risks such as flooding; the effect on infrastructure, the effect on employment opportunities;[72] the relationship of the inhabitants to land from a legal and cultural viewpoint;[73] and the impact on the rate base. As a result, standard adaptation measures for a large area, across a wide range of issues, may not be as appropriate as solutions for individual, local issues that allow a flexibility that accepts the variables and uncertainties.

It is clear that the larger cities of the world are all preparing for adaptation to the effects of climate change,[74] such as a super-levee for Tokyo, the Jakarta coastal defence strategy, and the water detention ponds in Staten Island. Climate change adaptation has a natural fit with planning, both at the plan-making stage and the decision-making stage in a system of development control. The wide concept of sustainability can be easily expanded to include adaptation at the local level as a relevant planning consideration.

---

67 Feenstra et al. 1998
68 Ayers and Dodman 2010.
69 Chatterjee 2010.
70 Nelson, Adger and Brown 2007.
71 Birkmann et al. 2010.
72 United Nations Environment Programme 2010.
73 Ahmed et al. 2008.
74 C40 Cities Climate Change Leadership Group 2011.

8.8 Best practice

As with mitigation, adaptation must be mentioned as a component of planning in all relevant documents. A good example is the strategic plan for New York City, *PlaNYC 2030*, which mentions that work must be carried out on adaptation. This has led to the establishment of a task force where these issues are being analysed. The mention of adaptation as an aspect of planning is sufficient as it will lead to further investigation and possible local solutions.

A strategic plan should also indicate how it is consistent with a national agenda or plan of action. As adaptation issues may transcend local interests, regional strategic planning must mention adaptation and, at the least, a regional association should be formed, either formally or informally, to analyse vulnerabilities and co-ordinate adaptation efforts in areas of overlapping concern.

There is no argument to be made that adaptation is not a valid planning issue. Adaptation fits within the concept of sustainability and should be listed as a sustainability goal. As it is a planning issue affecting the community, the adaptation choices should either be a result of community participation as part of the visioning process or as a separate exercise for sustainability purposes. Ideally, because there are so many issues involved in the concept of sustainability, the best practice, as already mentioned, is to have sustainability in a separate document and not in the strategic plan. The strategic plan, of course, should mention the sustainability plan and make the adaptation issues relevant considerations in both the making of a plan and in development control.

Flood risk should be considered as part of strategic planning and accounted for in the spatial plan. This is accomplished by setting up zones or an overlay on a zone that recognises the risk. The methods for inclusion are well established, such as areas where there is a one in 100-year chance of flooding. Flood risk is a formal consideration in a system of development control.

Conclusion

The primary realisation of this work is that the relationship of an individual to a city is multilayered and is essentially *independent* of land use planning. Planning exerts little control over the subjective experience of city living. It is not possible for planning to positively address the urban ills of the 21st century: income inequality apparent in all cities, loneliness, alienation, racism, noise, pollution, murders, homelessness, impassable traffic, crowded medical services and escalating costs, decaying infrastructure, corruption, and endemic drug use.

The myth that planning can make great cities is moribund. The grand visions based on pure aesthetics or high ideals, such as those of Le Corbusier, Ebenezer Howard or Georges-Eugène Haussmann, cannot be achieved through the control of the use of land in modern urban environments. The reasons for the failure of planning to deliver those ideals can be explained by the dominion of neoliberalism, where planning is oriented towards the exploitation of land for wealth creation rather than the establishment of any co-operative, compelling urban vision. The economic power of a city, its competitiveness in attracting business, its ability to foster personal wealth, coupled with the prevalent zeitgeist that accumulation of wealth is the measure of success, have made planning the servant rather than the master. The gleaming city, the grand homes, the displays of wealth, are the levers that control the planning process.

The thesis of this work is that the disconnect arises because the conscious values of harmony, order and higher ideals are no longer the real bases for planning and have been replaced by unarticulated neoliberal ideas and practices that support that ideology. The change from one set of ideals to another has gone relatively unnoticed because harmony and order, as well as neoliberal ideals, are both ruled by and receive their momentum from the same unconscious goals of ameliorating the fears arising from an unpredictable world. Obtaining wealth, preserving property values, maximising site yield, making grand cities to prove economic power, are a form of harmony and order and offer a chance to believe there is a buffer against the ill winds of urban chaos.

The planner who evokes the arguments of harmony and order and promises that we can make better communities through planning is connected to some historical dream that no longer applies in the same form as its progenitors. The idea of Jane Jacobs that the subjective experience can be improved through planning is now a barrier rather than an inspiration. Although her propositions sound so meaningful and aligned with our deepest hopes and fears, they wither in the face of contemporary urban problems, brought about by the inexorable progress of neoliberalism and its consequences. New Urbanism and Smart Growth are at least redeemed as planning devices because, and only because, they bring the focus back to the details of the physical surroundings, offering the possibility of a shared examination of community values.

Neoliberalism, through the creation of inequality and the push for reduced regulation, has been the catalyst for two processes that are now emerging. The first, which can be seen explicitly in post-communist regimes and in the *New urban agenda*, is the search for the return of power to the repressed community to be able to influence decisions. It can be observed in iconoclastic, anti-government political movements and heightened dissatisfaction with closed-door deals and corruption. The second effect is increasing distrust in the planning system as the vehicle to deliver a higher standard of living for the entire community and not just for the elite. In older cities, such as Utrecht or Copenhagen, where the underlying patterns are set by historical imprint, the community understands that the job of the planning authorities is not to allow that to erode, so there is less distrust. In newer cities, gripped by economic inequality, decisions are too often inexplicable and tainted by unaccountable decision making, bringing residents into the streets.

This is not to say that planning is not necessary. The absence of planning in modern urban centres creates insecure land tenure, speculation, erratic markets, confusion over urban futures, and individual conflicts. There is no better example than walking 30 minutes from the city centre of Bucharest to the wetlands of Văcărești Park, which are cut off by dykes and were previously unusable. The lack of planning of the Ceaușescu regime and his idea of using it for building created chaos among interested parties, uncertainty as to how to protect this unique area, individual and professional conflicts, and interagency confusion.[1] Planning was needed to provide a framework for conflicting interests, to set a path for decisions, preventing corruption and intimidation, and re-establishing a role for government in the formation of the city, which finally gave it protected conservation status.

In this century of mass migration and inequality, various practices have emerged that suggest a reorientation of the function and operation of urban land use planning. The idea of top-down planning on a grand scale for vast regions, based on the need to distribute population increases, no longer has the same imprimatur. The concept of the planner having a vast set of tools to fill in every piece of a regional puzzle is no longer as acceptable as a means to supply the best outcome.

The rise of localism, although more a concept at this point rather than a predominant form, suggests a movement away from top-down planning towards a concentration on local issues and details. The advantage of localism as the basis of planning is the engagement of the community so as to reach a consensus in line with local views, sustainability ideals, and the challenges of climate change. To see each local area as merely a cog in the regional machine has proven to be less effective than to agree on common state and regional goals and leave the implementation and details to local areas and involvement of its residents.

The rights of city dwellers cannot be adequately protected in a planning system that explicitly or implicitly primarily promotes economic growth. Community participation in these cases is inevitably weak or useless and ecological sustainability is rarely championed. Sustainability loses its way in the complexities of the planning process and, in most cases, is tokenised or ignored. Therefore, it is very clear in observing the functioning of planning

---

1 Ianoș, Sorensen and Merciu 2017.

regimes that the prime vehicle for participation and the exposition of community values is in a separate local process, most effectively *outside the planning process*, perhaps under the convenient rubric of a sustainability policy. Here, all the outcomes of community hopes and dreams can be included in one focused summary unpolluted by the strands of political or economic ideologies. This can then be used as the counterbalance for unarticulated power interests that seek wealth above efficacy.

Nothing in this conclusion deflates the importance of developers for an urban future. There must be a capitalist emphasis on profits and growth for a city to develop. However, the community are stakeholders as much as the developers. Accordingly, the voice of the community is as essential as any neoliberal ideal and a planning system that fails to accord equal weight to all stakeholders is inadequate. That voice of the residents can be accessed in several ways: the reduction of complex regulations that the community are unable to understand, abolishing behind-closed-door decision making, explicit recognition of participation at the formative stage, less abstracted decisions by state or regional authorities without consultation, preventing unaccountable metropolitan commissions, and providing an emphasis on trust of local decision making.

The inevitable, countervailing sentiment behind state control is that local authorities cannot be trusted because of corruption. There is no need to look far to say that state or federal politicians can be the subject of similar claims. There are many methods for mitigating corruption and influence in local decision making. These are preferable to removing the power of local governments and handing power to boards, regional authorities and independent decision makers.

The search for best practice is one for equity, transparency and effectiveness. A planning system must understand its limits and not venture into social issues directly or through the back door of creating 'vibrant' communities. The factors that make for that vibrancy are more complex than allowing coffee shops or mixed uses and include such factors as the cohesion of the community, faith in government, the juxtaposition of elements of the built form, the services available, the availability of familiar settings for foreign-born residents, and the degree to which social capital is developed over time. If a planning system is inclusive, if it can be understood by the community, if it does not foster conflicts and stakeholders are satisfied, that is enough.

C.1 Idealised systems

The best planning system, however configured and expressed, is one where the wishes, hopes and dreams of a community are able to be contained in a document that is outside the planning system yet is a reference point for planning decisions. This document is then the basis for all considerations in development decisions. As the whole notion of finding individuals to participate and setting up a process for information and scenario testing is so complex, this should receive prime attention as the absolute best practice in land use planning.

It is important to repeat and emphasise that the community vision is best when it is outside the planning system because the layers of that system, buried in regulations, policies and controls, are so dense that there is little room for the emergence of a community sentiment. This is why participation is often weak or merely tokenistic. When a zoning decision is to be made, or an application is considered for development consent, the external document must be examined for a narrative that explains what the community expects. This is not a system where the community values have to outweigh the cogency of a potential development at the time of impact, but rather it is an acknowledgement that the community is an equal partner in its future.

This is not a left-wing sentiment or based on any ideological foundation. Instead, it arises from a recognition that planning cannot enhance the subjective experience of inhabitants unless it provides them with an understanding of their community and a chance to express their hopes and dreams. Planning, with the acknowledgement that it cannot prevent inequality and the effects of urban ills, can at least become a forum for a shared understanding of community and can create empowerment. This was palpable in Latin America, where all conversations about planning returned again and again to the benefits of participation, not even in order to shape a city but just to be heard in an era of powerlessness.

Around this concept of providing forums for participation flow other effects on the planning system: narrowing the scale of planning to local issues, reducing regional and state guidance to essential matters, and providing very clear explanations of how the entire planning system works. Demystifying the process, providing line-of-sight analysis between local and regional documents, offering officials who can consult with the community and keep the public informed all lead to an idealised form of a planning system. As much planning is carried out by policies, it is equally essential that a guide or summary be provided that makes the policies able to be understood by anyone in the community and not only by planning experts.

The argument of the state is that complications arise and it alone understands the future spatial distribution of increased population. It must force local authorities to accept greater densities, so token participation is therefore enough. This occurs because of the long timeline of demography, suggesting 15–20 year plans, and also a lack of a champion for local issues in the larger state or regional context. These long-term decisions should be made on a shorter time scale, assessed after certain intervals, with gradual introduction of density targets and timing as matters of discussion and ongoing analysis, rather than imposed housing numbers. Whatever the form, they are best made in consultation with the community and with community representation on state and local planning authorities directly or by elected representatives.

The historical view of planning as a task for experts squirrelled away in the back room of a planning department poring over maps, drawing up zones and deciding uses, is no longer the contemporary approach to land use planning. On-the-ground examination of planning systems reveals that government planners are most comfortable with this process as a remnant of what they were taught in planning schools or because they are not sure where else to turn when there is no new developed planning theory. The realisation is, however, apparent that the experiments of planning systems in Vancouver, Portland, and England indicate that local involvement is what makes systems most effective, preserves worthy environments, and allows for engagement by the citizenry in their futures. It is not embracing a planning theory such as TOD or mixed uses that makes planning work, but rather public engagement from the beginning of every planning idea.

An idealised system would thus have limited top-down regional and state intervention. Where it exists, it must explain itself and be along regional or state lines and not for local issues. Regional intervention should be for the purpose of interconnectivity of local areas, as is the plan for Paris or Copenhagen. The region should be involved only in the historic concepts of urban growth, such as concentric growth, linearity, or new cities as attractors. It should not be a decision-making layer that overrides local concerns and forces outcomes, except in the case of state-significant infrastructure or iconic sites.

This ideal system would look at the process of planning as a tripartite collective bargaining exercise, with developer interests, local interests and local government weighing and balancing potential alternatives. The outcome of that balancing should provide for a large range of uses as of right, reflecting that the decisions have been made by consensus.

It must also be recognised that development control is essentially a system that reflects poor initial up-front planning and exists on the rationale that a decision should be temporally efficacious. However, it forces a rewrite of the consensus attained by tripartite collective bargaining and has too many levels of inefficiency and control. The movement to consensus-driven plan-led schemes far outweighs the apparent flexibility of development control. Where it is used for flexibility, as it must be, it should confine itself to those considerations which are not social in nature but fall under the essential elements of land use allocation in terms of placement of uses, the building standards and the impact on the amenity of an existing area.

C.2 Operational best practice

The goals and visions of the collective process may be too wide and vague to be operationalised into a planning system. A goal of a 'pleasant' community does not yield particular forms of land use. The goals and visions, to be the subject of a planning regime, must arise from a direct need identified by the community in relation to the physical environment and not as an attempt to direct subjective experience that is impossible to predict; it is just as much a guess that opening up land for a park will reduce alienation as it is that bumping into a neighbour on a multi-use street will have that effect. This can only occur when planning gets away from Jane Jacobs thinking; it must confine her work to fantasy, and concentrate on the needs of the community in terms of roads, social services, open space, and environmentally sensitive land. It should leave the social, aspirational goals to their proper place through social programs and the larger milieu of economic and political factors. It should rely on community participation as the only social statement.

Regional planning is not as focused as local planning but it has its own wider goals. In an ideal system, the regional goals should be subsumed, as much as possible, into local processes. This creates a need to focus regional planning on individual, discrete projects, such as urban renewal of overlapping local areas or revitalising a waterfront. The use of independent development corporations instead of local governments is contrary to good planning practice if they do not allow participation from the very beginning or if they keep their processes secretive. The use of municipal commissions has a long successful history but they operate properly when there is intense community engagement and not autocratic directing of outcomes. It is an observable phenomenon, perhaps traceable back to Max Weber, that members of commissions become captured by the possibility that the lofty ideals can be reached and so there is a history of *ex cathedra* statements by appointed luminaries on how to improve the city, such as piazza here or a monument there. Commissions need to be accountable and that can only occur where all members are elected and none are appointed.

Growth areas for future populations raise a particular set of problems and are the most difficult of all planning issues. The choice of areas and co-ordination with infrastructure are the loose ends of this process that lead to speculation, rising land and house prices. The time period and scope of the development of new areas should be absorbed into local agendas after consultation. When areas are designated, this reflects a regional need, and the local authority must report its progress on meeting those needs, but in a local context without a regional authority intervening.

The operational best practice derived from an examination of systems across the world results in two clear observations. The first is that the best practice is always towards a process for balancing stakeholder involvement. This is acceptance of the reality of allocation of land use being a form of collective bargaining with different, and often contrary, stakeholder interests. When this occurs, the 'users' of the system are satisfied with the imperfect result.

The second is that planning cannot deliberately affect subjective experience, or at least in a way that is measurable. This is a statement of the limited effect of planning to create a grand vision and a realisation that its role is reduced to balancing competing interests for land. Accordingly, any best practice that seeks to balance the interests of stakeholders has cogency and can be operationalised. Other practices that work against this framework, such as unaccountable decision makers, amendments without community involvement, development corporations acting on their own, state intervention in local matters, and complex policy and plan interactions, are not best practice. By failing to balance stakeholder interests, such systems are at the mercy of unarticulated ideologies, power struggles and improper influences, and yield a lack of faith in the process.

Looked at from this perspective, a planning scheme should be created in light of a community vision, it should be able to be understood completely by the community, the rights of individuals under the scheme should be settled as much as possible, and the decision makers should be local and elected. If there is a regional authority, the local, elected representatives should have a place. If there are regional decisions on growth areas or population projections, the elected representatives should be involved. Ideally, the regional authority should establish principles, such as sustainability, and a general growth pattern, at most.

C.3 Climate change

The last two chapters indicate how complicated it is inserting climate change issues into the planning process. However, most greenhouse gas emissions come from land-based activities or, as with transportation emissions, are a consequence of land use allocations. The control of the use of land to mitigate emissions and to adapt to the effects of global warming appears to be a logical, contemporary extension of planning. The fact that greenhouse gas emissions are virtually invisible has made it difficult for them to be regarded as an externality arising from the use of land. If a subdivision increases car use, the developer may be asked to contribute to an upgrade of a road but not to compensate for the increase in unseen emissions.

Even in this book, the climate change issues have been left to the end, as there is not a ready acceptance that planning is indeed the appropriate means to tackle issues relating to greenhouse gas emissions. As well, attempts to use planning controls for mitigation and adaptation have been sporadic and subsumed within other planning issues, such as the rise in sea levels being included within the known category of flooding; climate change issues are not given a separate identity.

The main difficulty in using planning for mitigation and adaptation is that the global warming agenda is addressed internationally and nationally, meaning it is seldom the central focus of local or regional government. Yet, it is clear that planning at the local level has a strong role to play by preventing uses that will irresponsibly increase emissions and by adopting planning laws that take into account the use of renewables. It is here, in the realm of global warming, that planning will find its foundation again and can recover its desire to better the community. Planning needs to become an essential aspect of the battle against global warming and it should not be left to the weaknesses of the *Paris agreement*.

C.4 The character of change

Travelling to various countries to study and observe their planning systems did not provide a clear picture of a perfect regime. It was not possible to say that any particular system satisfactorily delivers all the goals and concepts that amount to best practice. In some places, there was at least a consensus that the community was satisfied with the operation of the planning process, while in others there was distrust, fear, and disdain for planning. This was not dependent on the quality of the neighbourhoods, the juxtaposition of facilities or any other apparent indicia of what constitutes a good planning result; the community was often satisfied because conditions had improved rather than because residents felt excited about a grand vision.

The cultural nuances, unavailable to an outside observer, indicate what was 'good enough planning' – the most that can be said for any planning regime. These cultural nuances are often unknown to those within the system because they have no idea of any other viewpoint or what created the various threads that came together to form their world. Thus, it is not possible to look to other cultures for best practice by plucking out one practice or process. A recurring awareness while visiting the countries analysed for this work – which should not be a surprise – was that Western planners were exercising a cultural imperialism, justified by saying that the cities in the East are like those in the West: congested by traffic, haphazard, and in need of some order.

If any observation can claim universality, it is that participation by the community in the planning process really does create a sense of empowerment and a feeling that the result is a consensus rather than a forced conclusion. Attending a meeting in Ashland, Oregon, where the community was engaged, or seeing the enthusiasm in a meeting of a community in Rio, created the sense that there was a social bond that had formed and this was recognised by the planning authority. It seems so easy theoretically for there to be full participation and the lack of it was the most confusing observation. In almost all planning regimes, there is no countervailing force or constitutional barrier for participation to occur. The fear is still prevalent that participation will have the negative effect of delaying projects because of NIMBYism. The lessons of this work are that the planning system cannot deliver what it promises but, if there is consensus, there is a greater likelihood that planning can be seen to be working within cultural and social norms, granting it efficacy and legitimacy.

Appendix 1

Elements of a model community participation policy

1. Legal framework
   A. Community Participation Charter of Principles
   B. Community Participation Plan of Details
2. Application of the community participation plan
   A. Making of a local plan
   B. Amending or replacing a provision of a local plan
   C. Merit assessment (development control)
3. Timing for use of the community participation plan
   A. Resolution to make a local plan
   B. Resolution to amend or replace a local plan
   C. When application is made for merit assessment
4. Goals of the community participation plan
   A. General goals
      a. Community as collaborative partner
      b. What is to be accomplished
         I. Increased understanding of issues
         II. Determine possible options
         III. Generate new ideas
         IV. Discover and explore possible compromises
         V. Gauge the greater public's support for various solutions
         VI. Active participation
         VII. Diverse modes and venues of participation
         VIII. Consensus orientation
         IX. Build relationships
      c. Who is included and who is excluded
         I. Making of a local plan (the community as a whole)
         II. Amending and replacing a local plan (identified community)
         III. Merit assessment (identified community)
         IV. Participation exclusion (outside experts, non-community)
      d. Principle of inclusion
         I. Importance of capacity building (funding for local groups, snowballing, speakers bureau, available facilities)

Appendix 1

        II. Disadvantaged groups
       III. Informal groups
       IV. Flexible timing
        V. Training in participation
    e. Participant roles
        I. Community advisory group
       II. Council (drafting role, determination role)
       III. Stakeholders
       IV. Community
  B. In making a local plan
    a. Community vision
  C. In amending or replacing a provision in a local plan
    a. Community recommendations
  D. In merit assessment
    a. Community recommendations
5. Involvement of the community
  A. Community advisory group
    a. Functions
    b. Formation by random selection
  B. Community identification for making a plan
    a. Stakeholders
        I. Recruitment
       II. Registration
    b. Local groups
        I. Recruitment
       II. Listing
    c. Informal groups
    d. Youth / schools
    e. Senior citizens
    f. Those who have difficulty participating
  C. Community identification for amending or replacing provisions of a local plan
  D. Community identification for merit assessment
6. Council commitments
  A. Dedicated officer
  B. Points of contact
  C. Facilities for meetings
  D. Speakers bureau (experts when needed)
  E. Trained facilitators
7. Informing and educating the community
  A. Information
    a. Preparation of community information packet
        I. Nature of proposal
       II. Council or state studies
       III. Impact of proposal
       IV. Resources
        V. Inspection of documents
    b. Community information packet for making of local plan

Appendix 1

      c. Community information packet for all other plans or merit assessment
      d. Requests for information
          I. Duty of council
          II. Time to reply
   B. Education
      a. Community
          I. The scope of participation: participation roadmap (process, goals, timing, submissions, dedicated officer)
          II. The information pack
          III. Making complaints
      b. Council
          I. The scope of participation
          II. Council responsibilities
8. Notification to the community
   A. Responsibilities
      a. Community advisory group
      b. Dedicated officer
   B. Forms
      a. Advertisement
          I. Local newspapers
          II. Notice boards
          III. Social media
          IV. Website
          V. Registered stakeholder notification
          VI. Listed community organisations
      b. Outreach tools
          I. Multilingual notifications
          II. Attending special events / community gatherings
          III. Other community meetings
          IV. Street displays
          V. Fact sheet distribution
          VI. Newsletter
          VII. Blogs
9. Forms of participation
   A. Range of meetings
      a. Community forums
      b. Study circles
      c. Informal groups
      d. Focus groups
      e. Charrettes
      f. Stakeholder forum
      g. Local group forums
      h. Youth forums
      i. Senior citizen forums
      j. Process feedback meetings
   B. Electronic assistance
      a. Interactive website

Appendix 1

       b. Voting
       c. Completing questionnaires
       d. Blogs
       e. Online chat
       f. Social media
    C. Paper or electronic surveys
       a. Referendum
       b. Deliberative surveys
       c. Open-ended surveys
10. Application of alternative forms
    A. Making of a local plan
       a. Maximum devices
       b. Recommendations
    B. Making of amendment or replacement of provisions of local plan
    C. Merit assessment
11. Stages of participation
    A. Background information / identification of process
       a. Clarify legal requirements
       b. Determine efficient methods
    B. Determination of timeline
    C. Issue generation
    D. Scenario testing
    E. Establishing priorities
    F. Option testing
    G. Community vision analysis
    H. Evaluation
    I. Production of community vision
12. Evaluation of outcomes
    A. Individual outcome
       a. Improving knowledge
       b. Community social capital
    B. Community outcomes
       a. New solutions
       b. Community betterment
    C. Process-oriented outcomes
       a. Building trust between participants
       b. Inclusion of all stakeholders
       c. Inclusion of all other groups
    D. Content-oriented outcomes
       a. Better plan
    E. User outcomes
       a. Satisfaction with process

Appendix 2

Model community participation plan

Introduction

The emphasis of the [*Relevant Planning Act*] is for residents and council to partner together to plan your community. This community participation plan explains how that partnership is formed and how the residents will participate.

This plan explains the goals of participation, how the community is to be encouraged to participate, how the community will be informed, and the stages of the participation process.

This plan applies in two cases. The first is when a council decides to make a local plan, amend that plan, or replace any of its provisions. The second is when the council is called upon to assess the merits of an application for rezoning or for a development proposal.

The contact person for the council is:

Dedicated participation officer:

Address:

Email:

Phone:

Mobile/cell:

Appendix 2

Part A: The function of this community participation plan

Legal requirements

The [relevant *Planning Act* or policy] contains a *Community Participation Charter* with the following principles that form the basis of this plan:

> The community is to be provided with opportunities to participate in planning ... [etc.]

By the [*Planning Act*], these principles must be reflected in a community participation plan.

Situations when the community participation plan operates

Council will implement the community participation plan in two situations.
    Category 1: The first is where the council decides on its own initiative to create a new local plan for the entire local government area or a part of the area or to amend an existing local plan.
    Category 2: The second is where a landowner requests the council to amend an existing local plan or to replace provisions of that plan or a landowner has made an application to develop land that requires council to assess the merits of that application.

When this plan comes into effect

Category 1 (making a local plan or amending it): when the council passes a resolution that it desires to make a local plan or amend a plan or replace an existing plan provisions.
    Category 2 (an application by a landowner to amend a plan or a merit assessment): when the application is received.

Part B: The goals of the community participation plan

The essential goals

A working partnership between the residents and the council is the most important goal of this plan. In order to form this partnership, the [*Planning Act*] requires that residents be involved in creating the vision behind the local plan from the very beginning and not after that plan is created. Early, full, inclusive participation is the road to a working partnership.

To accomplish the partnership, everyone in the community affected should be offered and encouraged to participate. The participation should go beyond community activists and those who traditionally are involved to include every resident, even if they feel they lack the knowledge to participate meaningfully.

Inclusion of all residents is necessary because the purpose of participation is to build a consensus on community values, develop an understanding of the aspirations of residents, and make participation a means of bettering community relations among residents and between residents and council.

The practical goal is to generate ideas from the community in a non-confrontational setting, to allow the development of options, to discuss which values are important and which may give way to community needs, and to reach consensus on the vision for the future of the area. All of these discussions, to be useful, must be carried out in different venues at times that work for all residents in discussions that are constructive and not intimidating.

The goal of inclusion

The community is made up of diverse groups: business owners, landowners, community groups, sporting groups, youths, senior citizens, and loose-knit groups such as book clubs or even groups of friends. They are the community and, for participation to work, they must all be included. Council and the community advisory group (CAG) must therefore reach out to and encourage the participation of all groups including youth groups, senior citizens, charitable organisations, business associations, existing neighbourhood groups and every other organisation or group.

The opportunity must be given to participate to those unable to leave their homes, who are disabled, or those who work at irregular times. There are those may who feel reluctant to speak in a large forum or who would never think of coming to a meeting about the future of the community. All these are to be included.

The goal of representation: community advisory group

In spite of best efforts, there may be many in the community who do not participate in establishing a community vision to guide the making of a plan or to assist in determining the merits of a development application. The CAG is to be made up of a random sample of individuals across the community who are asked to serve for a three year term for the express purpose of being involved in the planning process by facilitating participation, by being involved in the participation exercises, and by having a representative voice in the assessment of development applications.

The CAG will consist of seven members chosen by council from every walk of life at random from diverse geographical locations in the local government area. They do not need any knowledge of local government procedures, or have expertise in planning matters but are chosen because they are, by the process of being chosen randomly, a cross-section of the community that is willing to give time and energy for their community. How they meet and organise is really up to them once they are chosen and council will provide a meeting space at times they desire.

Part C: Commitments and responsibilities under the plan

Council commitments

- To regard planning as a partnership between council and the community
- To follow this community participation plan in order to create an effective partnership
- To encourage participation of all affected residents in the making and amending of a local plan or in the assessment of an application for development to be determined on its merits.

Council responsibilities

- To provide meeting facilities for the community to discuss issues relating to planning, either at council offices or elsewhere, at flexible times
- To provide council officers, when requested by any group of individuals, to explain technical information and the participation process
- To provide a 'dedicated participation officer' who is the liaison between the council and the community
- To provide trained facilitators to conduct meetings initiated by council
- To provide translation services where necessary for any group or at any meeting to allow full participation by non-English speaking individuals
- To provide transportation for any disabled person who seeks to attend any meeting set out in this plan.

Community advisory group commitments

- To work with council to encourage participation in the community
- To assist council in carrying out this community participation plan.

Community advisory group responsibilities

- To make rules for the conduct of CAG meetings
- To meet at regular intervals to discuss planning matters or, where required, to convene a meeting by council
- To work with council to identify those that should be included in the participation process

Appendix 2

- To actively assist council in finding groups and organisations that may be able to participate under this plan
- To assist council in making arrangements for individuals to participate who have difficulties because of disability or other reasons
- To coordinate the completion of the community vision statement in category 1 matters
- To provide recommendations to council on category 2 matters
- To provide a summary of submissions of participants for council on category 2 matters.

Part D: Steps in the participation process for all planning matters

Upon the Community Plan having effect, these steps will take place for all planning matters in the following order:

1. Determination of the identified community
2. Locating participants in the identified community
3. Preparing information for the community
4. Preparing communication with the community
5. Determining the content of notification
6. Providing notification
7. Recruitment of participants.

Some issues that arise in planning may be very local in nature: an initiative by council to rezone a local reserve, while others may have implications across a community: a rezoning for a major shopping centre. It is important to identify the scope of the community that is potentially affected and should participate.

Defining the scope of the community is not straightforward or precise. It is clear that if the council is seeking to create a new plan or substantially amend an existing plan, the entire community should be involved. It is also clear that if the issue is local, the relevant community will be those who will be affected by a decision.

Council and the CAG must reach consensus on the scope of the community to participate.

When the council and CAG have reached consensus, the boundaries of the area that is identified should be determined with some precision.

If council and the CAG cannot reach consensus, then it is the identification that is the widest in coverage that should prevail.

Council, with the assistance of the CAG, should proceed to record the details of as many of the following (and other groups not listed) in the identified community:

- Social groups
- Youth groups
- Senior citizen groups and homes
- Religious groups
- Single parent groups
- School parent teacher groups
- Business associations
- Sporting clubs
- Ratepayers groups
- Groups concerned with health or disabilities.

Appendix 2

As soon as practicable after this plan has effect, council shall develop a community information packet for the identified community that contains at least:

- In the case of category 1 planning matters, the resolution of the council to make or amend the local plan
- In the case of category 2 planning matters, the application and accompanying documentation of the applicant
- Any studies in possession of council relating to the identified community area
- In the case of studies or applications that are too voluminous to reproduce, the location where they can be inspected
- This community participation plan
- The means of communicating with reference to web-based methods
- An invitation to make submissions on any aspect of process at any time
- The names and addresses of the CAG members.

Council will provide the following:
   Interactive website containing:

- a blog
- an opportunity for online chat with the dedicated planning officer
- a chance to make written submissions on a form provided
- the capacity to vote on questions posed by council
- the capacity to provide and receive questionnaires
- the capacity to view meetings electronically and in real time.

Social media presence:

- A Facebook page or pages
- A Twitter account
- A Google+ group.

Record of meetings:

- YouTube channel
- Integrated video on council website.

As soon as practicable after this community participation plan has effect and the members of the identified community are compiled, the identified community will be notified by the council and that notification shall contain, in plain language:

- Nature of the planning matter that will be considered
- Scope of the identified community according to its boundaries
- This community participation plan
- Reference to the first process meetings to explain the participation process
- Reference to the electronic means of communicating.

An example of a category 1 notification is:

An invitation to participate in
The making of a new plan for X City

Council has decided to make a new local plan for the area bounded by […].

Those of you working or living in this area are invited to partner with council to create this new local plan.

Council has adopted a community participation plan that will guide the process of your involvement. You can obtain that plan by requesting a copy from council by phone call, picking a copy up at council offices or any library, or by reading the plan on the council website.

The process of partnership begins with this notice and will take many months of care, thought and your input to find a vision for the community that can be used to create the local plan.

The first meeting to discuss how this process works will be on the following three days […] at council offices.

Call [the dedicated participation officer] on […] for further information or transportation assistance or go to council's website at [www …] and see the information there and the various electronic means to communicate with council.

An example of a category 2 notification is:

An invitation to participate in
> **Determining an application for [rezoning/development]**

Council has received an application for [rezoning/development] for […] in X City.

Those of you working or living in the area bounded by […] and […] are invited to partner with council to determine this application.

Council has adopted a community participation plan that will guide the process of your involvement. You can obtain that plan by requesting a copy from council by phone call, picking a copy up at council offices or any library, or by reading the plan on the council website at [www …].

The process of partnership begins with this notice and will seek your opinions to find the proper determination to benefit the community.

The first meeting to discuss how this process works will be on the following three days […] at council offices.

Call [the dedicated participation officer] on […] for further information or transportation assistance or go to council's website at [www …] for more information and for the various electronic means to communicate with council.

Council shall use as many of the methods listed as possible to provide notification to the identified community as is practicable but including at least:

- Mailing to those recognised as being in the identified community
- Weekly or daily advertisements in the local newspaper for two weeks
- Notice on the council website
- Notice on council Facebook page and Google+ page
- A notice by Twitter
- Posting in the public library and other public places
- Posting in shops that are willing to display the notice
- Multi-lingual notices where there are areas known to include residents from non-English-speaking backgrounds.

Appendix 2

The dedicated participation officer and members of the CAG should meet with as many groups as possible to explain the community participation plan and to encourage attendance at the initial process meetings.

Further recruitment of participants should take place at, at least:

- A community special event (such as a barbecue) attended by CAG members and the dedicated officer to publicise the notification and participation process
- Regular meetings of groups in the identified community
- Street displays in shopping areas
- Distribution at random places of the notification and the community participation plan.

Part E: Additional steps for category 1 matters

In addition to the steps in the participation process for all matters, the following other steps are necessary for category 1 (making and amending a local plan):

1. Initial process meetings
2. Community vision meetings.

Meetings shall be held on at least three occasions over a two-week period, varying the times to account for those who cannot attend at normal business hours.

The meetings shall be at a venue supplied by council.

The following, at least, should be raised at each meeting by the dedicated participation officer:

- The CAG and its function
- The goals of this community participation plan
- The contents of the council resolution
- The process in detail that will be adopted for participation having regard to this plan
- The availability of the community information packet and its content
- The ability to make written submissions at any time
- The availability and contents of the website
- The availability of experts from council to speak to any group that is part of the identified community
- The availability of transportation facilities for those unable to attend or translation facilities when needed
- The timetable of meetings that will follow.

Community vision meetings are to be carried out (in conjunction with interactions on the website and social media) for the purpose of full participation by the identified community in the following ten stages:

Stage 1: Background information provided

- The legal requirements of the [*Planning Act*]
- The nature and form of the community vision meetings
- Information on the background of the area displayed by maps including uses, transportation, infrastructure and other relevant matters that explain the function and operation of the area

- Experts or council officers to set out any findings or explain any reports for the area
- Timeline for the process (number of meetings and intervals).

Stage 2: Issue generation
- Elicit from the identified community the issues that confront the community in its function and operation;
- Identify with the community those issues that have priority.

Stage 3: Goals and hopes
- Elicit from the community their goals and hopes for the planning area
- Examine the goals and hopes from the point of view of different residents such as youth, senior citizens, and immigrants.

Stage 4: Scenario testing
- Discuss possible solutions and alternatives to reach the goals and hopes having regard to the issues.

Stage 5: Priorities
- Analyse with the community which of the possible solutions and alternatives should have priority.

Stage 6: Option testing
- Examine whether the prioritised solutions will meet the issues and goals and hopes
- Examine the impact of the prioritised solutions.

Stage 7: Establishing the principles of the community vision statement
- Work to produce the principles that will go into the community vision statement
- Reach consensus as to the statements that should be included in the community vision statement

Stage 8: Preparation of the community vision statement
- The community vision statement is to be completed by the CAG having regard to the consensus in Stage 7 and having regard to any written submissions received by council or electronic communications.

Stage 9: Analysis of the community vision statement
- Analyse with the identified community the adequacy of the community vision statement in recording the effect and contents of the meetings
- Send the community vision plan to council to form the basis for the draft plan.

Stage 10: Draft local plan

- After the draft local plan is completed by council, discuss the contents and the extent that the plan fulfils the community vision statement.

There should be at least the following meetings organised by council:

1. Five identified community forums inclusive of stages 1 through 8.
2. One meeting for stage 9
3. One meeting for stage 10
4. A youth forum and a senior citizens' forum relating to stage 3
5. A business community forum relating to stage 3.

The dedicated planning offer and the CAG where possible will organise the following as needed or requested:

- Focus groups on particular issues
- Guest speakers on particular issues
- Speakers for groups in the identified community.

The meetings should be conducted by a facilitator provided by council in conjunction with the dedicated planning officer and the members of the CAG.

The goal is to have meetings that are non-confrontational, that allow all participants a chance to offer opinions, and that yield a constructive community vision.

The object of the community vision meetings is to reach consensus on a community vision statement that will form the basis for the draft local plan.

The community vision statement should include at least:

- The steps that were taken to provide information to the identified community
- The electronic means that were used to provide information and for communication
- A summary of any written submissions that were received
- A summary of the results of any questionnaires or voting on the website
- The date and attendance of the meetings that were held and the manner in which the community participation plan was implemented
- The proposal the subject of the category 1 planning matter
- The issues for the identified community
- The goals and hopes for that community
- The priorities of that community
- The principles that were used to form the community vision
- The community vision for the identified community.

Part F: Additional steps for category 2 matters

In addition to the steps in the participation process for all matters, the following other steps are necessary for category 2 (application for rezoning or a merit assessment):

1. Initial process meetings
2. Assessment meetings

Appendix 2

Meetings shall be held at a venue supplied by council on at least three occasions over a one-week period, varying the times to account for those who cannot attend at normal business hours.

The following, at least, should be raised at each meeting by the dedicated participation officer:

- The basis for the determination of the identified community
- The role of the community in rezoning and merit assessment
- The CAG and its function
- The goals of this community participation plan
- The details of the application for rezoning or merit assessment
- The process in detail that will be adopted for participation having regard to this plan
- An invitation to make written submissions at any time prior to a decision and to use any opportunities on the website
- The availability of the community information packet and it content
- The availability of experts from council to speak to any group that is part of the identified community
- The availability of transportation facilities for those unable to attend or translation facilities when needed.

At least three meetings should be held over two weeks at venues supplied by council where the following should occur:

Stage 1: Understanding the application

- The legal requirements of the [*Planning Act*]
- The nature and form of the assessment meetings
- Information on the background of the area displayed by maps including uses, transportation, infrastructure and other relevant matters that explain the function and operation of the area
- Experts or council officers to set out any findings or explain any reports for the area
- A briefing by the applicant if the applicant so desires
- Timeline for the process (number of meetings and intervals).

Stage 2: Community assessment

- Council to present an analysis of the consistency of the application with the community vision statement
- Elicit from the identified community their goals for the planning area the subject of the application if the community vision statement is more than three years old
- Obtain the views of the CAG as to the proposal
- Elicit identified community views and recommendations as to the proposal.

Stage 3: Post-meeting submission

The CAG shall prepare a submission to council that shall contain:

- The views of the CAG

- A summary of the recommendations of the identified community as to the project in the evaluation meetings and by written submissions or the results of any questionnaires or voting on the website.

Stage 4: Decision

The council shall notify the identified community of its decision that shall be accompanied by a statement that sets out:

- The detailed reasons for the decision
- The manner in which the decision in consistent or inconsistent with the community vision statement
- The response to the views of the CAG
- A response to any written submissions or communications from the website
- A response to the recommendations of the identified community to the project.

Part G: Evaluation of the participation process

At the completion of the Part D and Part E participation processes, Council shall as soon as is practicable evaluate the process and publish the results by the notification methods in this plan.

Council by survey or other means will determine at least the following:

Individual outcomes

- Improving knowledge: did the participation improve an individual's understanding of the process of council?
- Community social capital: does the individual now have a closer relationship with others in his community?

Community outcomes

- New solutions: did the participation process result in a new approach to the future of the community?
- Community betterment: did the participation result in a better community?

Process outcomes

- Building trust between participants: did the participation process result in greater trust of the council?
- Inclusion: were all participants encouraged to participate and did they participate?

Content outcomes

- Better plan: did the participation process result in a better plan or decision than if this plan had not been used?

Appendix 2

User outcomes

- Satisfaction with process: was the council and the identified community satisfied with the process?

Works cited

Abbott, C. (1997). The Portland region: where city and suburbs talk to each other – and often agree. *Housing Policy Debate* 8(1): 28.
Abdullah, J. (2012). City competitiveness and urban sprawl: their implications to socio-economic and cultural life in Malaysian cities. *Procedia – Social and Behavioral Sciences* 50: 20–9.
Abrantas, P., I. Fontes, E. Gomes and J. Rocha (2016). Compliance of land cover changes with municipal land use planning: evidence from the Lisbon metropolitan region, 1990–2007. *Land Use Policy* 51: 120–34.
Adler, A. (1930). *The problems of neurosis*. New York: Cosmopolitan Book Corporation.
Ahmad, I., I.U. Bajwa, S.M. Mayo, M.B. Sharif and A.U. Qazi (2012). Urban sewerage planning through community participation. *Pakistan Journal of Science* 64(1): 24–6.
Ahmed, F., I. Mohd, S. L. Maidin, N. M. Noor and R.i Zainol (2013). Malaysian development plan system: issues and problems, one decade after its reform (2001–2011). *Planning Malaysia: Journal of the Malaysian Institute of Planners* XI: 1–20. https://ssrn.com/abstract=2559001.
Ahmed, I., J. Deaton, R.l Sarker and T. Virani (2008). Wetland ownership and management in a common property resource setting: a case study of Hakaluki Hoar in Bangladesh. *Ecological Economics* 68(1–2): 429–36.
Aiginger, K. and A. Guger (2006). The ability to adapt: why it differs between the Scandinavian and continental European models. *Intereconomics* 41(1): 14–23.
Albrechts, L. (2006). Shifts in strategic spatial planning? Some evidence from Europe and Australia. *Environment and Planning A* 38(6): 1149–70. doi:10.1068/a37304.
Albrechts, L. (2004). Strategic (spatial) planning reexamined. *Environment and Planning B: Planning and Design* 31(5): 743–58.
Albrechts, L., P. Healey and K. Kunzmann (2003). Strategic spatial planning and regional governance in Europe. *Journal of the American Planning Association* 69(2): 113–29.
Alderson, A.S., J. Beckfield and J. Sprague-Jones (2010). Intercity relations and globalisation: the evolution of the global urban hierarchy, 1981–2007. *Urban Studies* 47(9): 1899–923.
Alexander, E. (2002). The public interest in planning: from legitimation to substantive plan evaluation. *Planning Theory* 1(3): 226–49. doi: 10.1177/147309520200100303.
Alterman, R. (2011). Comparative research at the frontier of planning law: the case of compensation rights for land use regulations. *International Journal of Law in the Built Environment* 3(2): 100–12. https://ssrn.com/abstract=2116268.
Alterman, R. (2010). *Takings international: a comparative perspective on land use regulations and compensation rights*. Chicago: American Bar Association.
Alterman, R. (1976). Implementation of urban land use plans in Israel and the attitudes of the decision-makers. Haifa: Center for Urban and Regional Studies, Technion, Israel Institute of Technology.

Works cited

Amdam, J. (2014). Flexible local planning: linking community initiative with municipal planning in Volda, Norway. In N. Gallent and D. Ciaffi, eds, *Community action and planning: contexts, drivers and outcomes*. Bristol: Policy Press. doi: 10.1332/policypress/9781447315162.003.0015.

Amdam, R. (2010). Empowerment planning in regional development. *European Planning Studies* 18(11): 1806–19.

American Planning Association (2002). *Growing smart legislative guidebook: model statutes for planning and the management of change*. Chicago: APA.

Amsler, L.B. (2010). The next generation of administrative law: building the legal infrastructure for collaborative governance. *Wisconsin Law Review* 2010: 297–350. https://ssrn.com/abstract=1646725.

Anderson, J.L., A.E. Brees and E.C. Reninger (2008). A study of American zoning board composition and public attitudes toward zoning issues. *Urban Lawyer* 40(4): 689–745.

Arciniegas, G. and R. Janssen (2012). Spatial decision support for collaborative land use planning workshops. *Landscape and Urban Planning* 107(3): 332–42.

Arku, G. (2009). Rapidly growing African cities need to adopt smart growth policies to solve urban development concerns. *Urban Forum* 20(3): 253–70.

Arnold, C.A. (2007). The structure of the land use regulatory system in the United States. *Journal of Land Use and Environmental Law* 22(2): 441–523. https://ssrn.com/abstract=1020305.

Arnott, R.J. and J.E. Stiglitz (1979). Aggregate land rents, expenditure on public good, and optimal city size. *Quarterly Journal of Economics* 93(4): 471–500. http://www.jstor.org/stable/1884466.

Arnstein, S.R. (1969). A ladder of citizen participation. *Journal of the American Institute of Planners* 35(4): 216–24.

Artibise, A.C, K. Cameron and J.H. Seelig (2004). Metropolitan organization in Greater Vancouver: 'Do It Yourself' regional government. In D. Phares, ed., *Metropolitan governance without metropolitan government*. Burlington, VT: Ashgate Publishing. 195–211.

Arts, J. and F. van Lamoen (2005). Before EIA: defining the scope of infrastructure projects in the Netherlands. *Journal of Environmental Assessment Policy and Management* 7(1): 51.

Ashe, M., G. Bennett, C. Economos, E. Goodman, J. Schilling, L. Quintiliani, et al. (2009). Assessing coordination of legal-based efforts across jurisdictions and sectors for obesity prevention and control. *Journal of Law, Medicine and Ethics* 37 (suppl. s1): 45–54.

Attinger, S. (2011). US cities get serious about sustainability. *International Journal of Innovation Science* 3(1): 29–38.

Aurand, A. (2010). Density, housing types and mixed land use: smart tools for affordable housing? *Urban Studies* 47(5): 1015–36.

Austin, S., S. Melly, B.N. Sanchez, A. Patel, S. Buka and S.L. Gortmaker (2005). Clustering of fast-food restaurants around schools: a novel application of spatial statistics to the study of food environments. *American Journal of Public Health* 95(9): 1575–81.

Ayers, J. and D. Dodman (2010). Climate change adaptation and development I: the state of the debate. *Progress in Development Studies* 10(2): 161–8.

Backer, L.C. (2013). The co-operative as a proletarian corporation: the global dimensions of property rights and the organization of economic activity in Cuba. *Northwestern Journal of International Law and Business* 33(3): 527–618.

Baker, D.C., N.G. Sipe and B.J. Gleeson (2006). Performance-based planning: perspectives from the United States, Australia, and New Zealand. *Journal of Planning Education and Research* 25(4): 396–409.

Baker, M. (1998). Planning for the English regions: a review of the secretary of state's regional planning guidance. *Planning Practice and Research*. 13(2): 153–69.

Bafarasat, A.Z. (2016). Exploring new systems of regionalism: an English case study. *Cities* 50: 119–28.

Balducci, A. (2011). Strategic planning as exploration. *Town Planning Review* 82(5): 529–46.

Balducci, A. (2008). Constructing (spatial) strategies in complex environment. In J. van den Broeck, F. Moulaert and S. Oosterlynck, eds, *Empowering the planning fields: ethics, creativity and action*. Leuven: Acco. 79–99.

Ball, M. (2011). Planning delay and the responsiveness of English housing supply. *Urban Studies* 48(2): 349–62.
Barker, K. (2004). *Review of housing supply. Delivering stability: securing our future needs*, London: Barker Review.
Barnstable County Assembly of Delegates (2012). *Proposed Ordinance 12–07: Amendment of the Regional Policy Plan per Section 8H of Chapter 716 of the Acts of 1989, as amended May 24, 2012.* Cape Cod, MA: Cape Cod Commission. http://bit.ly/2tUP6zq.
Bartelmus, P. (2007). SEEA-2003: accounting for sustainable development? *Ecological Economics* 61(4): 613–6. doi:10.1016/j.ecolecon.2006.09.008.
Beauregard, R. (2012). Planning with things. *Journal of Planning Education and Research* 32(2): 182–190. doi:10.1177/0739456X11435415.
Belsky, E.S., N. DuBroff, D. McCue, C. Harris, S. McCartney and J. Molinsky (2013). *Advancing inclusive and sustainable urban development: correcting planning failures and connecting communities to capital.* Cambridge, MA: Joint Center for Housing Studies of Harvard University. http://bit.ly/2vi2Ffy.
Bendixsen, S. and P. de Guchteneire (2003). Best practices in immigration services planning. *Journal of Policy Analysis and Management* 22(4): 677–82. doi:10.1002/pam.10163.
Bengston, D.N., J.O. Fletcher and K.C. Nelsen (2004). Public policies for managing urban growth and protecting open space: policy instruments and lessons learned in the United States. *Landscape and Urban Planning* 69(2–3): 271–86. doi:10.1016/j.landurbplan.2003.08.007.
Benioff, R., S. Guill and J. Lee, eds (1996). *Vulnerability and adaptation assessments: an international handbook*. Dordrecht: Kluwer Academic Publishers.
Benson, D. and A. Jordan (2004). Sustainability appraisal in local land-use planning: patterns of current performance. *Journal of Environmental Planning and Management* 47(2): 269–86. doi:10.1080/0964056042000209076.
Bentley, G. and L. Pugalis (2013). New directions in economic development: localist policy discourses and the localism act. *Local Economy* 28(3): 257–74. doi:10.1177/0269094212473940.
Berke, P.R. and M.M. Conroy (2000). Are we planning for sustainable development? *Journal of the American Planning Association* 66(1): 21–33. doi:10.1080/01944360008976081.
Berke, P.R. and D.R. Godschalk (2009). Searching for the good plan: a meta-analysis of plan quality studies. *Journal of Planning Literature* 23(3): 227–40. doi:10.1177/0885412208327014.
Biesbroeck, G. R., R. Swart, T.R. Carter, C. Cowan, T. Henrichs, H. Mela, et al. (2010). Europe adapts to climate change: comparing national adaptation strategies. *Global Environmental Change* 20(3): 440–50. doi:10.1016/j.gloenvcha.2010.03.005.
Bingham, L.B., T. Nabatchi and R. O'Leary (2005). The new governance: practices and processes for stakeholder and citizen participation in the work of government. *Public Administration Review* 65(5): 547–58. doi:10.1111/j.1540-6210.2005.00482.x.
Bingham, M. (1998). A plan-led system? The potential and actual role of development plans in development control (with particular reference to planning appeals). PhD thesis, University of Cambridge.
Birdsong, B.C. (2002). Adjudicating sustainability: New Zealand's environment court. *Ecology Law Quarterly* 29(1): 1–70. doi:10.15779/Z38WR8N.
Birkmann, J., M. Garschagen, F. Kraas and Q. Nguyen (2010). Adaptive urban governance: new challenges for the second generation of urban adaptation strategies to climate change. *Sustainability Science* 5(2): 185–206. doi:10.1007/s11625-010-0111-3.
Bithas, K. and M. Christofakis (2006). Environmentally sustainable cities: critical review and operational conditions. *Sustainable Development* 14(3): 177–89. doi:10.1002/sd.262.
Boardman, A.E., M. Siemiatycki and A.R. Vining (2016). The theory and evidence concerning public–private partnerships in Canada and elsewhere. *University of Calgary School of Public Policy Research Papers* 9(12). https://ssrn.com/abstract=2804683.
Bodansky, D., E. Diringer and X. Wang (2004). *Strawman elements: an assessment. Possible approaches to advancing international climate change efforts*. Arlington, VA: PEW Center on Global Climate Change. https://www.c2es.org/docUploads/Strawman%20Elements.pdf.

Works cited

Bohringer, C. and P. Jochem (2007). Measuring the immeasurable – a survey of sustainability indices. *Ecological Economics* 63(1): 1–8. doi:10.1016/j.ecolecon.2007.03.008.

Bollens, S.A. (1993). Restructuring land use governance. *Journal of Planning Literature* 7(3): 211–26. doi:10.1177/08854122930070030.

Booth, P. (2009). Managing land-use change. Supplement 1, *Land Use Policy* 26 (suppl.1): S154–59. doi:10.1016/j.landusepol.2009.08.011.

Booth, P. (2003). *Planning by consent: the origins and nature of British development control*. London: Routledge.

Booth, P. (2002). A desperately slow system? The origins and nature of the current discourse on development control. *Planning Perspectives* 17(4): 309–23. doi:10.1080/02665430210154731.

Booth, P. (1995). Zoning or discretionary action: certainty and responsiveness in implementing planning policy. *Journal of Planning Education and Research* 14(2): 103–12. doi:10.1177/0739456X9501400203.

Booth, P. (1993). The cultural dimension in comparative research: making sense of development control in France. *European Planning Studies* 1(2): 217–29. doi:10.1080/09654319308720210.

Booth, P. and T.F. Stafford (1994). Revisions and modifications: the effect of change on French *plans d'occupation des sols*. *Environment and Planning B: Planning and Design* 21(3): 305–22. doi:10.1068/b210305.

Bossel, H. (1996). Deriving indicators of sustainable development. *Environmental Modeling and Assessment* 1(4): 193–218. doi:10.1007/BF01872150.

Botes, L. and D. van Rensburg (2000). Community participation in development: nine plagues and twelve commandments. *Community Development Journal* 35(1): 41–58. doi:10.1093/cdj/35.1.41.

Boudreau, J., P. Hamel, B. Jouve and R. Keil (2007). New state spaces in Canada: metropolitanization in Montreal and Toronto compared. *Urban Geography* 28(1): 30–53. doi:10.2747/0272-3638.28.1.30.

Brabham, D. (2009). Crowdsourcing the public participation process for planning projects. *Planning Theory* 8(3): 242–62. doi:10.1177/1473095209104824.

Bragagnolo, C. and D. Geneletti (2012). Addressing cumulative effects in strategic environmental assessment of spatial planning. *Aestimum* 60: 39–52. doi:10.13128/Aestimum-11270.

Brand, R. and F. Gaffikin (2007). Collaborative planning in an uncollaborative world. *Planning Theory* 6(3): 282–313. doi:10.1177/1473095207082036.

Briffault, R. (2000). Localism and regionalism. *Columbia Law School: Public Law and Legal Theory*. doi:10.2139/ssrn.198822.

Brody, S.D., D.R. Godschalk and R.J. Burby (2003). Mandating citizen participation in plan making: six strategic planning choices. *Journal of the American Planning Association* 69(3): 245–64. doi:10.1080/01944360308978018.

Brown, G. and R. Gifford (2001). Architects predict lay evaluations of large contemporary buildings: whose conceptual properties? *Journal of Environmental Psychology* 21(1): 93–9. doi: 10.1006/jevp.2000.0176.

Brown, R., R. Ashley and M. Farrelly (2011). Political and professional agency entrapment: an agenda for urban water research. *Water Resources Management* 25(15): 4037–50. doi:10.1007/s11269-011-9886-y.

Bruegmann, R. (2005). *Sprawl: a compact history*. Chicago: University of Chicago Press.

Brunick, N. (2003). *The impact of inclusionary zoning on development*. Chicago: Business and Professional People for the Public Interest. http://www.bpichicago.org/documents/impact_iz_development.pdf.

Buitelaar, E. (2009). Zoning, more than just a tool: explaining Houston's regulatory practices. *European Planning Studies* 17(7): 1049–65. doi:10.1080/09654310902949588.

Buitelaar, E., M.e Galle and N. Sorel (2011). Plan-led planning systems in development-led practices: an empirical analysis into the (lack of) institutionalisation of planning law. *Environment and Planning A* 43(4): 928–41. doi:10.1068/a43400.

Works cited

Bunce, S. (2009). Developing sustainability: sustainability policy and gentrification on Toronto's waterfront. *Local Environment* 14(7): 651–67.
Burton, I. and M. van Aalst (1999). *Come hell or high water: integrating climate change vulnerability and adaptation into bank work.* Washington, DC: The World Bank. http://www.start.org/Projects/AIACC_Project/resources/ele_lib_docs/burton_WBreport.pdf.
Buttimer, R.J., S.P. Clark and S.H. Ott (2008). Land development: risk, return and risk management. *The Journal of Real Estate Finance and Economics* 36(1): 81–102. doi:10.1007/s11146-007-9077-z.
Buxton, M. and E. Taylor (2011). Urban land supply, governance and the pricing of land. *Urban Policy and Research* 29(1): 5–22. doi:10.1080/08111146.2011.537605.
C40 Cities Climate Change Leadership Group (2011). *Climate action in megacities: C40 cities baseline and opportunities.* New York: ARUP. http://www.c40.org/researches/arup-c40-baseline-report.
Calavita, N. (1984). Urbanization, public control of land use and private ownership of land: the development of Italian planning law. *Urban Lawyer* 16(3): 459–88.
Calavita, N. and A. Mallach, eds (2010). *Inclusionary housing in international perspective: affordable housing, social inclusion, and land value recapture.* Cambridge: Lincoln Institute of Land Policy.
California Environmental Protection Agency (CEPA) (2007). *Proposed early actions to mitigate climate change in California.* http://bit.ly/2ufWjcN.
Callahan, K. (2002). The utilization and effectiveness of citizen advisory committees in the budget process of local governments. *Journal of Public Budgeting, Accounting & Financial Management* 14(2): 295–319.
Campos, I., J. Guerra, J.F. Gomes, L. Schmidt, F. Alves, A. Vizinho and G.P. Lopes (2017). Understanding climate change policy and action in Portuguese municipalities: a survey. *Land Use Policy* 62: 68–78.
Capkova, S. (2005). *The local government and public service reform initiative of the Open Society Institute.* Budapest: Open Society Institute. http://bit.ly/2whKfcd.
Carbone, M. (2009). Mission impossible: the European Union and policy coherence for development. In Maurizio Carbone, ed., *Policy Coherence and EU Development Policy.* New York: Routledge.
Carina, E., H. Keskitalo and M. Pettersson (2016). Can adaptation to climate change at all be mainstreamed in complex multi-level governance systems? A case study of forest-relevant policies at the EU and Swedish levels. In W.L. Filho et al., eds, *Implementing climate change adaptation in cities and communities: integrating strategies and educational approaches.* Cham: Springer. 53–74.
Carriere, S.M. et al. (2012). Rio+20, biodiversity marginalized. *Conservation Letters* 6(1): 6–11.
Carruthers, J. (2002). Evaluating the effectiveness of regulatory growth management programs: an analytic framework. *Journal of Planning Education and Research* 21(4): 391–405.
Carter, T., M. Parry, H. Harasawa and S. Nishioka (1994). IPCC technical guidelines for assessing climate change and impacts and adaptation. London: University College London and Center for Environmental Research. http://bit.ly/2w2pYbh.
Center for Housing Policy (2008). The effects of inclusionary zoning on local housing markets: lessons from the San Francisco, Washington, DC and suburban Boston areas. New York: Furman Center for Real Estate and Urban Policy. http://bit.ly/2uRLn8Q.
Chang, T. (2016). 'New uses need old buildings': gentrification aesthetics and the arts in Singapore. *Urban Studies* 53(3): 524–39. doi:10.1177/0042098014527482.
Chatterjee, M. (2010). Slum dwellers response to flooding events in the megacities of India. *Mitigation Adaptation Strategies for Global Change* 15: 337–53.
Chee, S. and S.N. Pang (1992). *The role of residents, non-governmental organizations and quasi-public agencies in local government in Malaysia.* Comparative Studies of Public Administration. Tokyo: EROPA Local Government Centre.
Chen, Y., X. Li, W. Su, and Y. Li (2008). Simulating the optimal land-use pattern in the farming-pastoral transitional zone of Northern China. *Computers, Environment and Urban Systems* 32(5): 407–14.
Chien, D. (2005). US transportation models forecasting greenhouse gas emissions: an evaluation from a user's perspective. *Journal of Transportation and Statistics* 8(2): 43–58.

Works cited

Chiodelli, F., and S. Moroni (2015). Corruption in land-use issues: a crucial challenge for planning theory and practice. *Town Planning Review* 86(4): 437–55.

Churchman, A. (1999). Disentangling the concept of density. *Journal of Planning Literature* 13(4): 389–411.

City of Westminster (2011). *Core strategy*. Westminster: City of Westminster. http://bit.ly/2w6k7Un.

Coase, R.H. (1960). The problem of social cost. *Journal of Law and Economics* 3: 1–44.

Colijn, C.J. and A.C. Binnendijk (1998). Physical planning in the coastal region of Zeeland, Netherlands. *Journal of Coastal Conservation* 4(2): 135–42.

Commission of the European Communities (2009). *Adapting to climate change: towards a European framework for action*. Brussels: Commission of the European Communities. http://bit.ly/2oXDTOz.

Commission of the European Communities (1997). Urban development, legislation, and planning in post-socialist Zagreb. *GeoJournal Library* 92: 385–412.

Communities and Local Government Committee (2012). *Guidance on information requirements and validation*. London: The Stationery Office. http://bit.ly/2f5B7Ee.

Communities and Local Government Committee (2011). *The National Planning Policy Framework: Eighth Report of Session 2010–12*. London: The Stationery Office. http://bit.ly/2tXHAnc.

Conroy, M. and J. Evans-Cowley (2006). E-participation in planning: an analysis of cities adopting online citizen participation tools. *Environment and planning C: Government and Policy* 24: 371–384.

Cooper, E. and G. Smith (2012). Organizing deliberation: the perspectives of professional participation practitioners in Britain and Germany. *Journal of Public Determination* 8(1): article 3. http://www.publicdeliberation.net/jpd/vol8/iss1/art3/.

Coriolis Consulting Corporation (2007). *Increased housing density in single detached neighbourhoods*. Vancouver: Metro Vancouver.

Costonis, J. (1982). Law and aesthetics: a critique and a reformation of the dilemmas. *Michigan Law Review* 80: 355–461. http://bit.ly/2vlYDmx.

Coulson, A. (2011). Scrutiny in English local government and the role of councillors. *The Political Quarterly* 82(1): 102–11.

Cowell, R. (2013). The greenest government ever? Planning and sustainability in England after the May 2010 elections. *Planning Practice and Research*. 28(1): 27–44.

Cowell, R. and S. Owens (2006). Governing space: planning reform and the politics of sustainability. *Environment and Planning C: Government and Policy* 24(3): 403–21.

Crook, T., J. Henneberry and C. Whitehead (2016). *Planning Gain*. Hoboken, NJ: John Wiley & Sons.

Crosby, N., P. McAllister and P. Wyatt (2013). Fit for planning? An evaluation of the application of development viability appraisal models in the UK planning system. *Environment and Planning B: Planning and Design* 40: 3–22.

Cullingworth, J.B. (1994). Alternate planning systems: is there anything to learn from abroad? *Journal of the American Planning Association* 60(2): 162–73.

Curry, N. (2012). Community participation in spatial planning: exploring relationships between professional and lay stakeholders. *Local Government Studies* 38(3): 345–66.

Dalal-Clayton, B. (1993). Modified EIA and indicators of sustainability: first steps towards sustainability analysis. Paper presented to the 12th annual meeting of the International Association of Impact Assessment (IAIA), Washington, DC, 19–29 August. http://bit.ly/2uWQxP0.

Daniel, C. (2001). Land use planning – the twin cities metropolitan council: novel initiative, futile effort. *William Mitchell Law Review* 27(3): 1941–70.

Daniel, S. (2012). Situating private equity capital in the land grab debate. *The Journal of Peasant Studies* 39(3–4): 703–29.

Dassopoulos, A. and S. Monnat (2011). Do perceptions of social cohesion, social support, and social control mediate the effects of local community participation on neighborhood satisfaction? *Environment and Behavior*. 43(4): 546–65.

Davis, P. (2006). Spatial competition in retail markets: movie theaters. *RAND Journal of Economics* 37(4): 964–82.

Works cited

Dawson, M. (1996). The best laid plans: the rise and fall of growth management in Florida. *Journal of Land Use and Environmental Law* 11(2): 325–74.

DeGrove, J. (2005). *Planning policy and politics: smart growth and the states.* Cambridge, MA: Lincoln Institute of Land Policy.

Deloitte Real Estate (2015). *London office crane survey: construction activity boost.* London: Deloitte LLP. http://bit.ly/2vlP9rG.

Department for Communities and Local Government (2012). *National planning policy framework.* London: Department for Communities and Local Government. http://bit.ly/1gGu8KY.

Department for Communities and Local Government (2008). *Planning applications: a faster and more responsive system: final report of the Killian Pretty Review.* London: Department for Communities and Local Government. http://bit.ly/2vm0Gat.

Department for Communities and Local Government (2000). *Our towns and cities: the future – delivering an urban renaissance.* London: Department for Communities and Local Government. http://bit.ly/2wcW5FP.

Department of City Planning (1988). *The master plan of the City and County of San Francisco.* San Francisco: Department of City Planning.

Dieringer, J. and R. Sturm (2010). *Regional governance in EU-Staaten.* Germany: Barbara Budrich Publishing.

Dilworth, R., R. Stokes, R. Weinberger and S. Spatari (2011). The place of planning in sustainability metrics for public works: lessons from the Philadelphia region. *Public Works Management and Policy* 16(1): 20–39.

Diossy, L. (2009). The Hungarian national climate change strategy: its principles, assignments and special case study on maize production. *Environment, Development and Sustainability* 11: 1135.

Dissart, J. and S. Deller (2000). Quality of life in the planning literature. *Journal of Planning Literature.* 15(1): 135–61.

Doak, J. and G. Parker (2005). Networked space? The challenge of meaningful participation and the new spatial planning in England. *Planning, Practice and Research* 20(1): 23–40.

Domingo, I. and R. Beunen (2012). Regional planning in the Catalan Pyrenees: strategies to deal with actors' expectations, perceived uncertainties and conflicts. *European Planning Studies* 21(2): 1–17.

Donnelly, A., B. Dalal-Clayton and R. Hughes (1998). *A directory of impact assessment guidelines.* 2nd edition. London: International Institute for Environment and Development.

Duany, A. and E. Talen (2001). Making the good easy: the smart code alternative. *Fordham Urban Law Journal* 29: 1445–68.

Dulal, H.B. and S. Akbar (2013). Greenhouse gas emission reduction options for cities: finding the 'coincidence of agendas' between local priorities and climate change mitigation objectives. *Habitat International* 38: 100–5. http://bit.ly/2uidmLa.

Dupont, V. (2015). Secured residential enclaves in the Delhi region: impact of indigenous and transnational models. *City, Culture and Society* 7(4): 227–36.

Eckert, R., C. Voigt and T. Kien (2009). Developing guidelines for energy and climate efficient urban structures a new planning instrument for adapting Ho Chi Minh City to the impacts of climate change. Paper presented to the fifth Urban Research Symposium. Marseille, 28–30 June 2009. http://bit.ly/2f096hj.

Ehrenfeld, J. (2000). Industrial ecology: paradigm shift or normal science? *American Behavioral Scientist* 44(2): 229–44.

Eran, B. (2005). *The code of the city: standards and the hidden language of place-making.* Cambridge, MA: MIT Press.

Eriksson, M. and B. Lindström (2005). Validity of Antonovsky's sense of coherence scale: a systematic review, *Journal of Epidemiology and Community Health.* 59(6): 460–66. http://bit.ly/2wjCJ0s.

Espinosa, A. and T. Velázquez (2015). Introduction: community psychology and the need for community participation in Peru. *Journal of Prevention and Intervention in the Community* 43(4): 235–37.

Works cited

European Commission (1999a). *European spatial development perspective 2000–2009.* http://bit.ly/2vvySQQ.

European Commission (1999b). *The EU compendium of spatial planning systems and policies: Germany.* Regional Development Studies Series, Luxembourg: Office for Official Publications of the European Communities. http://bit.ly/2w3TRbv.

European Commission (2000). *Communication from the Commission on the precautionary principle.* http://bit.ly/2hSshWF.

European Commission (2010). *Europe 2020: A strategy for smart, sustainable and inclusive growth.* Brussels: European Commission. http://bit.ly/KMnOnV.

European Environmental Agency (2015). *National monitoring, reporting and evaluation of climate change adaptation in Europe.* EEA Report No. 20. Luxembourg: Office for Official Publications of the European Communities. http://bit.ly/1LQA0eK.

European Environmental Agency (2014). *National adaptation policy processes in European countries - 2014.* EEA Report No. 4. Luxembourg: Office for Official Publications of the European Communities. http://bit.ly/10eT4mp.

European Environmental Agency (2007). *Greenhouse gas emissions trends and projections in Europe 2007.* EEA Report No. 5. Luxembourg: Office for Official Publications of the European Communities. http://bit.ly/2wjJU8V.

European Environmental Agency (2006). *Urban sprawl in Europe: the ignored challenge.* EEA Report No. 10. Luxembourg: Office for Official Publications of the European Communities. http://bit.ly/2vrfdT1.

European Network of Environmental Law Organizations (2006). *Implementation of the Aarhus Convention in EU member states.* Brno: Justice and Environment European Network of Environmental Law Organisations. http://bit.ly/2vlOjez.

European Union (2007). *Leipzig charter on sustainable European cities.* http://bit.ly/2vxV9K3.

Ezeabasili, A.C.C., B.U. Okoro and A.I. Ezeabasili (2014). Water resources: management and strategies in Nigeria. *AFRREV STECH: International Journal of Science and Technology* 3(1): 35–54.

Fahmi, F.Z., M. Prawira, D. Hudalah and T. Firman (2016). Leadership and co-operative planning: a case study of Surakarta, Indonesia. *Planning Theory* 15(3): 204–315.

Faludi, A. (1987). *A decision-centred view of environmental planning.* Oxford and New York: Pergamon Press.

Farret, R. (2001). Urban and regional planning in Brazil: the role of the federal government. *disP: The Planning Review* 37(147): 8–13. 10.1080/02513625.2001.10556782.

Farris, J.T. (2001). The barriers to using infill development to achieve smart growth. *Housing Policy Debate* 12(1): 1–30.

Federal Department of Town and Country Planning (2010). *National physical plan 2.* Kulala Lumpur: Ministry of Housing and Local Government.

Federal Highway Administration (2010). *Livability in transportation guidebook: planning approaches that promote livability.* Washington, DC: Department of Transportation.

Feenstra, J.F., I. Burton, J.B. Smith and R.S.J. Tol, eds (1998). *Handbook on methods for climate change impact assessment and adaptation strategies.* United Nations Environment Programme, Nairobi and77 Institute for Environmental Studies Vrije Universiteit, Amsterdam. http://bit.ly/2vlDCs6.

Feiock, R. (2013). The institutional collective action framework. *Policy Studies Journal* 41(3) 397–425. doi: 10.1111/psj.1202310.

Field, P., K. Harvey and M. Strassberg (2010). Integrating mediation in land use decision making: a study of Vermont. *Land Lines* (January): 14–19. http://bit.ly/2wjG6ET.

Fishkin, J.S. (2009). *When the people speak: deliberative democracy and public consultation.* Oxford and New York: Oxford University Press.

Fitzgerald, J. and J. Lenhart (2016). Eco-districts: can they accelerate urban climate planning? *Environment and Planning C: Politics and Space.* 34(2): 364–80. doi::10.1177/0263774X15614666.

Works cited

Fitzgerald, J. and J. Wolak (2016). The roots of trust in local government in Western Europe. *International Political Science Review* 37(1): 130–46.

Fleurke, F. and R.Willemse (2004). Approaches to decentralization and local autonomy: a critical appraisal. *Administrative Theory & Praxis* 26(4): 523–44. doi: 10.1080/10841806.2004.11029467.

Flyvbjerg, B. (2001). Beyond the limits of planning theory: Response to my critics. *International Planning Studies* 6(3): 285–92.

Foley, J. et al. (2005). Global consequences of land use. *Science* 309(5734): 570–4. doi: 10.1126/science.1111772.

Foster, K. (2010). Challenges ahead for US regional planning governance. *The Town Planning Review* 81(5): 485–503. doi: http://dx.doi.org/10.3828/tpr.2010.21.

Foy, G. (1990). Economic sustainability and the preservation of environmental assets. *Journal of Environmental Management* 14(6): 771–78. doi: 10.1007/BF02394171.

French, C. and M. Gagne (2010). Ten years of community visioning in New Hampshire: the meaning of 'success'. *Community Development* 41: 223–39. doi: 10.1080/15575330903446742.

Friedmann, J. (2005). Planning cultures in transition. In S. Bishwapriya, ed., *Comparative planning cultures*. New York: Routledge.

Friedmann, J. et al. (2004). Strategic spatial planning and the longer range. *Planning Theory and Practice* 5(1):49–67. doi: 10.1080/1464935042000185062.

Frug, G. (2002). Beyond regional government. *Harvard Law Review* 115(7): 1763. doi: 10.2307/1342596.

Fung, A. and E.O. Wright, eds (2003). *Deepening democracy: institutional innovations in empowered participatory governance*. London and New York: Verso Press.

Gagnon-Lebrun, F. and S. Agrawala (2006). *Progress on adaptation to climate change in developed countries: an analysis of broad trends*. Paris: Organisation for Economic Co-operation and Development. http://www.oecd.org/env/cc/37178873.pdf.

Gallent, N. (2008). Strategic-local tensions and the spatial planning approach in England. *Planning Theory and Practice* 9(3):307–23. doi: 10.1080/14649350802277795.

Garcia-Lopez, M., A. Sole-Olle and E. Viladecans-Marsal (2015). Does zoning follow highways? *Regional Science and Urban Economics* 53:148–55. doi: 10.1016/j.regsciurbeco.2015.05.008.

Garrelts, H. and H. Lange (2011). Path dependencies and path change in complex fields of action: climate adaptation policies in Germany in the realm of flood risk management. *AMBIO* 40(2): 200–9. doi: 10.1007/s13280-010-0131-3.

Geoghegan, M. and F. Powell (2009). Community development and the contested politics of the late modern agora: of, alongside or against neoliberalism? *Community Development Journal* 44(4): 430–47. doi: 10.1093/cdj/bsn020.

Gillette, C. (2001). Regionalization and interlocal bargains. *New York University Law Review* 76(1): 190. http://bit.ly/2wjZSjo.

Godschalk, D. (2004). Land use planning challenges: coping with conflicts in visions of sustainable development and livable communities. *Journal of the American Planning Association* 70(1): 5–13. doi: 10.1080/01944360408976334.

Gordon, P. and H. Richardson (2000). Defending suburban sprawl. *Public Interest* 139: 65–71. http://bit.ly/2uU1Yc2.

Görg, C. (2010). Adaptive governance within Europe the need for integrated adaptation strategies. *Nova Acta Leopoldina* 384: 71–6.

Grant, J. (2009a). Experiential planning: a practitioner's account of Vancouver's success. *Journal of the American Planning Association* 75(3): 358–70 doi: 10.1080/01944360902965875.

Grant, J. (2009b). Theory and practice in planning the suburbs: challenges to implementing new urbanism, smart growth, and sustainability principles. *Planning Theory and Practice* 10: 11–33. doi:10.1080/14649350802661683.

Grant, J. (2002). Mixed use in theory and practice: Canadian experience with implementing a planning principle. *Journal of the American Planning Association* 68: 71–84. doi: 10.1080/01944360208977192.

Works cited

Greater London Authority (2014). *Sustainable design and construction: supplementary planning guidelines*. London: Greater London Authority. http://bit.ly/2wdq4xs.
Green, R. (1999). Meaning and form in community perception of town character. *Journal of Environmental Psychology* 19(4): 311–29. doi: 10.1006/jevp.1999.0143.
Griffith, J. (2001). Smart governance for smart growth: the need for regional governments. *Georgia State University Law Review* 17(4): 1019–62. http://bit.ly/2vrl1fa.
Guillermo Aguilar, A. (2008). Peri-urbanization, illegal settlements and environmental impact in Mexico City. *Cities* 25(3): 133–45. doi: 10.1016/j.cities.2008.02.003.
Gunder, M. and J. Hillier (2009). *Planning in ten words or less: a Lacanian experiment with spatial planning*. Farnham, UK: Ashgate Publishing.
Gupta, A. (2012). *Red tape: bureaucracy, structural violence, and poverty in India*. Durham, NC: Duke University Press.
Guy, S. and S. Marvin (2000). Models and pathways: the diversity of sustainable urban futures. In K. Williams, M. Jenks and E. Burton, eds, *Achieving Sustainable Urban Form*. London: Spon Press.
Haar, C. (1957). Regionalism and realism in land-use planning. *University of Pennsylvania Law Review* 105(4): 515–37. doi: 10.2307/3310367.
Haase, D., N. Kabisch and A. Haase (2013). Endless urban growth? On the mismatch of population, household and urban land area growth and its effects on the urban debate. *PloS One* 8(6). doi:10.1371/journal.pone.0066531.
Habermas, J. (1970). On systematically distorted communication. *Inquiry: An interdisciplinary Journal of Philosophy*. 13(1–4): 205–18.
Hadden, S. (1981). Technical information for citizen participation. *Journal of Applied Behavioral Science* 17(4): 537–49.
Hajer, M. (2011). *The energetic society: in search of a governance philosophy for a clean economy*. Netherlands Environmental Assessment Agency: The Hague. http://bit.ly/2fBxcOh.
Hajer, M. and W.H. Zonneveld (2000). Spatial planning in the network society – rethinking the principles of planning in the Netherland. *European Planning Studies* 8(3): 337–55.
Hall, E. (2007). Divide and sprawl, decline and fall: a comparative critique of Euclidean zoning. *University of Pittsburgh Law Review* 68(4): 915–50.
Halleux, J., S. Marcinczak and E. van der Krabben (2012). The adaptive efficiency of land use planning measured by the control of urban sprawl: the cases of the Netherlands, Belgium and Poland. *Land Use Policy* 29(4): 887–98.
Hallisey, C. (2013). The care of the past: the place of pastness in transgenerational projects. In B. Hellemans, O. Willemien and P. Burcht, eds, *On Religion and Memory*. New York: Fordham University Press. 89–99.
Halpern, B. et al. (2013). Achieving the triple bottom line in the face of inherent trade-offs among social equity, economic return, and conservation. *PNAS* 110(15): 6229–34. doi: 10.1073/pnas.1217689110.
Hardwicke Parish Council (2013). Stroud District Council Planning Permission: Crest Nicholson Operations. Planning Ref: S.13/2774/FUL.
Harless, J. (1992). Local government environmental advisory boards. *National Civic Review* 81(1): 9–18.
Harrison, J. (2012). Life after regions? The emergence of city-regionalism in England. *Regional Studies* 46(9): 1243–59.
Haslauer, E., M. Biberacher and T. Blaschke (2015). A spatially explicit backcasting approach for sustainable land-use planning. *Journal of Environmental Planning and Management* 59(5): 1–25.
Hatcher, C. and S. Thieme (2016). Institutional transition: internal migration, the *propiska*, and post-socialist urban change in Bishkek, Kyrgyzstan. *Urban Studies* 53(10): 2175–91.
Healey, P. (2016). Territory, Integration and Spatial Planning. In M. Tewdwr-Jones and P. Allmendinger, eds, *Territory, identity and spatial planning: spatial governance in a fragmented nation*. London: Routledge. 64–79.

Healey, P. (2007). Re-thinking key dimensions of strategic spatial planning: sustainability and complexity. In G. de Roo and G. Porter, eds, *Fuzzy planning: the role of actors in a funny governance environment*. Aldershot, UK: Ashgate Publishing. 21–41.

Healey, P. (2008). Making choices that matter: the practical art of situated strategic judgement. In J. van den Broeck, F. Moulaert and S. Oosterlynck, eds, *Spatial strategy-making: empowering the planning fields – ethics, creativity and action*. Leuven: Acco. 23–41.

Hellemans, B., W. Otten and B. Pranger (2013). *On religion and memory*. New York: Fordham University Press.

Henderson, J. and J. Thisse (2000). On strategic community development. *Journal of Political Economy* 109: 546–69.

Hickley, D. (2011). Porritt slates pickles for planning 'smear campaign'. *Planning Resource*, 14 June. http://bit.ly/2vhnb0B.

Hidalgo, M.C. and B. Hernandez (2001). Place attachment: conceptual and empirical questions. *Journal of Environmental Psychology* 21(3): 273–81.

Hilber, C.A.L. and W. Vermeulen (2010). *The impacts of restricting housing supply on house prices and affordability: final report*. London: Department for Communities and Local Government.

Hill, E. (2006). *SANDAG: an assessment of its role in the San Diego region*. Sacramento: Legislative Analyst's Office.

Hillier, J. (2007). *Stretching beyond the horizon: a multiplanar theory of spatial planning and governance*. Aldershot, UK: Ashgate Publishing.

Hiltgartner, K. (2007). The right to compensation for declines in property values due to a planning or zoning decision in Austria. *Global Studies Law Review* 6(1): 103–20.

Hirt, S. (2012). Mixed use by default: how the Europeans (don't) zone. *Journal of Planning Literature* 27(4): 375–93.

Hirt, S. (2014a). Home, sweet home: American residential zoning in comparative perspective. *Journal of Planning Education and Research* 33(3): 292–309.

Hirt, S. (2014b). *Zoned in the USA: the origins and implications of American land use regulation*. New York: Cornell University Press.

Hirt, S. (2013). Form follows function? How America zones. *Planning Practice a Research* 28(2): 204–30.

HM Treasury (2006). *Stern Review on the Economics of Climate Change*. http://bit.ly/1Mvzl3o.

Hodge, G. and I. Robinson (2001). *Planning Canadian regions*. Vancouver: University of British Columbia Press.

Hofstede, J. (2008). Climate change and coastal adaptation strategies: the Schleswig-Holstein perspective. *Baltica* 21(1–2): 71–8.

Hogan, R. (2003). *The failure of planning: permitting sprawl in San Diego suburbs, 1970-99*. Columbus: Ohio State University Press.

Holden, M. (2012). Urban policy engagement with social sustainability in metro Vancouver. *Urban Studies* 49(3): 527–42.

Holden, M. and A. Scerri (2015). Justification, compromise and test: development a pragmatic sociology of critique to understand the outcomes of urban redevelopment. *Planning Theory* 14(4): 360–83.

Holden, S. and K. Otsuka (2014). The roles of land tenure reforms and land markets in the context of population growth and land use intensification in Africa. *Food Policy* 48: 88–97.

Holman, N. and Y. Rydin (2013). What can social capital tell us about planning under localism? *Local Government Studies* 39(1): 71–88.

Hopwood, B., M. Mellor and G. O'Brien (2005). Sustainable development: mapping different approaches. *Sustainable Development* 13(1): 38–52.

Howland, M. and J. Sohn (2007). Has Maryland's priority funding areas initiative constrained the expansion of water and sewer investments. *Land Use Policy* 24(1): 175–86.

Hoyler, M., T. Freytag and C. Mager (2006). Advantageous fragmentation? Reimagining Metropolitan Governance and Spatial Planning in Rhine-Main. *Built Environment* 32(2): 124–36.

Works cited

Huang, J., X.X. Lu and J. Sellers (2007). A global comparative analysis of urban form: applying spatial metrics and remote sensing. *Landscape and Urban Planning*. 82(4): 184–97.

Ianos?, I, A. Sorensen and C. Merciu (2017). Incoherence of urban planning policy in Bucharest: its potential for land use conflict. *Land Use Policy* 60: 101–12.

Innes, J. and D. Booher (2004). Reframing public participation: strategies for the 21st century. *Planning Theory and Practice* 5(4): 419–36.

Innes, J. and J. Gruber (2005). Planning styles in conflict: the metropolitan transportation commission. *Journal of the American Planning Association* 71(2): 177–88.

Intergovernmental Panel on Climate Change (2014). *Climate change 2014: mitigation of climate change : Working group III contribution to the fifth assessment report of the intergovernmental panel on climate change.* Edited by O. Edenhofer et al. Cambridge: Cambridge University Press.

Intergovernmental Panel on Climate Change (2007). *Climate change 2007: impacts, adaptation, vulnerabilities, contribution of working group II to the fourth assessment report of the Intergovernmental Panel on Climate Change.* Edited by M.L. Parry et al. Cambridge: Cambridge University Press.

Irazabal, C. (2009). *Revisiting urban planning in Latin America and the Caribbean.* Nairobi: United Nations Human Settlements Programme.

Jacobs, J. (1961). *Death and life of great American cities.* New York: Random House

James, S. and T. Lahti (2004). *The natural step for communities: how cities and towns can change to sustainable practice.* Vancouver: New Society Publishers.

Jepson, E. and A. Haines (2014). Zoning for sustainability: a review and analysis of the zoning ordinances of 32 cities in the United States. *Journal of the American Planning Association* 80(3): 239–52.

Johar, F. (2007). Managing sustainable development through planning conditions. *Malaysian Journal of Environmental Management* 8: 3–15.

Kalupahana, D. (1974). The Buddhist conception of time and temporality. *Philosophy East and West.* 24(2): 181–91.

Kantor, P. and H.V. Savitch (2005). How to study comparative urban development Politics: a research note. *International Journal of Urban and Regional Research* 29(1) 135–51.

Kasanko, M. et al. (2006). Are European cities becoming dispersed? A comparative analysis of 15 European urban areas. *Landscape and Urban Planning* 77(1–2): 111–30.

Kathi, P. and T. Cooper (2005). Democratizing the administrative state: connecting neighborhood councils and city agencies. *Public Administration Review* 65(5): 559–67.

Keil, R. (2009). The urban-politics of roll-with-it neoliberalization. *City* 13(2–3): 230–45.

Kelly, G.A. (1963). *The psychology of personal constructs.* New York: W.W. Norton.

Kelly, K. and T. Stirling (2011). *Welsh housing policy: where next?* Cambridge, UK: Joseph Rowntree Foundation.

Keogh, G. and E. D'Arcy (1999). Property market efficiency: an institutional economics perspective. *Urban Studies* 36(13): 2401–14.

Khan, S. and M. S. H. Swapan (2013). From blueprint master plans to democratic planning in South Asian cities: Pursuing good governance agenda against prevalent patron-client networks. *Habitat International* 38: 183–91.

Kiefer, L. (1961). Comprehensive plan requirement in zoning. *Syracuse Law Review* 12: 342–47.

Kiisel, M. (2013). Local community participation in the planning process: a case of bounded communicative rationality. *European Planning Studies* 21(2): 232–50.

Kink, J. and R. Denaldi (2012). Metropolitan fragmentation and neo-liberalism in the periphery. *Urban Studies* 49(3): 543–61.

Kirschbaum, M. (2003). Can trees buy time? An assessment of the role of vegetation sinks as part of the global carbon cycle. *Climate Change* 58(1–2).

Klein, R., R. Nicholls and N. Mimura (1999). Coastal adaptation to climate change: can the IPCC technical guidelines be applied? *Mitigation and Adaptation Strategies for Global Change* 4(3–4): 239–52.

Knieling, J. and F. Othengrafen (2009). *Planning cultures in Europe. Decoding cultural phenomena in urban and regional planning.* London: Routledge.

Works cited

Knight-Lenihan, S. (2007). A critique of the influence of sustainable development on ecological sustainability: a New Zealand application. Doctoral dissertation, University of Auckland. http://bit.ly/2uin2p1.

Korcelli-Olejniczak, E. et al (2005). *Urban policies on diversity in Warsaw, Poland*. EU Seventh Framework Programme SSH.2012.2.2.2–1: Translation of Strategia Rozwoju Województwa.

Kropf, K. (1996). An alternative approach to zoning in France: typology, historical character and development control. *European Planning Studies* 4(6): 717–37.

Kryvobokov, M. (2004). Urban land zoning for taxation purposes in Ukraine: possible methods under an immature land market. *Property Management* 22(3): 214–29.

Kumar, S. (2005). Urban design decision-making: a study of Ontario municipal board decisions in Toronto. *Canadian Journal of Urban Research* 14(2): 3–24.

Kweit, R. and M. Kweit (1980). Bureaucratic decision making: impediments to citizen participation. *Polity* 12(4): 647–66.

Laidley, T. (2015). Measuring sprawl: a new index, recent trends, and future research. *Urban Affairs Review* 52(1): 66–97.

Land Use Subgroup of the California Climate Action Team (2008). Draft submission to the CARB Scoping Plan on Local Government, Land Use and Transportation. http://bit.ly/2wjyMZQ.

Langhelle, O. (2000). Why ecological modernization and sustainable development should not be conflated. *Journal of Environmental Policy and Planning* 2(4): 303–22.

Larsson, G. (2006). Planning systems. In G. Larsson, *Spatial planning systems in Western Europe: an overview*. Amsterdam: IOS Press. 21–54.

Latha, S. and M. Prasad (2010). Current state of coastal zone management practices in India. In A.L. Ramanthan et al., eds, *Management and sustainable development of coastal zone environments*. Berlin: Springer Science and Business Media.

Le Corbusier (1991). *Precisions on the present state of architecture and city planning: with an American prologue, a Brazilian corollary followed by the temperature of Paris and the atmosphere of Moscow*. Cambridge, MA: MIT Press.

Lei, S. (2016). Plan-based decision making for urban complexity. *Journal of Urban Management* 5(1): 1–2.

Lemmen, D. and F. Warren (2004). *Climate change impacts and adaptation: a Canadian perspective*. Ottawa: Natural Resources Canada.

Lenferink, S. and J. Arts (2009). Government strategies for market involvement in road infrastructure planning: an international overview. Paper delivered to the Changing Roles Conference, Noordwijk ann Zee, The Netherlands, 5–9 October 2009.

Lewinnek, E. (2014). *The working man's reward: Chicago's early suburbs and the roots of American sprawl*. Oxford: Oxford University Press.

Lewis, R., G. Knaap and J. Sohn (2009). Managing growth with priority funding areas: a good idea whose time has yet to come. *Journal of the American Planning Association* 75(4): 457–78.

Li, G., X. Luan, J. Yang and X. Lin (2013). Value capture beyond municipalities: transit-oriented development and inter-city passenger rail investment in China's Pearl River Delta. *Journal of Transport Geography* 33: 268–77.

Light, M. (1999). Different ideas of the city: origins of metropolitan land-use regimes in the United States, Germany, and Switzerland. *Yale Journal of International Law* 24(2): 577–611.

Lindblom, C. (1959). The science of 'muddling through'. *Public Administration Review* 19(2): 79–88.

Litman, T. (2016). Evaluating criticisms of smart growth. Victoria, British Columbia: Victoria Transport Policy Institute, 2016. http://bit.ly/2vrE5K6.

Lloyd, M.G. and D. Peel (2007). Shaping and designing model policies for land use planning. *Land Use Policy* 24(1): 154–64.

Lombardi, D.R., L. Porter, A. Barber and C. Rogers (2011). Conceptualizing sustainability in UK urban regeneration: a discursive formation. *Urban Studies* 48(2): 273–96.

Works cited

Lombardi, D.R., et al. (2011). Elucidating sustainability sequencing, tensions, and trade-offs in development decision making. *Environment and Planning B: Planning and Design* 38(6): 1105–21.

Ludwig, F. and R. Swart (2010). *Tools for climate change adaptation in water management: inventory and assessment of methods and tools*. Utrecht: Knowledge for Climate.

Lurcott, R. (2005). *Regional visioning public participation: best practices*. Pittsburgh: Sustainable Pittsburgh. http://bit.ly/2wjS3KJ.

Lüthi, S., A. Thierstein and V. Goebel (2010). Intra-firm and extra-firm linkages in the knowledge economy: the case of the emerging mega-city region of Munich. *Global Networks* 10(1): 114–37. doi:10.1111/j.1471-0374.2010.00277.x.

Luyet, V., R. Schlaepfer, M. Parlange and A. Buttler (2012). A framework to implement stakeholder participation in environmental projects. *Journal of Environmental Management* 111: 213–19. doi:10.1016/j.jenvman.2012.06.026.

Lynn, M. F. and G.J. Busenberg (1995). Citizen advisory committees and environmental policy: what we know, what's left to discover. *Risk Analysis* 15(2): 147–62. doi: 10.1111/j.1539-6924.1995.tb00309.x.

MacCallum, D. (2010). *Discourse dynamics in participatory planning: opening the bureaucracy to strangers*. Burlington, VT: Ashgate Publishing.

MacGregor, B. and A. Ross (1995). Master or servant? The changing role of the development plan in the British planning system. *Town Planning Review* 66(1): 41–59. doi:10.3828/tpr.66.1.d674066035273q30.

MacLeod, G. (2013). New urbanism/smart growth in the Scottish highlands: mobile policies and post-politics in local development planning. *Urban Studies* 50(11): 2196–221. doi:10.1177/0042098013491164.

Maidin, A. (2011). Access to public participation in the land planning and environmental decision making process in Malaysia. *International Journal of Humanities and Social Science* 1(3): 148–64. http://bit.ly/2woeYo0.

Maier, K. (2000). The role of strategic planning in the development of Czech towns and regions. *Planning Practice and Research*. 15(3): 247–55. doi:10.1080/713691901.

Mallet, S. (2004). 'Understanding home: a critical review of the literature. *Sociological Review* 52(1): 62–89. doi: 10.1111/j.1467-954X.2004.00442.x.

Mandelker, D. (1963). Delegation of power and function in zoning administration. Washington University Law Quarterly 1963(1): 60–101. http://openscholarship.wustl.edu/law_lawreview/vol1963/iss1/4

Mandelker, D. (2010). Designing Planned Communities. New York: IUniverse. http://law.wustl.edu/landuselaw/BookDPC/Designing%20Planned%20Communities.pdf.

Manderscheid, K. (2012). Planning sustainability: intergenerational and intragenerational justice in spatial planning strategies. *Antipode* 44(1): 197–216. doi:10.1111/j.1467-8330.2011.00854.x

Marin County Community Development Agency (2007). *Marin Countywide Plan* Policy CD-1.1.

Marquart-Pyatt, S. (2012). Contextual influences on environmental concerns cross-nationally: a multilevel investigation. *Social Science Research* 41(5): 1085–099. doi:10.1016/j.ssresearch.2012.04.003

Martin, J., R. Puentes and R. Pendall (2006). *From traditional to reformed: a review of the land use regulations in the nation's 50 largest metropolitan areas*. Washington, D.C.: The Brookings Institution. https://www.brookings.edu/wp-content/uploads/2016/06/20060802_Pendall.pdf

Martínez, M. (2011). The citizen participation of urban movements in spatial planning: a comparison between Vigo and Porto. *International Journal of Urban and Regional Research* 35(1): 147–71. doi:10.1111/j.1468-2427.2010.00956.x

Marwedel, J. (1998). Opting for performance: an alternative to conventional zoning for land use regulation. *Journal of Planning Literature* 13(2): 220–31. doi:10.1177/088541229801300205.

Mavrommati, G. and C. Richardson (2012). Experts' evaluation of concepts of ecologically sustainable development applied to coastal ecosystems. *Ocean and Coastal Management* 69: 27–34. doi:10.1016/j.ocecoaman.2012.07.016.

Works cited

Mavrommati, G. and K. Bithas (2013). Ecologically sustainable economic development in aquatic ecosystems: from theory to environmental policy. *Sustainable Development* 21(1): 60–72. doi: 10.1002/sd.504.

Mawdsley, G. (2015). Devolution of power to local governments. Paper presented to the CIPFA Scotland Conference, St Andrews, 24 September. http://bit.ly/2w9p5xW.

McAuslan, P. (1980). *The ideologies of planning law*. Oxford: Pergamon Press.

McCormick, K. (2009). An overview of distributed energy in the EU and USA. *Victorian Eco-Innovation Lab (VEIL)* 1. http://portal.research.lu.se/ws/files/5493611/3814722.pdf.

McKain, K. et al. (2012). Assessment of ground-based atmospheric observations for verification of greenhouse gas emissions from an urban region. *Proceedings of the National Academy of Sciences of the United States of America* 109(22): 8423–8. doi: 10.1073/pnas.1116645109

McMillan, D. and D. Chavis (1986). Sense of community: a definition and theory. *Journal of Community Psychology* 14(1): 6–23. doi: 10.1002/1520-6629(198601)14:1<6::AID-JCOP2290140103>3.0.CO;2-I.

McQuillin, E. (1983). *Municipal corporations vol. 8*, revised 3rd edition. Chicago: Callaghan & Co.

Mearns, R. and A. Norton, eds (2010). *Social dimensions of climate change: equity and vulnerability in a warming world*. Washington, DC: The World Bank. http://hdl.handle.net/10986/2689.

Measham, T.G. et al. (2011). Adapting to climate change through local municipal planning: barriers and challenges. *Mitigation and Adaptation Strategies for Global Change* 16(8): 889–909. doi:10.1007/s11027-011-9301-2.

Menichini, T. and F. Rosati (2013). A managerial tool for environmental sustainability. *ABCBEE Procedia* 5(2013): 551–6. doi: 10.1016/j.apcbee.2013.05.092

Midgely, J., A. Hall, M. Hardiman and D. Narine (1988). Community participation, social development and the state. *Public Administration and Development* 8(3): 365–6. doi: 10.1002/pad.4230080310

Milfont, T. and C. Sibley (2012). The big five personality traits and environmental engagement: associations at the individual and societal level. *Journal of Environ. Psychology* 32(2):187–95. doi:10.1016/j.jenvp.2011.12.006

Miller, J. and L. Hoel (2002). The 'smart growth' debate: best practices for urban transport planning. *Socio-economic planning sciences* 36(1): 1–24. doi: 10.1016/S0038-0121(01)00017-9

Ministry of Environment, Forest and Nature Agency (2004). *Regional planning in Finland, Iceland, Norway and Sweden*. Denmark: Special Planning Department. http://bit.ly/2vlPN8v.

Mitchell, B. (2005). Integrated water resource management, institutional arrangements, and land-use planning. *Environment and Planning A* 37(8): 1335–52. doi:10.1068/a37224

Mitra, A. (2003). *Painting the town green: the use of urban sustainability indicators in the United States*. London: RICS Foundation.

Mittelman, J. (2000). *The globalization syndrome: transformation and resistance*. Princeton, NJ: Princeton University Press.

Mohan, G. and K. Stokke (2000). Participatory development empowerment: the dangers of localism. *Third World Quarterly* 21(2): 274–86. doi:10.1080/01436590050004346

Monkkonen, P (2013). Urban land-use regulations and housing markets in developing countries: evidence from Indonesia on the importance of enforcement. *Land Use Policy* 34: 255–64. doi:10.1016/j.landusepol.2013.03.015

Monno, V. and A. Khakee (2012). Tokenism or political activism? Some reflections on participatory planning. *International Planning Studies* 17(1): 85–101. doi:10.1080/13563475.2011.638181

Mookherjee, D. and E. Hoerauf (2015). Is it sprawling yet? A density-based exploration of sprawl in the urban agglomeration region around the mega city of Delhi. In R.B. Singh, ed., *Urban development challenges, risks and resilience in Asian mega cities*. Tokyo: Springer.

Morgan, Ed (2012). The sword in the zone: fantasies of land use planning law. *University of Toronto Law Journal* 62(2): 163–99. doi:10.3138/utlj.62.2.163

Mori, K. and A. Christodoulou (2012). Review of sustainability indices and indicators: towards a new city sustainability index (CSI). *Environmental Impact Assessment Review* 32(1): 94–106. doi:10.1016/j.eiar.2011.06.001

Municipal Department, Urban Development and Planning (2014). *STEP 2025: urban development plan Vienna*. Vienna: Vienna City Administration. http://bit.ly/2xBEHtP.

Murdoch, J., and M. Tewdwr-Jones (1999). Planning and the English regions: conflict and convergence amongst the institutions of regional governance. *Environment and Planning C* 17(6): 715–29. http://epc.sagepub.com/content/17/6/715.abstract

Murray, C. (2011). Planning: sustainable development. *Architects Journal* 234(17): 42. http://bit.ly/2xlOC7J.

Musil, T. (2007). What development regulatory variables say – or don't say – about a municipality. *Journal of Real Estate Research* 29(2): 159–72. doi: 10.5555/rees.29.2.h8u877q577m42423

Nadin, V. (2000). European spatial planning and spatial development. Paper presented to the European Council of Town Planners Conference, London, 1 December.

National Climate Commission (2010). Austrian national report of the 27th session of the EFC Working Party on the Management of Mountain Watersheds. Štrbské Pleso, 7–10 April. http://www.fao.org/forestry/20824-0b45fa2bf2a47c2d7ccf2b65f9c176de.pdf.

National Observatory for the Impacts of Global Warming (2009). *Climate change: costs of impacts and lines of adaptation*. Paris: ONERC.

National Observatory for the Impacts of Global Warming (2007). *Stratégie Nationale d'Adaptation au Changement Climatique*. Paris: ONERC.

Nedović-Budić, Z., D. Djordjević and T. Dabović (2011). The mornings after … Serbian spatial planning legislation in context. *European Planning Studies* 19(3): 429–55. doi: 10.1080/09654313.2011.548448

Nelson, A. and J. Duncan (1995). *Growth management principles and practices*. Washington, D.C: Planners Press, American Planning Association.

Nelson, D., W. Adger and K. Brown (2007). Adaptation to environmental change: contributions of a resilience framework. *Annual Review of Environment and Resources* 32: 395–419. doi:10.1146/annurev.energy.32.051807.090348

Neuvonen, A. and P. Ache (2017). Metropolitan vision making – using backcasting as a strategic learning process to shape metropolitan futures. *Futures* 86: 73–83. doi: 10.1016/j.futures.2016.10.003

Department of Environmental Services (2008). *Innovative land use planning techniques: a handbook for sustainable development*. Concord, NH: New Hampshire Department of Environmental Services. https://www.des.nh.gov/repp/documents/ilupt_complete_handbook.pdf

Ngetich, J., G. Opata, and L. Mulongo (2014). A study on the effectiveness of urban development control instruments and practices in Eldoret Municipality, Kenya. *Journal of Emerging Trends in Engineering and Applied Sciences* 5(2): 83–91. http://hdl.handle.net/10520/EJC152928

Nilsson, A.E. (2009). Climate change, community response and multilevel governance. Final report for the CIRCLE-ERA-Net Project. http://bit.ly/2un6jRf.

Norton, R. (2011). Who decides, how, and why? Planning for the judicial review of local legislative zoning decisions. *The Urban Lawyer* 43(4): 1085–105.

Nunes Correia, F., M. Saraiva, F.N. Da Silva and I. Ramos (1999). Floodplain management in urban developing areas: urban growth scenarios and land use controls. *Water Resources Management* 13(1): 1–21.

O'Keefe, P., G. O'Brien, Z. Gadema and T. Devisscher (2008). From vulnerability to resilience: the adaptation continuum. Paper presented to the 3rd Asian Ministerial Conference on Disaster Risk Reduction, Kuala Lumpur, 2–3 December. http://nrl.northumbria.ac.uk/9432/1/Malaysia_Presentation_Final_%281%29.pdf.

O'Leary, R. and L.B. Bingham (2003). *The promise and performance of environmental conflict resolution*. Washington, DC: Resources for the Future.

Obermaier, M. et al. (2009). Adaptation to climate change in Brazil: the Pintadas pilot project and multiplication of best practice examples through dissemination and communication. Paper presented to

Works cited

Rio 9: World Climate and Energy Event, Rio de Janeiro, 17–19 March. http://www.rio12.com/rio9/programme/Book_of_Proceedings/31_ECB_Obermaier.pdf.

Office of the Deputy Prime Minister (2005). *Planning policy statement 1: delivery sustainable development*. London: The Stationery Office. http://bit.ly/2wCev1M.

Oppermann, E. (2011). The discourse of adaptation to climate change and the UK climate impacts programme: describing the problematization of adaptation. *Climate and Development* 3(1): 71–85.

Orenstein, D., L. Jiang and S.P. Hamburg (2011). An elephant in the planning room: political demography and its influence on sustainable land-use planning in drylands. *Journal of Arid Environments* 75: 596–611.

Organisation for Economic Co-operation and Development (2016). Mainstreaming adaptation in national development planning. http://bit.ly/2ubBezV.

Organisation for Economic Co-operation and Development (2010). Recent OECD work on climate Change adaptation. http://www.oecd.org/dataoecd/34/39/46533473.pdf

Organisation for Economic Co-operation and Development (2006). *Applying strategic environmental assessment: good practice guidance for development co-operation*. Paris: OECD Publishing. http://bit.ly/2vkMP52.

Organisation for Economic Co-operation and Development (2001a). *Cities for citizens: improving metropolitan governance*. Paris: OECD Publications Service. http://www.ocs.polito.it/sostenibilita/dwd/oecd_gov-2001.pdf

Organisation for Economic Co-operation and Development (2001b). *Engaging citizens in policy-making: information, consultation and public participation*. PUMA Policy Brief no. 10. http://library.deeep.org/record/1300/files/DEEEP-PAPER-2015-014.pdf.

Othengrafen, F. (2010). Spatial planning as expression of culturised planning practices: the examples of Helsinki, Finland and Athens, Greece. *Town Planning Review* 81(1): 83–110.

Ownes, D. (2004). The zoning variance: reappraisal and recommendations for reform of a much-maligned tool. *Columbia Journal of Environmental Law* 29(2): 279–322.

Özer-Kemppainen, O., H. Hentilä, L. Soudunsaari and R. Suikkari (2010). *Participatory urban planning: best practices (PUP)*. Oulu, Finland: University of Oulu. http://jultika.oulu.fi/files/isbn9789514263958.pdf.

Ozuduru, B., C. Varol, and O. Yalciner Ercoskun (2014). Do shopping centers abate the resilience of shopping streets? The co-existence of both shopping venues in Ankara, Turkey. *Cities* 36(10): 145–57.

Pacific Island Climate Change Assistance Programme (1999). *Training course on climate change vulnerability and adaptation assessment for Pacific Island countries*. CD-ROM. Hamilton, New Zealand: International Global Change Institute, University of Waikato.

Palhano, A. (2010). The role of municipal planning secretariats in strengthening collaborative metropolitan governance: a comparative case study approach from the metropolitan region of Belo Horizonte. In T. McGee and E. de Castro, eds, *Inclusion, collaboration and urban governance: challenges in metropolitan regions of Brazil and Canada*. Vancouver: University of British Columbia, 2010.

Papadopolous, R.K. (2002). *Therapeutic care for refugees: no place like home*. London: Karnac Books.

Parson, E.A., P.M. Haas and M.A. Levy (1992). A summary of the major documents signed at the Earth summit and the global forum. *Environment* 34(4): 12–15, 34–36.

Paterson, R. and D. Saha (2010). The role of the 'new' political culture in predicting city sustainability efforts. Working paper series, University of Texas at Austin. http://soa.utexas.edu/libraries-centers/center-sustainable-development/research/working-papers.

Paulsen, K. (2013). The effects of growth management on the spatial extent of urban development, revisited. *Land Economics* 89(2): 193–210.

Pawson, H., G. Davison and I. Wiesel (2012). *Addressing concentrations of disadvantage: policy, practice and literature review*. AHURI Final Report No. 190. Melbourne: Australian Housing and Urban Research Institute.

Pearce, G. and S. Ayres (2006). New patterns of governance in the English region: assessing their implications for spatial planning. *Environment and Planning C: Government and Policy* 24: 909–27.

Peet, R. (2011). Neoliberalism, inequality, and development. In W. Ahmed, A. Kundu and R. Peet, eds, *India's new economic policy: a critical analysis*. New York: Routledge. 11–32.

Peña, D. Information and communication technologies in citizen participation mechanisms in the local sphere. *Revista Venezolana de Gerencia* 43: 398–416.

Penney, J. and T. Dickenson (2009). Climate change adaptation in Toronto: progress and challenges. Paper presented to the Fifth Urban Research Symposium, Marseilles, 28–30 June.

Perec, G. (1997). *Species of spaces and other pieces*. Translated by John Sturrock. London: Penguin.

Phares, D., ed. (2004). *Metropolitan government without metropolitan governance?* Burlington, VT: Ashgate Publishing.

Pielke, R. (2005). Misdefining 'climate change': consequences for society and action. *Environmental Science and Policy* 8(6): 548–61.

Pinter, L., P. Hardi and L. McRorie-Harvey (1995). *Performance measurement for sustainable development: a compendium of experts, initiatives and publications*. Winnipeg: International Institute for Sustainable Development.

Pizer, W. (2006). *Economics versus climate change*. Washington, DC: Resources for the Future. http://www.cetesb.sp.gov.br/wp-content/uploads/sites/28/2014/05/economicsversusclimatechange.pdf.

Planning and Economic Development Committee (2011). *Report No. 1 of the Planning and Economic Development Committee Meeting Held on January 12, 2011*. York: Regional Municipality of York. http://archives.york.ca/councilcommitteearchives/pedc%20rpt%201-3.html.

Plummer, J. and J.G. Taylor, eds (2013). *Community participation in China: issues and processes for capacity building*. London: Earthscan.

Pojani, D. and D. Stead (2015). Going Dutch? The export of sustainable land-use and transport planning concepts from the Netherlands. *Urban Studies* 52(9): 1558–76.

Portney, K. (2005). Civic engagement and sustainable cities in the United States. *Public Administration Review* 65(5): 579–91.

Patt, A. and R. Zeckhauser (2000). Action bias and environmental decisions. *Journal of Risk and Uncertainty* 21(1): 45–72.

Preston, B.L., R.M. Westaway and E.J. Yuen (2011). Climate adaptation planning in practice: an evaluation of adaptation plans from three developed nations. *Mitigation and Adaptation Strategies for Global Change* 16(4): 407–38.

Punter, J.V. (1988). Planning control in France. *Town Planning Review* 59(2): 159–81.

Purcell, M. (2009). Resisting neoliberalization: communicative planning or counter-hegemonic movements? *Planning Theory* 8(2): 140.

Raepple, C. (1997). Florida's expedited permit review process: streamlining the development of Florida's economy. *Florida State Law Review* 25: 309–13

Ranger, N. et al. (2010), *Adaptation in the UK: a decision-making process*. Grantham Research Institute for Climate Change and the Environment and The Center for Climate Change Economics and Policy. http://www.lse.ac.uk/GranthamInstitute/wp-content/uploads/2014/03/PB-Ranger-adaptation-UK.pdf.

Real Estate Research Corporation (1974). *The costs of sprawl: environmental and economic costs of alternative residential development patterns at the urban fringe: prepared for the Council on Environmental Quality, the Office of Policy Development and Research, Department of Housing and Urban Development, and the Office of Planning and Management, Environmental Protection Agency*. Washington, DC: US Government Printing Office.

Reckien, D. et al. (2014). Climate change response in Europe: wha'ts the reality? Analysis of adaptation and mitigation plans from 200 urban areas in 11 countries. *Climatic Change* 122 (1): 331–40.

Reed, M.S. (2008). Stakeholder participation for environmental management: a literature review. *Biological Conservation* 141(10): 2417–31.

Works cited

Reimer, M., P. Getimis, and H. Blotevogel, eds (2014). *Spatial planning systems and practices in Europe: a comparative perspective on continuity and changes.* New York: Routledge.

Renn, O., T. Webber, and P. Wiedemann, eds (1995). *Fairness and competence in citizen participation: evaluating models for environmental discourse.* Dordrecht, The Netherlands: Kluwer Academic Publishers.

Resosudarmo, B., A. Nawir, I. Resosudarmo, and N. Subiman (2012). Forest land use dynamics in Indonesia. In A. Booth, C. Manning and T.K. Wie, eds, *Land, livelihood, the economy and the environment in Indonesia: essays in honour of Joan Hardjono.* Jakarta: Yayasan Obor. 20–50.

Revi, A. (2008). Climate change risk: an adaptation and mitigation agenda for Indian cities. *Environment and Urbanization* 20(1): 207–29.

Rittel, H.W.J., and M.M. Webber (1973). Dilemmas in a general theory of planning. *Policy Sciences* 4(2): 155–69.

Robinson, J. et al. (2011). Envisioning sustainability: recent progress in the use of participatory backcasting approaches for sustainability research. *Technological Forecasting and Social Change* 78(5): 756–68.

Robinson, J. (2004). Squaring the circle? Some thoughts on the idea of sustainable development. *Ecological Economics* 48(4): 369–84.

Rogers, R. (1979). Land-use planning: a prerequisite to effective zoning. *St Mary's Law Journal* 11: 161–75.

Root, L., E. van der Krabben, and T. Spit (2015). Between structures and norms: assessing tax increment financing for the Dutch spatial planning toolkit. *Town Planning Review* 86(3): 325–49.

Rose, J. (1969). Industrial zoning and beyond: compatibility through performance standards. *Journal of Urban Law* 46: 723–72.

Runhaar, H., P.P.J. Driessen and L. Soer (2009). Sustainable urban development and the challenge of policy integration: an assessment of planning tools for integrating spatial and environmental planning in the Netherlands. *Environment and Planning B: Urban Analytics and City Science* 36(3): 417–31.

Ryan, E. (2002). Zoning, taking, and dealing: the problems and promise of bargaining in land use planning conflicts. *Harvard Negotiation Law Review* 7: 337–86.

Salet, W. and A. Faludi (2000). *The revival of strategic spatial planning.* Amsterdam: Royal Netherlands Academy of Arts and Sciences.

Salkin, P. (2009). Sustainability and land use planning: greening state and local land use plans and regulations to address climate change challenges and preserve resources for future generations. *William and Mary Environmental Law and Policy Review* 34(1): 121–70.

Salkin, P. (2011). Failure to articulate clear ethics rules and standards at the local level continues to haunt local land use decision makers. *The Urban Lawyer* 43(3): 757–73.

Sampson, R. (2007). Theory and practice in the granting of dimensional land use variances: is the legal standard conscientiously applied, consciously ignored, or something in between? *The Urban Lawyer* 39(4): 877–958.

San Diego Association of Governments (2011). *Regional housing needs assessment plan: fifth housing element cycle planning for housing in the San Diego region, 2010-2020.* San Diego: SANDAG.

San Diego Association of Governments (2004). *Regional comprehensive plan for the San Diego* Region. San Diego: SANDAG. http://bit.ly/2wopDzT.

Sanyal, B. (2005). *Comparative planning cultures.* New York: Routledge.

Sarkar, C., J. Gallacher and C. Webster (2013). Urban built environment configuration and psychological distress in older men: results from the Caerphilly study. *BMC Public Health* 13: 695–705. doi: 10.1186/1471-2458-13-695.

Sartorio, F.S. (2005). Strategic spatial planning: a historical review of approaches, its recent revival, and an overview of the state of the art in Italy. *disP: The Planning Review* 41(162): 26–40. doi: 10.1080/02513625.2005.10556930

Sawyer, W. and F. Schmidt (2004). Citizen advisory groups. *Citizen participation strategies for municipal planning in Vermont, No. 5.* Burlington: University of Vermont. http://bit.ly/2vk1jC5.

Works cited

Saxer, S.R. Ross (1997). Local autonomy or regionalism? Sharing the benefits and burdens of suburban commercial development. *Indiana Law Review* 30(3): 659–92.

Scannell, L., and R. Gifford (2010). Defining place attachment: a tripartite organizing framework. *Journal of Environmental Psychology*. 30(1): 1–10. doi: 10.1016/j.jenvp.2009.09.006.

Scott, J. (1998). *Seeing like a state: how certain schemes to improve the human condition have failed*. New Haven, CT: Yale University Press.

Scottish Executive Development Department (2003). *Your place, your plan; a white paper on public involvement in planning*. Edinburgh: Scottish Executive Development Department. http://www.gov.scot/Publications/2003/03/16913/21151.

Selmi, D.P. (2011). The contract transformation in land use regulation. *Stanford Law Review* 63(3): 591–645.

Shah, A. (2014). *Decentralized provision of public infrastructure and corruption*. International Center for Public Policy Working Paper Series, paper 14–18. Atlanta: Andrew Young School of Policy Studies, Georgia State University.

Shahumyan, H. and R. Moeckel (2016). Integration of land use, land cover, transportation, and environmental impact models: expanding scenario analysis with multiple modules. *Environment and Planning B: Urban Analytics and City Science* 44(3): 531–52.

Shatkin, G. (2007). *Collective action and urban poverty alleviation: community organizations and the struggle for shelter in Manila*. Aldershot, UK: Ashgate Publishing.

Shaw, K. and F. Robinson (2012). From 'regionalism' to 'localism': opportunities and challenges for North East England. *Local Economy: Journal of the Local Economy Policy Unit* 27(3): 232–50.

Shrestha, P. and R. Aranya (2015). Claiming *invited* and *invented* spaces: contingencies for insurgent planning practices. *International Planning Studies* 20(4): 424–43.

Sik, C.I., and B. Križnik (2017). *Community-based urban development: evolving urban paradigms in Singapore and Seoul*. Singapore: Springer.

Silva, E.R. (2011). Deliberate improvisation: planning highway franchises in Santiago, Chile. *Planning Theory* 10(1): 35–52.

Simpson, F., and M. Chapman (1999). Comparison of urban governance and planning policy: East looking West. *Cities*. 16(5): 353–64.

Slaton, C.D. (1992). *Televote: expanding citizen participation in the quantum age*. New York: Praeger.

Smith, H.A. (2010). Choosing not to see: Canada, climate change and the Artic. *International Journal* 65(4): 931–42.

Smith, N. (1995). Remaking scale: competition and co-operation in prenational and postnational Europe. In Heikki Eskelinen and Folke Snickars, eds, *Competitive European peripheries*. Berlin: Springer. 59–74.

Smithsimon, G. (2008). Dispersing the crowd: bonus plazas and the creation of public space, *Urban Affairs Review* 43(3): 325–51.

Song, Y. and C. Ding, eds (2009). *Smart urban growth for China*. Cambridge, MA: Lincoln Institute of Land Policy.

Sorensen, A. (2011).Toronto megacity: growth, planning institutions and sustainability. In A. Sorensen and J. Okata, eds, *Megacities: urban form, governance, and sustainability*. Tokyo: Springer. 245–71.

Sovacool, B.K., B. Linnér, and R.J.T. Klein (2017). Climate change adaptation and the least development countries fund (LDCF): qualitative insights from policy implementation in the Asia-Pacific. *Climate Change*, 140(2): 209–26.

Spash, C.L. (2012). New foundations for ecological economics. *Ecological Economics* 77: 36–47.

Springett, D. (2013). Editorial: critical perspectives on sustainable development. *Sustainable Development* 21(2): 73–82.

Sridhar, K.S. (2010). Impact of land use regulations: evidence from India's cities. *Urban Studies* 47(7). 1541–69.

Works cited

Stanghellini, P.S.L., and D. Collentine (2008). Stakeholder discourse and water management – implementation of the participatory model CATCH in a Northern Italian alpine sub-catchment. *Hydrology and Earth System Sciences* 12(2): 317–31.
Statistisches B. (2012). *Sustainable development in Germany: indicator report 2014*. Wiesbaden: Federal Statistical Office. https://www.destatis.de/EN/Publications/Specialized/EnvironmentalEconomicAccounting/Indicators2014.pdf
Stein, L. (2015). Global warming: inaction, denial, and psyche. *Spring* 88: 23–46.
Stein, L. (2014). The efficacy of the forms of climate change adaptation. In S. Leckie, ed., *Land solutions for climate displacement*. London: Routledge.
Stein, L. (2013). Domestic law for resettlement of persons displaced by climate change. In M.B. Gerrard and G.E. Wannier, eds, *Threatened island nations: legal implications of rising seas and a changing climate*. Cambridge: Cambridge University Press.
Stein, L. (2010). The legal and economic bases for an emissions trading scheme. *Monash University Law Review* 36(1): 192–214.
Stein, L. (1982). Density controls and the use of space. *Urban Law and Policy* 1.
Steinberg, F. (2005). Strategic urban planning in Latin America: experiences of building and managing the future. *Habitat International* 29(1): 69–93.
Sullivan, E.J. (2000). The evolving role of the comprehensive plan. *Urban Lawyer* 32(4): 813–37.
Sullivan, E. (2010). Recent developments in comprehensive planning law. *Urban Lawyer* 43(3): 665–76.
Sung, H., S. Lee, and S. Cheon (2015). Operationalizing Jane Jacobs's urban design theory: empirical verification from the great city of Seoul, Korea. *Journal of Planning Education and Research* 35(2): 117–30.
Susskind, L., and M. Elliot (1981). Learning from citizen participation and citizen action in Western Europe. *Journal of Applied Behavioral Science* 17(4): 497–517.
Talen, E. (2012). Zoning and diversity in historical perspective. *Journal of Planning History* 11(4): 330–47.
Tang, B. and L.H. Choy (2000). Modelling planning control decisions: a logistic regression analysis on office development applications in urban Kowloon, Hong Kong. *Cities* 17(3): 219–25.
Tang, Z. (2009). How are California local jurisdictions incorporating a strategic environmental assessment in local comprehensive land use plans? *Local Environment* 14(4): 313–38.
Tanguay, G.A., J. Rajaonson, J. Lefebvre, and P. Lanoie (2010). Measuring the sustainability of cities: an analysis of the use of local indicators. *Ecological Indices* 10(2): 407–18.
Taylor, J. (1999). *Energy efficiency: no silver bullet for global warming. Policy analysis no. 356*. Washington, DC: Cato Institute.
Thomas, D. et al. (1983). *Flexibility and commitment in planning: a comparative study of local planning and development in the Netherlands and England*. The Hague: Martinus Nijhoff Publishers.
Tian, L., and T. Shen (2011). Evaluation of plan implementation in the transitional China: a case of Guangzhou city master plan. *Cities* 28(1): 11–27.
Tocqueville, A. (1968). *Democracy in America* [1835]. London: Fontanfa.
Tolley, R. and B.J. Turton (2013). *Transport systems, policy and planning: a geographical approach*. Second edition. New York: Routeledge.
Tomalty, R. (2002). Growth management in the Vancouver region. *Local Environment: The International Journal of Justice and Sustainability* 7(4): 431–55.
Tomalty, R., and A. Skaburskis (2003). Development charges and city planning objectives: the Ontario disconnect. *Canadian Journal of Urban Research* 12(1): 142–61.
Toronto Environment Office (2008). *Ahead of the storm . . . Preparing Toronto for climate change: development of a climate change adaptation strategy*. Toronto: The City of Toronto. http://www.toronto.ca/teo/pdf/ahead_of_the_storm.pdf.
Transportation Research Board (2009). *Driving and the built environment: the effects of compact development on motorized travel, energy use, and CO2 emissions. Special report 298*. Washington, DC: National Academies Press.

Works cited

Transportation Research Board (2004). *Transit-oriented development in the United States: experiences, challenges, and prospects (Transit Co-operative Research Program report 102)*. Washington, DC: National Academies Press.

Troutman, P. (2004). A growth machine's plan B: legitimating development when the value-free growth ideology is under fire. *Journal of Urban Affairs* 26(5): 611–22

Turowski, G. (2002). *Spatial planning in Germany: structures and concepts. Studies in spatial development, no. 1*. Hannover: Akademie für Raumforschung und Landesplanung. http://hdl.handle.net/10419/59969.

United Kingdom Interdepartmental Liaison Group on Risk Assessment (2002). Third Report prepared by the Interdepartmental Liaison Group on Risk Assessment. London: UK-ILGRA.

United Nations (2016). *New urban agenda*. Habitat III Secretariat: 2017. http://bit.ly/2ujfrr0.

United Nations (2015a). *International guidelines on urban and territorial planning*. Nairobi: United Nations Human Settlements Programme (UN-Habitat). http://bit.ly/2wH3Ere.

United Nations (2015b). *Transforming our world: the 2030 agenda for sustainable development*. http://bit.ly/1OTd4Sr.

United Nations (2012). *The future we want*. Outcome document of the Rio+20 Conference on Sustainable Development, Rio de Janeiro, 20–22 June. http://bit.ly/1BGlIee.

United Nations (1992). *Report of the United Nations Conference on Environment and Development (Rio declaration on environment and development)*. http://www.un.org/documents/ga/conf151/aconf15126-1annex1.htm.

United Nations (1987). *Our common future: report of the World Commission on Environment and Development*. http://www.un-documents.net/our-common-future.pdf.

United Nations et al. (2003). *Handbook of national accounting: integrated environmental and economic accounting*. http://bit.ly/2uksY5A.

United Nations Environment Programme (2011). *Towards a green economy: pathways to sustainable development and poverty eradication – a synthesis for policy makers*. www.unep.org/greeneconomy.

International Recovery Program and United Nations Development Programme India (2010). *Guidance note on recovery: climate change*. Kobe: IRP.

United Nations Framework Convention on Climate Change (2008). *The Nairobi work programme on impacts, vulnerability and adaptation to climate change*. Bonn: UNFCCC.

van Klink, B. (2016). Symbolic legislation: an essentially political concept. In B. van Klink, B. van Beers and L. Poort, eds, *Symbolic legislation theory and new developments in biolaw*. Bonn: Springer International.

van Minnen, J.G. et al. (2008). Quantifying the effectiveness of climate change mitigation through forest plantations and carbon sequestration with an integrated land-use model. *Carbon Balance and Management* 3(3). doi: 10.1186/1750-0680-3-3.

Vandergeest, P. and N.L. Peluso (1995). Territorialization and state power in Thailand. *Theory and Society* 24(3): 385–426.

van Vuuren, Detlef P. et al. (2017). Energy, land-use and greenhouse gas emissions trajectories under a green growth paradigm. *Global Environmental Change* 42: 237–50.

Vermuelen, S. (2009). Needed: an intelligent and integrated vision for Brussels' urban planning. Paper presented to the 4th International Conference of the International Forum on Urbanism. Delft, The Netherlands, 26–28 November.

Viguié, V. and S. Hallegatte (2012). Trade-offs and synergies in urban climate policies. *Nature Climate Change* 2(5): 334–7.

Walters, L.C. (2013). Land value capture in policy and practice. *Journal of Property Tax and Assessment and Administration* 10(2): 5–21.

Warrick, R. (2000). Strategies for vulnerability and adaptation assessment in the context of national communications. Paper presented at the second AOSIS Workshop of Climate Change Negotiations. Apia, Samoa, 31 July–3 August. http://bit.ly/2hg1iZC.

Works cited

Waterhout, B., F. Othengrafen, and O. Sykes (2012). Neo-liberalization processes in spatial planning in France, Germany and the Netherlands: an exploration. *Planning Practice and Research* 28(1): 141–59.

Weaver, C.L. and R.F. Babcock (1979). *City zoning: the once and future frontier*. Chicago: Planners Press, American Planning Association.

Weber, E.M., R. Cowie and the Center for Substance Abuse Treatment (1995). *Siting drug and alcohol treatment programs: legal challenges to the NIMBY syndrome*. Technical Assistance Publication, issue 14. Rockville, MD: US Department of Health and Human Services.

Webler, T., and S. Tuler (2000). Fairness and competence in citizen participation: theoretical reflections from a case study. *Administration and Society* 32(5): 566–95.

Wegener, M., F. Gnad and M. Vannahme (1986). The time scale of urban change. In B. Hutchinson and M. Batty, eds, *Advances in urban systems modelling*. Amsterdam: North Holland. 175–97.

Weible, C.M. and P.A. Sabatier (2005). Comparing policy networks: marine protected areas in California. *Policy Studies Journal* 33(2): 181–201.

Wekerle, G.R. and T.V. Abbruzzese (2010). Producing regionalism: regional movements, ecosystems and equity in a fast and slow growth region, *GeoJournal* 75(6): 581–94.

Westerhoff, L., et al. (2010). Planned adaptation measures in industrialized countries: a comparison of select countries within and outside the EU. In E.C.H. Keskitalo, ed., *Developing adaptation policy and practice in Europe: multi-level governance of climate change*. Dordrecht: Springer Netherlands. 271–338.

Western Australian Planning Commission (2006). *Statement of planning policy no. 1: state planning framework variation no. 2*. https://www.planning.wa.gov.au/publications/1160.aspx.

White, M.J. (1988). *American neighborhoods and residential differentiation*. New York: Russell Sage Foundation. jstor.org/stable/10.7758/9781610445580.

White, W. and P. Allmendinger (2003). Land-use planning and the housing market: a comparative review of the UK and the USA. *Urban Studies* 40(5–6): 953–72.

Whiteside, K. (2006). *Precautionary politics: principle and practice in confronting environmental risk*. Cambridge, MA: MIT Press.

Wieglib, G. et al. (2012). Ecological restoration as precaution and not as restitutional compensation. *Biodiversity and Conservation* 22(9): 1931–48.

Wilde, J., L. Boydell and J. Rugkåsa (2006). Integrating sustainable development and public health on the island of Ireland. *Public Health* 120(7): 601–3

Willows, R., R. Connell, N. Reynard and I. Meadowcroft (2003). *Climate adaptation: risk, uncertainty and decision-making*. Oxford: UK Climates Impacts Programme.

Wilson, E. and J. Piper (2010). *Spatial planning and climate change*. Oxon: Routledge.

Wood, C. (1996). Environmental planning. In J.B. Cullingworth, ed., *British planning: 50 years of urban and regional planning*. London: Athlone Press.

Woodhead, R.M. (2000). Investigation of the early stages of project formulation. *Facilities 18(13/14)*: 524–35.

World Bank (2013). *Doing business in Italy*. Washington, DC: The World Bank.

Wu, F. (2015). Planning for growth: urban and regional planning in China. New York: Routledge.

Yates, E. (2003). Central planning meets the neighborhood: land-use law and environmental impact assessment in Cuba *Tulane Environmental Law Journal* 16: 653–58.

Ye, L., S. Mandpe, and P.B. Meyer (2005). What is 'smart growth' – really? *Journal of Planning Literature* 19(3): 301–15.

Yetano, A., S. Royo, and B. Acerete (2010). What is driving the increased presence of citizen participation initiatives? *Environment and Planning C: Politics and Space* 28(5): 783–802.

Yiftachel, O. (2006). Re-engaging planning theory? Towards 'south-eastern' perspectives. *Planning Theory* 5(3): 211–22.

Yu, H. (2004). Knowledge and climate change policy coordination in China *East Asia* 21(3):58–77.

Works cited

Zokaei, K. et al. (2010). *Lean and systems thinking in the public sector in Wales: report for the Wales Audit Office*. Cardiff: Lean Enterprise Research Centre, Cardiff University. http://bit.ly/2vvySQQ.

Index

adaptation for climate change 227–244
  and planning 206–208, 208, 210–211
    externality 206–208
    planning processes 240–243
  best practice 244
  bottom-up approach 227, 228, 237–240
    city-level approaches 239–240
    regional approaches 237–239
  local-level planning 240–241
  NAPA (National Adaptation Programmes of Action) 229, 242
  NAS (National Adaptation Strategy) 227
  alternatives to 234–236
  and governance 232–233
  goals of 230–231
  immaturity of 228–230
  problems with implementation 236–237
  risk reduction 230–230
  national failures to adapt for climate change 227
  top-down approach 227, 228–230, 234–236
aesthetics 14–16, 77, 245
  city beautiful movement 14
  garden city movement 14
affordable housing 191–192
Australia 124, 139, 149, 165
  New South Wales 135, 209, 241; *see also* sustainability: examples of use in planning: Coffs Harbour, Australia
  Queensland 51
  Victoria 114
    Melbourne 108; *see also* sustainability: examples of use in planning: Melbourne, Australia
  Western Australia
    Perth 13; *see also* United States, The: New York: unsaid goals
Austria 144, 237

Balkans 178
Bangladesh 17
Belgium 75, 237
  Brussels 19
Better life index 131
Bolivia 58
Brazil 65, 177
  Rio de Janeiro 139, 241
Bulgaria 178, 238

Canada 124, 151, 233, 235
  British Columbia 31–32, 155
    Vancouver 32, 52–53, 60, 64, 67, 80–80, 97, 130, 133, 182, 218
  Manitoba
    Winnipeg 186
  Nova Scotia 114
  Ontario 63, 130, 173, 178, 212
    Ottawa 42, 104
    Toronto 32, 59, 63, 239
  Quebec
    Montreal 103, 125
Chile
  Santiago 184
China 75, 126, 234
  Shanghai 149
Columbia 59, 178
community participation 9–10, 19, 34, 123, 163, 246, 251
  access to information 108–110
  advisory panels 113–115

Index

citizen advisory groups 113–115
and development control 176–180, 200
and land laws 92
best practice 118–119
collaborative planning 108
  consensus 185, 251–251
  democracy as basis 91, 119
  draft plans 117–118
  emotionality 107, 135
  forms of participation 97
  implementing participation 98–102
    models for implementation 100–101
  in regional planning 116–117
  local stakeholders 115–116
  meaning 91
  methods of participation 110–113
  phases of participation 102–105
    formative stage 102–103
    submission phase 105
    visioning stage 103–105
  principles 105–106
  ujamma 92
  social capital 94, 133
  vision 9–9, 103–104, 123, 129, 148–150, 247
    vision statements 16
Croatia
  Zagreb 112–113
Cuba 144–145
Czech Republic 149
climate change mitigation 40, 205–226, 238, 239, 250, 250; *see also* GHGE (greenhouse gas emissions): mitigation
  best practice 224–226
  bottom-up approach 205
  common public good 131
  emissions trading scheme 205, 206
  Kyoto protocol 205, 220
  Paris climate agreement 205, 211, 220
  precautionary principle 208–210
  Rio declaration 21–22, 209
  top-down approach 205, 224

Denmark
  Copenhagen 42
density 4, 71–72, 80
  perceived density 71
developers, the role of 163, 182, 191–194, 247
  bonuses 194
development control 85, 105, 124–126, 220–221, 241, 249
  and localism 176–180
  and strategic planning 165–166, 169, 170–173
  best practice 198–201
    considerations 198
    decision makers 199
    plan-led systems 199–201
    processing 201
    United Kingdom system 198
  changing from plan-led approach to development control approach 173–176
  compared to zoning 169
  decision-making bodies 178
  decision-making responsibility 188–191
    delegation of decision-making power 188
    biases 189–190
  definition 163–163
  delays in 180–181
  development applications 164, 181–184, 201
    conditions 191–194
    factors to consider 187–188
    good procedures on 184–185
    time to determine 185–186
  development standards 140
  efficacy of 169–170
  English land use system 164–165
  exceptions to plans
    exemptions 167–167
    special permits 168, 177, 180
    variances 167–168, 177–181, 188
  flexibility 171, 174
  performance standards 195–198
  standards for 194–198

European Union 10, 95

Finland 56, 60, 97
  Helsinki 56
flood risk 87, 236, 241, 243, 244
France 60, 86, 98, 172, 228, 238

gentrification 15
  Little India 15
Germany 28–28, 57, 60, 151, 236–236
  Bavaria 31
  Berlin 135
  Stuttgart 242
GHGE (greenhouse gas emissions) 205–226, 250
  as pollutant 208
  emitters 220–221
  mitigation 210–213, 217
    through building efficiency 215–216
    through planning 213–214, 220, 224–225

Index

through transportation planning 216–220
through governance 221–224
governance 54–59, 65, 177, 232–233
growth areas 71–82, 89, 250

Hong Kong 51, 171
Hungary 238

India 166, 235
  Delhi 75
infrastructure 146–147
  value capture 12, 146–147
Ireland 50–51
Italy 228
  Faenza 242

Jacobs, Jane 5, 128, 245
Japan
  Tokyo 147

Kenya 169
  Nairobi 193, 230

land market 145
Lithuania 68, 178
localism 54–55, 57, 175, 176–180, 190–191, 246

Malaysia 55, 75, 124
Mexico
  Mexico City 125
Mozambique 92

neoliberalism 16–20, 245, 246
Nepal
  Kathmandu 6
Netherlands 28, 80, 83, 152, 174–174
New Urbanism 19, 31, 33, 76–78, 90, 134, 195, 214, 246
  New Zealand 27–28
    Auckland 42
  NGOs (non-government organisations) 6
  Nigeria 85, 124
  Norway 107, 147

Pakistan 107, 150
Peru 92, 178
Philippines
  Manila 107
planners 4–4, 11, 170
planning authorities 151, 177, 183–184
  best practice 87–90

conducting economic analysis 187–187
conflict 66–70
corruption 178, 199
  interrelationship between 49–50, 61–62, 69–70
  metropolitan governments 63–66
    models of 63–65
  plan alignment 50–53
planning culture 66, 68, 173
planning
  anxiety, a source of 127–136
  best practice 249–250
  cultural variety in planning systems 251–251
  harmony and order 245
  idealised planning systems 247–249
property rights of individuals 92–93, 167, 169
private property 7
population forecasting 45
policies 180–180, 181–182
Poland 89, 137, 178
Portugal 98
  Lisbon 62
  Porto 92

quality of life 4, 132–134

regional planning 49–50, 53, 59–61, 68, 249
regionalism 60
regulatory controls 123–136
  best practice 134–135
  consistency in 125
  land use policies 124
  legal controls 125–126
  limitations of 125, 133
  planning aspirations and 130–134, 135
  planning controls, reasons for 127–130
  regulatory provisions 124, 173
  relationship between strategic plans and regulatory provisions 124–126
  spatial plan 124, 126
right to the city 6, 33, 246
right to participate 93–93, 94–95
right to develop 164–164, 165
residential zones 139–139, 141
Romania
  Bucharest 246
Russia 178
  Moscow 41

Serbia 105
Singapore 98, 130, 149, 184
Slovakia 178

Index

smart growth 72, 74–75, 78–79, 90, 190, 213
South Africa 58, 95, 106
   Johannesburg 125
South Korea 62
South-East Asia 92
Spain 90, 141
   Vigo 92
spatial planning 6, 7, 29, 147
   cumulative impacts of 157
   map 137–139, 140
sprawl 5, 73–76
Sri Lanka 124, 166
state intervention 55–56, 57, 65, 73, 87–88
   scope of 58–59
Strategic Environmental Assessment 155–157
strategic planning 3–47, 49, 66–71, 86, 163
   and development control 170–173
   best practice 43–47
      goals and visions 44–45
         timing 45–46
            sustainability 46–46
               content 46–47
   culturally determined 7–9
   for economic development 17–19
   formal contents 39–42
   goals 170–171, 195–195
   line of sight principle 52–53, 88, 248
   popularity 9–11, 49
   timeframe of plan 42–43
subjective experience
   of architecture 132–133
   of city living 245
sustainability 152–155, 187–188, 198, 243, 244
   and economic growth 29
   approaches to 24–31
   assessment 155–157
   balance 23, 36, 38
   ecological sustainability 23–35
   examples of use in planning
      Albany, New York 34
      Buffalo, New York 34
      Coffs Harbour, Australia 34
      Eugene, Oregon 34
      Long Island, New York 34
      Melbourne, Australia 34
   external forms 31–33
   goals of 20–24
   legal definition 37–38
   metrics 31
   overarching plan for 34–35
   smart cities 20–24

TBL (triple bottom line) 33–35, 155, 210
terminology 36

Tanzania 92
Thailand 50
   Bangkok 7
tokenism in planning 92, 98, 104, 247
transport 82–85, 141, 216–220
   public transport 219–219, 225
   TOD (transport-oriented design) 216–219, 225

Uganda 92
United Kingdom, The 181, 182, 190, 193
   England 62–63, 67, 83, 124, 164–165
      London 25, 230
      Sheffield 143, 165
   Northern Ireland 26
   Scotland 88–88, 96, 101, 109–110
      Scottish Highlands 77
   Wales 180
United States, The 83, 123, 167–167
   Arizona
      Phoenix 168
   Arkansas
      Little Rock 152
   California 30, 37, 82, 83, 185, 211–211, 217, 219, 223
      Berkeley 130
      Los Angeles 149, 230
      Sacramento 116
      San Diego 61, 69, 81, 114
      San Francisco 30, 82, 179, 187
   Colorado 37–37
      Boulder 38
      Denver 37
      Pueblo 4
   Florida 132, 154, 186
      Miami 173
   Georgia
      Atlanta 67, 83
   Idaho 184
   Illinois
      Chicago 70
   Louisiana
      New Orleans 101
   Maine 84, 195
   Maryland 73
   Massachusetts
      Boston 42, 69–69, 70
      Cambridge 211
   Michigan

Index

Albion 38
New Hampshire 130
New Jersey 67, 167
New York 33–34, 222
    Albany *see* sustainability: examples of use in planning: Albany, New York
    Buffalo *see* sustainability: examples of use in planning: Buffalo, New York
    Hudson Yards 47
    Manhattan 11; *see also* United States, The: New York: unsaid goals
    New York City 140, 147, 180, 244
      North Carolina
        Charlotte 83
        Greensboro 200–200
      Ohio
        Cleveland 128
        Kent 111
      Oregon 58, 68, 111
        Bend 61
        Eugene *see* sustainability: examples of use in planning: Eugene, Oregon
        Hillsboro 185
        Portland 35, 98, 105–106, 111, 148, 154
      Pennsylvania
        Bucks County 197
        Philadelphia 30
        Pottstown 39–41
      South Carolina
        Charleston County 138
      Texas
        Houston 141
      Vermont 74, 113
      Washington
        Seattle 123, 191
      Wisconsin 52–52, 177
        Madison 38
unsaid goals 11–16, 245
unrealistic goals 5–6
urban problems 4–5, 33, 149, 245
urban sprawl 62
US Housing and Urban Development Department (HUD) 96–97

value 146–147
Vietnam 140
    Ho Chi Minh City 13, 242; *see also* United States, The: New York: unsaid goals
Venezuela 109

water management 85–87, 90, 233

Yemen 178

zoning amendments 147–150
zoning 124, 164
  and property rights 144–145
  best practice 158–161
    amendments 159–159
    explanation of zoning 158–158
    policies 159–160
    positive uses of zones 158
    strategic environmental assessments 160–161
    value capture 160
  boundaries 138–138
  contract zoning 183
  designation of 140–142
  goals 152–155
  inclusionary zoning 191–192
  legal controls and 140–140
  negative effects of 142
  policies 150–152
  rezoning 142, 168–168, 172
  up-zoning 146–147
zoning ordinances 143, 150–151, 152, 167

www.ingramcontent.com/pod-product-compliance
Lightning Source LLC
Chambersburg PA
CBHW081416230426
43668CB00016B/2253